AF539569

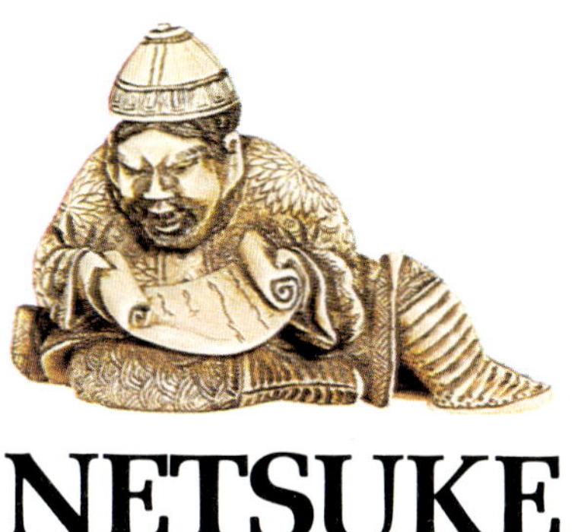

NETSUKE

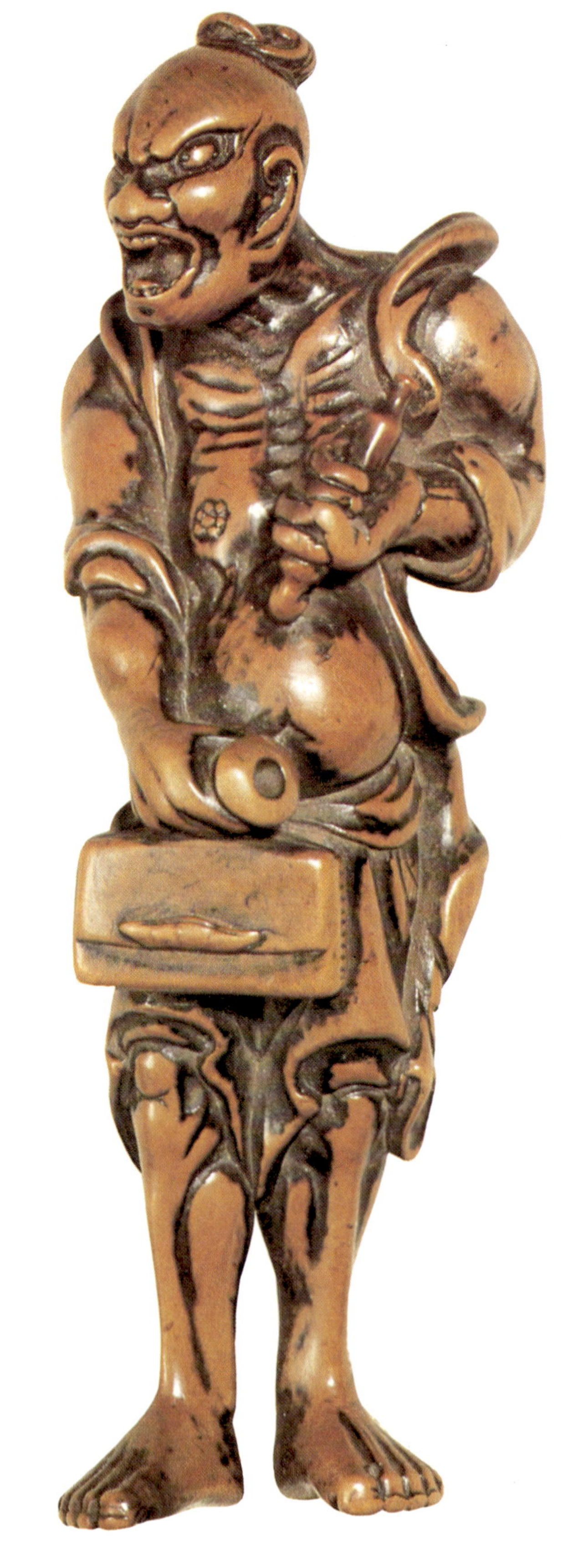

Richard Barker & Lawrence Smith

NETSUKE

The Miniature Sculpture of Japan

Published for
The Trustees of the British Museum
by
British Museum Publications Limited

ISBN 0 7141 1409 X
Published by British Museum Publications Ltd
6 Bedford Square, London WC1B 3RA
Reprinted 1983

Designed by Patrick Yapp
Set in Monophoto Melior by Tradespools Ltd,
Frome Somerset
Litho reproduction by Adroit Photo Litho Ltd,
Birmingham
Printed in Great Britain by
Ashdown Printing Services Ltd.

Contents

Preface

This exhibition of the British Museum's collection of netsuke has been arranged to coincide with the London Netsuke Convention of 1976, when many of the world's netsuke collectors and scholars will be gathered in the capital. The selection has been made to cover as far as possible all aspects of the art, its history, subjects, materials and schools of carvers. The catalogue, which illustrates every piece in the exhibition and all signatures, is intended as a permanent record of the major part of the collection.

The formation of the collection is due entirely to the gifts and bequests of benefactors, of whom Sir A. W. Franks, Mrs H. Seymour Trower, James Hilton, Oscar Raphael and Mrs Helen Epstein are the most important.

It is gratifying to acknowledge that this tradition of fruitful collaboration between the Museum and private generosity continues. The Organising Committee of the London Netsuke Convention – Luigi Bandini, Richard Barker, Neil Davey, Gerard Hawthorn, Richard Marchant, Geoffrey Moss, Jens S-Rasmussen, William Tilley and Douglas Wright – not only proposed the exhibition but subsidized all the photography for the catalogue. Richard Barker and Neil Davey, with Lawrence Smith of the Department, made the selection and wrote the catalogue entries. Jens S-Rasmussen, a specialist in this field of miniature sculpture, did all the black and white photography (over 400 pieces), while Sally Oxenham did the colour photography. Luigi Bandini and Douglas Wright advised on the choice of colour-plates.

The secretarial work was done by Susan Armstrong-MacDonnell, Ellen Bernfeld of the Department, and David MacFarlane.

Douglas Barrett
Keeper
Department of Oriental Antiquities
5 April 1976

Introduction

The use of netsuke

The traditional outdoor dress of the Japanese, both men and women, consisted basically of a long wrap-around garment with sleeves, secured by a sash, and a shorter jacket with short sleeves over it, loosely secured at the front by ties or a hook-and-toggle. There were no pockets, and only the women's garment had places in the sleeves to keep small objects in. Men needed to carry things around with them, including by the seventeenth century seal-cases (*inrō*) used by the warrior class (*samurai*), tobacco pouches, purses, pipes in cases, and a combination of writing-brush and ink-well called a *yatate*.

The natural place to hang such objects was from one of the two swords the *samurai* thrust through his sash, and this was done at all periods. But as a method it lacked elegance, except perhaps when a young blood ostentatiously hung letters to his lady-friends from his sword. A more convenient way, and the only one for the classes not allowed to carry swords, was to suspend the object on a cord from the sash. All objects hung from the sash in this way were called *sagemono* ('hanging things'). To stop the cord slipping a small toggle was obviously necessary at the other end, and this toggle was called a *netsuke*.

Early history

These devices must have been used very early, for similar things appeared naturally in widely scattered cultures throughout the world wherever things were suspended from a belt or sash. The illustrated handscrolls of the Kamakura Period (AD 1185–1333) and later occasionally show a *sagemono*, but not the netsuke, and there seems to be no illustration of them in use until the seventeenth century. One may infer, therefore, that netsuke were insignificant objects and rarely of artistic interest until that period, and that they were worn very unobtrusively. Probably they were conveniently-shaped natural objects, such as pieces of wood. The name netsuke, meaning 'root-fix', supports this inference. The small double-gourd was were probably always the commonest type of netsuke. The Japanese delight in simulating one material with another led to gourds being carved in wood.

The social climate of the Edo period

The history of netsuke as an art form is largely restricted to the Edo Period (AD 1601–1867). After 1867 their practical use declined with the introduction of Western dress.

In 1601 the *Shōgun* (generalissimo) Tokugawa Ieyasu defeated his last important rivals at the Battle of Sekigahara and established his family as hereditary dictators. He moved his centre of government from the ancient capital of Kyoto, where the Emperors continued to languish powerless and short of funds as they had done for many centuries, and settled it at the remote village of Edo, some five hundred kilometres to the east. It grew quickly into a huge city, and was renamed Tokyo ('The Eastern Capital') in 1867 when the restored Emperors finally moved there. Edo did not dominate higher cultural life, which remained centred on the Kyoto area, but as a great consumer society it provided both a market and an alternative way of life, marked by the haste, sharp wit, and passion for novelty and entertainment which are common to all metropolises. It was a natural haven for newer forms of art, and among them was the netsuke. Although Edo became the greatest consumer and producer of netsuke, they probably began as an art form in the great commercial port of Ōsaka, near Kyoto. There and in other far-flung centres, such as Nagoya, Kyoto, Wakayama, Kanazawa, and Fukuoka they flourished.

Urbanization reflected the increasing prosperity of Japan, which grew out of the country's stability. From the fall of Ōsaka Castle in 1614 the only internal rebellion was that of the remote Shimabara Christians in 1639. Thus freed from uncertainty, Japan's industries and agriculture all increased their production many times, and Ōsaka, Nagoya and Edo became the centres of a great trade in all commodities. These more and more included luxury goods, which increasing wealth put within the grasp of more people, and among them were netsuke.

Edo Period Japan was a feudal society, divided strictly into nobility, *samurai*, farmers, artisans, and merchants in order of precedence. The feudal lords and their *samurai* retainers were compelled to make periodic visits to Edo, where they could be checked on by the government and forced to live in a style befitting their status, so that they should not get too rich. This resulted in much money being spent on expensive clothes and accoutrements, which must have included fine netsuke for use with the *inrō* (seal-cases) which were the prerogative of the *samurai* class. At the bottom of the formal scale were the merchants, who were nevertheless often very rich and enlightened patrons of the arts. Unlike the *samurai*, they were not allowed to flaunt their riches. This tended to make their tastes more refined and quieter than is usual among the new rich of any society. Fine netsuke were one of the means through which such a merchant could express his wealth in a not too noticeable form. Below them in wealth, if not status, were the artisans and farmers who often fled illegally from their places of work to a freer and more lucrative life in the great urban centres. They too were continually coming into the income range which could afford netsuke.

Opposite

176 201

206 212

186 182

Overleaf page 12

38 14

17 23

31

24 3

Overleaf page 13

341 326

342

230 338

The Isolation, native taste, and early netsuke

The most significant fact of Japanese society was its isolation from the outside world. From 1639 onwards, all foreigners were excluded from Japan except for certain licensed Chinese and Dutch traders confined to parts of Nagasaki, and the occasional Korean embassy to Edo. At the same time Japanese were forbidden to go abroad, and the import of foreign books was banned. The reasons for the Isolation were complex, but it was basically designed to protect the ruling Tokugawa family's position against foreign alliances with their domestic enemies, and to save Japan from European colonialism and Christian missionaries.

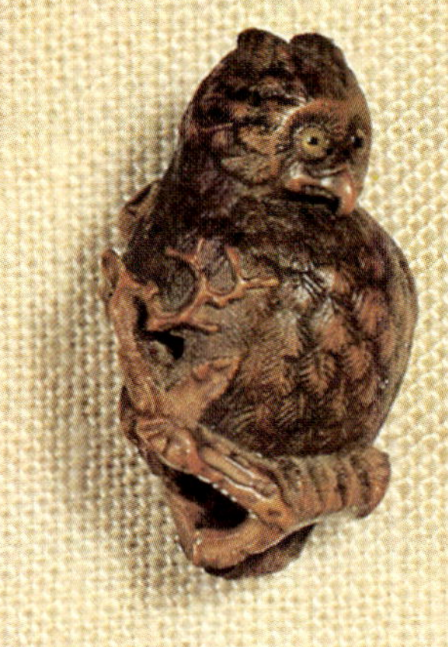
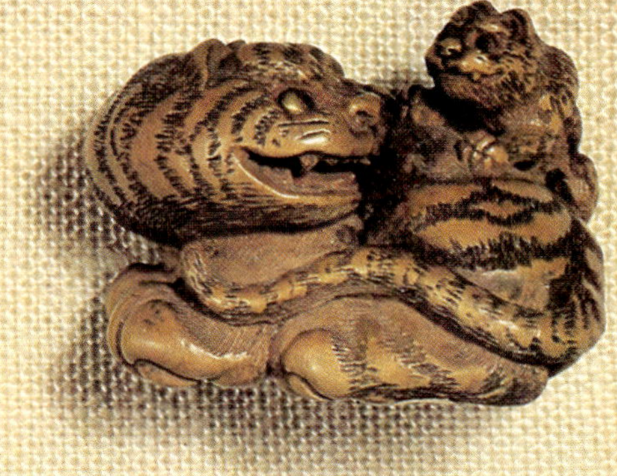
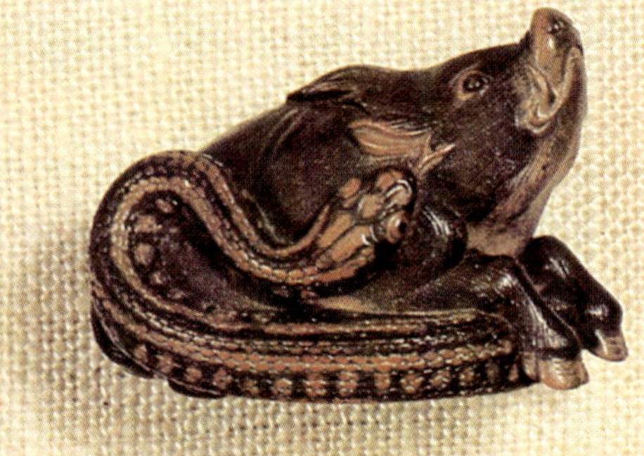
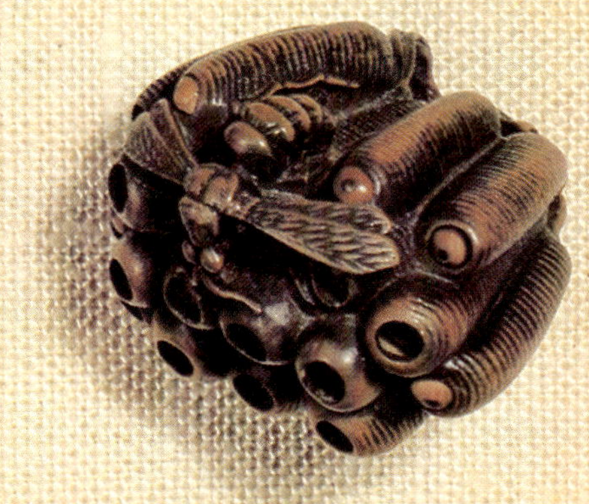
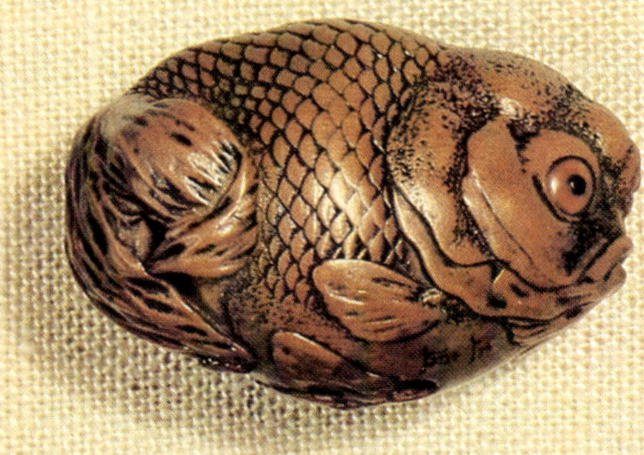
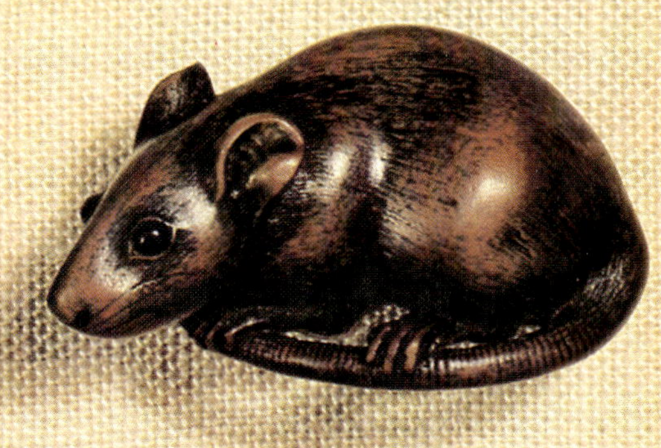

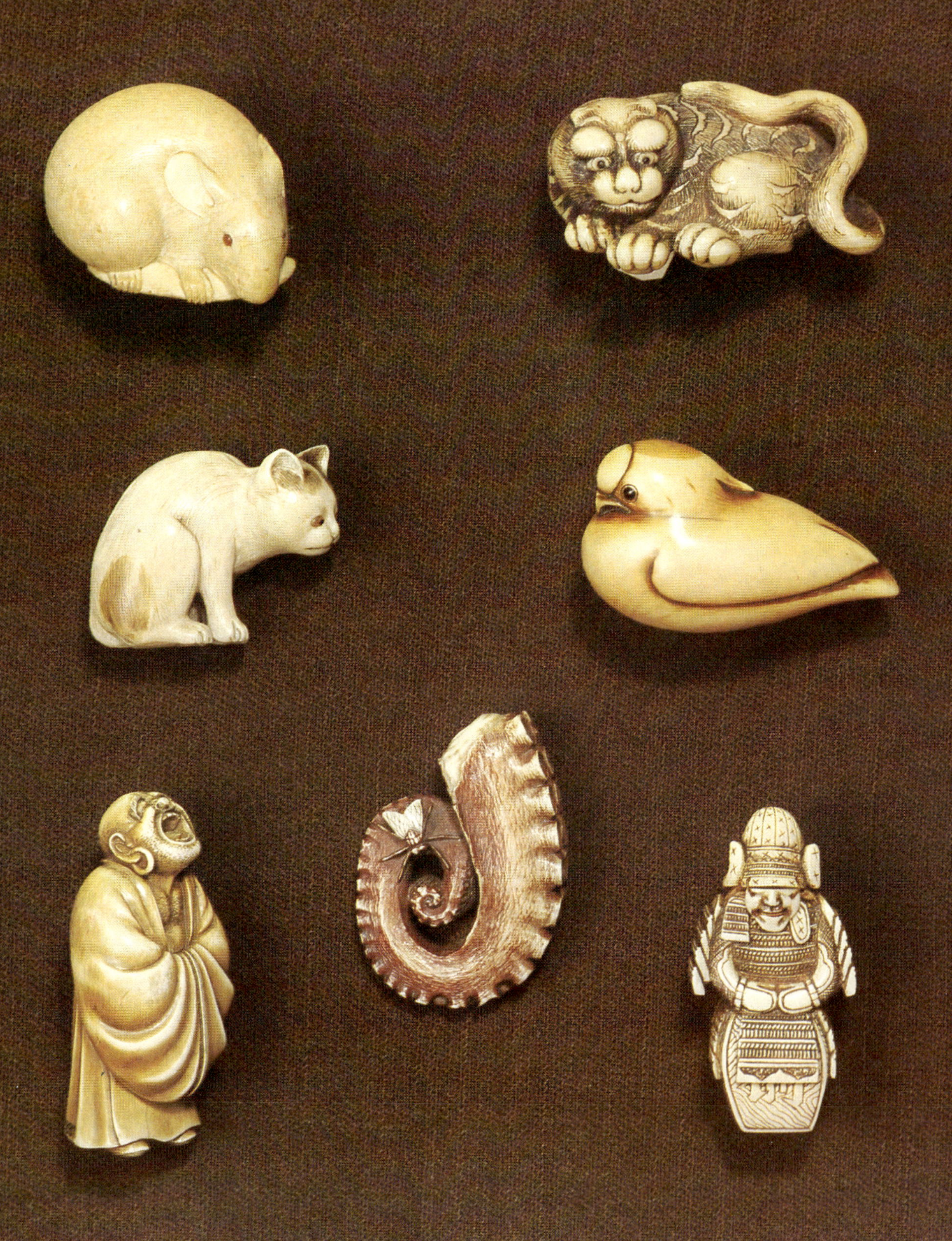

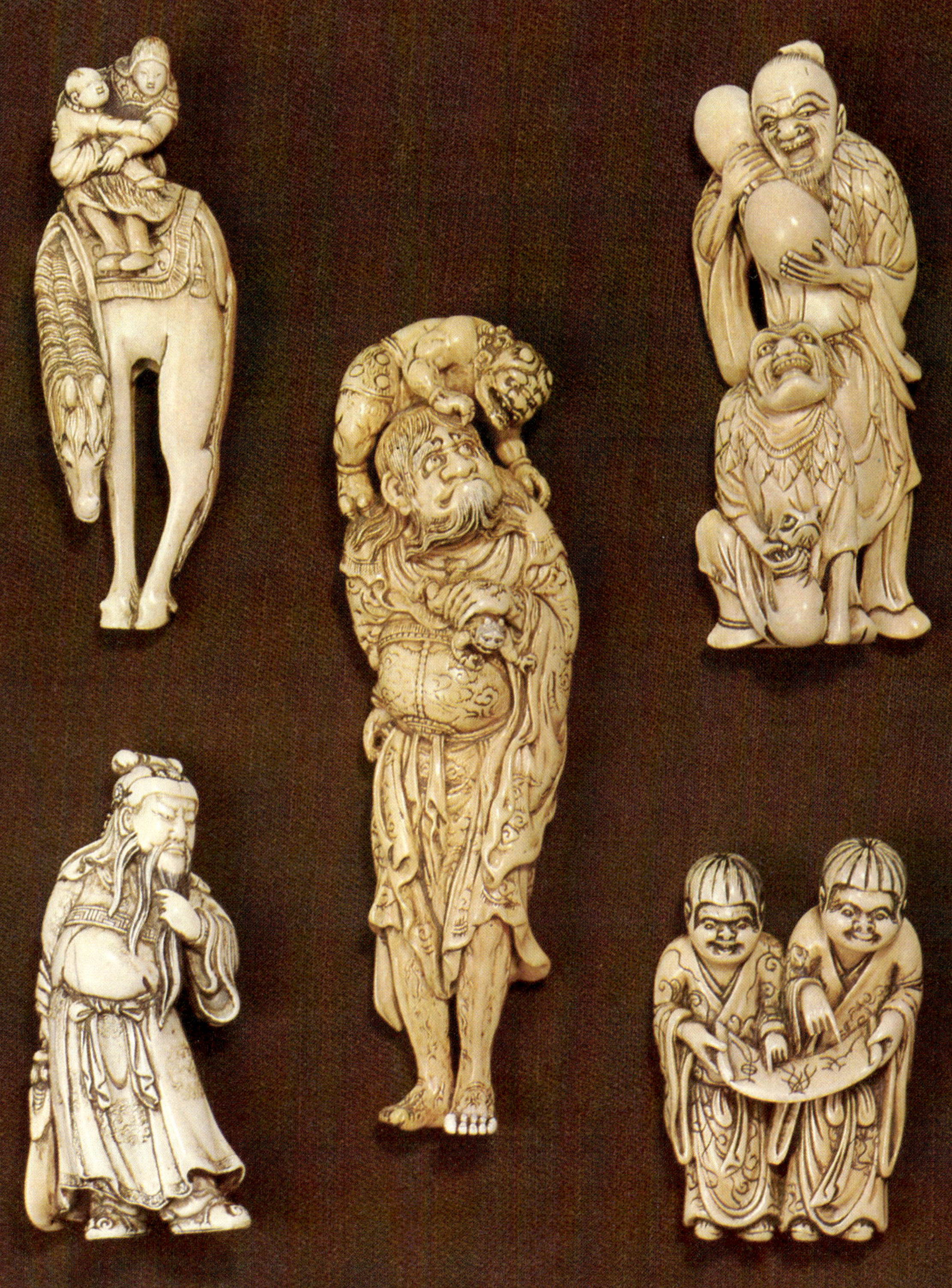

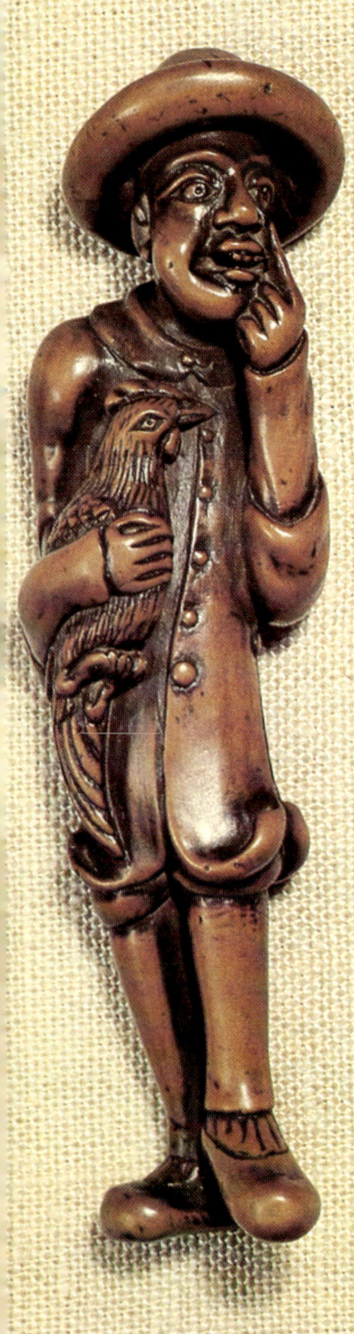
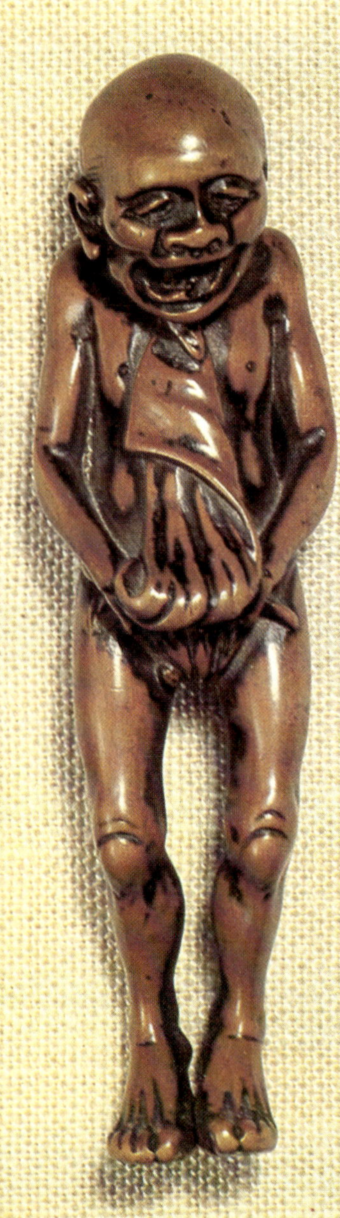
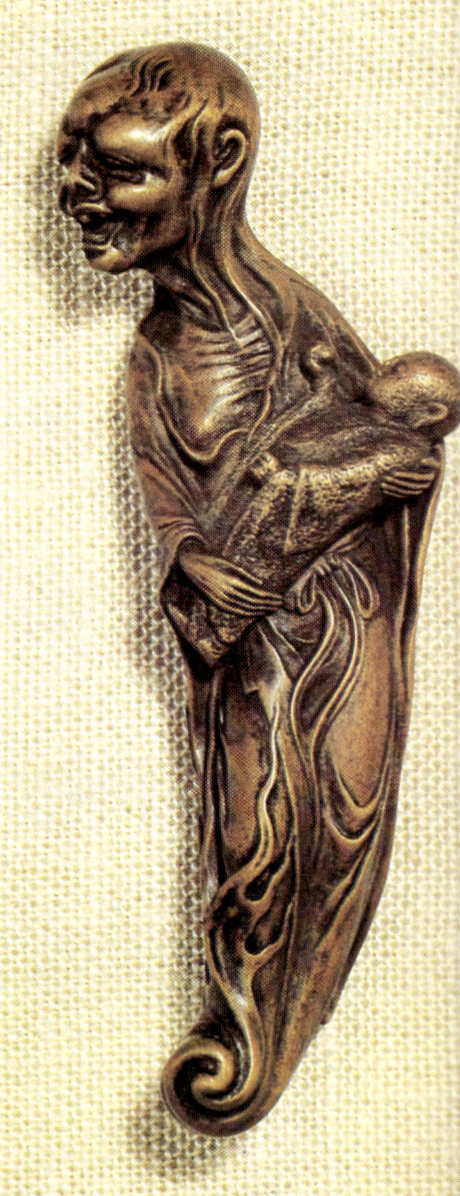

The first effects were to cause a great proliferation of native styles and techniques, especially in lacquer, metalwork, and woodblock printing, which culminated in the cultural flowering of the *Genroku* period (1688–1703). Decorative netsuke have not survived which can be dated definitely so early, but it seems likely that they were mostly in lacquer, designed *en suite* with the *inrō* which were then at their height of refinement. These would have been in the *hako* and *manjū* shapes. The *hako* was in the traditional shape of a small, flat lidded box which sometimes opened to be used as an extra container. The *manjū* was round and flat, in the shape of the rice-cake which gave it its name. In both of these the cord passed through a central hole and was fixed to a ring inside. The *manjū* remained popular and were made in large quantities. They were the perfect shape for netsuke, lying flat and smooth against the sash with no projections. Most *manjū* were probably undecorated discs of wood, lacquer or ivory and have not been preserved.

Chinese taste, tobacco, and early carved netsuke

By the end of the seventeenth century the smoking of tobacco, first introduced by the Portuguese in the previous century, had increased greatly, and a tobacco pouch or pipe-case was carried by every man of means. The merchant classes were now in need of fine netsuke, and something more in harmony with the wood or leather pouch developed. At about the same time Chinese learning began to spread in status downwards from the *samurai* who maintained the government and clan Confucian schools, a process much hastened in 1720 when Chinese and other foreign books were again permitted, though references to Christianity stayed on the black list. The Chinese had long used carved toggles of hardstone, and also larger seals in ivory, often surmounted by a carving of a lion-dog or other auspicious creature. Imported seals must soon have been copied, and these and other curios like the Goanese Christ Child or the Chinese medical figures (used by modest women to show where the trouble was), set a fashion for ivory, which had not been much used in Japan until then.

The earliest carved netsuke produced in any quantity are the tall figures in wood and ivory which reflect this foreign taste. They are mostly unsigned, of great skill, and clearly belong to a period before carvers and collectors began to place more faith is names than in quality. They usually had two holes bored in the back, through which the cord would pass. The knot would rest on the larger hole. From this time onwards most netsuke used holes for attaching the cord. The British Museum collection is particularly rich in these rare pieces. It is not known for certain why they are so much bigger (often as much as fifteen cm long) than at later periods, but it may be that their large size implied the lack of haste which was the ideal of the Chinese scholar. The subjects of these pieces were often the Taoist Immortals (*Sennin* in Japanese) illustrated in woodblock books such as the *Ressenden* ('Traditions of all the *Sennin*'), the Buddhist saints (*rakan*), or figures of the Chinese or Dutch merchants who were segregated in their own quarter at Nagasaki. The Chinese are often shown as effeminate and the Dutch as buffoons with large noses; but it is fair to state that native Japanese also are usually shown in a ridiculous light. The keynote of netsuke is detached humour.

Netsuke carving as an industry

303 301 89 The earliest account of netsuke carvers is in the book *Sōken Kishō* (1781)

by Inaba Tsūryū, an Ōsaka sword-merchant. The sixth and seventh volumes deal with *sagemono* and netsuke respectively. Inaba mentions fifty-seven carvers, mostly from Ōsaka, Kyoto and Edo, but also from a number of widely scattered provincial towns. This suggests that the industry had been in full swing for several generations. On the other hand, he feels the need to describe what netsuke are, which implies that they were still not commonly used articles among all classes. Inaba gives pride of place to an amateur carver, Yoshimura Shūzan (died 1776). The prestige of this *Kanō* school artist, who carved mostly Chinese figures in wood which he used his knowledge of pigments to paint with brilliant lustre and depth, still reflects the Chinese inspired cult of the gentleman amateur, though we may be sure Shūzan, like his contemporary 'amateur' painters of the scholar school, did not lose by presenting a fine piece to a rich patron. Yet it is clear from the other fifty-six carvers mentioned that a fully professional industry had already developed in the centres which continued to dominate for the next century. If Ōsaka has the most quoted, it is probably because Inaba came from that city. In later periods, when a great many netsuke were signed, we can estimate the relative density of production. As one might expect, it tends to go with population; Edo being the most productive, followed by the other great cities of Ōsaka, Kyoto, and Nagoya, with at least some from all major centres of population.

The fact that the signatures of only about one third of the carvers in the *Sōken Kishō* have been found on actual pieces supports the theory that eighteenth-century netsuke tended to be unsigned. Certainly Shūzan never signed a piece for all his fame, and many other great carvers, such as the creators of most of the unsigned eighteenth century figures in this catalogue, are never likely to be identified.

The origins of the early carvers

It is a fact of great interest to art historians that the natural sculptural genius of the Japanese, which produced the grand and dynamic Buddhist sculpture of the Kamakura Period (1185–1333), and the subtly restrained Zen portrait figures and Nō drama masks of the Muromachi Period (1392–1568), should have produced from the sixteenth century onwards so little of real interest. By the seventeenth century Buddhist sculptors were already producing miniature shrines for private devotions which exhibit that fineness of detail which was to grace the netsuke. These carvers were certainly among the first makers of netsuke in wood, and though the new form rarely achieved grandeur because of its utilitarian nature it certainly had the vitality of inspiration which the old forms could no longer provide. Thus it is true to say that in the period 1700–1850, netsuke for all their smallness of scale were the main vehicle of Japanese sculptural genius. Other craftsmen who may have turned to netsuke included the seal-makers and makers of plectrums for stringed instruments – they were acquainted with the use of ivory which was not used in Buddhist work – and the makers of bamboo and wooden pipes, combs, hair-pins and tea utensils. Netsuke in other materials, such as lacquer, pottery, porcelain, and metalwork, were usually made as a side industry of old established crafts.

The great age, and later developments

The period of major production of high quality netsuke lies roughly in the years 1800–50. Netsuke lost their scholarly bias, became smaller, rounder and more humorous, took on a much wider range of subjects and materials, and reached surprising heights of technical perfection or brilliant cleverness. Kagetoshi, for example, produced architectural fantasies in ivory in which every detail is perfect even under a magnifying glass. It has been said that some of the finest netsuke took as long as two months to complete. Obviously such pieces must have been very expensive, and, as noted before, they were a useful vehicle for the quiet ostentation forced on the rich of that period. But they also reflected that perfectionism which has been a characteristic of the best Japanese craftsmen at all periods.

In the mid-nineteenth century social and historical circumstances caused netsuke to decline as an art form. In 1853 and 1854 the American Commander Perry's gunboats broke the Isolation, and from then on Western goods and ideas poured into Japan. The effects were twofold, neither of them beneficial to netsuke. On the one hand Japanese taste was for a while thoroughly confused by the flood of Western innovations, and for a generation there was a real crisis of confidence in native aesthetic values. On the other hand, Western visitors began to arrive and collect netsuke. A few were discriminating and began the great collections which still exist in Europe and America. Among them were Sir Augustus Franks, a Keeper at the British Museum, who did not go to Japan himself but acquired things from people who did. But unfortunately the greater number of Westerners were easily impressed by the supposed quaintness of low-grade netsuke while blind to their poor craftsmanship. Thus began the large-scale production of low-grade pieces, nearly always in ivory or cheap substitutes for it, which has continued ever since.

On top of this, the great Ansei fire at Edo in 1857 destroyed great quantities of property, including netsuke. To replace them quickly, the easily-turned *manjū* in ivory were produced in great numbers, often rather sketchily engraved, and this too caused artistic standards to decline. Then in 1867 came the great political upheaval which destroyed the Tokugawa government and restored the Emperors to at least theoretical power in Edo, now renamed Tokyo. With the Restoration came a commitment to Westernization, the abolition of the *samurai* class as such, the wearing of Western clothes, and a rapid decline in all traditional crafts. Thus in a period of only fifteen years the netsuke received a series of blows which virtually destroyed it as a craft relevant to contemporary life.

Traditional carvers and the practical demand for their work did not die away all at once, and some fine pieces continued to be made in the Meiji period (1867–1912). Alongside them developed gradually the self-conscious art-netsuke, made for example at the Tokyo Art School which was founded to preserve old crafts but was nevertheless very influenced by Western artistic ideas. Many of the carvers of both types turned to making *okimono* ('ornaments'), larger works, usually in ivory, and often with a strong bias towards Western naturalism. The smaller *okimono* (up to about twenty cm long) were often bored with holes at a later date, so that they could be passed off as the more saleable netsuke. Among the art-carvers was Kōseki, whose mask and ghost are sculpturally the most impressive works in the British Museum's netsuke collection. They have in miniature a quality approaching grandeur, made possible by the artist's studies of ancient sculpture and his freedom from the whims of taste. Fine art-netsuke have continued to be made, but the British Museum has no examples later than Kōseki's work.

The principal schools of makers, and their most famous carvers, are briefly listed at the end of the catalogue.

Types of netsuke

The commonest type of netsuke was the three-dimensional carving (*katabori*) of a subject which could be a deity, a human being, a mythical creature or apparition, any member of the animal and vegetable kingdoms, or any object. The scale could range from a life-sized copy of a nut to a group of palaces, the actual size from about fifteen cm down to about 2.5 cm. Bigger than fifteen cm the netsuke would be too heavy and cumbersome, below 2.5cm too small to be effective in its job. However long the netsuke might be, it would always be slim enough to lie flush against the belt. Many longer netsuke were made from pieces of ivory of triangular section discarded by other craftsmen, one facet providing a flat back for a figure-subject to lie comfortably. In fully carved pieces the two holes for the cord (*himotoshi*) were sometimes bored in the back or base, sometimes formed by natural elements in the design. These netsuke provide a gallery in miniature of all aspects of Japanese life of the Edo Period.

Manjū netsuke, in the shape of a round rice-cake flattened at the edges, were common. They could be in unadorned lacquer, ivory or wood and then engraved, inlaid, or carved in semi-relief. The cords were attached to a ring inside, passing out through a central hole, or if the piece were carved in the solid, were tied to a metal ring fixed on one side.

Kagamibuta ('mirror lid') netsuke consisted of a *manjū* case, into one side of which fitted a decorated metal plate. It was held in position by the cord, which was attached to the back of the plate and passed out through a hole in the *manjū* case. This type became especially popular in Tokyo in the later nineteenth century when the makers of sword-furniture, put out of business by the ban on the wearing of swords by civilians in 1876, turned to other forms to make their living.

Mask-netsuke were very popular in Edo, and were the speciality of the Deme studio or family. They represented the ceremonial Buddhist *gigaku* and *bugaku* masks, the masks of the *Nō* drama, those used in popular festivals, and some which are probably imaginary. It is not known why they were so popular in Edo, which had no ancient mask tradition. It is a question of some interest whether actual mask-makers turned their hands to mask-netsuke.

A rarer type, perhaps because it was less often decorated, was the *sashi*-netsuke which hooked over the sash. Only one is included in this catalogue.

Real objects, suitably polished and sometimes with cord-rings attached, were used; the jaw of a wolf is a striking example in this collection. Natural objects like gourds, shells and nuts, were of course used from an early period, though they have not been collected.

A most interesting class of netsuke were those which had a primary use. The earliest of these were the seals with carved handles, though Medieval literature suggests that the flint and tinder set was used as a netsuke from very early on. These useful netsuke included watches, sun-dials, flint-lighters, small knives, utensils for the tea ceremony, and ash-trays. The last-named, common with tobacco pouches, were usually in metal; the comic figure of a guardian king is shown wearing one of them Occasionally foreign articles, like the Chinese 'medical' figures, were used as netsuke.

The main subjects depicted in netsuke are outlined in the glossary. Subjects which appear only once are described in the entry for that piece.

Materials

As netsuke had to be light, organic materials were preferred. Of these the most important were wood, ivory and lacquer. The most popular softwoods were boxwood and cedar, but many others were used. Hardwoods were used in great profusion, many of them imported from China and South East Asia. Because of the danger of wrong identification, no attempt has been made, with a few exceptions, to name in the catalogue the types of wood used. Similarly, the many kinds of ivory – elephant, walrus, narwhal, tooth, etc. – are easily confused, especially when stained; and only the narwhal has been identified in the catalogue where its rough outer shell has been left intact by the carver proud of using this most expensive of ivories. The eyes of animals and people are often inlaid ebony, horn, amber, metal, glass or tortoiseshell. It is very difficult to identify all of these because of their very small size, and the catalogue names them only when they are quite certain. Lacquer included the highly polished native style, with gold lacquer (*makie*) and other decoration, and carved red work in Chinese style.

Other organic materials employed were nuts, horn, antler, coral, amber, and the fossilized sea-pine called *umimatsu* much used by Ganbun to simulate vegetables.

Ceramics, stones and metals were less often used because of their weight, and tended to be small for that reason. There was a slight vogue for porcelain figures in the Hirado style during the nineteenth century, apparently made mainly for the Western market.

Signatures and authenticity

The problems of authenticity in netsuke are the same as in any field of Japanese art. The works of a great master were copied by his pupils and by more remote descendants in his studio. These copies included exact reproductions of the signature. If the practice known to have been used by painters was followed, a master would even put his signature on a pupil's work which he particularly approved of. At a further remove were the copies made by contemporary carvers of other schools to sell to unwary buyers more interested in a great name than in an original work. Further away still were the fakes and reproductions made in the Meiji and later periods with Western collectors in mind. In our present state of knowledge it is possible to separate the genuine from the copy only by guesswork based on relative quality. While it is undeniable that a master like Tomotada or Minkō must have produced great work to acquire his reputation, it is not easy to place a pupil who may have been his equal in skill. In this catalogue the attributions, as in most publications to date, are aesthetically based. Certainly there is very little documentation available on any major carver before the Meiji period.

The signatures of all the pieces are reproduced, and are romanized according to the Hepburn system in the catalogue entries. Where they consist of the maker's name or names they are simply quoted, but where extra information is included, such as a date or place of work, this is translated. Makers sometimes add seals, or use them alone. These, too, are reproduced and are romanized where it has been possible to read them. The *kakihan*, which are highly cursive seal-like forms of characters related to the *bonji* (Sanskrit characters) found on metalwork, are virtually unreadable, and only one has been certainly deciphered.

The British Museum's netsuke collection

The collection, of which this catalogue records about one third, was built up very largely by the bequests and donations of five collectors. The first and most important was Sir Augustus Wollaston Franks (1826–97) who joined the British Museum in 1851. In 1866 he became Keeper of the British and Medieval and of the Ethnographical sections, and was in fact in charge of all antiquities of the world except those of Greece, Rome, Egypt and the ancient Middle East. Franks was interested in everything, and had a wonderful eye for a fine or interesting object even when he knew little of the subject. He probably began collecting netsuke in the 1860s when he is known to have become interested in Japan. His large collection was bequeathed to the British Museum, but he had a habit of leaving things in the building during his lifetime, and it is not possible in every case to say whether it was a gift or a bequest. In the catalogue all his pieces are referred to simply as 'Franks Collection'. Franks' sure instincts told him that the unsigned eighteenth century figures, never popular with more than a handful of collectors, were sculpturally the finest netsuke, and he acquired many of these rare pieces.

In 1912 the prominent collector Harry Seymour Trower gave some of his best netsuke, which he had been collecting since 1876, and in 1930 the James Hilton bequest added a further very fine group, including more of the eighteenth century tall figures. The Oscar Raphael Bequest of 1945 included among Japanese arts of all sorts many netsuke of the finest quality, again with a good number of early figures. Raphael also collected a few pieces by late art-netsuke makers, among them the two magnificent carvings by Kōseki. The last great bequest was by Mrs Helen Epstein in 1953. Almost all the British Museum's netsuke came from these benefactors and from a few smaller bequests, and it is to their enthusiasm and discrimination that the nation is indebted for the existence of this fine collection.

L.R.H. SMITH

Notes on the Catalogue

Names and inscriptions are given in the Hepburn Romanization. Chinese names are given in their Japanese readings, as used in Japanese reference books. Measurements are given in centimetres with the equivalent in inches in brackets. The British Museum registration number of each piece is given, and should be quoted in correspondence with the Museum. All the pieces in the catalogue and their signatures are illustrated. For terms and names not explained in the individual entries, please consult the glossary.

The order of the catalogue is by place of origin, artists of unknown schools, masks, *kagamibuta*, unsigned wood and ivory netsukes and unusual materials.

Opposite

264 269

88

267 260

Overleaf

377 140

161 151 215

158

135 144

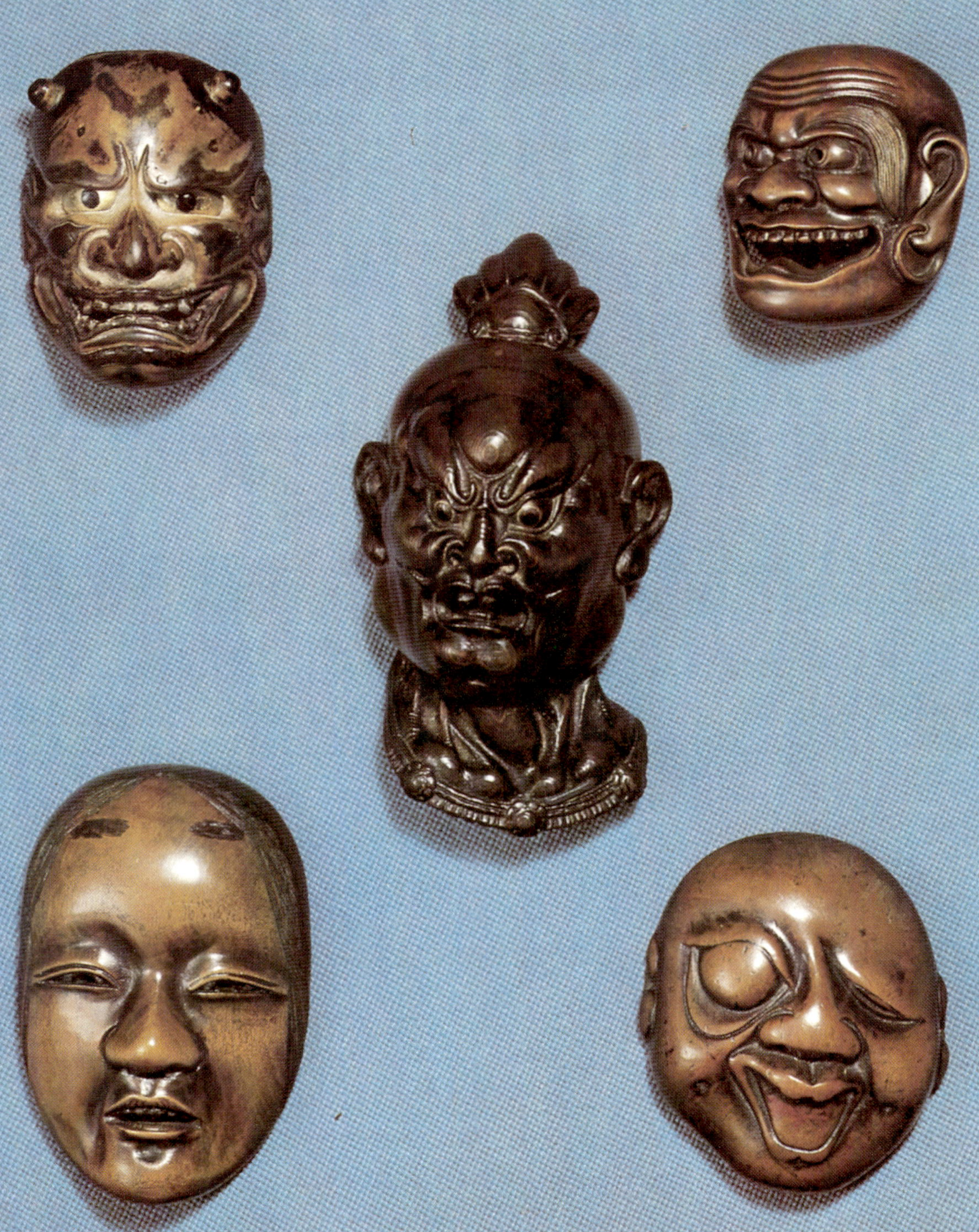

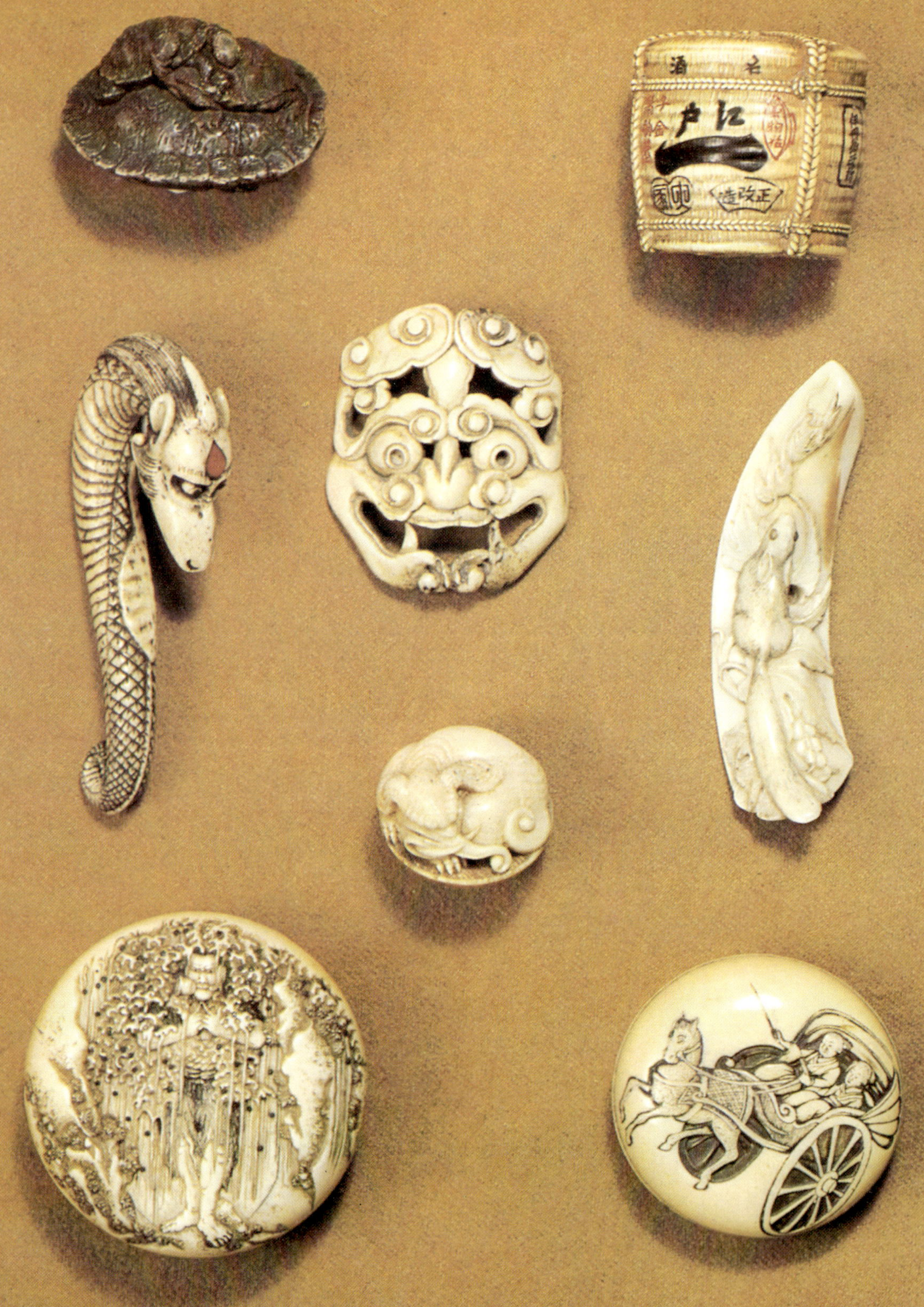
名酒
江戸一
正改造

The Catalogue

Ōsaka

1
Gama Sennin, holding the leg of the toad on his shoulder with one hand and a cluster of peaches with the other. Wood, details in ivory, partly stained.
Signed Tsuji at the hem of the robe.
18th century, the ivory inlay added at a later date.
Height 8.1cm ($3\frac{1}{4}$in).
1912 10-12 4. Given by Mrs H. Seymour-Trower.

2
Suit of armour, mounted on its storage box, the helmet and mask detachable, and held on by the cord. Ivory.
Signed Hidemasa.
Early 19th century.
Height 4.75cm ($1\frac{7}{8}$in).
F.1127. Franks Collection.
Colour plate, page 12

3
The monkey Songoku on a cloud, holding a staff to the hand of Buddha which appears before him. Ivory.
Signed Gyokuōsai Shūgyoku, in a rectangular cartouche on the base.
19th century.
Height 4.25cm ($1\frac{3}{4}$in).
F.967. Franks Collection.
Songoku is said to have helped the seventh-century Buddhist monk Sanzō in his 108 tests of holiness.

4
Shoki and two demons coming to life from a hanging painting, the 'demon-queller' piercing the mount of the painting with his sword, nearly impaling a demon who has escaped round the back.
Ivory, the scroll-ends in wood.
Signed Shūosai with seals Shōmei and Fujimoto.
19th century.
Height 3.75cm ($1\frac{1}{2}$in).
F.928. Franks Collection.
For a similar example, see R. Bushell, *Collectors' Netsuke*, p. 112, no. 173.

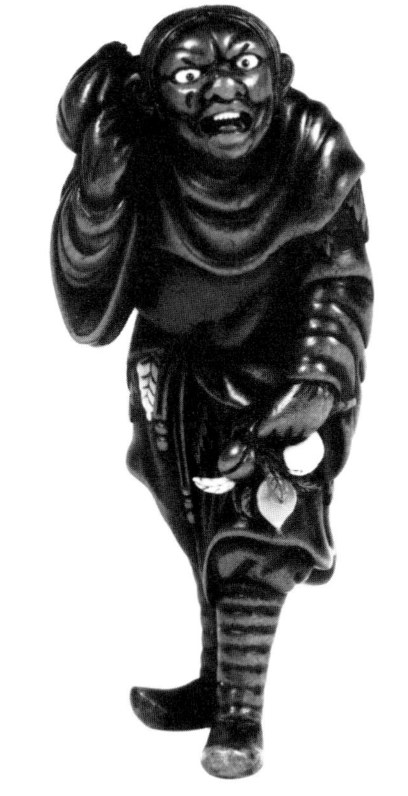

1
2

5
Gama Sennin seated on a giant toad.
Ivory, the toad's eyes inlaid with ebony.
Signed Masakazu in a leaf-shaped cartouche on the base.
19th century.
Length 4.75cm ($1\frac{1}{8}$in).
F.990. Franks Collection.
Gama Sennin is usually shown with his toad on his shoulder. This piece reverses their positions.

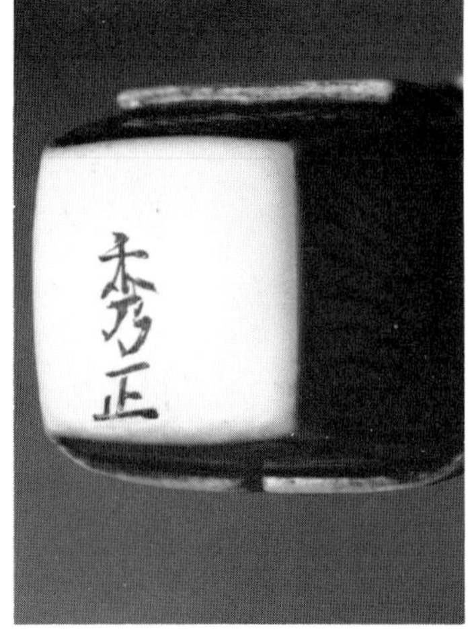

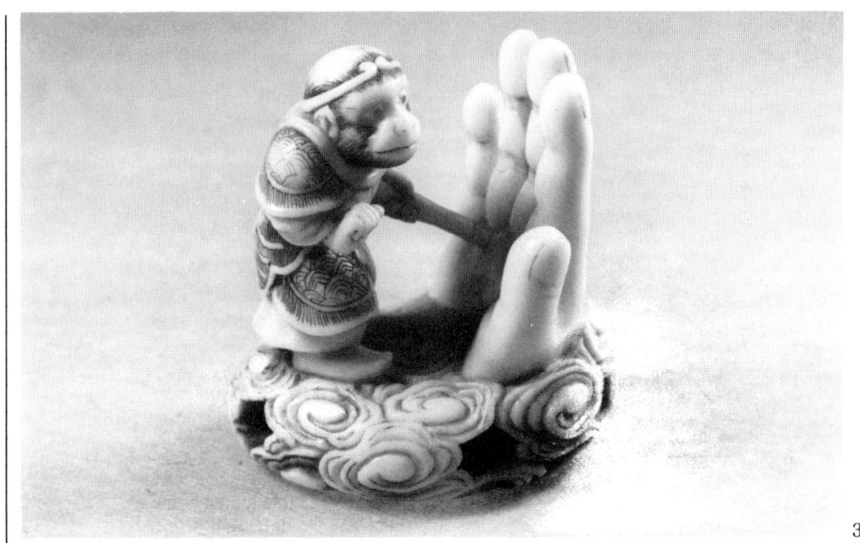

3

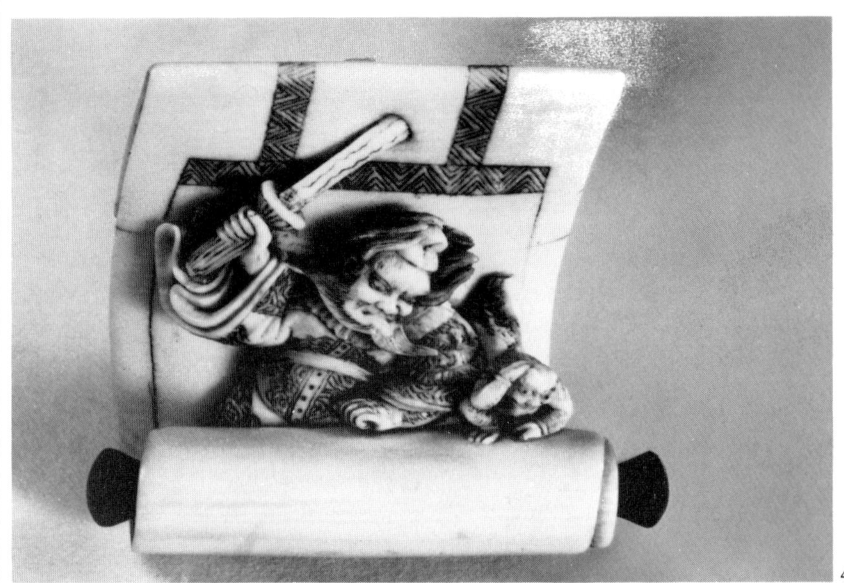
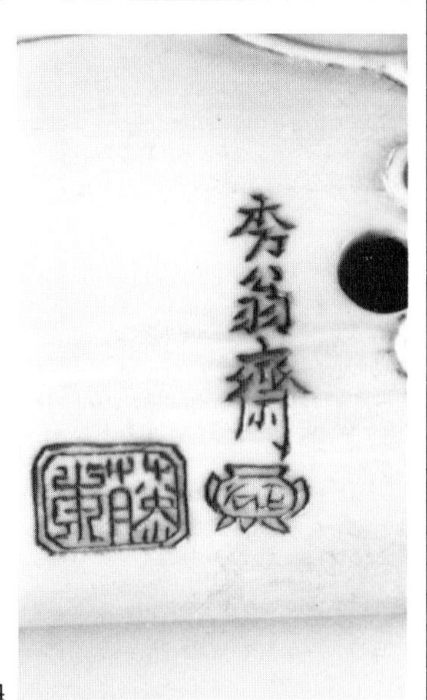

4

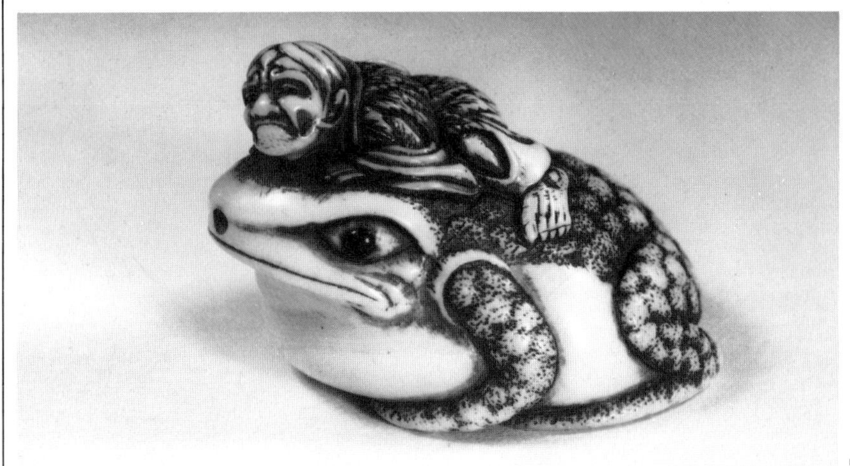
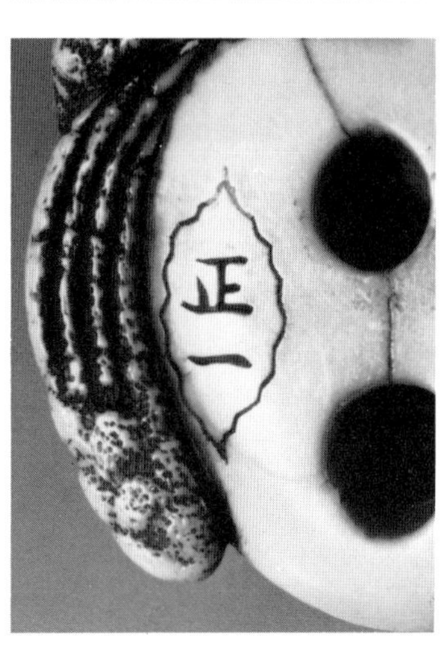

5

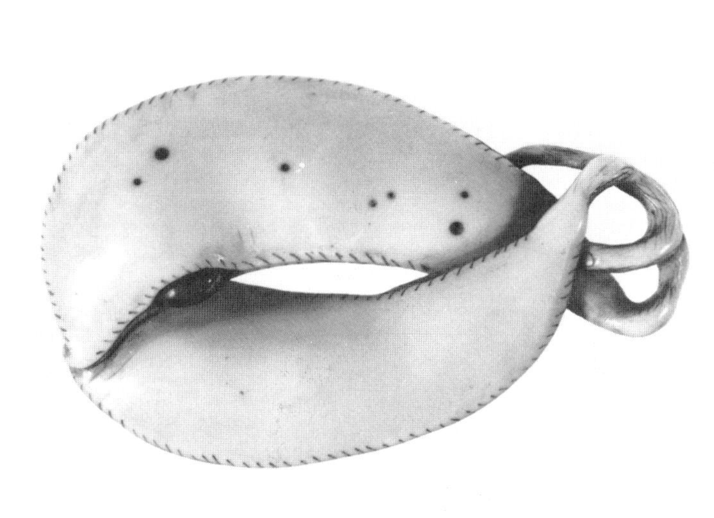

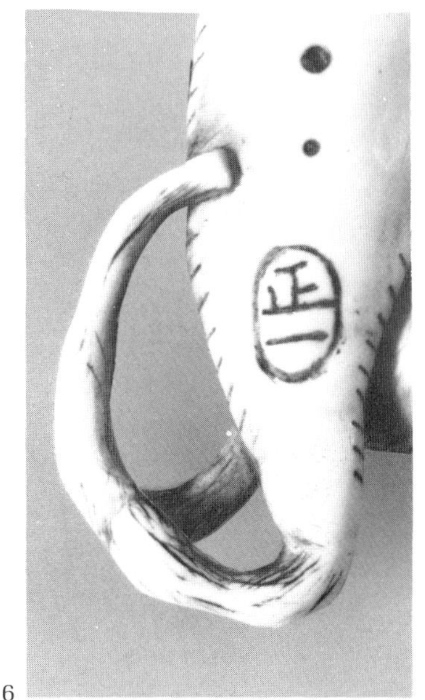

6

7

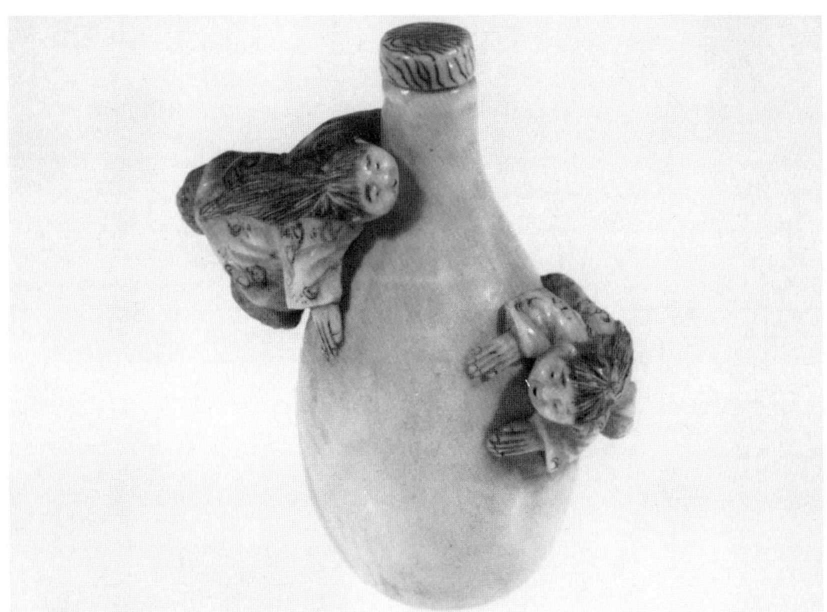

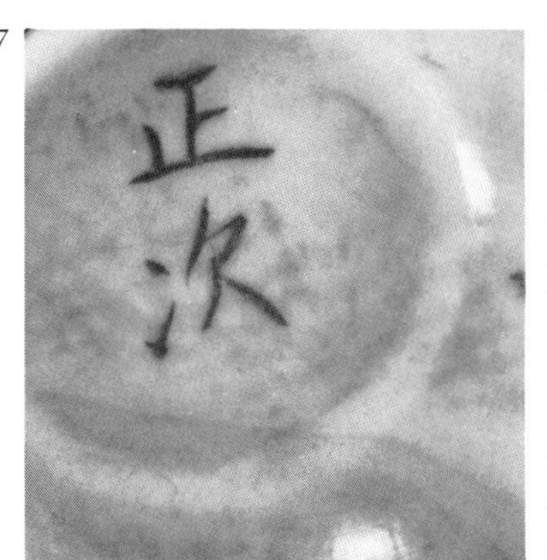

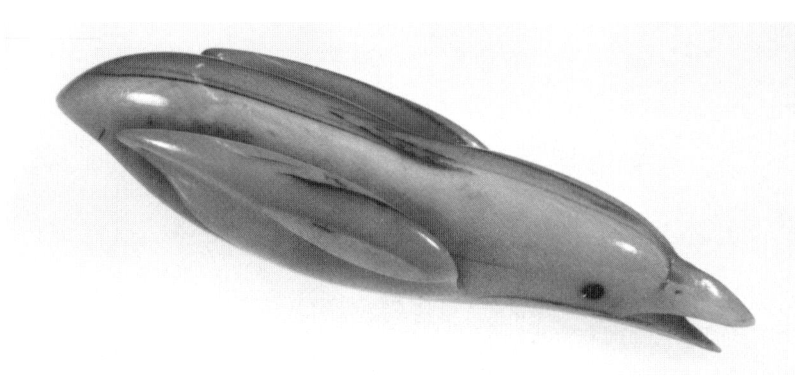

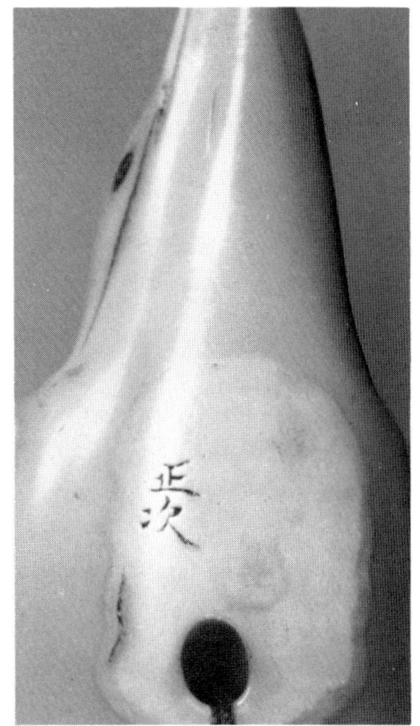

8

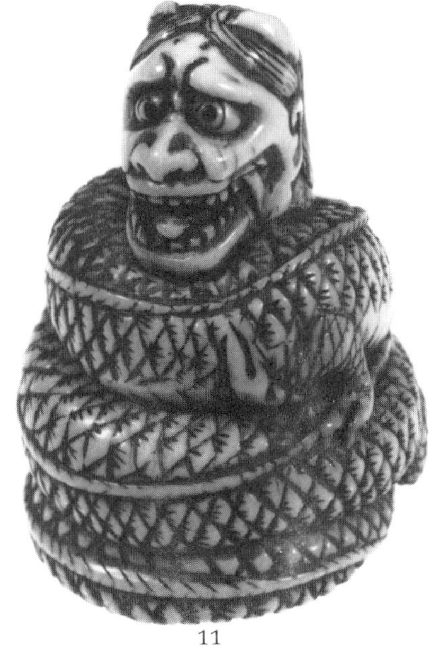

11

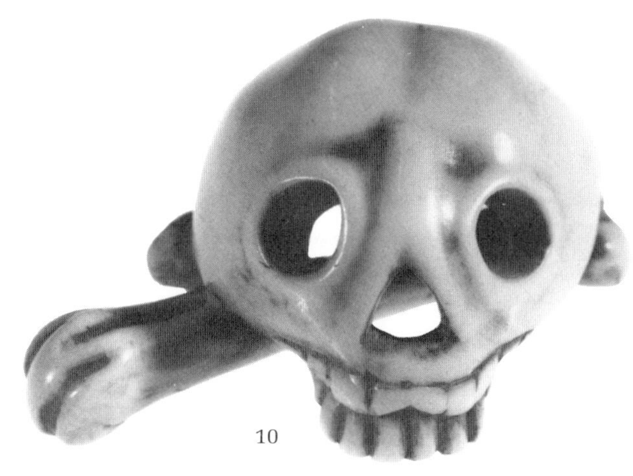

10

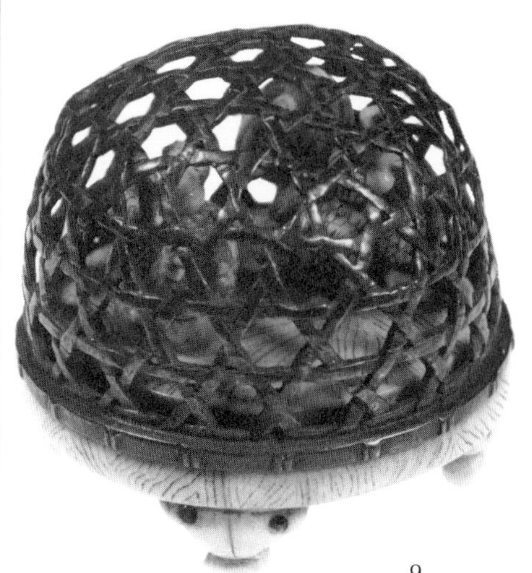

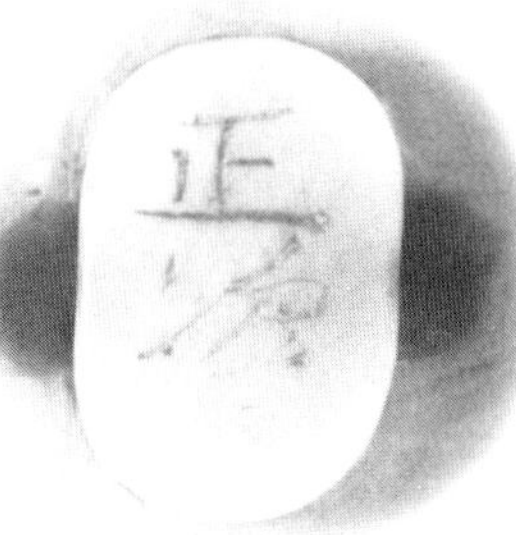

9

6
Two bean pods, one splitting to reveal a bean which is inlaid and stained purplish-green. Ivory.
Signed Masakazu in an oval cartouche.
19th century.
Length 5.3cm (2in)
F.1112. Franks Collection.

7
Two Shōjō (mythical drunken creatures), climbing round a large saké bottle. Ivory.
Signed Masatsugu.
19th century.
Length 4.5cm ($1\frac{3}{4}$in).
S.48.

8
Kingfisher in the act of diving. Ivory, the eyes inlaid with ebony.
Signed Masatsugu.
19th century.
Length 6.4cm ($2\frac{1}{2}$in).
1945 10-17 605. Bequeathed by Oscar Raphael.

9
Cock and hen with chicks in a cage, supported on four short legs and with a detachable steel basket-work cover. Ivory.
Signed Masatsugu.
19th century.
Height 3.5cm ($1\frac{1}{4}$in).
OA + 312.

10
Human skull and bone. Ivory.
Unsigned.
19th century.
Length 4.5cm ($1\frac{3}{4}$in).
1953 12-17 6. Bequeathed by Mrs Helen Epstein.

11
Kiyohime, already changed to a serpent, coiled round the invisible bell where Anchin hides. Ivory.
Signed Masatoshi in an irregular cartouche on lowest coil.
19th century.
Height 5.1cm (2in).
F.884. Franks Collection.

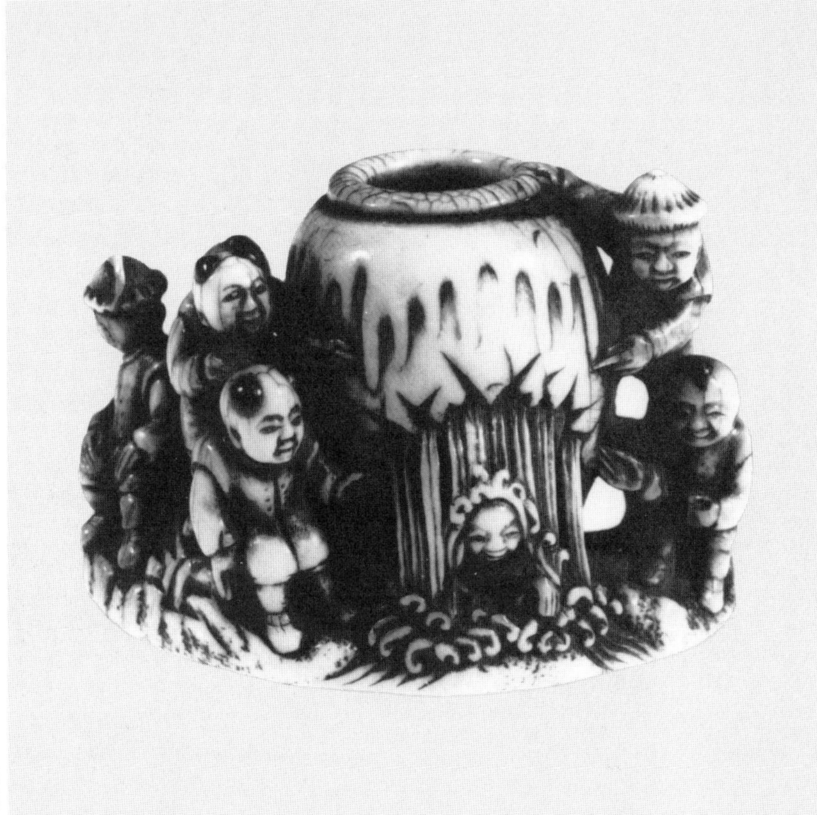

12 △

▽ 14

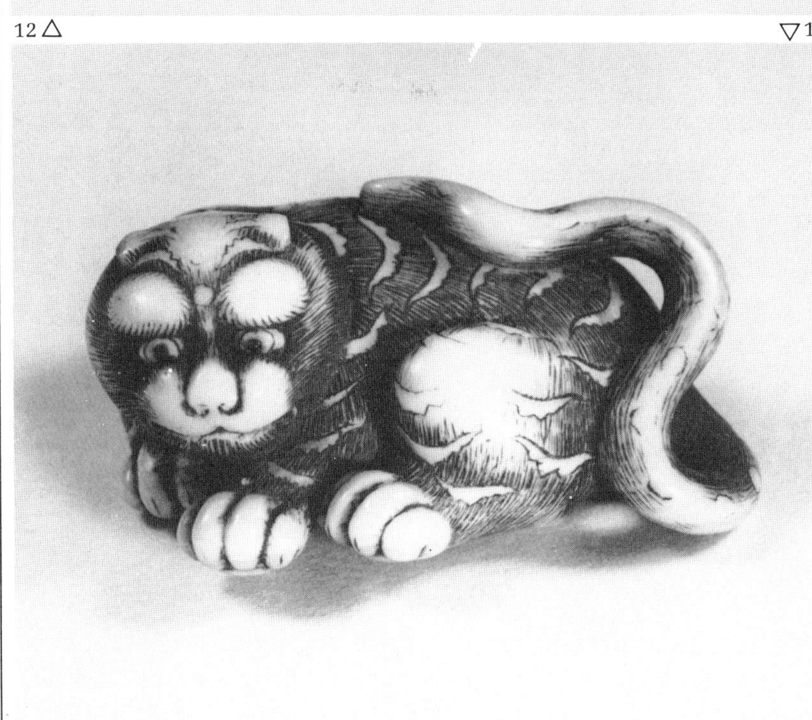

12
Shiba Onkō, the Chinese boy hero, breaking a large jar to release his drowning friend, who pours out on a flood of water, while other boys look on.
Ivory, boys' hair-knots inlaid in ebony.
Unsigned.
19th century.
Length 4.5cm (1¾in).
1945 10-17 516. Bequeathed by Oscar Raphael.

13
Seal-netsuke, the base surmounted by a standing tortoise. The seal has an unread grass-script name in relief.
Ivory, partly stained, eyes inlaid.
Signed Garaku on top of the base.
Early 19th century.
Height 3cm (1¼in).
F.268. Franks Collection.

14
Reclining tiger.
Ivory, the eyes inlaid with ebony.
Unsigned, probably school of Garaku.
Early 19th century.
Length 4.5cm (1¾in).
1972 1-14 19. Bequeathed by Mrs Rosina Maria Howe.
Colour plate, page 12.

15
Chick emerging from its egg.
Ivory, the eyes inlaid.
Signed Dōraku in an irregular cartouche on the base.
19th century.
Height 3.75cm (1½in).
F.791. Franks Collection.

16
Netsuke in the shape of a flat box, the cover carved in relief with the bust of a *rakkan* on a diaper ground. Ivory.
Signed Dōraku on the base.
19th century.
Length 4.5cm (1¾cm).
1945 10-17 551. Bequeathed by Oscar Raphael.

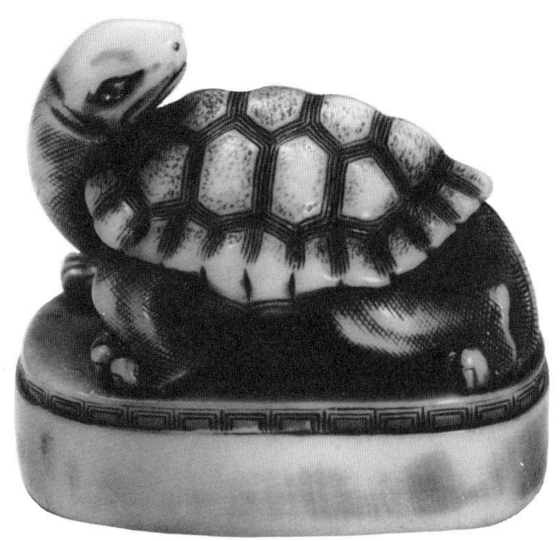

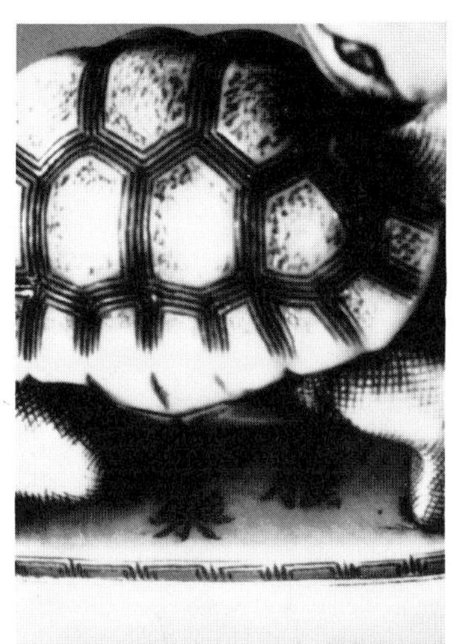

13

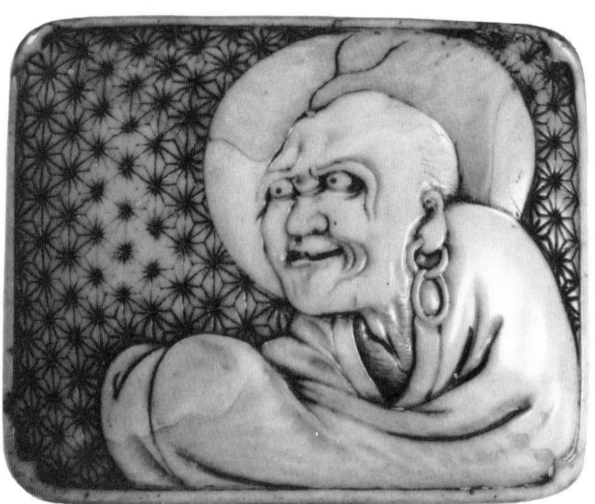

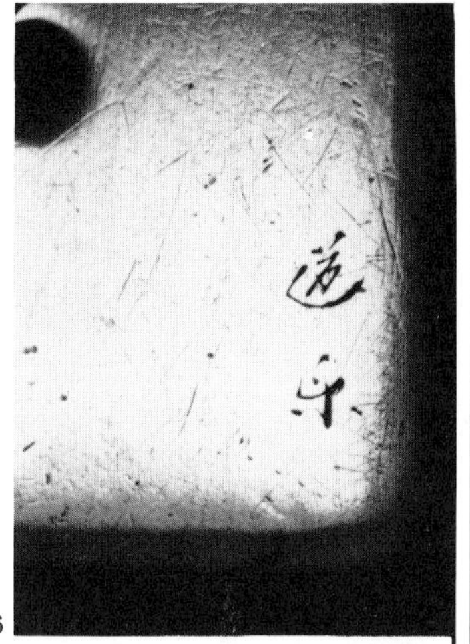

16

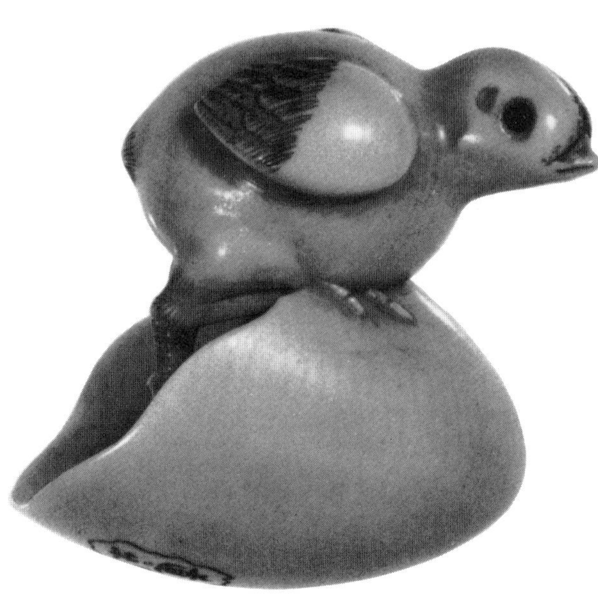

15

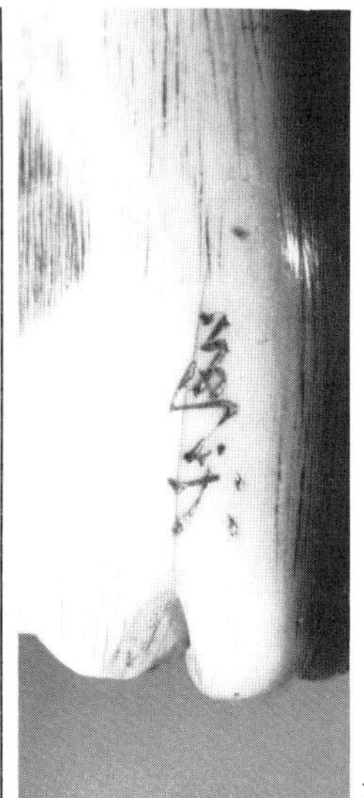
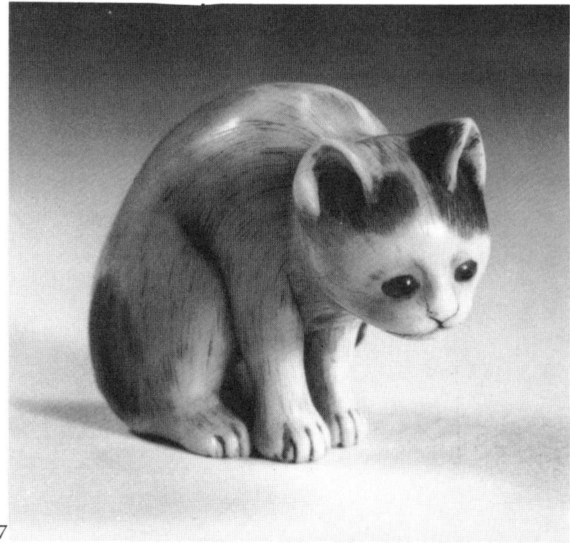
17

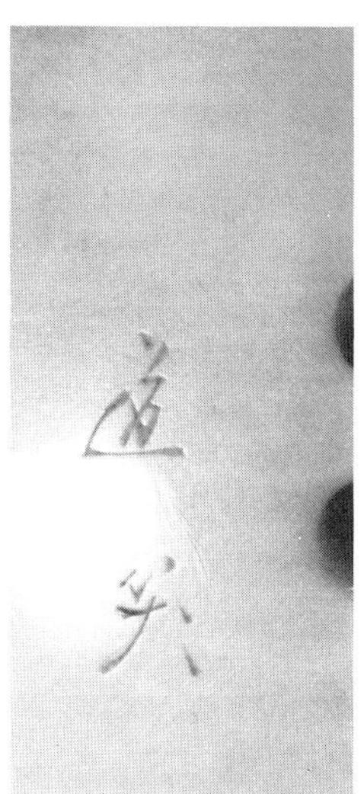
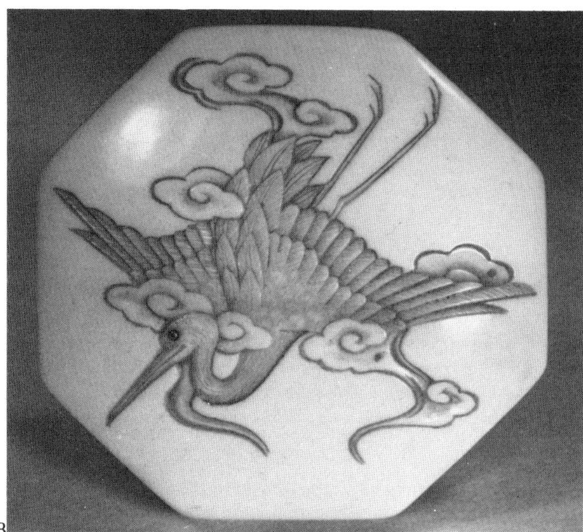
18

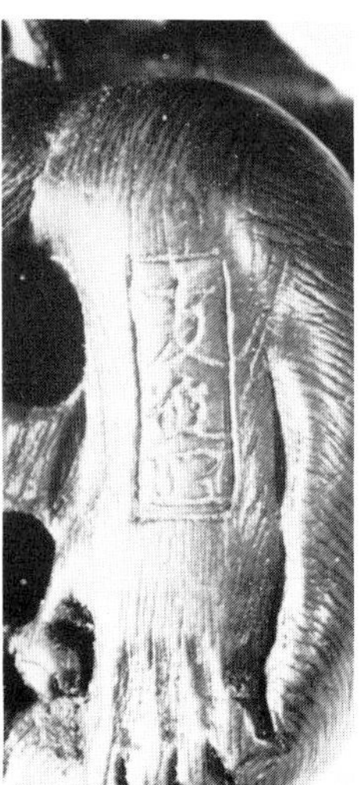
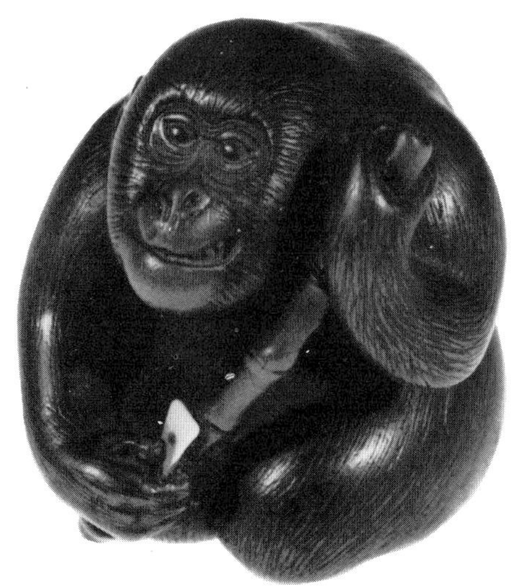
21

17
Seated cat.
Ivory, eyes inlaid with horn.
Signed Dōshō at top of tail.
19th century.
Height 2.5cm (1in).
1945 10-17 663. Bequeathed by Oscar Raphael.

Exhibited Red Cross, London, 1915, no. 199, illustrated in the catalogue, pl. L.
Colour plate, page 12.

18
Manjū, of octagonal form, carved in low relief with a crane flying among stylized clouds.
Ivory, bird's eye inlaid in metal.
Signed Dōshō on back.
19th century.
Diameter 3.25cm ($1\frac{1}{4}$in).
F.437. Franks Collection.

19
Stylized sparrow in flight, childrens' toys resting on its back, including a fishing line and a rattle.
Ivory, with horn and coral inlays.
Signed Dōshōsai on back.
19th century.
Length 5cm (2in).
F.794. Franks Collection.

20
Cooper making a bucket. Ivory.
Signed Gechū.
Late 18th–early 19th century.
Height 4.25cm ($1\frac{3}{4}$in).
F.202. Franks Collection.

21
Seated monkey, holding a bamboo stick and an ivory plectrum as if playing a stringed instrument.
Wood, with ivory plectrum.
Signed Tomochika in rectangular cartouche, with *kakihan*.
19th century.
Height 3.5cm ($1\frac{3}{4}$in)
F.679. Franks Collection.

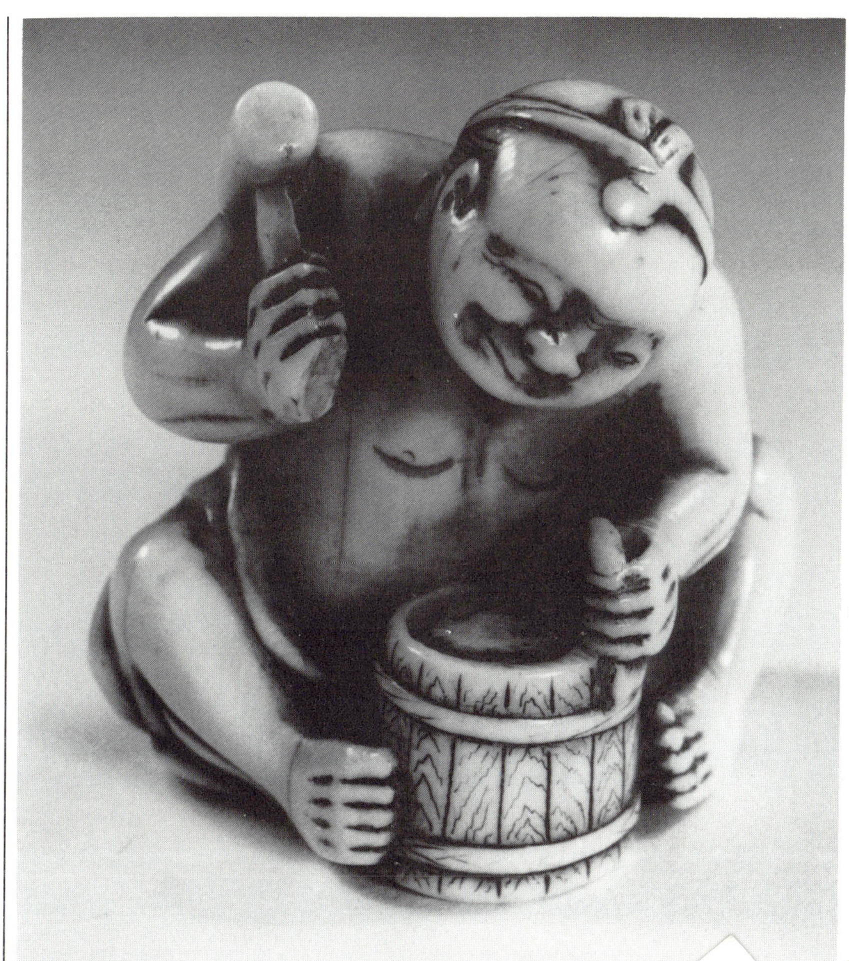

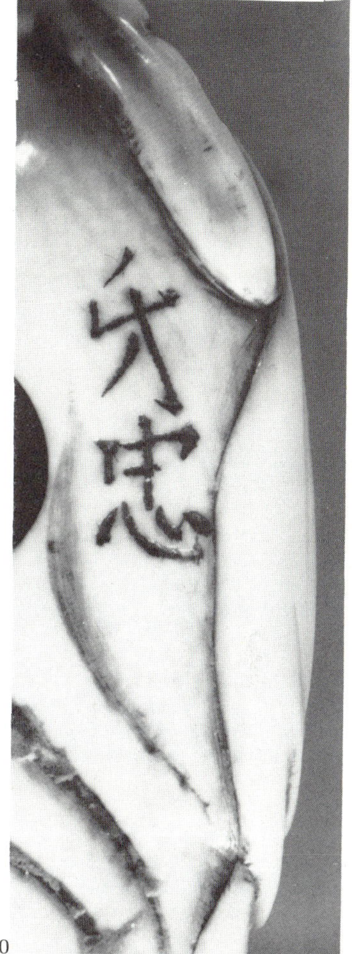

20

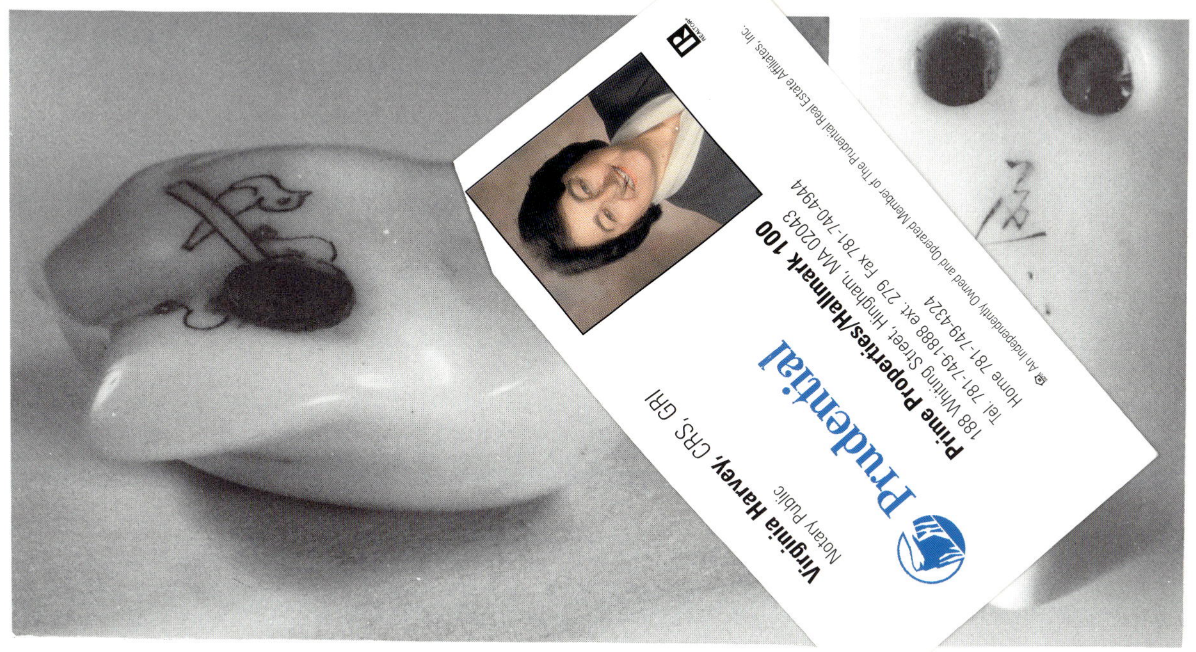

22
Manjū, carved in low relief with two puppies playing with a shell.
Ivory, puppy's mouth reddened.
Signed Kōgetsusai on back.
19th century.
Diameter 3.75cm ($1\frac{1}{2}$in).
F.411. Franks Collection.

23
Seated mandarin duck.
Ivory, deliberately stained, eyes inlaid.
Signed Ōhara Mitsuhiro, with *kakihan* on base.
19th century.
Length 4.5cm ($1\frac{3}{4}$in).
1945 10-17 592. Bequeathed by Oscar Raphael.
Colour plate, page 12.

24
Daruma, standing and yawning after his nine-year meditation.
Ivory, deliberately stained.
Signed Mitsuhiro with seal Ōhara, on back.
19th century.
Height 5cm (2in).
F.897. Franks Collection.
Colour plate, page 12

25
Peach, engraved with the immortal Tōbōsaku standing on clouds and holding a peach.
Ivory.
Signed Mitsuhiro with seal Ōhara, on back.
19th century.
Height 3.75cm ($1\frac{1}{2}$in).
F.1115. Franks Collection.

26
Mokugyō (temple bell) in the form of a carp. Ivory.
Signed Mitsuhiro in an oval cartouche with double outline.
19th century.
Length 7cm ($2\frac{3}{4}$in).
1945 10-17 606. Bequeathed by Oscar Raphael.

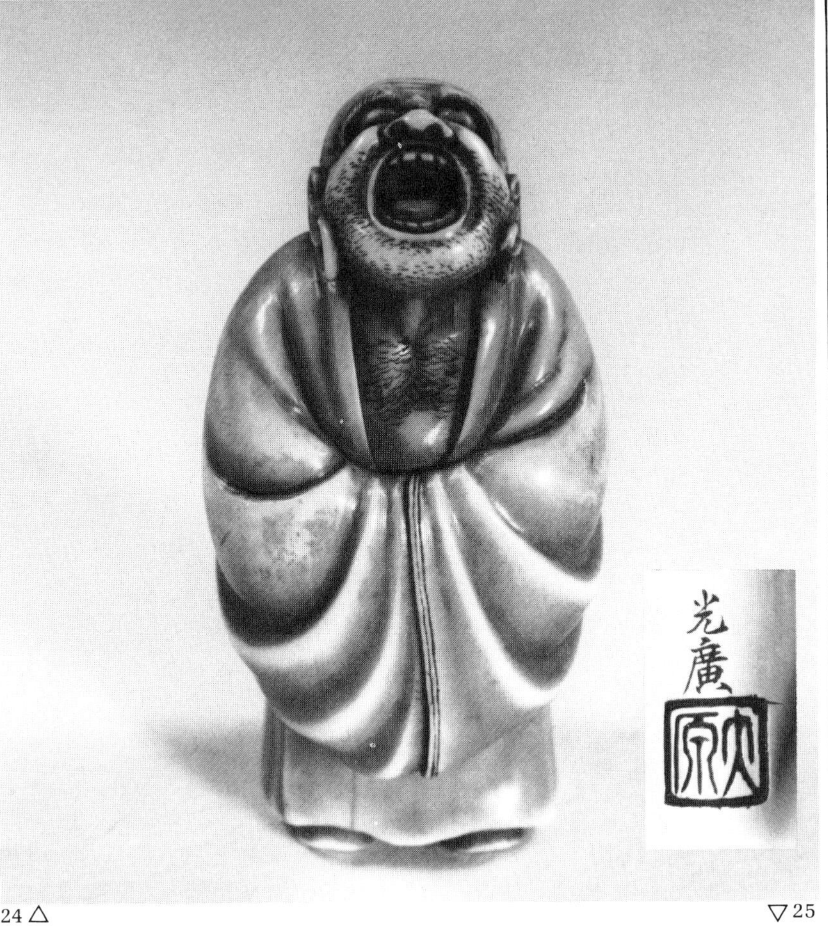

24 △

▽ 25

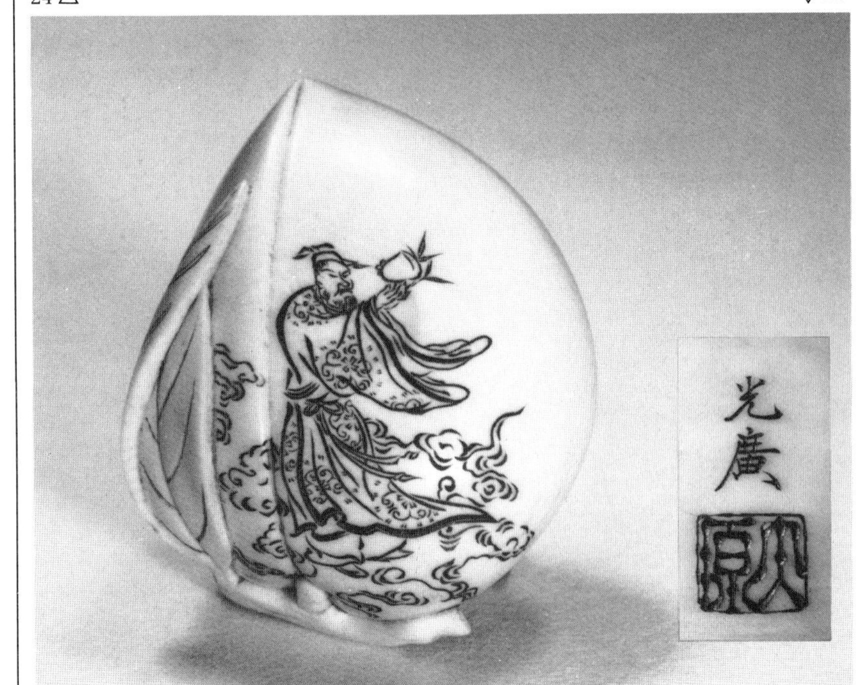

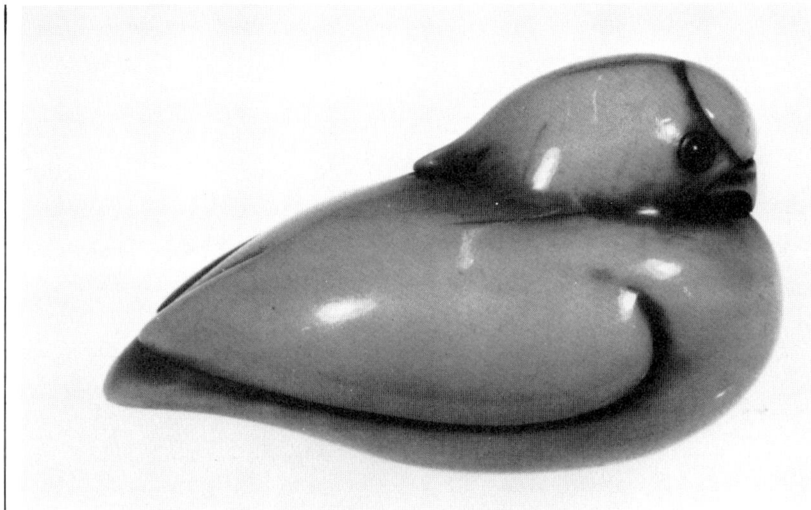

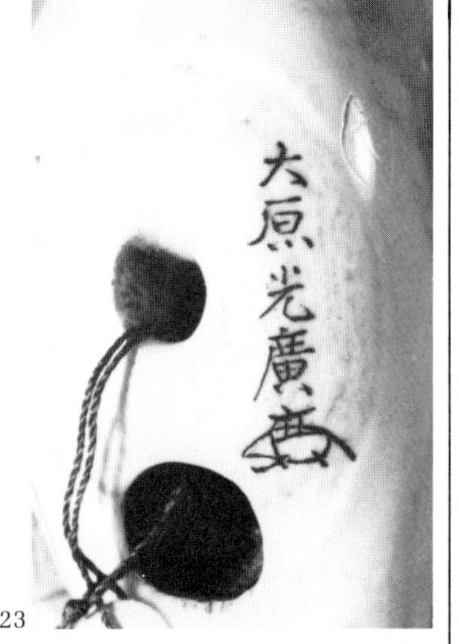

23

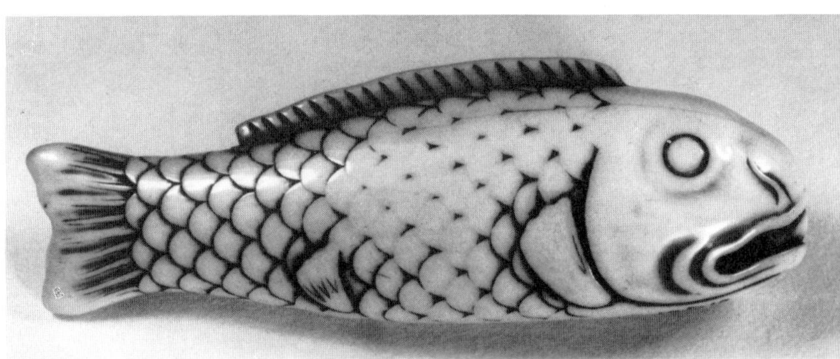

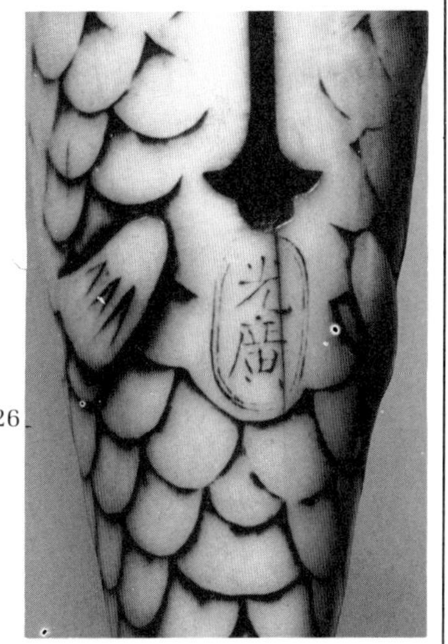

26

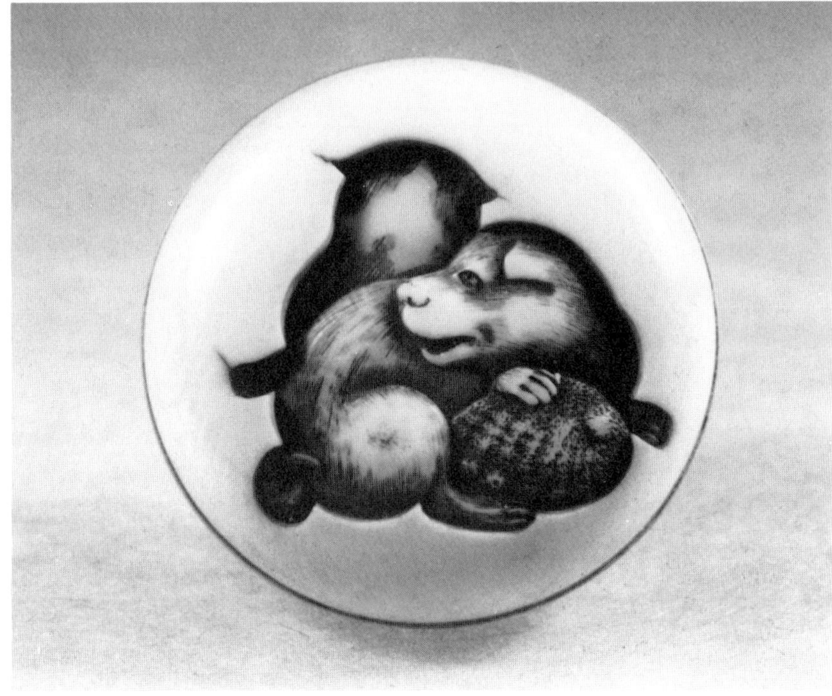

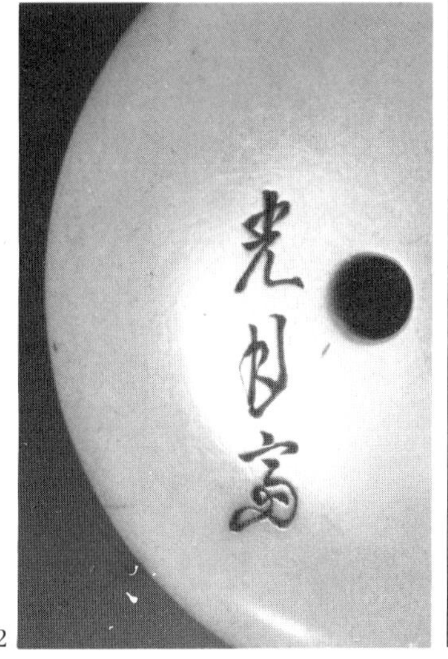

22

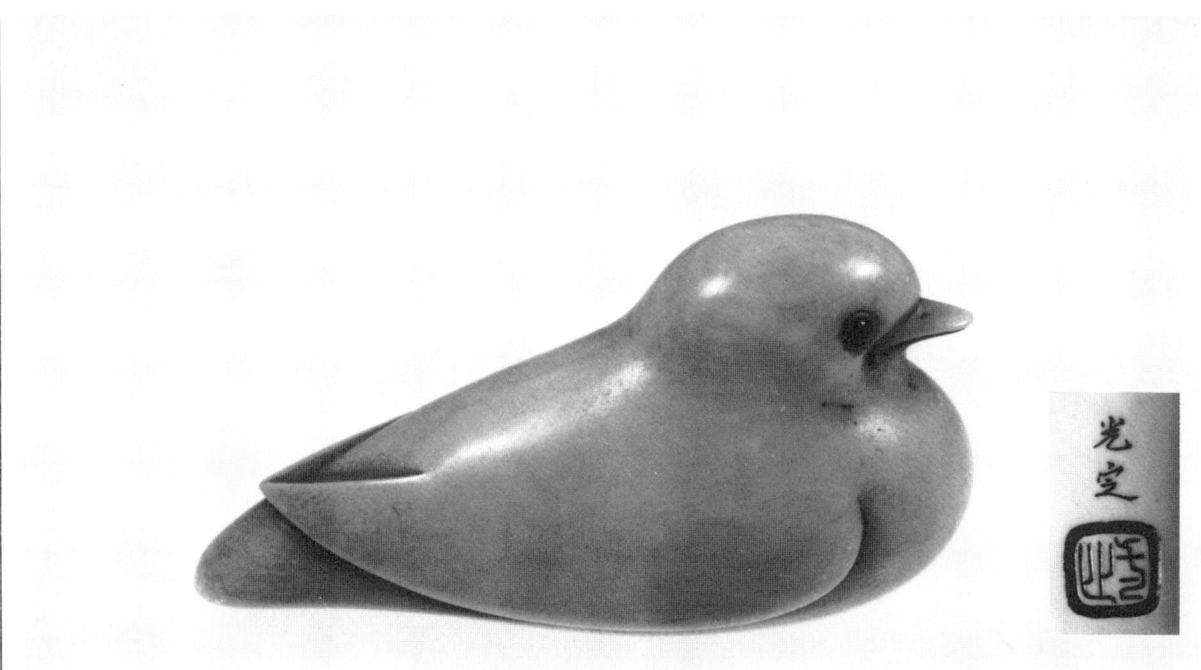

28▽

△30

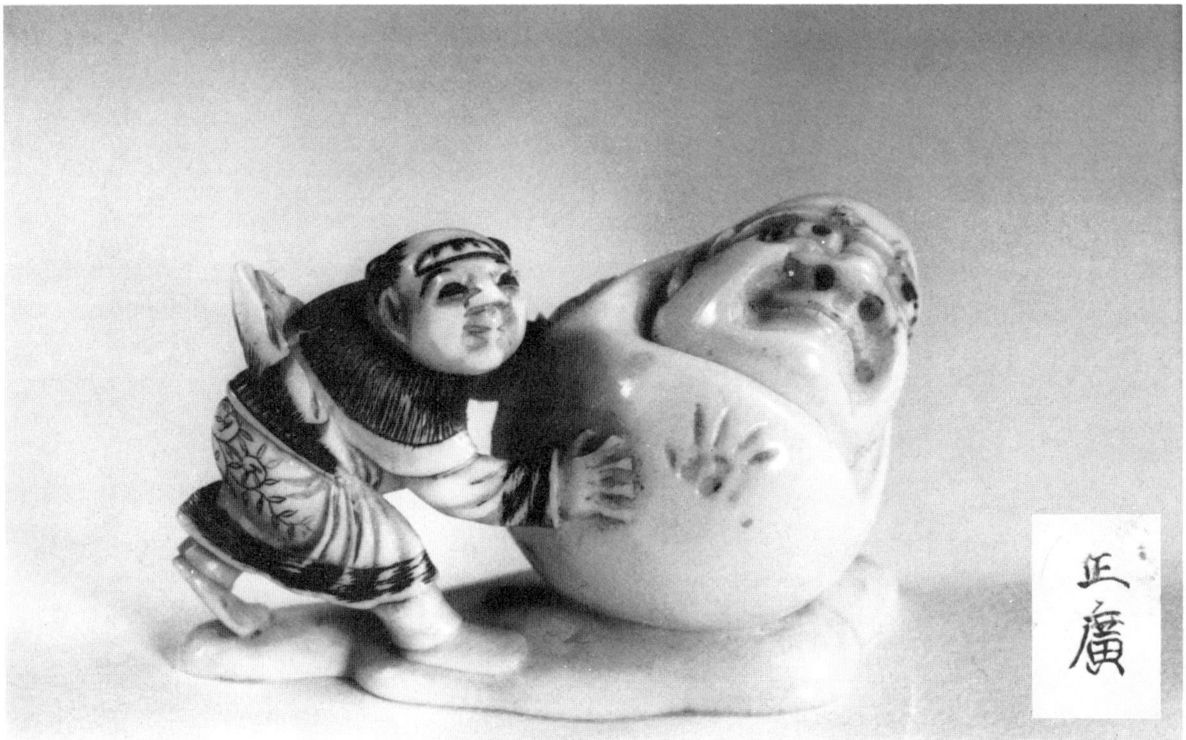

正廣

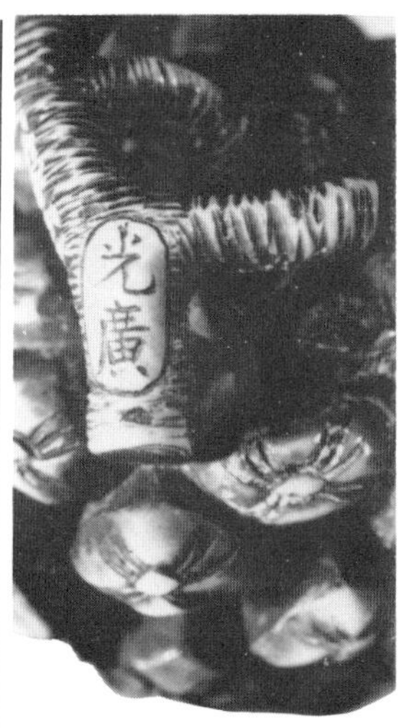

27

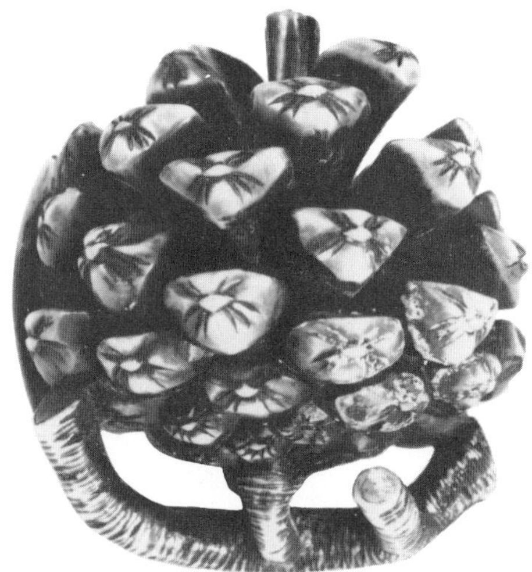

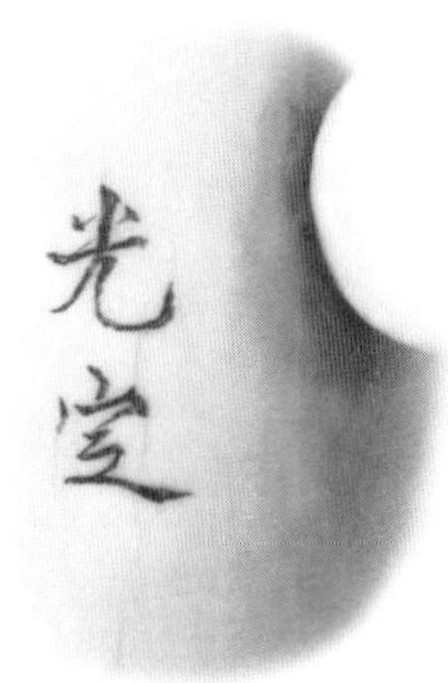

29

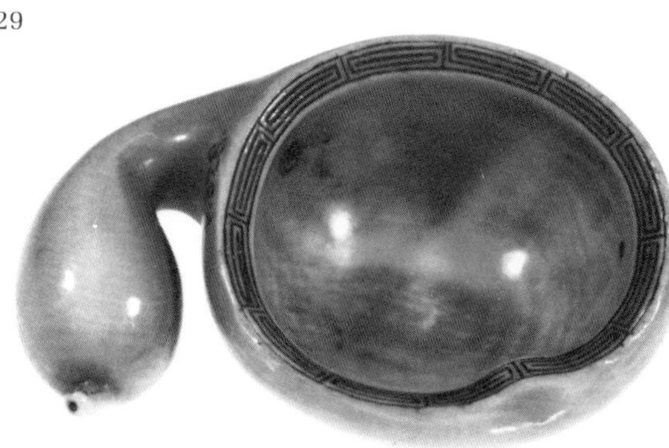

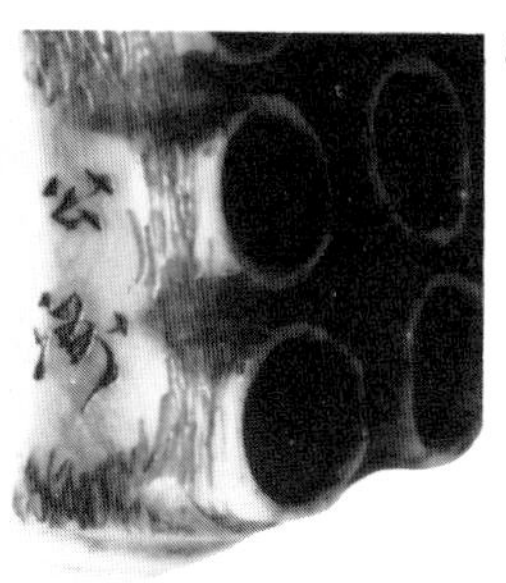

31

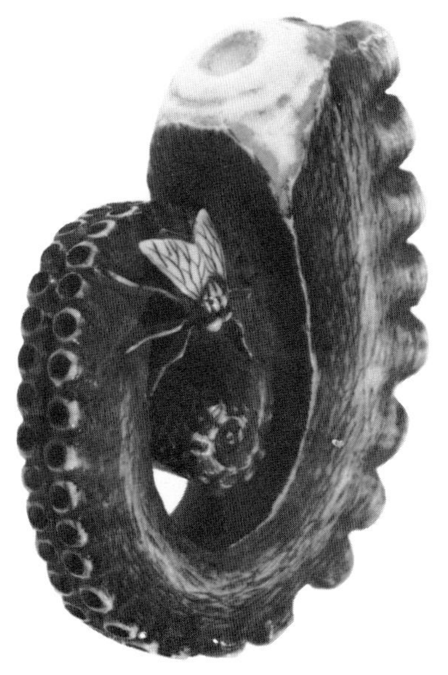

27
Pine cone, partly open, with two pine needles attached.
Ivory, deliberately stained.
Signed Mitsuhiro, in oval cartouche on base of twig.
19th century.
Height 3.25cm ($1\frac{1}{4}$in).
1945 10-17 661. Bequeathed by Oscar Raphael.

Ex. W. L. Behrens Collection, no. 2430, illustrated in the catalogue, pl. XXXII. Exhibited Red Cross, London, 1915, no. 186, pl. L.

28
Chinese boy pushing a Daruma snowman, on an irregular base, the snow bearing imprints of the child's hands.
Ivory, boy's and snowman's eyes inlaid.
Signed Masahiro, on base.
19th century.
Length 4.25cm ($1\frac{3}{4}$in).
F.1046. Franks Collection.

29
Saké-cup gourd, the rim with a key fret design, supported by a smaller gourd.
Ivory, deliberately stained.
Signed Mitsusada, on base.
19th century.
Length 3.75cm ($1\frac{1}{2}$in).
F. 328. Franks Collection.

For a similar example by Mitsuhiro, *see* R. Bushell, *Collectors' Netsuke*, p. 99, no. 133.

30
Seated bird.
Ivory, the eyes inlaid.
Signed Mitsusada with unread seal, on base of tail.
19th century.
Length 2.5cm (1in).
F.795. Franks Collection.

31
Fly resting on a severed octopus tentacle.
Ivory, partly stained a natural dark red.
Signed Kōshū, on edge of base.
19th century.
Length 4.5cm ($1\frac{3}{4}$in).
1930 12-17 60. Bequeathed by James Hilton.
Colour plate, page 12.

32
The Chinese general Kanyū, seated, leaning on an arm-rest and stroking his beard.
Ivory, deliberately stained.
Signed Mitsushige, on base of arm-rest.
19th century.
Width 3.25cm ($1\frac{1}{4}$in).
1972 1-14 47. Bequeathed by Mrs Rosina Maria Howe.

33
Hossu (fly-switch), with a small Daruma doll resting on it. Ivory.
Signed Shigemasa in an irregular cartouche with double outline, on base.
19th century.
Length 5cm (2in).
F.874. Franks Collection.

34
Seated heron.
Ivory, eyes inlaid.
Unsigned; school of Mitsuhiro.
19th century.
Height 3.75cm ($1\frac{1}{2}$in).
1953 12-17 8. Bequeathed by Mrs Helen Epstein.

35
Daruma, standing on the reed on which he crossed the sea to Japan. Ivory.
Unsigned; school of Mitsuhiro.
19th century.
Height 4.5cm ($1\frac{3}{4}$in).
1945 10-17 589. Bequeathed by Oscar Raphael.

Exhibited at the Red Cross Exhibition, London, 1915, no. 12, pl. XLVII.

36
Chrysanthemum bloom, the *himotoshi* formed by the stalk.
Ivory.
Signed Kōhōsai.
Late 19th century.
Length 4.5cm ($1\frac{3}{4}$in).
F.319. Franks Collection.

For a similar example, see the catalogue of the W. L. Behrens Collection, no. 1955.

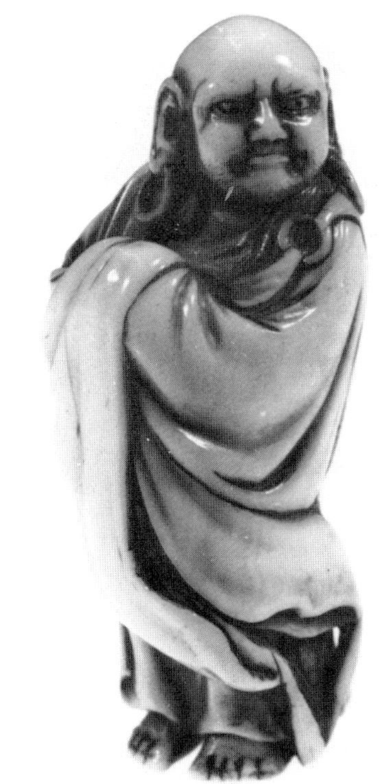

35

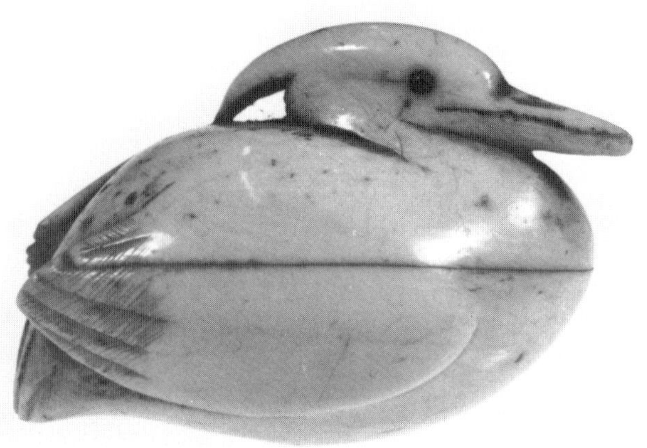

34

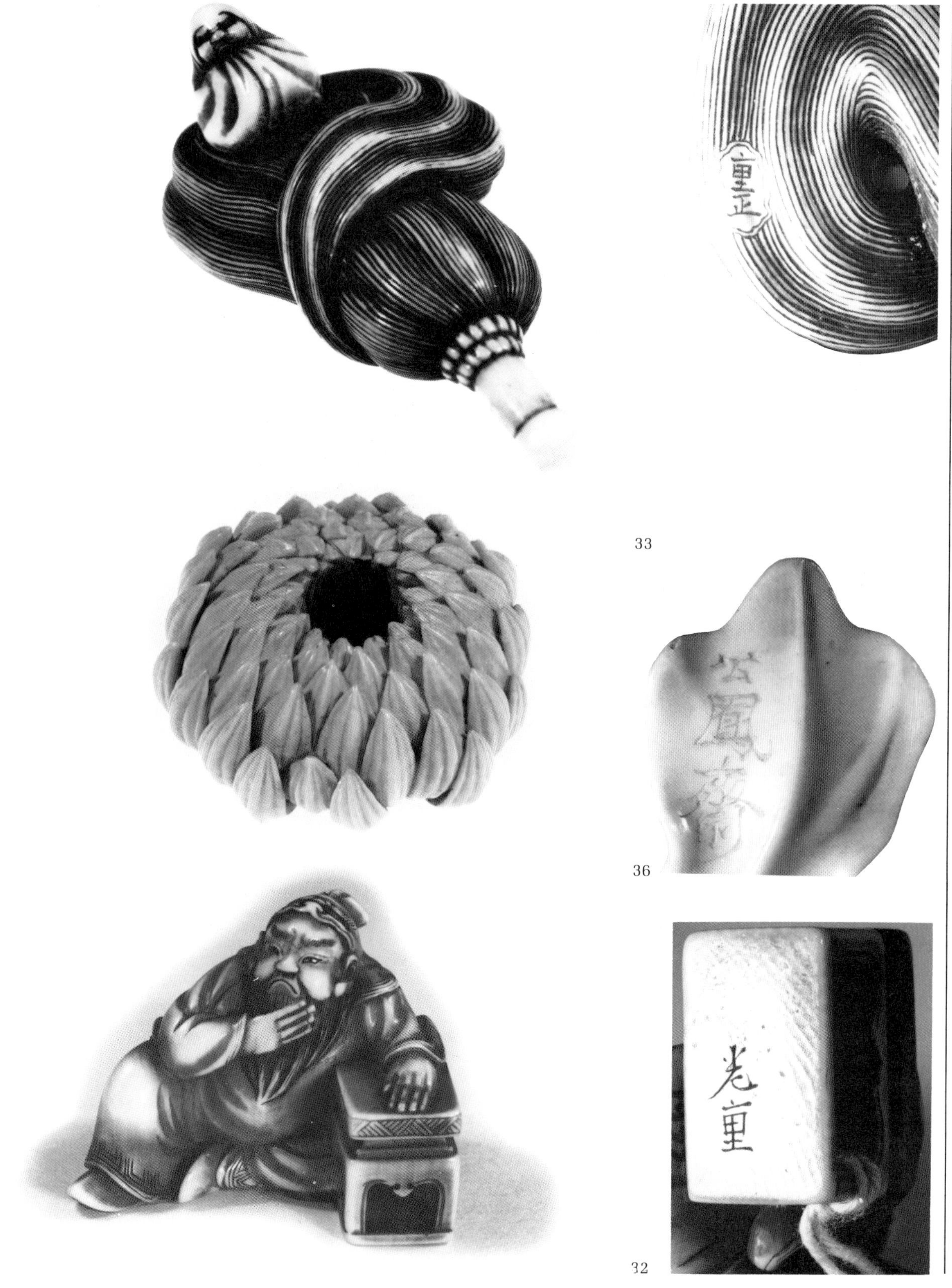

33

36

32

37
Cowering devil, protecting himself from beans thrown at him during the New Year Festival.
Ivory, eyes inlaid.
Signed Kōhōsai.
Late 19th century.
Length 3.25cm ($1\frac{1}{4}$in).
F.842. Franks Collection.

38
Rat holding a bean pod in its paws. The facial whiskers are carved in relief.
Ivory, eyes inlaid in amber.
Signed on the base Kaigyokusai in a rectangular cartouche with double outline and sealed Masatsugu.
19th century.
Length 3.75cm ($1\frac{1}{2}$in).
1953 12-17 1. Bequeathed by Mrs Helen Epstein.
Colour plate, page 12.

39
Clam, opening to reveal a minutely carved scene of a Shintō shrine among trees, the upper part carved with scrolling clouds, part of which form the *himotoshi*. Ivory.
Signed Kaigyokusai Masatsugu on base.
19th century.
Length 4.5cm ($1\frac{3}{4}$in).
1945 10-17 601. Bequeathed by Oscar Raphael.

For a similar example, see the catalogue of the Red Cross Exhibition, London, 1915, no. 175, pl. XCIX.

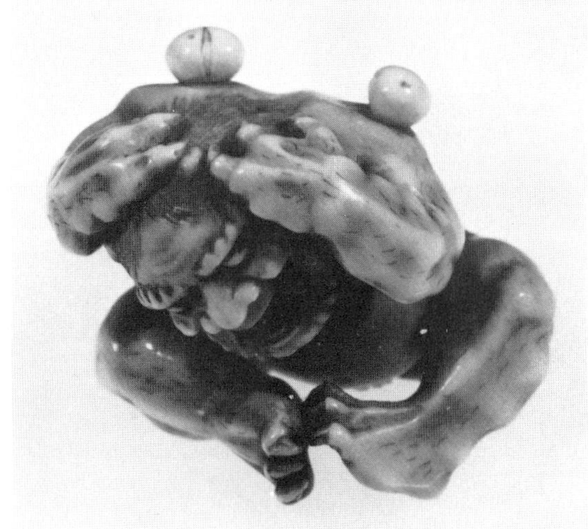

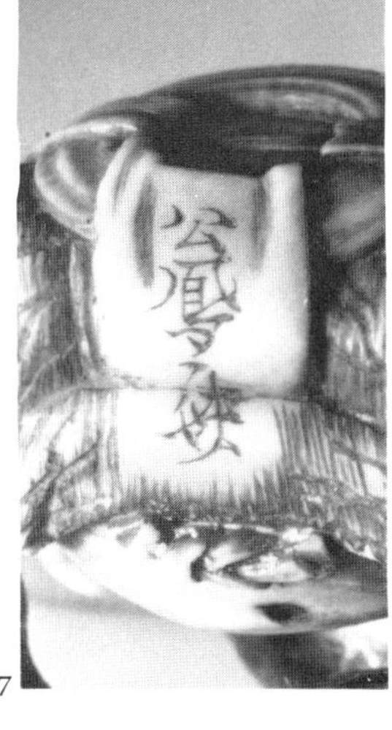

37

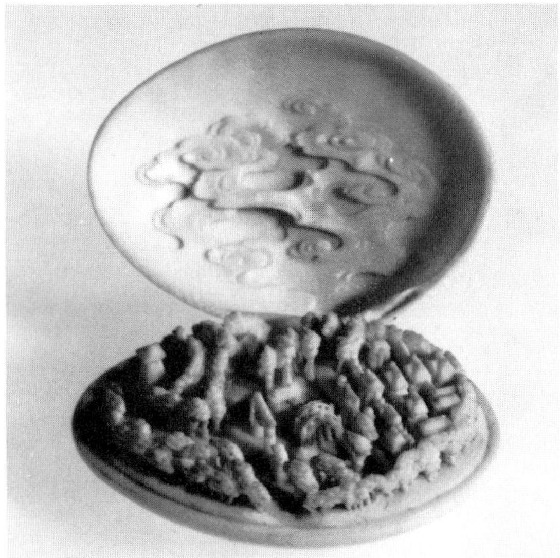

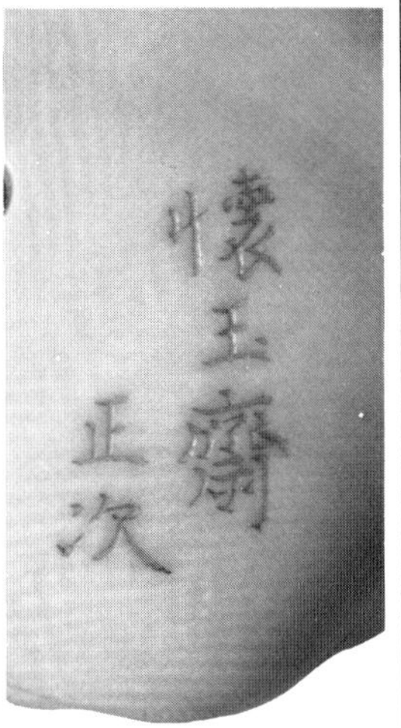

39

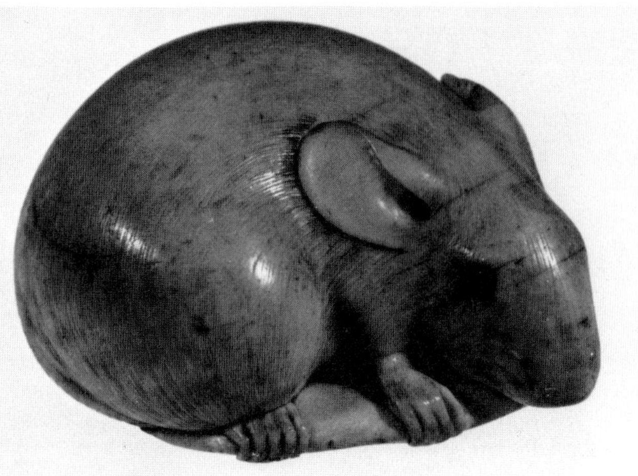

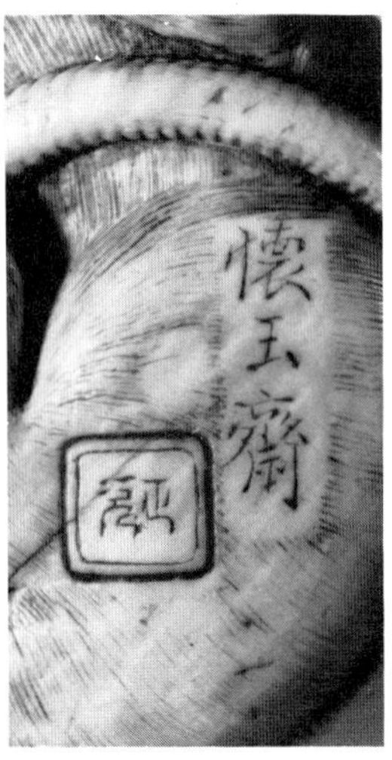

38

40
Nō drama actor, holding a fan and a rosary, painted with various colours in the style of Nagamachi Shūzan. Wood. Signed Shin'ichi in an elongated oval cartouche on the hem of the robe.
19th century.
Height 5.1cm (2in).
F.346. Franks Collection.

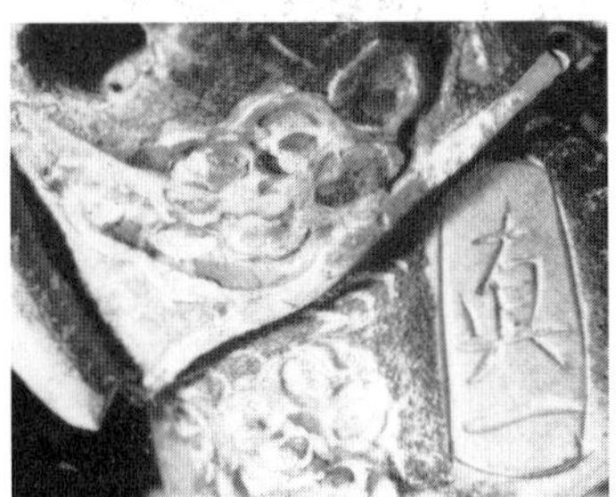

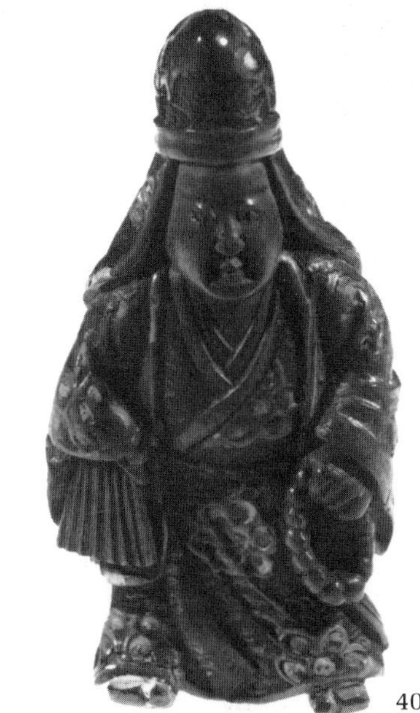

40

41
Rakkan holding a *hossu* (fly switch), his tongue protruding to touch the nose.
Wood, the tongue in ivory.
Signed Kokeisai and sealed Sanshō in red, on back.
About 1900 AD.
Height 8.9cm ($3\frac{1}{2}$in).
1912 10-12 6. Given by Mrs H. Seymour-Trower.

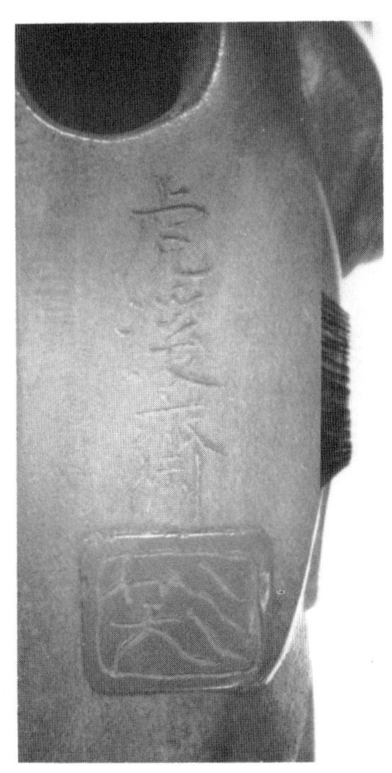

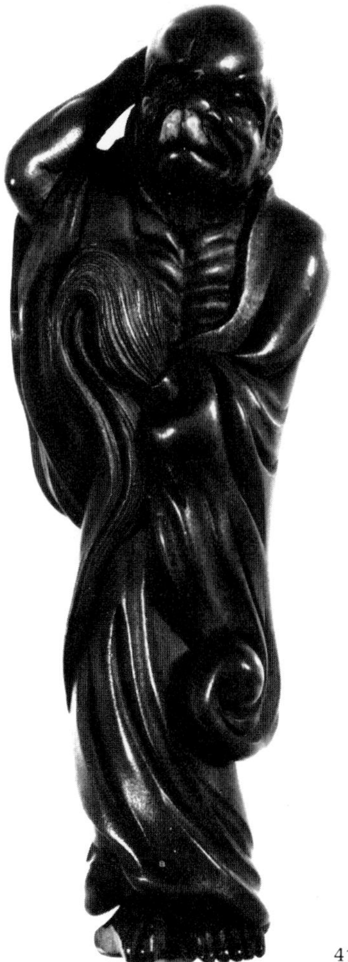

41

Kyoto

42
Severed hawk's claw. Ivory.
Signed Masanao in oval cartouche on lower talon.
18th century.
Length 5.75cm ($2\frac{1}{4}$in).
1945 10-17 628. Bequeathed by Oscar Raphael.

Ex Seymour-Trower Collection no. 684, and illustrated in the catalogue, pl. III. Exhibited Red Cross, 1915, no. 189, and illustrated in the catalogue, pl. LI.

43
Sleeping rat. Ivory.
Signed Masanao in an oval cartouche on the base.
18th century.
Length 5.5cm ($2\frac{1}{4}$in).
F.782. Franks Collection.

44
Kudan, a mythical creature with a semi-human head, ox's body, bushy tail, and eyes and horns distributed in several places. Ivory.
Signed Masanao in oval cartouche on base. The signature is not convincing and was probably added at a later date.
18th century.
Height 3.75cm ($1\frac{1}{2}$in).
F.816. Franks Collection.

Recorded in the Meinertzhagen Card Index.

45
Chinese warrior. Ivory.
Signed Masanao in oval cartouche on the back, the signature probably added later.
18th century.
Height 5.8cm ($2\frac{1}{2}$in).
1945 10-17 565. Bequeathed by Oscar Raphael.

Ex. W. L. Behrens Collection no. 851, illustrated pl. XVII. Exhibited Red Cross, 1915, no. 20, illustrated in the catalogue, pl. XLVII.

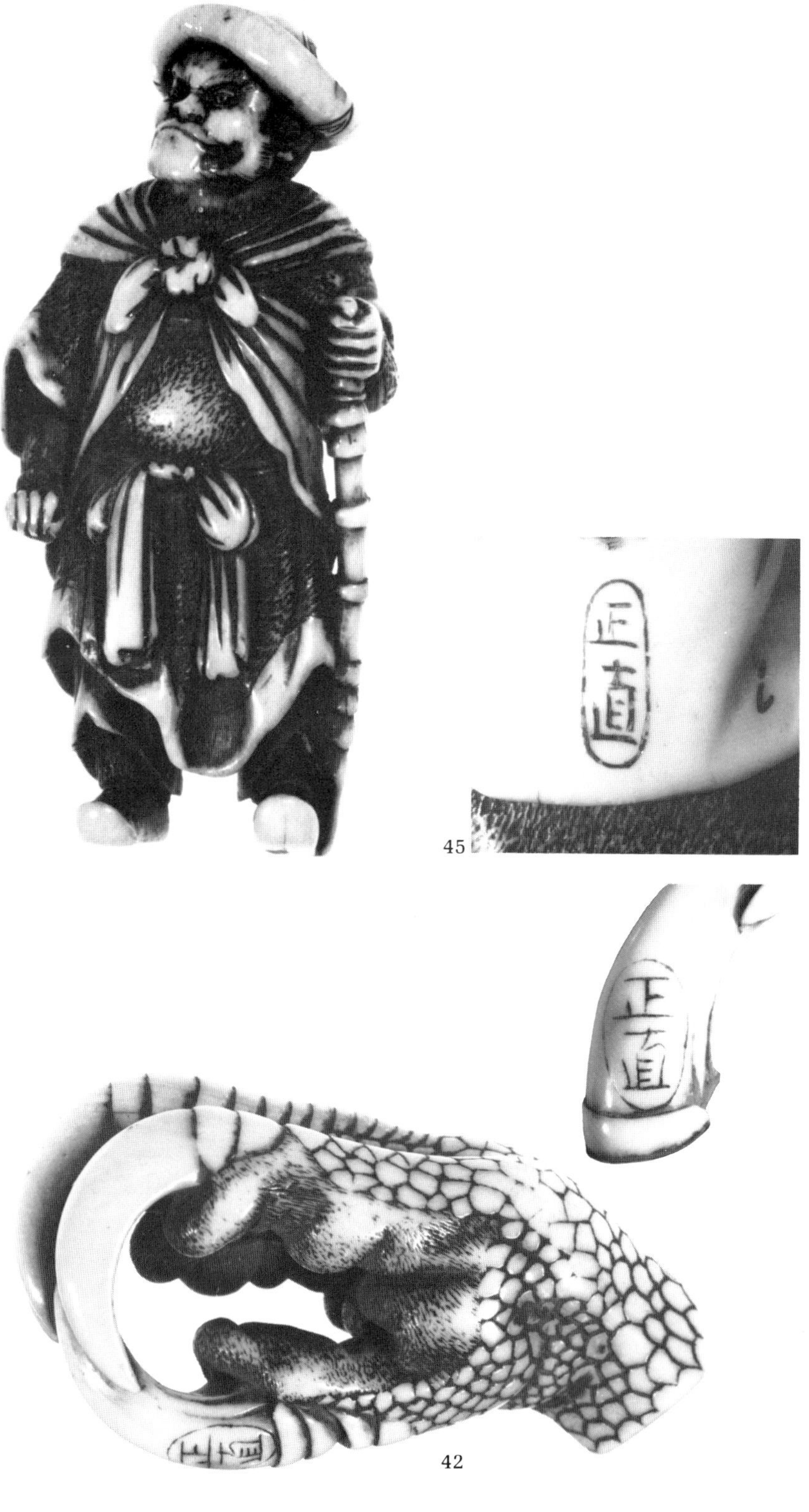

45

42

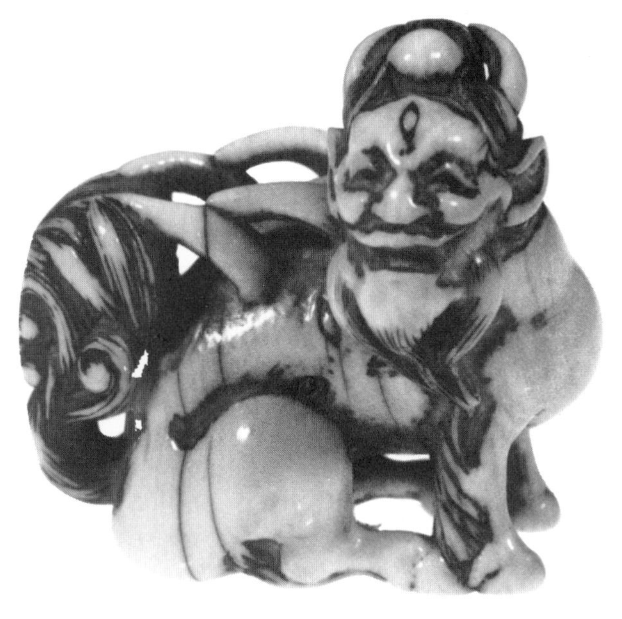

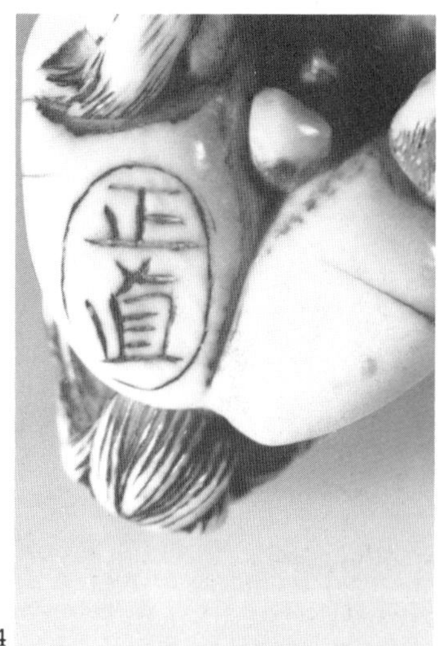

44

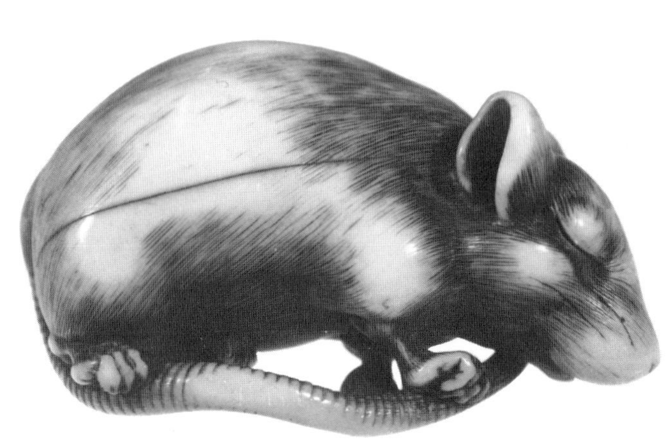

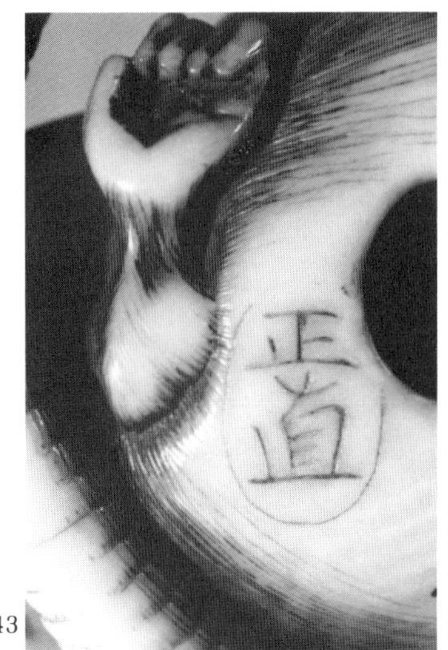

43

46
Sitting dog. Ivory.
Signed Masanao in an oval cartouche on the base, but probably school of Masanao.
19th century.
Height 4.8cm (1¾in).
F.772. Franks Collection.

47
Tartar warrior seated reading a scroll. Ivory.
Signed Yoshinaga in an elongated oval cartouche on base.
18th century.
Height 3.75cm (1½in).
F.577. Franks Collection.

The engraved design on the robe is typical of Yoshinaga and his school.
Colour plate, Half-title page

48
Dragon emerging from its egg. Wood.
Signed Tomotada in an oval cartouche on the base.
Late 18th century.
Diameter 3.25cm (1¼in).
F.1090. Franks Collection.

49
Reclining ox and calf.
Ivory, ox's eyes inlaid.
Signed Tomotada in a rectangular cartouche. The signature is placed, unusually for this carver, between the *himotoshi*.
18th century.
Length 7.75cm (3in).
F.763. Franks Collection.

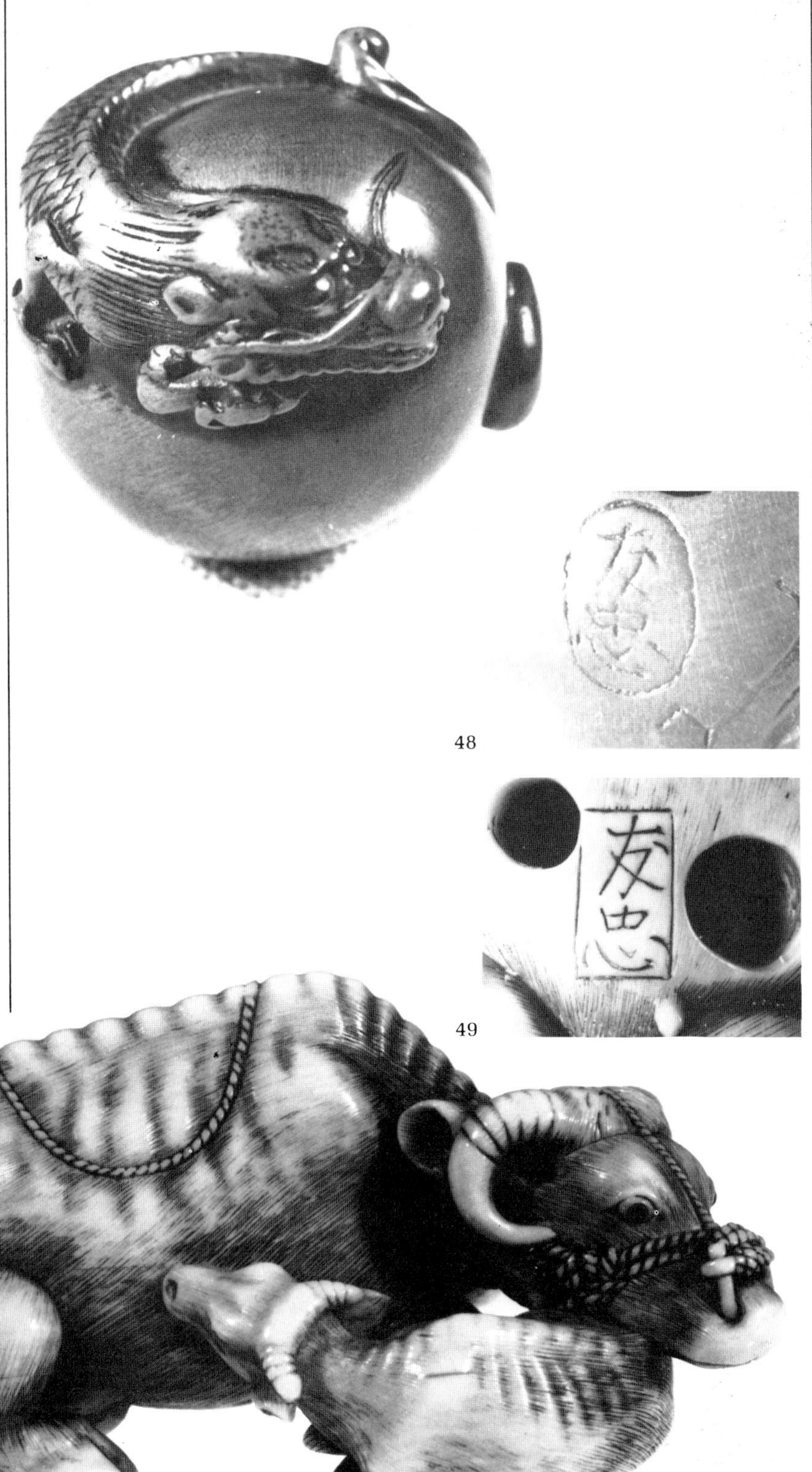

48

49

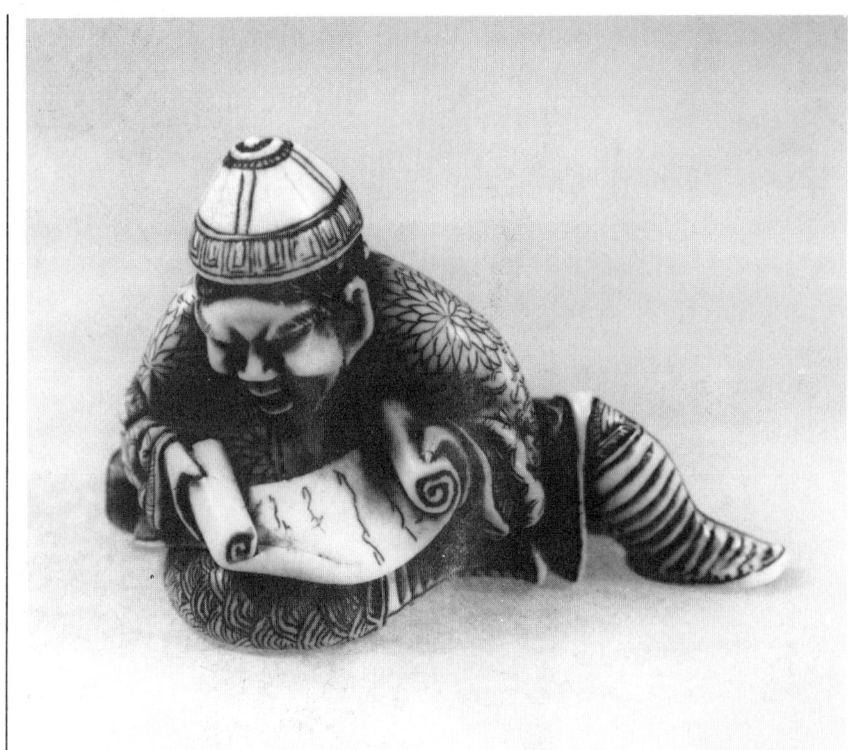

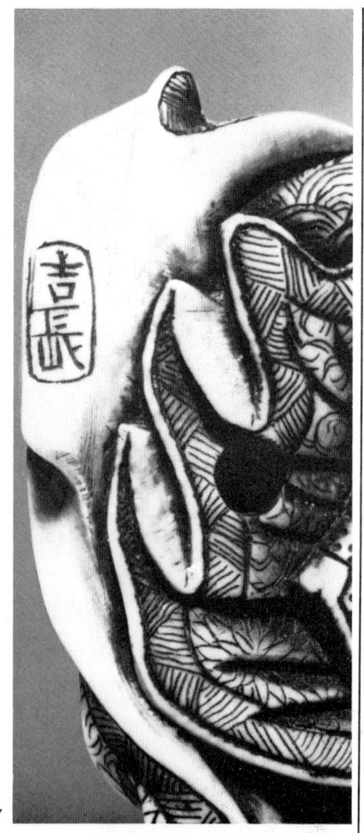

47

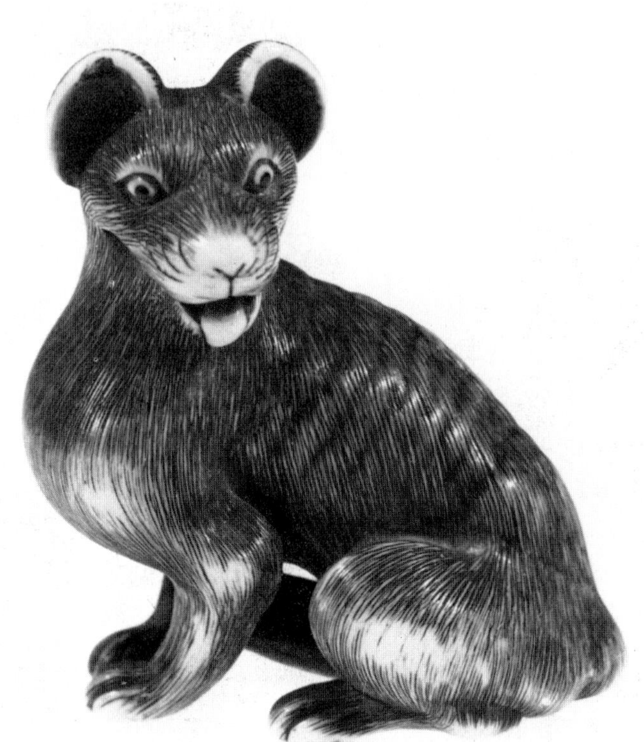

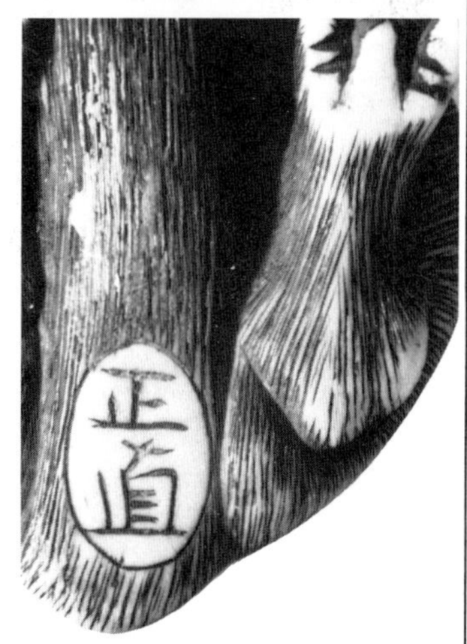

46

45

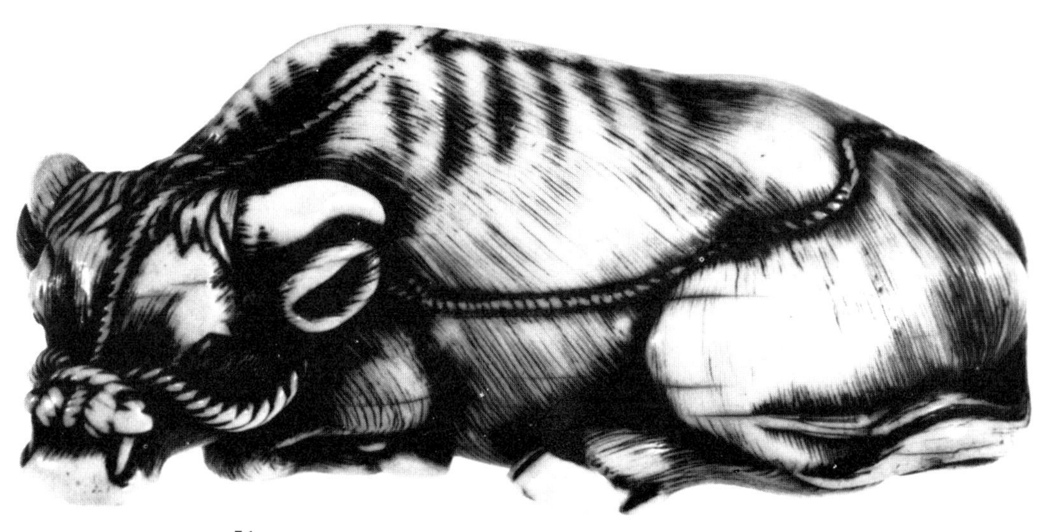

51

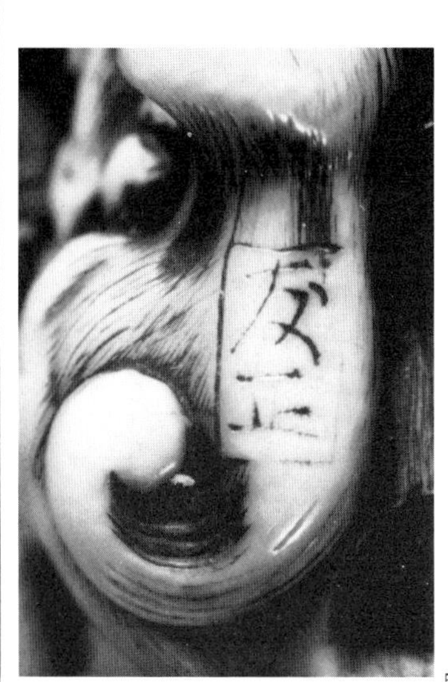

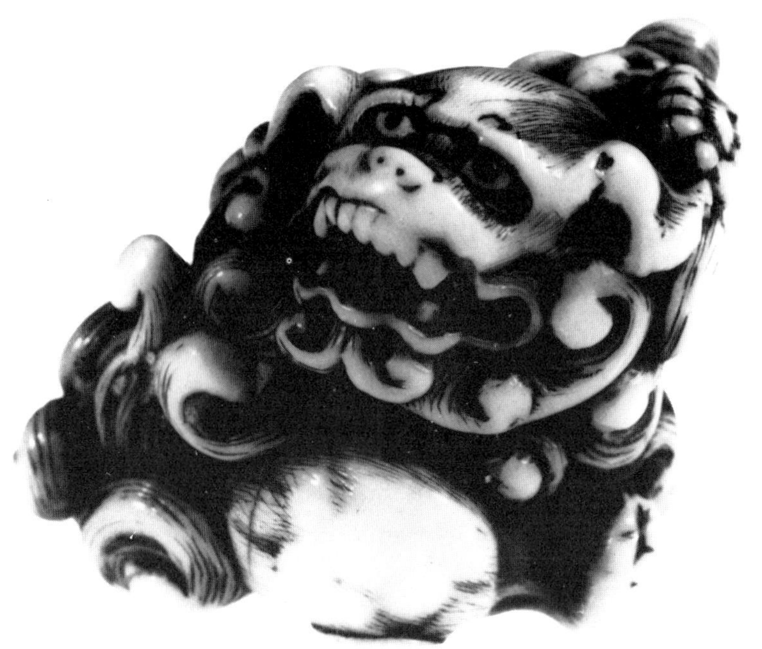

50

50
Shishi with its left forepaw raised.
Ivory, the eyes inlaid.
Signed Tomomasa in a rectangular cartouche under one leg.
19th century.
Height 3.75cm (1½in).
1930 12-17 93. Bequeathed by James Hilton.

51
Reclining ox.
Ivory, the eyes inlaid.
Unsigned; school of Tomotada
18th century.
Length 5.25cm (2in).
1930 12-17 74. Bequeathed by James Hilton.

52
Shishi's head with moveable jaw. Ivory.
Unsigned, probably by Tomotada.
Early 19th century.
Height 3.75cm (1½in).
F.1102. Franks Collection.

53
Coiled snake.
Ivory, the eyes inlaid.
Signed Okatomo in a rectangular cartouche on the base.
Late 18th century.
Diameter 4.25cm (1¾in).
1945 10-17 603. Bequeathed by Oscar Raphael.

Ex Gilbertson Collection. Exhibited Red Cross, 1915, no. 188, and illustrated in the catalogue, pl. LI.

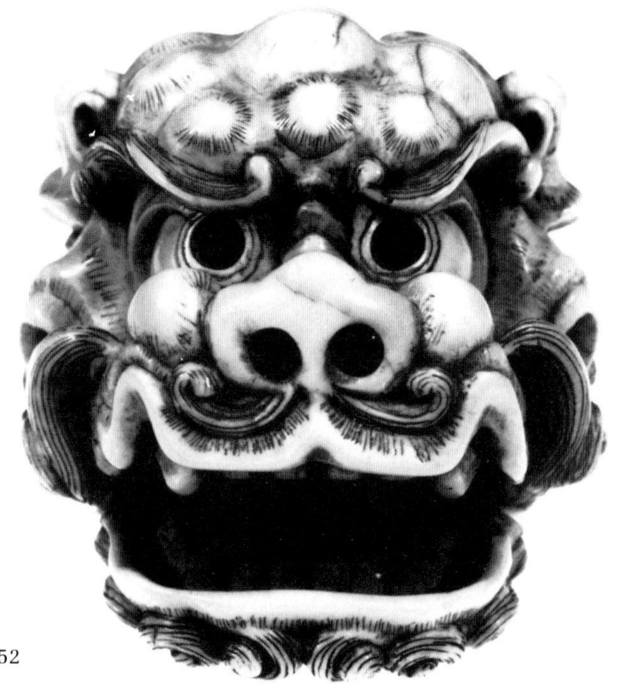

52

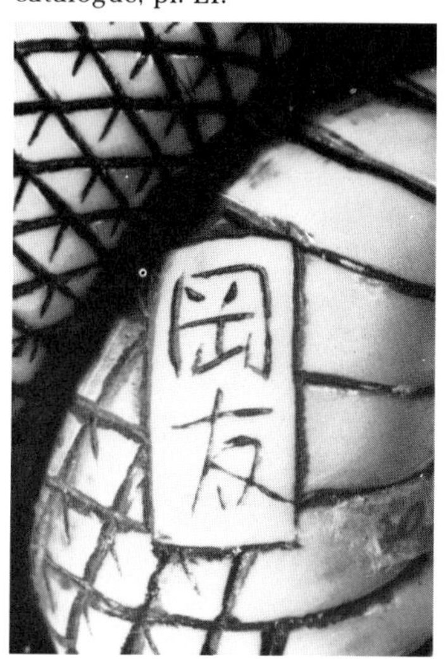

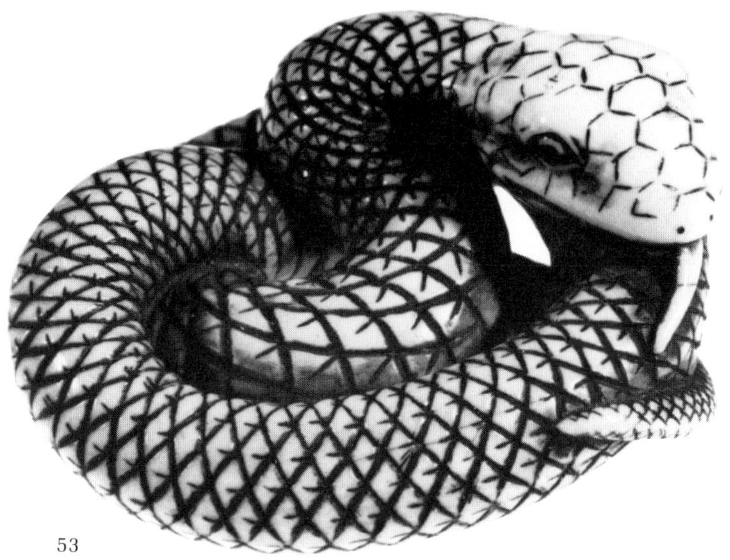

53

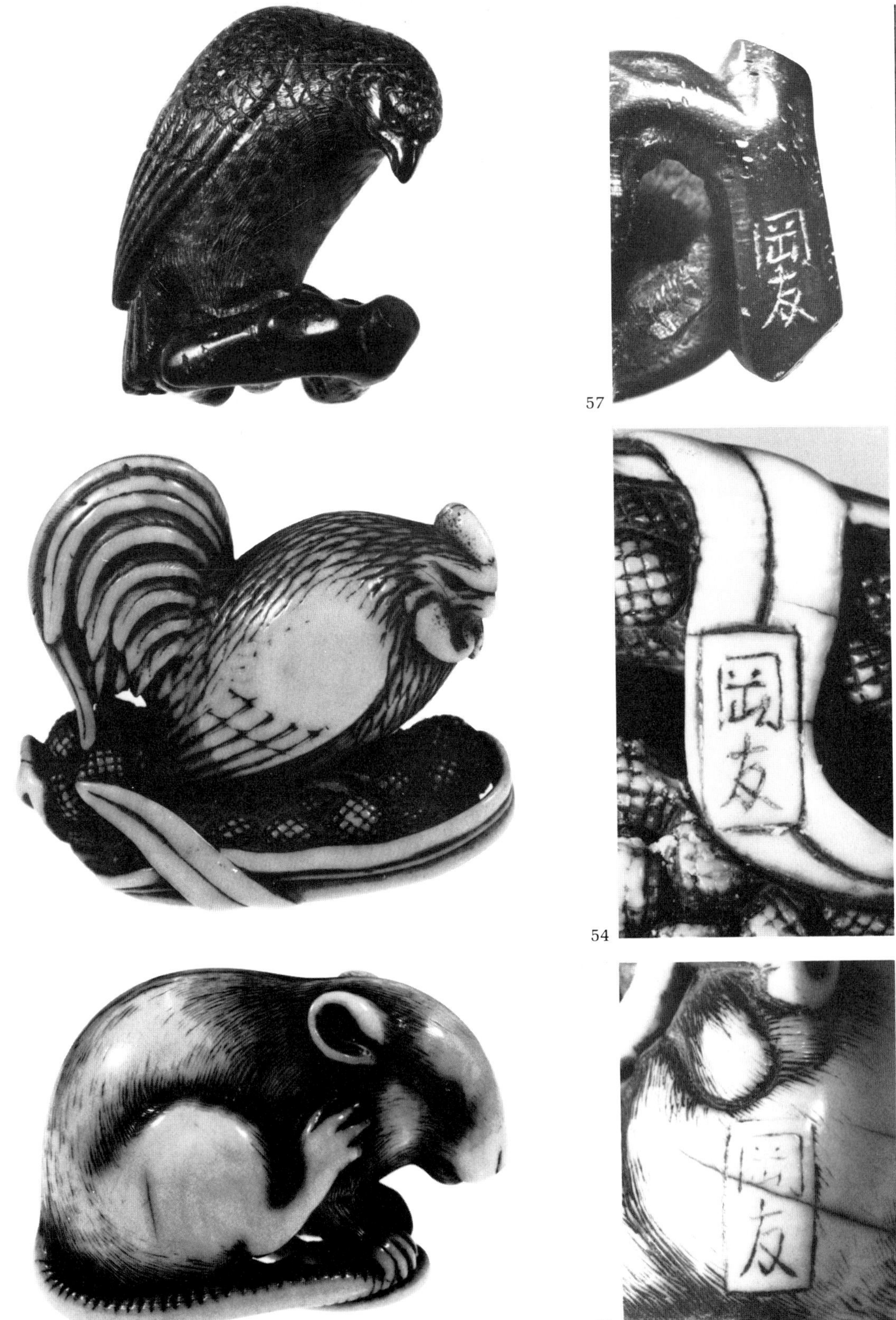

57

54

55

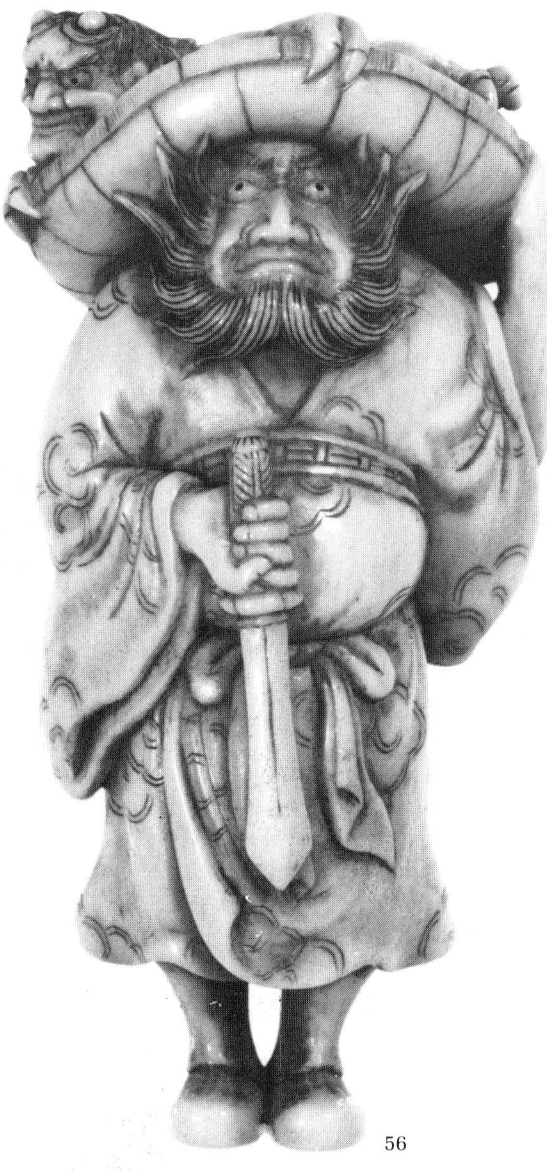

56

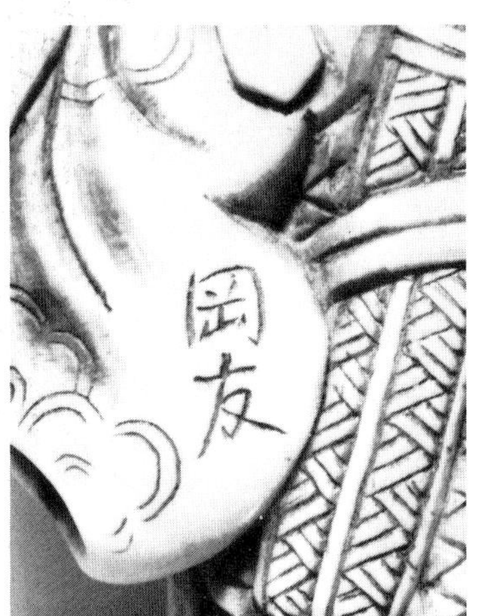

54
Cockerel seated on heads of millet.
Ivory, the eyes inlaid.
Signed Okatomo in a rectangular cartouche on the base.
18th century.
Height 3.75cm ($1\frac{1}{2}$in).
F.789. Franks Collection.

55
Rat, scratching, sitting on a horse-bit.
Ivory, the eyes inlaid.
Signed Okatomo in a rectangular cartouche by the tail.
18th century.
Length 3.75cm ($1\frac{1}{2}$in).
1945 10-17 520. Bequeathed by Oscar Raphael.

56
Shoki, the demon queller, standing wearing a large hat on top of which hides the demon.
Ivory.
Signed Okatomo on the back of a sleeve, but this piece is closer to the style of Yoshinaga.
Late 18th century.
Height 7cm ($2\frac{3}{4}$in).
F.693. Franks Collection.

57
Eagle perched on a tree-branch.
Wood, the eyes inlaid.
Signed Okatomo on the base, but this piece probably by his school.
Early 19th century.
Length 3.25cm ($1\frac{1}{4}$in).
F.135. Franks Collection.

58
Monkey holding down a tortoise. Ivory, the eyes inlaid. Signed Okatomo in a rectangular cartouche on the base, but this piece by his school. Early 19th century. Length 4.25cm ($1\frac{3}{4}$in). F.236. Franks Collection.

59
Deer giving voice. Ivory. Unsigned; Kyoto School, close to the style of Okatomo. 18th century. Height 9.25cm ($3\frac{3}{4}$in). 1945 10-17 519. Bequeathed by Oscar Raphael.

Ex Behrens Collection no. 1542A, illustrated in the catalogue, pl. XXVI Exhibited Red Cross, 1915 no. 190, and illustrated in the catalogue, pl. L.

60
Seated Kirin, a mythical creature of happy omen. Ivory. Unsigned; Kyoto School. Late 18th century. Height 8.25cm (3in). 1930 12-17 91. Bequeathed by James Hilton.

61
Quail on heads of millet. Ivory, the eyes inlaid. Signed Okatori in a rectangular cartouche on the base. Late 18th–early 19th century. Length 3.25cm ($1\frac{1}{4}$in). F.790. Franks Collection.

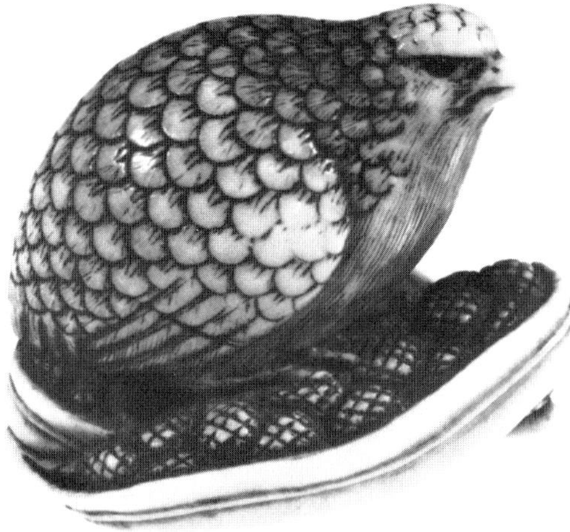

61

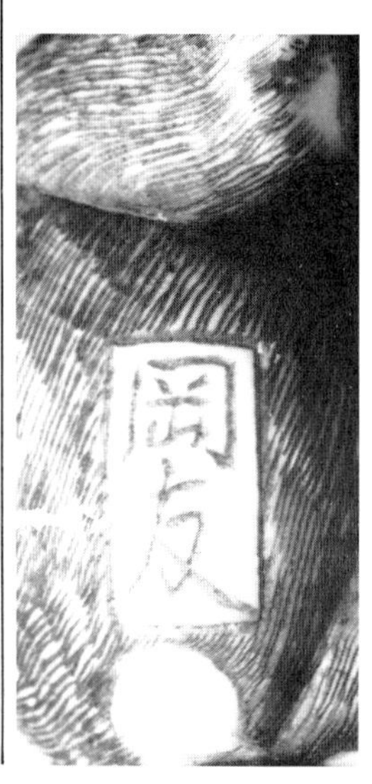

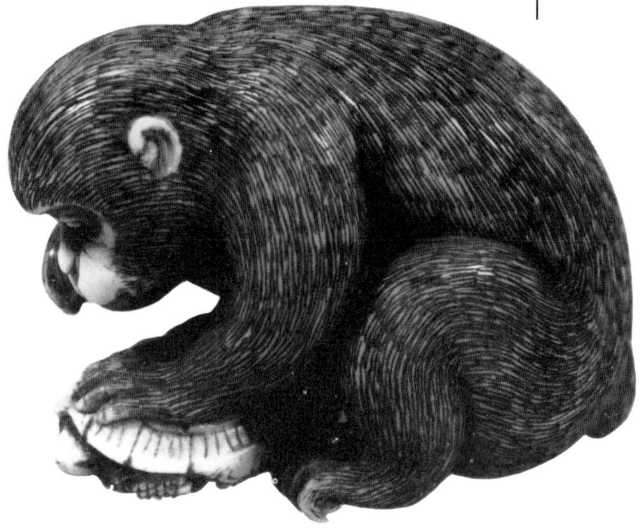

58

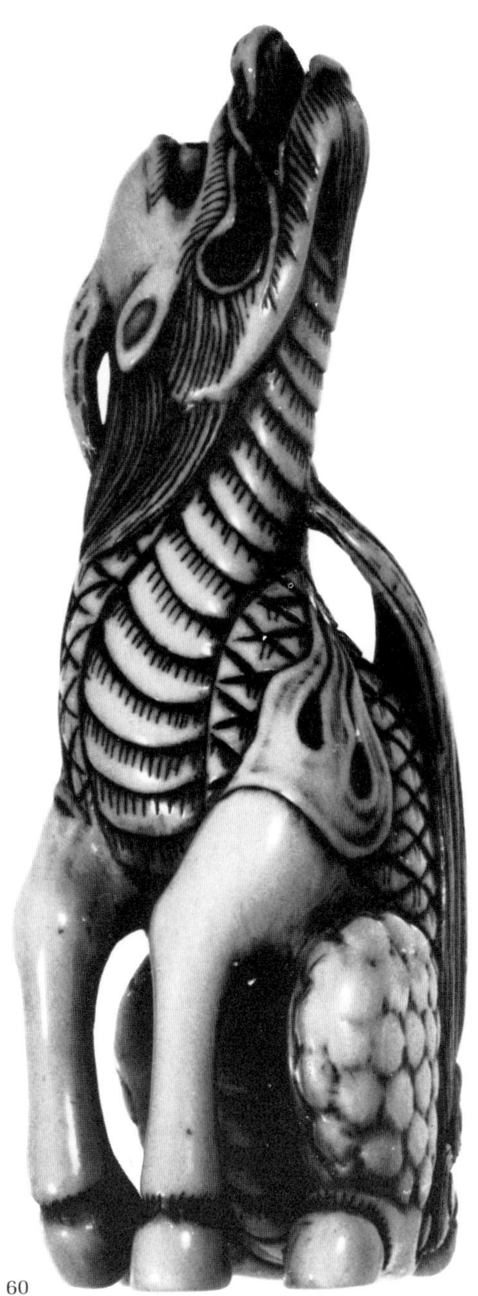
60

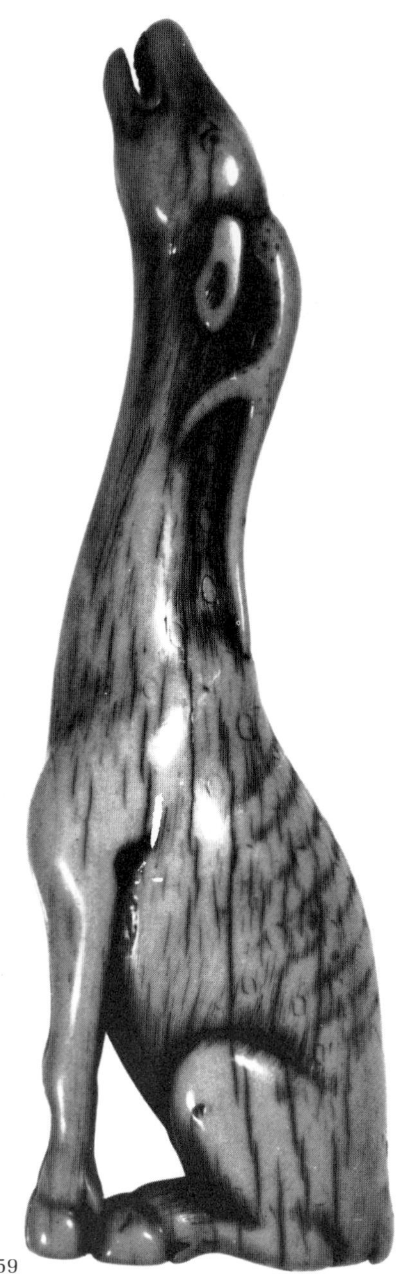
59

62

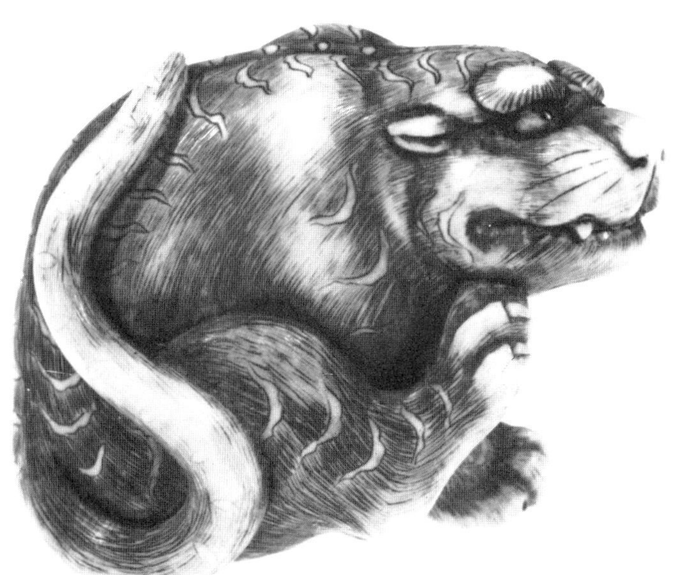

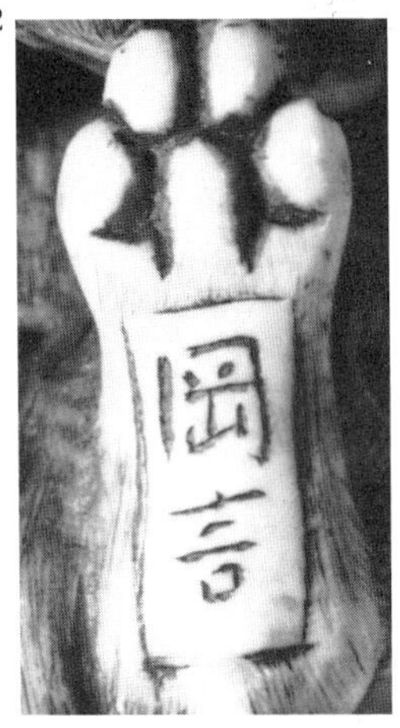

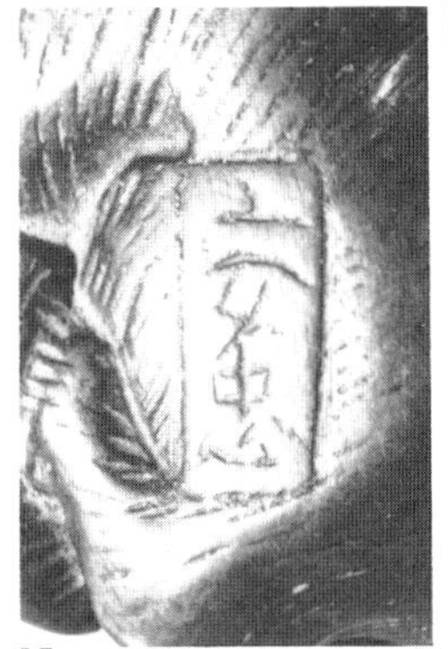

65

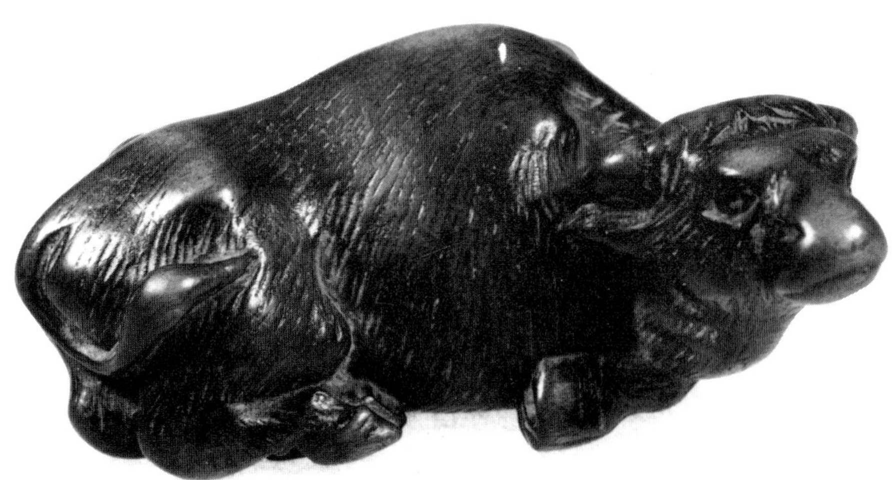

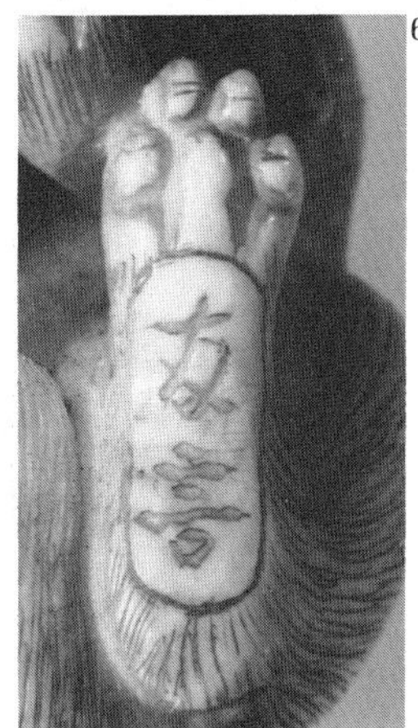

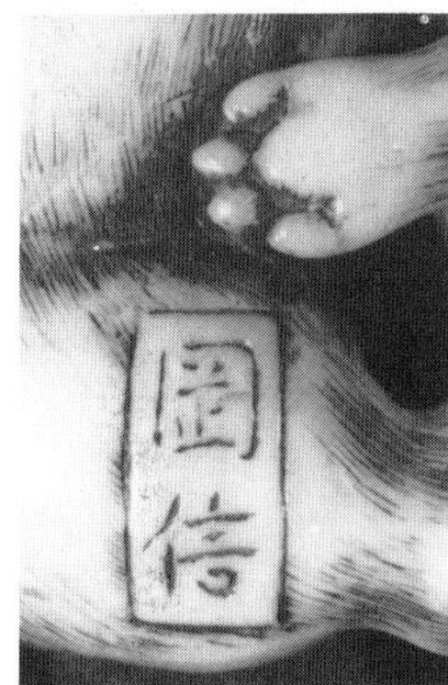

64

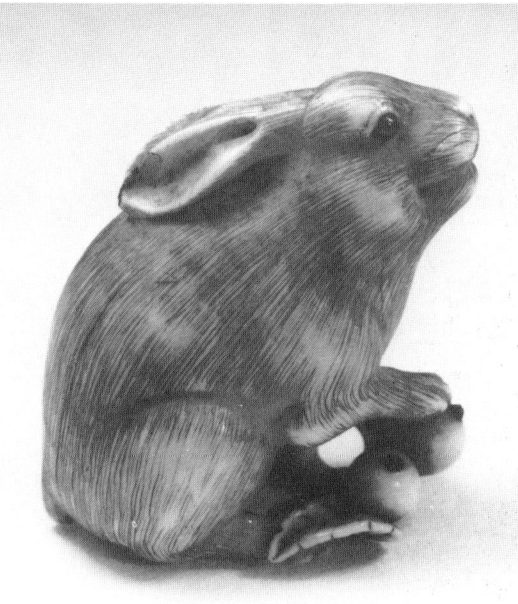

63

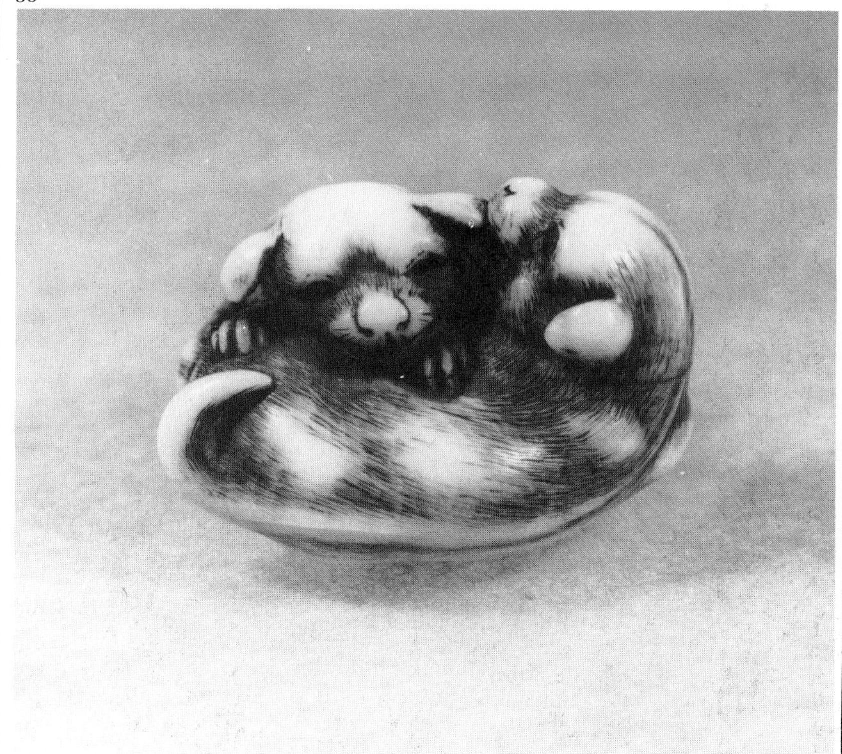

62
Tiger scratching its chin.
Ivory, the eyes inlaid.
Signed Okakoto in a rectangular cartouche under one leg.
Late 18th–early 19th century.
Height 3.75cm ($1\frac{1}{2}$in).
F.670. Franks Collection.

63
Two puppies playfully fighting.
Ivory, the eyes inlaid.
Signed Okanobu in a rectangular cartouche on the base.
Late 18th–early 19th century.
Width 3.5cm ($1\frac{1}{4}$in).
F.774. Franks Collection.

The artist was a member of the Okatomo school; his work is rare.

64
Rabbit with its paw on a cluster of fruit.
Ivory, the eyes and fruits inlaid.
Signed Tomokoto in an elongated oval cartouche under one leg.
Late 18th–early 19th century.
Height 3.25cm ($1\frac{1}{4}$in).
1953 12-17 10. Bequeathed by Mrs Helen Epstein.

65
Reclining ox. Wood.
Signed Yasutada in a rectangular cartouche on the base.
18th century.
Length 5.75cm ($2\frac{1}{4}$in).
F.221. Franks Collection.

Meinertzhagen Index stated that this artist was of the Tomotada school, a theory which this netsuke supports.

66
Goat and kid.
Ivory, the eyes inlaid.
Unsigned; Kyoto School.
Early 19th century.
Height 4.7cm ($1\frac{3}{4}$in).
F.770. Frank Collection.

67
Seated goat.
Ivory, the eyes inlaid.
Signed Mitsuharu in an oval cartouche on the base.
18th century.
Height 3.75cm ($1\frac{1}{2}$in).
F.77A. Franks Collection.

68
Grazing horse.
Wood, the eyes inlaid.
Signed Mitsuhide in an oval cartouche on the back flank.
Early 19th century.
Height 5.2cm (2in).
F.765. Franks Collection.

69
Rat and two young on a cluster of nuts.
Ivory, the eyes inlaid.
Signed Takenobu in a rectangular cartouche on the base.
Late 18th century.
Length 7cm ($2\frac{3}{4}$in).
F.256. Franks Collection.

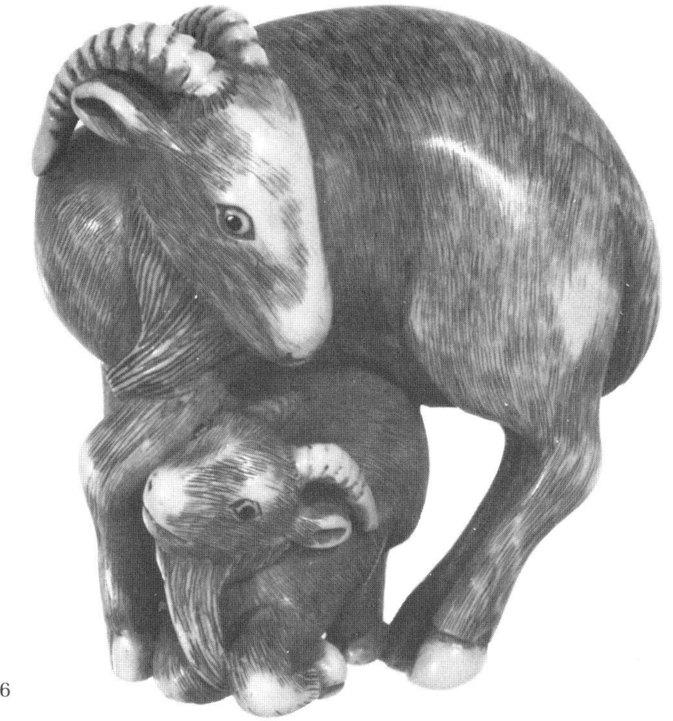

66

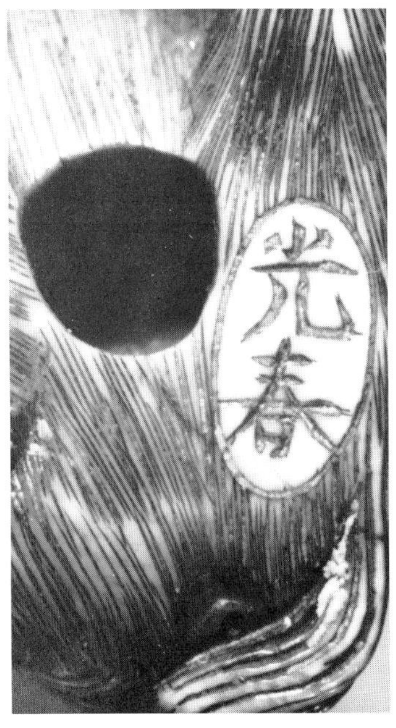

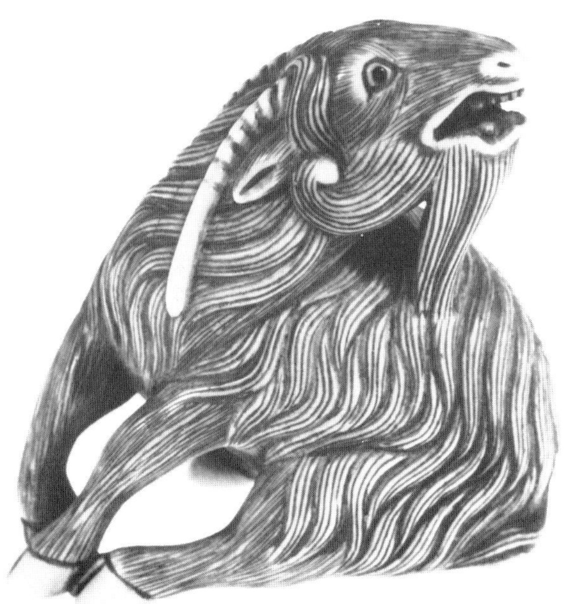

67

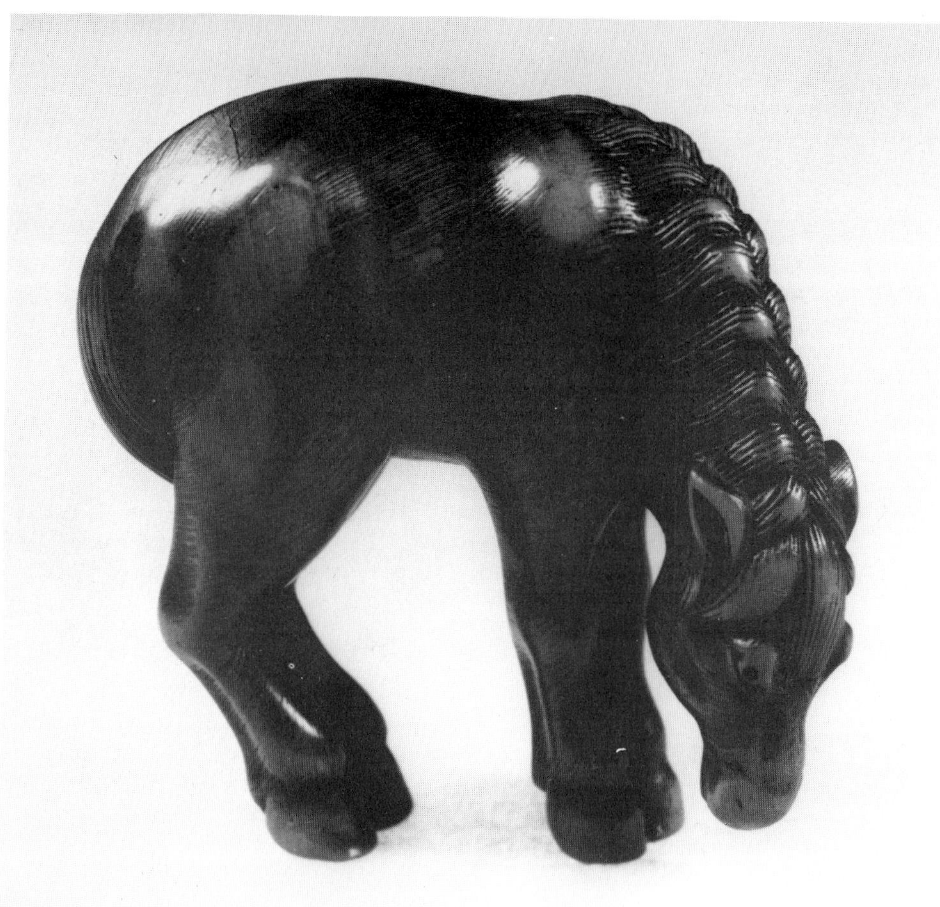

68

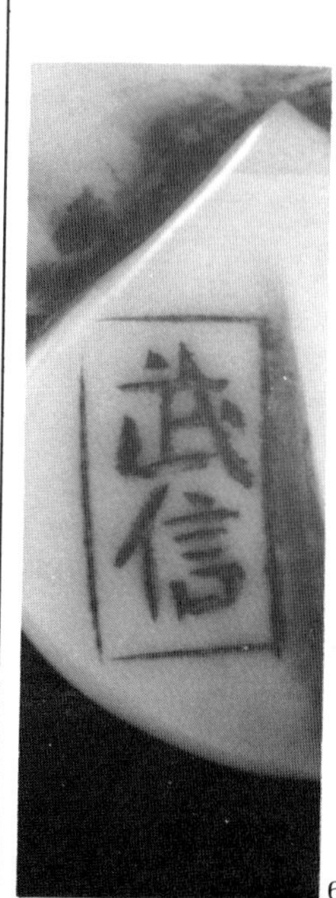

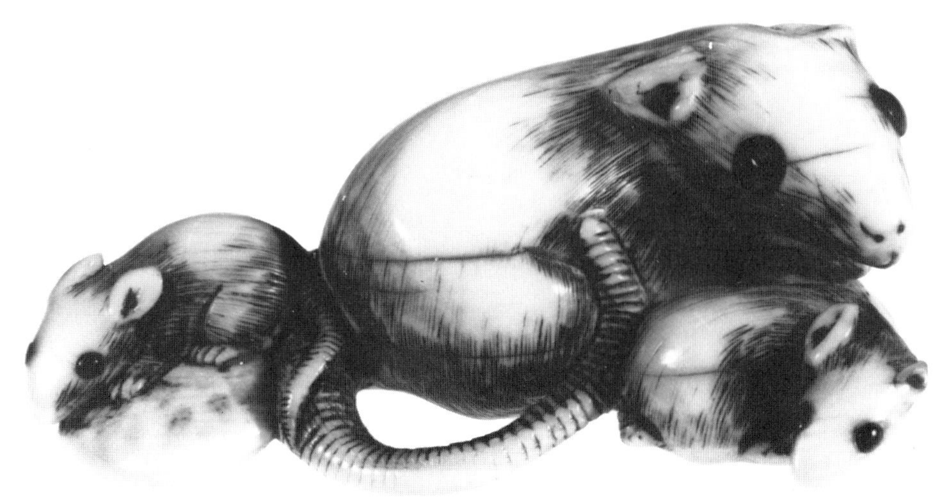

69

70
Three bean pods. Ivory.
Signed Kiyokatsu on the base.
Early 19th century.
Length 5.25cm ($2\frac{1}{4}$in).
1945 10-17 591. Bequeathed by Oscar Raphael.

Ex W. L. Behrens Collection. Ex Thacher Clarke Collection. Exhibited Red Cross, 1915, no. 149, and illustrated in the catalogue, pl. LIV.

71
Nine ginkgo nuts. Ivory.
Signed Kiyokatsu on the base.
Early 19th century.
Length 3.1cm (2in).
F.1108. Franks Collection.

Groups of ginkgo nuts were among Kiyokatsu's most frequent subjects.

72
Tea Ceremony utensils.
Ivory, the charcoal inlaid in ebony.
Unsigned, possibly by Kiyokatsu.
Early 19th century.
Length 8.25cm ($3\frac{1}{4}$in).
F.1119. Franks Collection.

73
Bushy-tailed rat on an upturned mushroom.
Ivory, the eyes inlaid.
Unsigned.
19th century.
Length 5.1cm (2in).
F.686. Franks Collection.

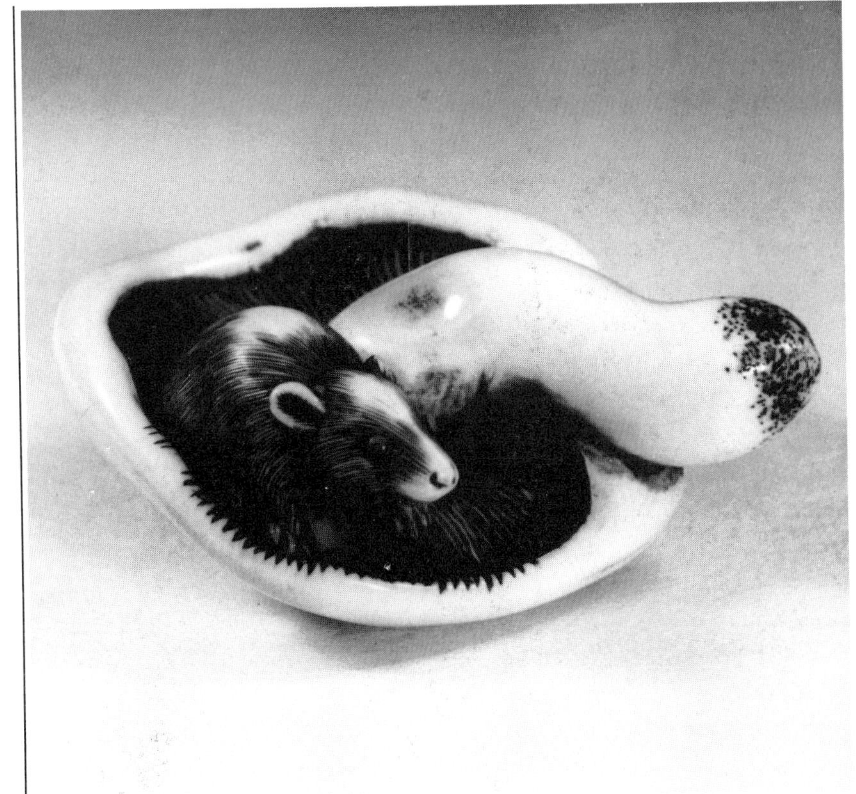

73

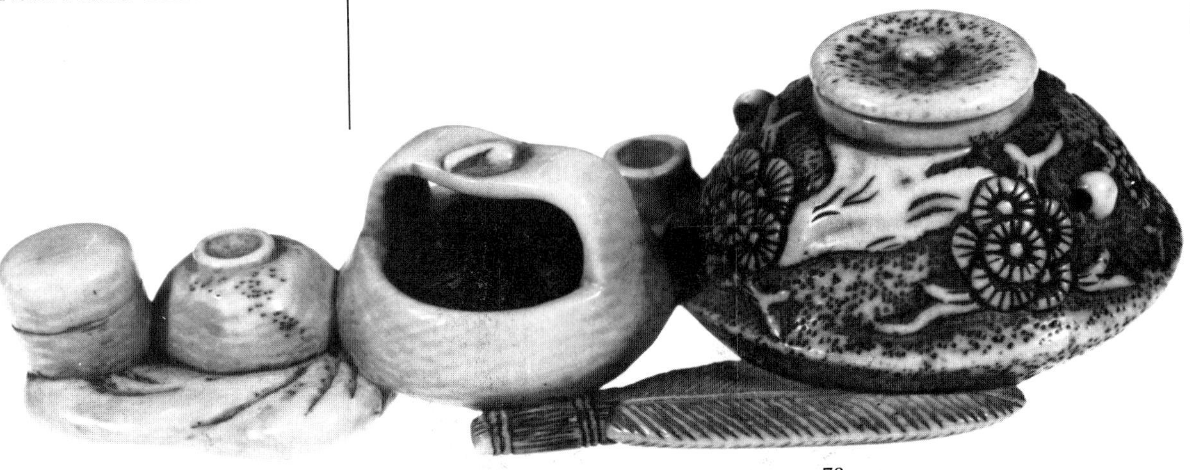

72

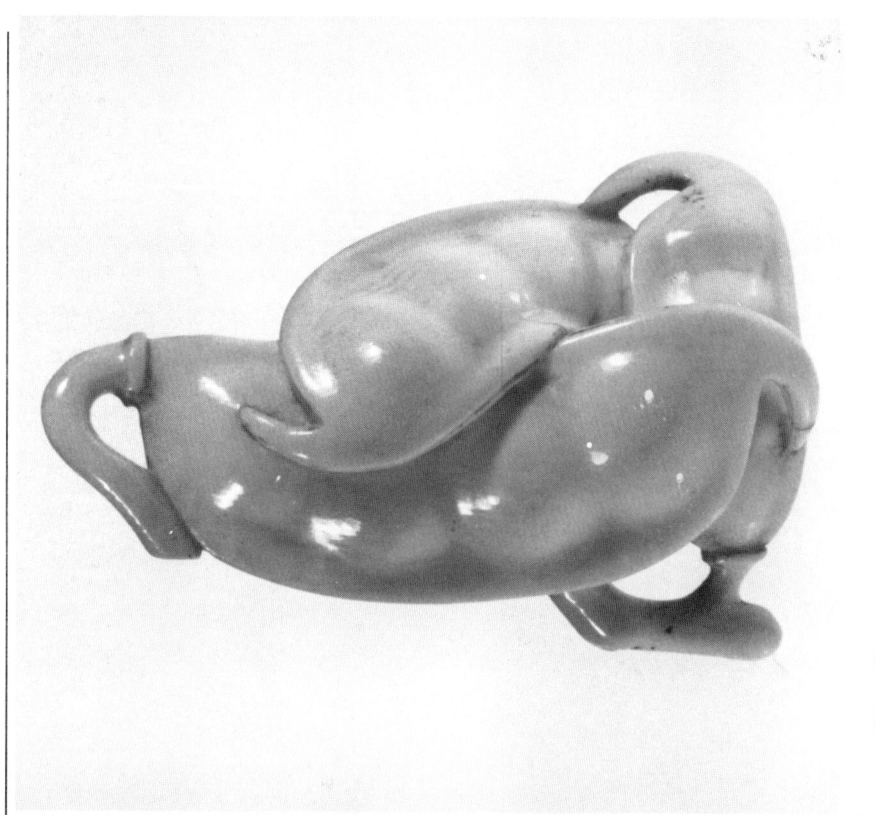

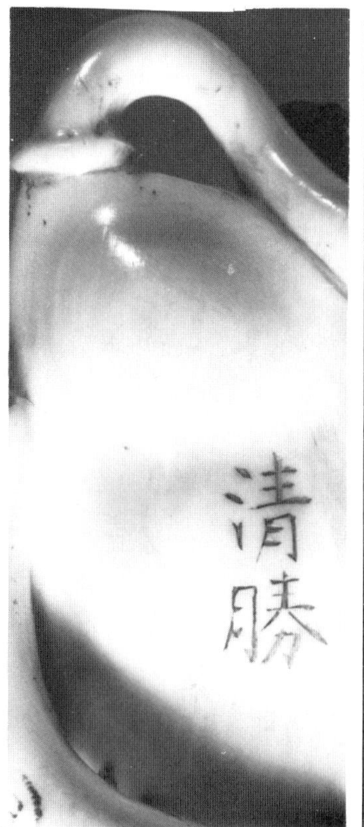

70

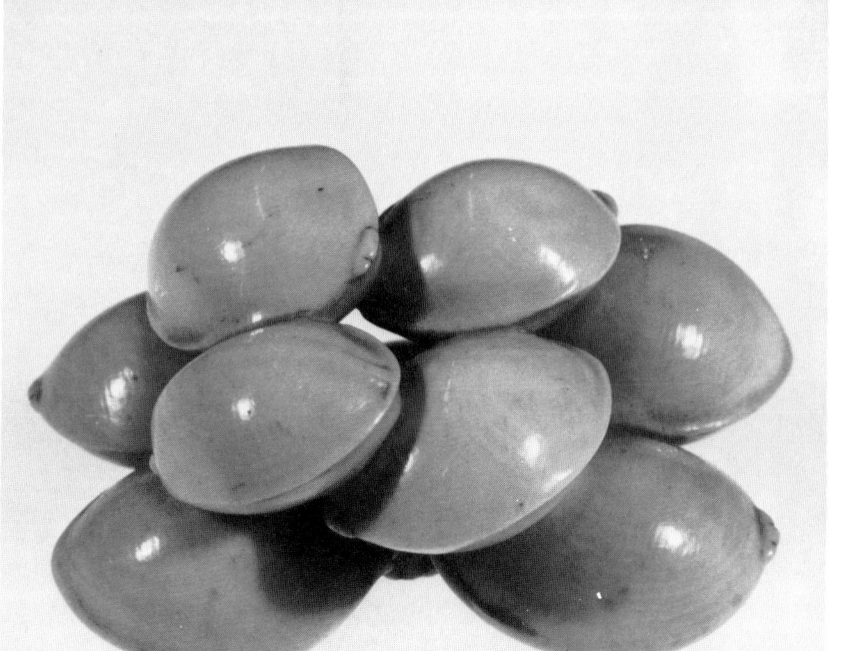

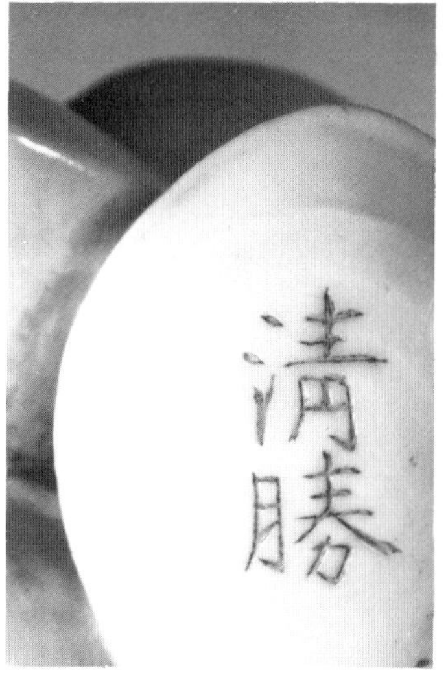

71

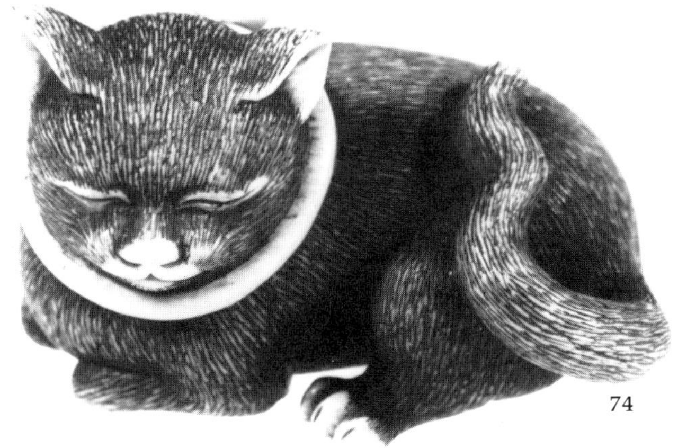
74

74
Dozing cat. Ivory.
Unsigned.
19th century.
Length 3.75cm ($1\frac{1}{2}$in).
F.778. Franks Collection.

75
Fox on a *mokugyō* (small temple bell). Ivory.
Signed Rantei in an irregular cartouche on the base.
Early 19th century.
Height 3.25cm ($1\frac{1}{4}$in).
F.806. Franks Collection.

76
Sitting deer.
Ivory, the eyes inlaid.
Signed Ran'ichi in an oval cartouche on the base.
19th century.
Length 3.25cm ($1\frac{1}{4}$in).
1972 1-14 6. Bequeathed by Mrs Rosina Maria Howe.

77
Two rats on a candle.
Ivory, the eyes inlaid and the wick deliberately blackened.
Signed Ransen in an elongated oval cartouche on the base.
19th century.
Height 3.75cm ($1\frac{1}{2}$in).
F.683. Franks Collection.

78
Two rabbits.
Ivory, partly stained, the eyes inlaid.
Signed Ransen in an elongated oval cartouche on the base.
19th century.
Length 4.25cm ($1\frac{3}{4}$in).
F.253. Franks Collection.

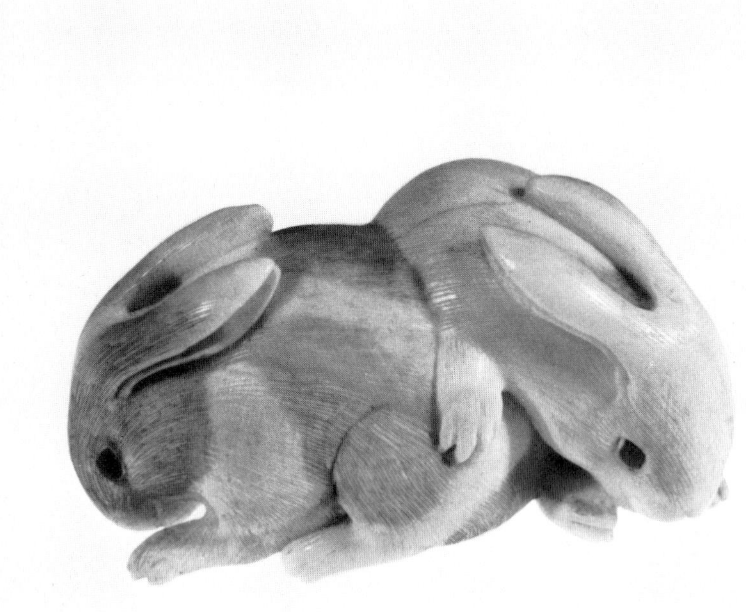

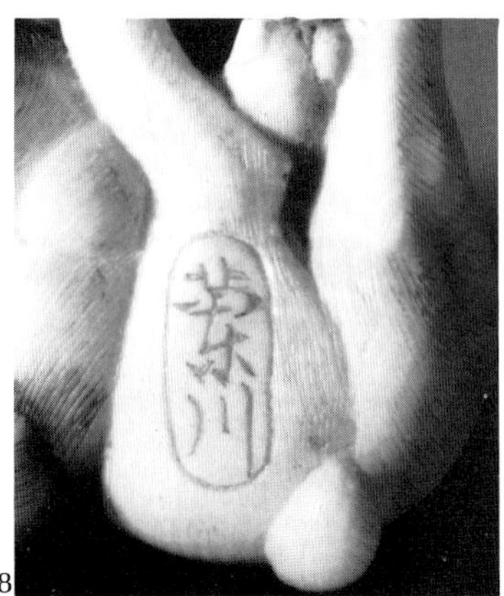
78

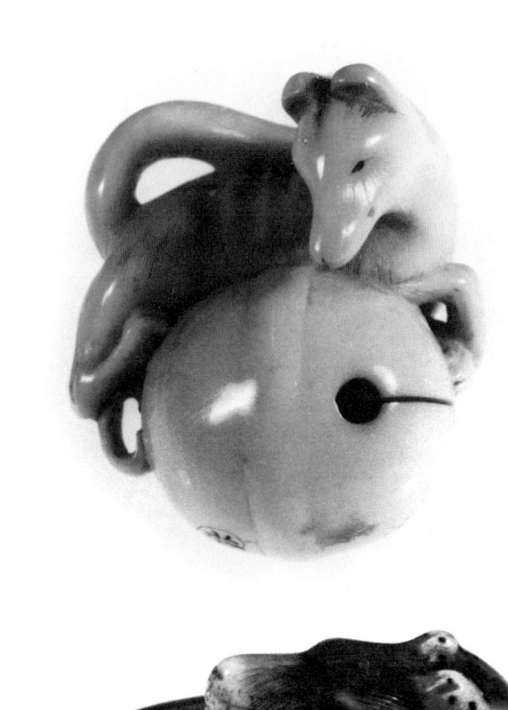

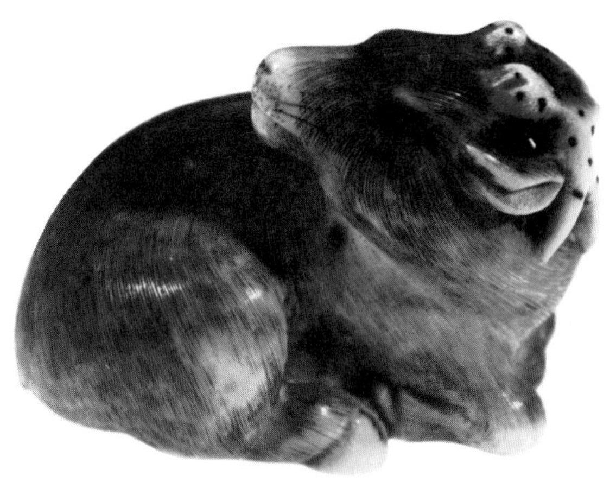

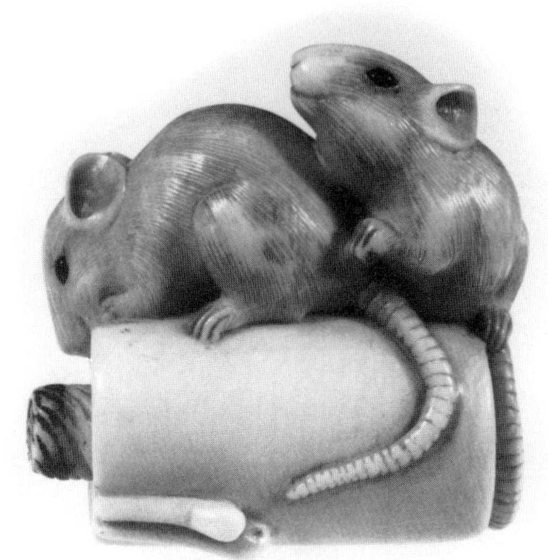

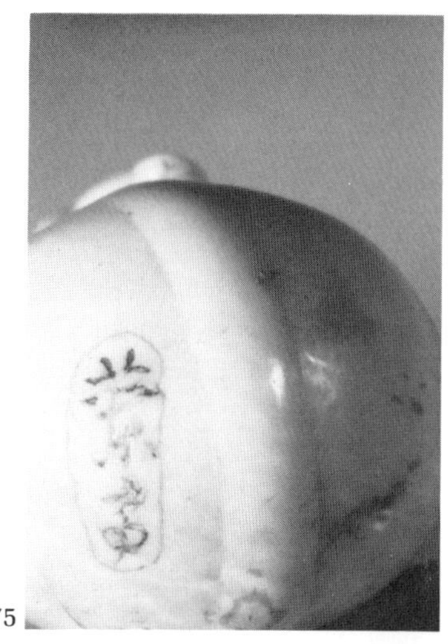

75

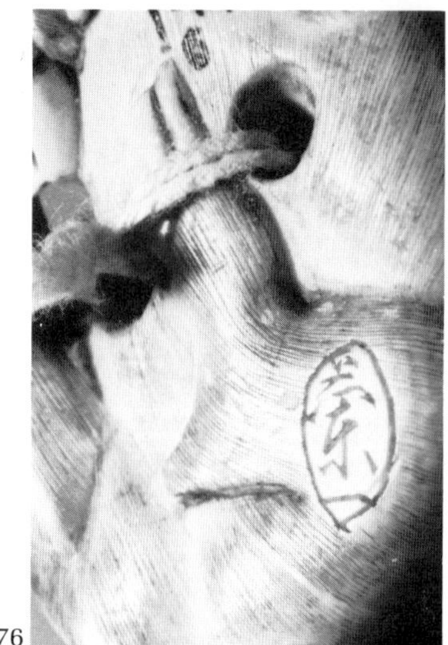

76

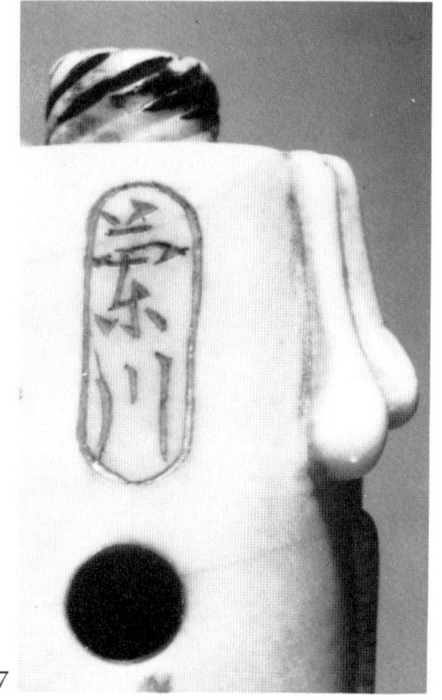

77

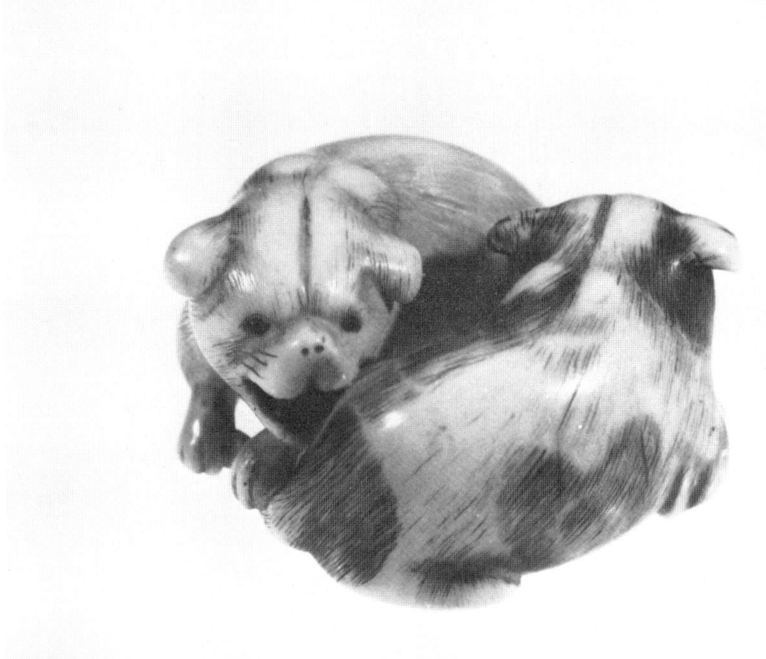

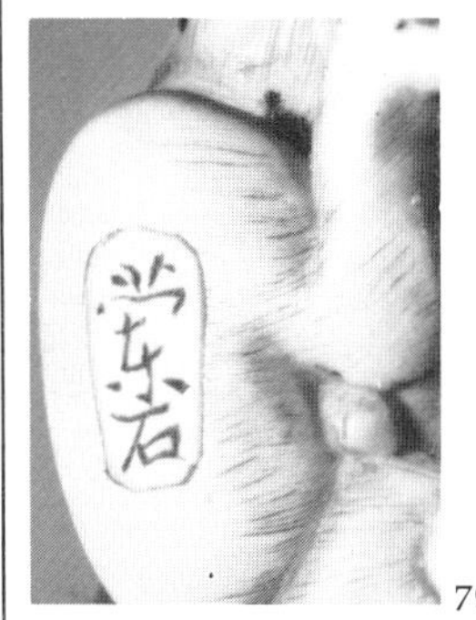

79

82

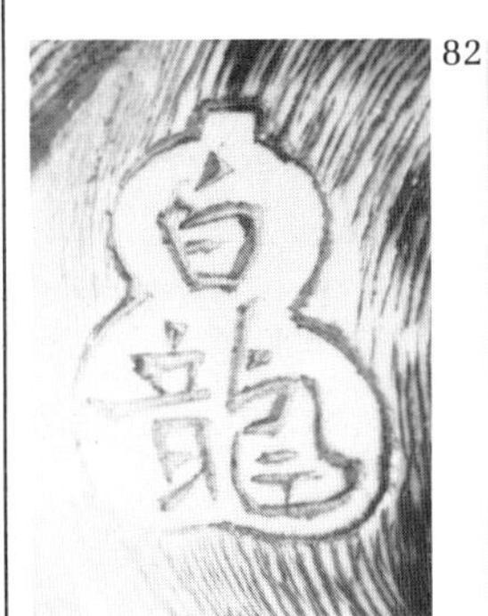

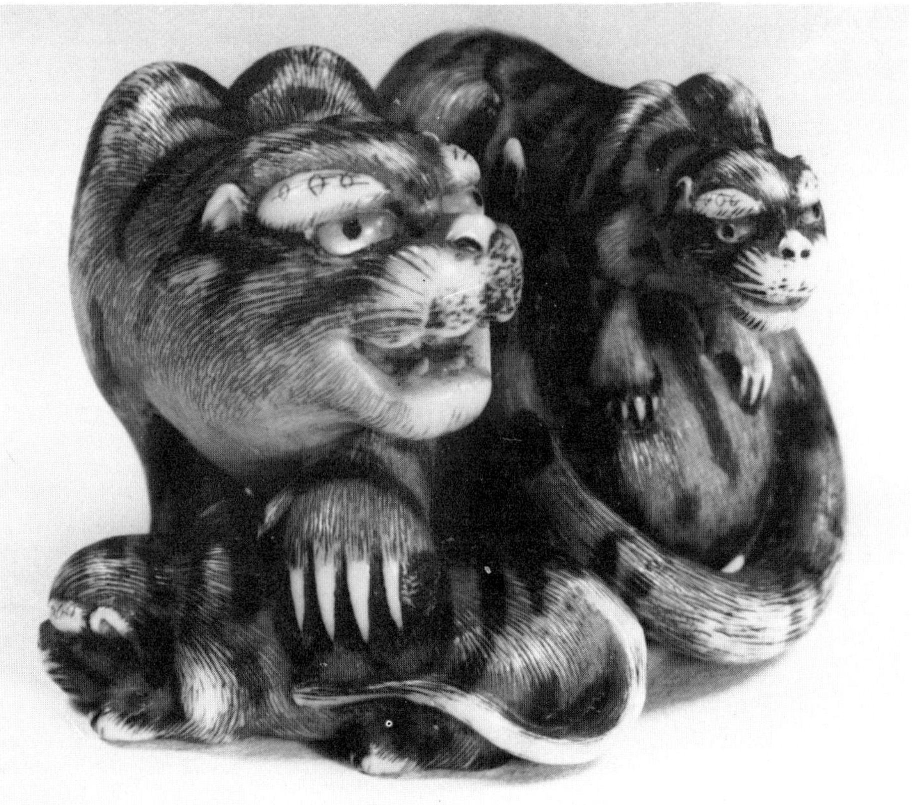

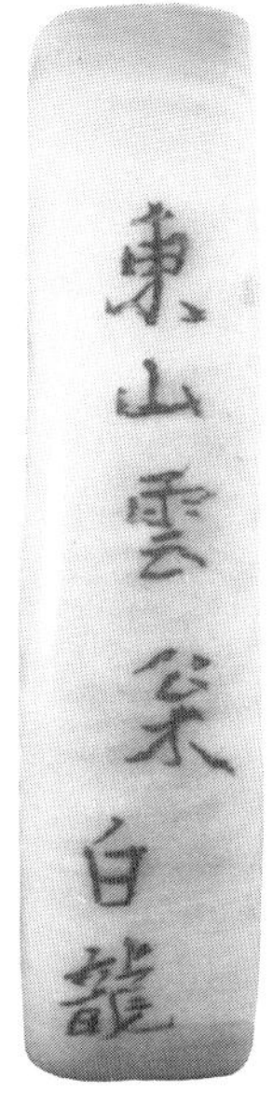

81

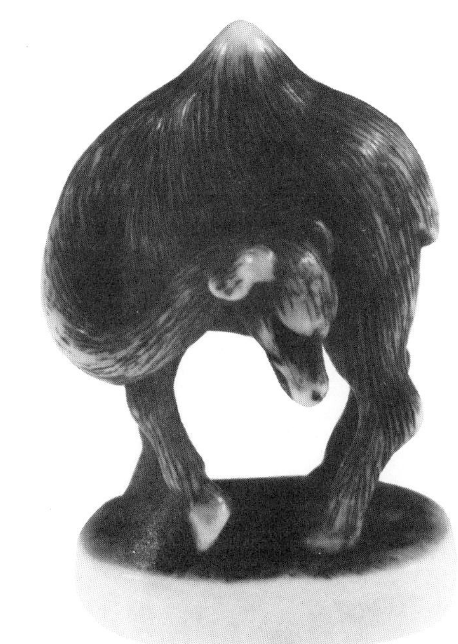

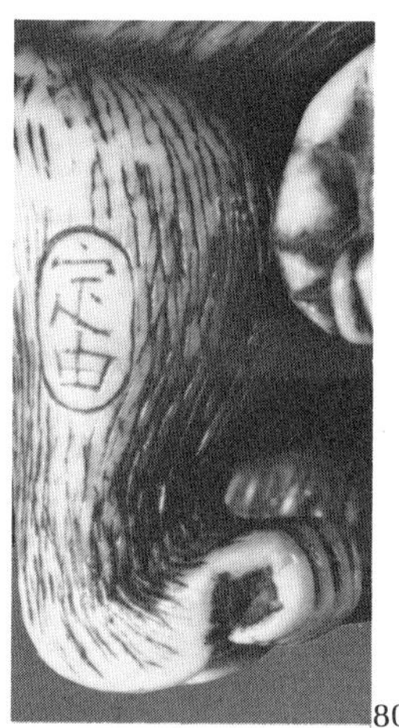

80

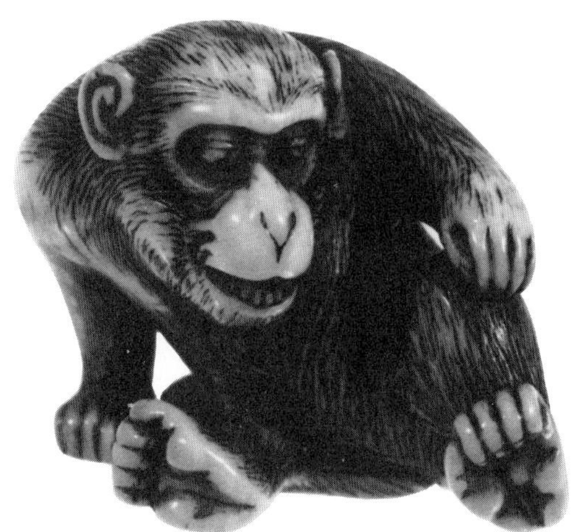

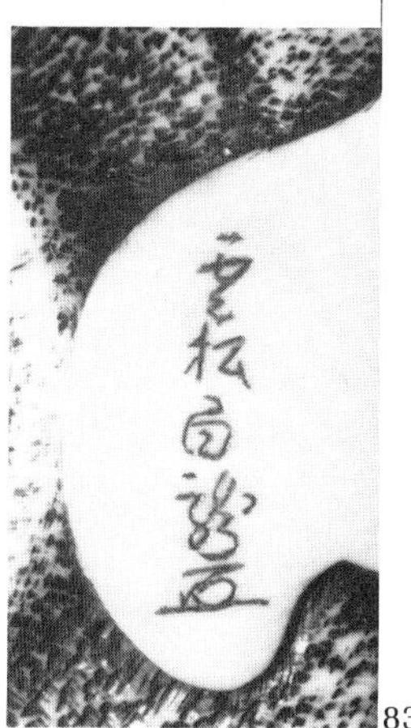

83

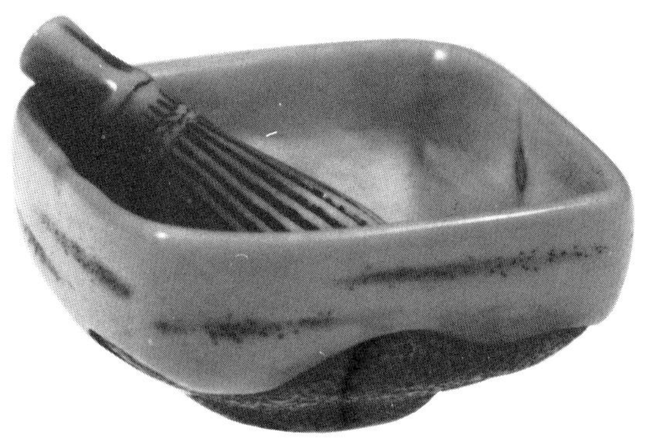

79
Two puppies fighting head to tail. Ivory, partly stained, the mouths reddened and the eyes inlaid. Signed Ranseki in an elongated oval cartouche on the base.
19th century.
Width 3.75cm ($1\frac{1}{2}$in).
F.231. Franks Collection.

80
Monkey scratching.
Ivory, the eyes inlaid.
Signed Sadayoshi in an oval cartouche under a leg.
Early 19th century.
Height 3cm ($1\frac{1}{2}$in).
OA + 124.

81
Camel on an oval base.
Ivory, the eyes inlaid.
Signed Tōzan Unshō Hakuryū on side of base.
19th century.
Height 4.25cm ($1\frac{3}{4}$in).
F.1070. Franks Collection.

82
Tigress and two cubs.
Ivory, stained brown and yellow, the mouths reddened, the eyes inlaid in mother-of-pearl.
Signed Hakuryū in a gourd-shaped cartouche on the tigress's behind.
19th century.
Length 4.5cm ($1\frac{3}{4}$in).
1972 1-14 9. Bequeathed by Mrs Rosina Maria Howe.

This example is by Hakuryū II.

83
Model of a pottery teabowl and bamboo tea-whisk. Ivory.
Signed Unshō Hakuryū with *kakihan* on the base.
19th century.
Width 3.25cm ($1\frac{1}{4}$in).
F.1174. Franks Collection.

84
Architectural fantasy, the base carved in relief with a Japanese waterside scene. Ivory.
Signed Kagetoshi in a rectangular cartouche on the base.
Early 19th century.
Height 2.75cm (1in).
Length 3.75cm ($1\frac{1}{2}$in).
1945 10-17 635. Bequeathed by Oscar Raphael.

85
Palaces and an official procession, as dreamed by Rosei who is carved lying on a bed to one side. The base is carved in sunken relief with clouds.
Ivory.
Signed Kagetoshi in a rectangular cartouche on the base.
Early 19th century.
Height 2.75cm (1in).
Length 3.75cm ($1\frac{1}{2}$in).
1945 10-17 634. Bequeathed by Oscar Raphael.

Rosei was a T'ang Dynasty Chinese who dreamed that he rose to be Emperor.

86
Palace revealed in the 'Clam's Breath', the clam carved at one corner. The base represents waves in sunk relief.
Wood, the clam in ivory.
Signed Kagetoshi in a rectangular cartouche on the base.
Early 19th century.
Height 2.60cm (1in).
Length 2.75cm ($1\frac{1}{2}$in).
F.994. Franks Collection.

For an almost identical example *see* W. L. Behrens Collection, Catalogue no. 1359, illustrated pl. XXIV.

87
Chinese boat on waves. Wood.
Signed Kagetoshi in a rectangular cartouche on the base.
Early 19th century.
Height 3cm ($1\frac{1}{2}$in).
Length 3.75cm ($1\frac{3}{4}$in).
1953 12-17 17. Bequeathed by Mrs Helen Epstein.

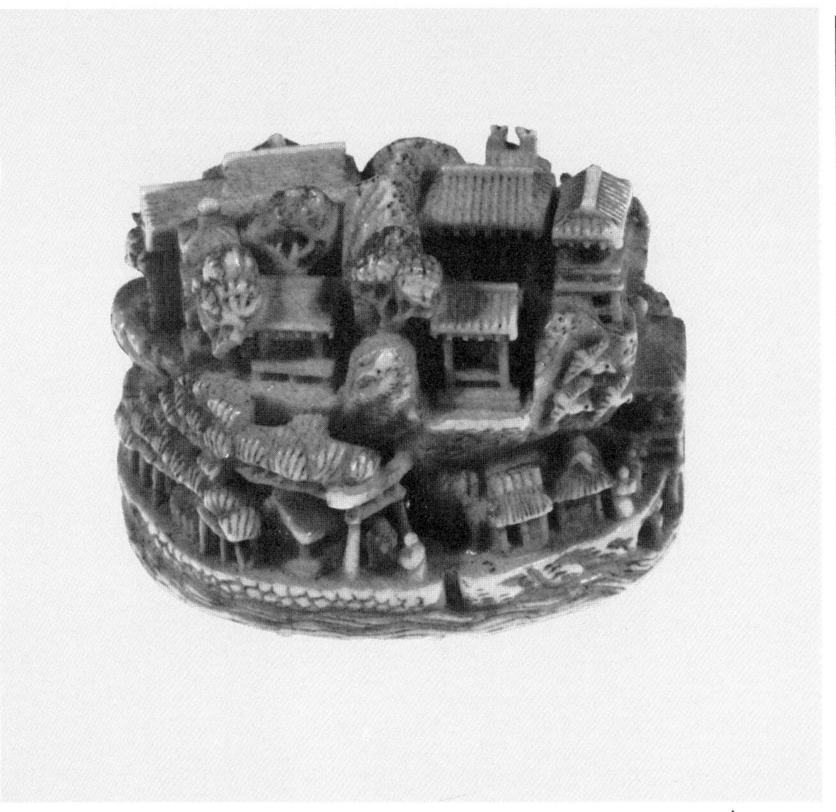

84 △ 85 ▽

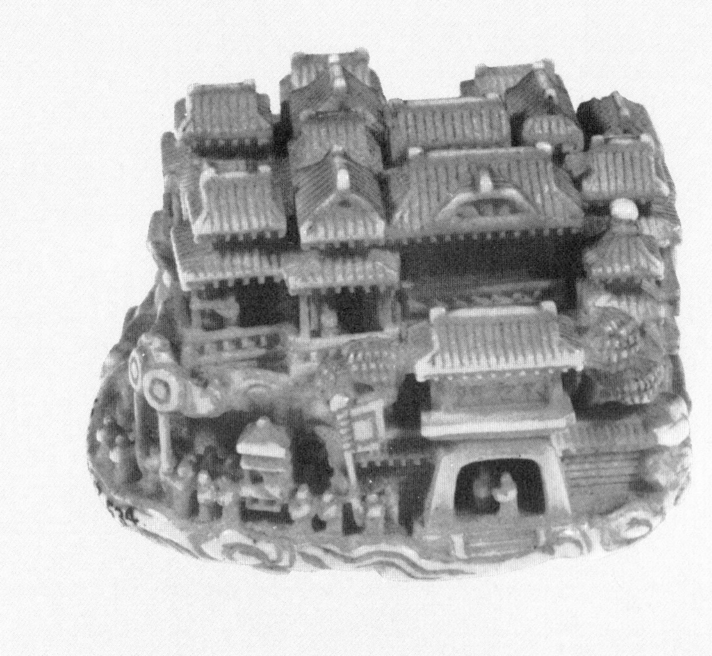

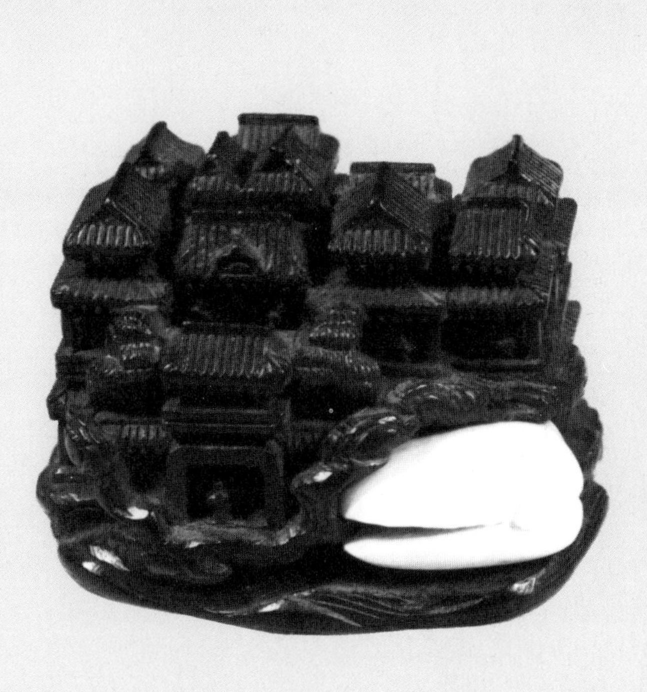

86 △ 87 ▽

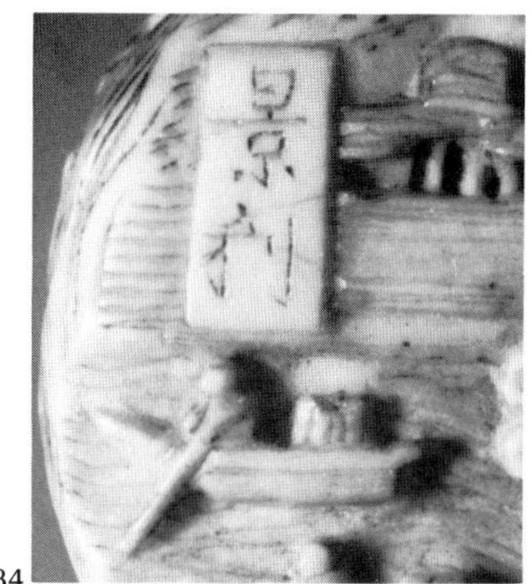

84

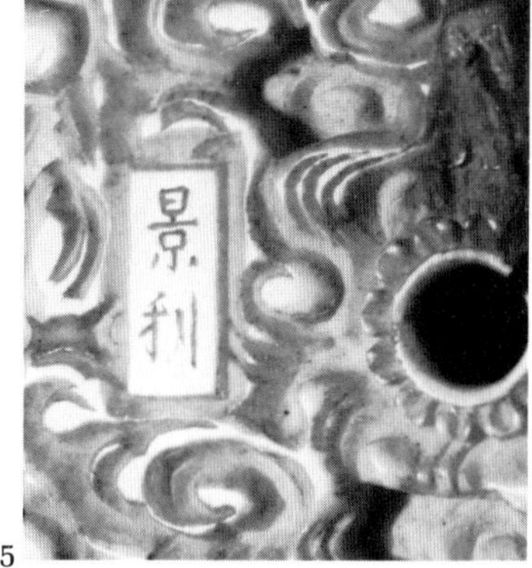

85

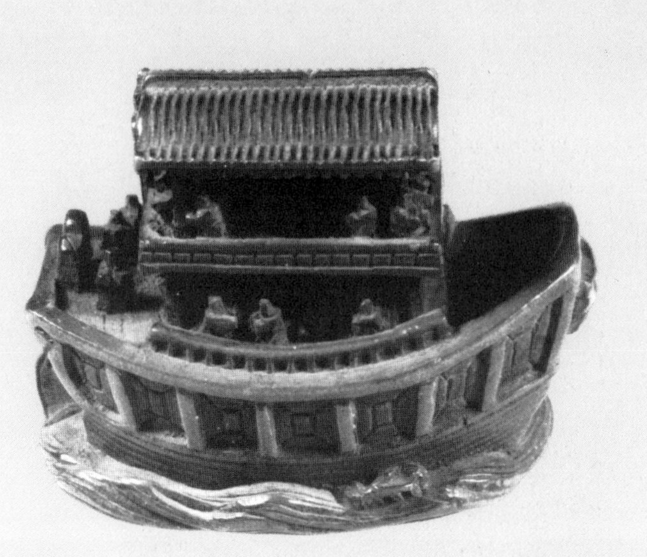

87

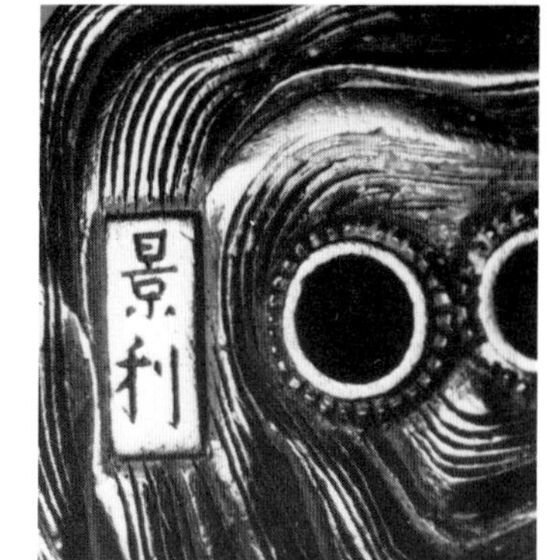

86

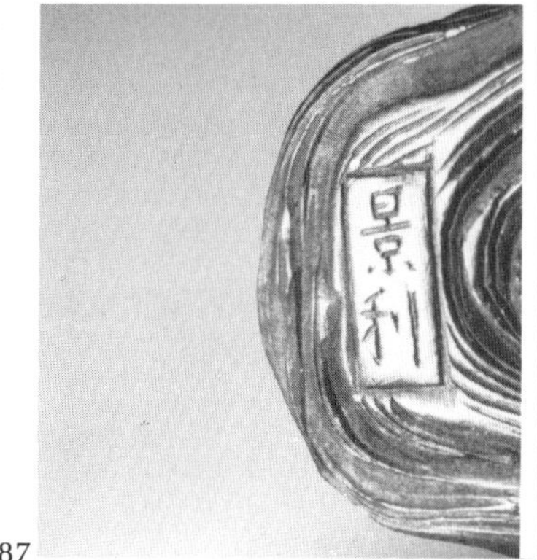

87

88
Head of a Buddhist Guardian King, in the form of a mask. Wood, the eyes inlaid and ringed in gold lacquer.
Signed Kōseki.
Late 19th–early 20th century.
Height 8.8cm ($3\frac{1}{2}$in).
1945 10-17 530. Bequeathed by Oscar Raphael.

This is one of the *Niō* ('Two Kings') who guard the main gate of many temples.
Colour plate, page 23

89
Ghost of an old woman rising out of flames, holding in her arms a stone sculpture of the Boddhisattva Jizō. Wood.
Signed Shin Kōseki.
Late 19th–early 20th century.
Height 10.2cm (4in).
1945 10-17 614. Bequeathed by Oscar Raphael.

The merciful Jizō comforts the denizens of the Buddhist hell. His stone image is also seen by cross-roads in Japan as the patron of travellers.
Colour plate, page 14

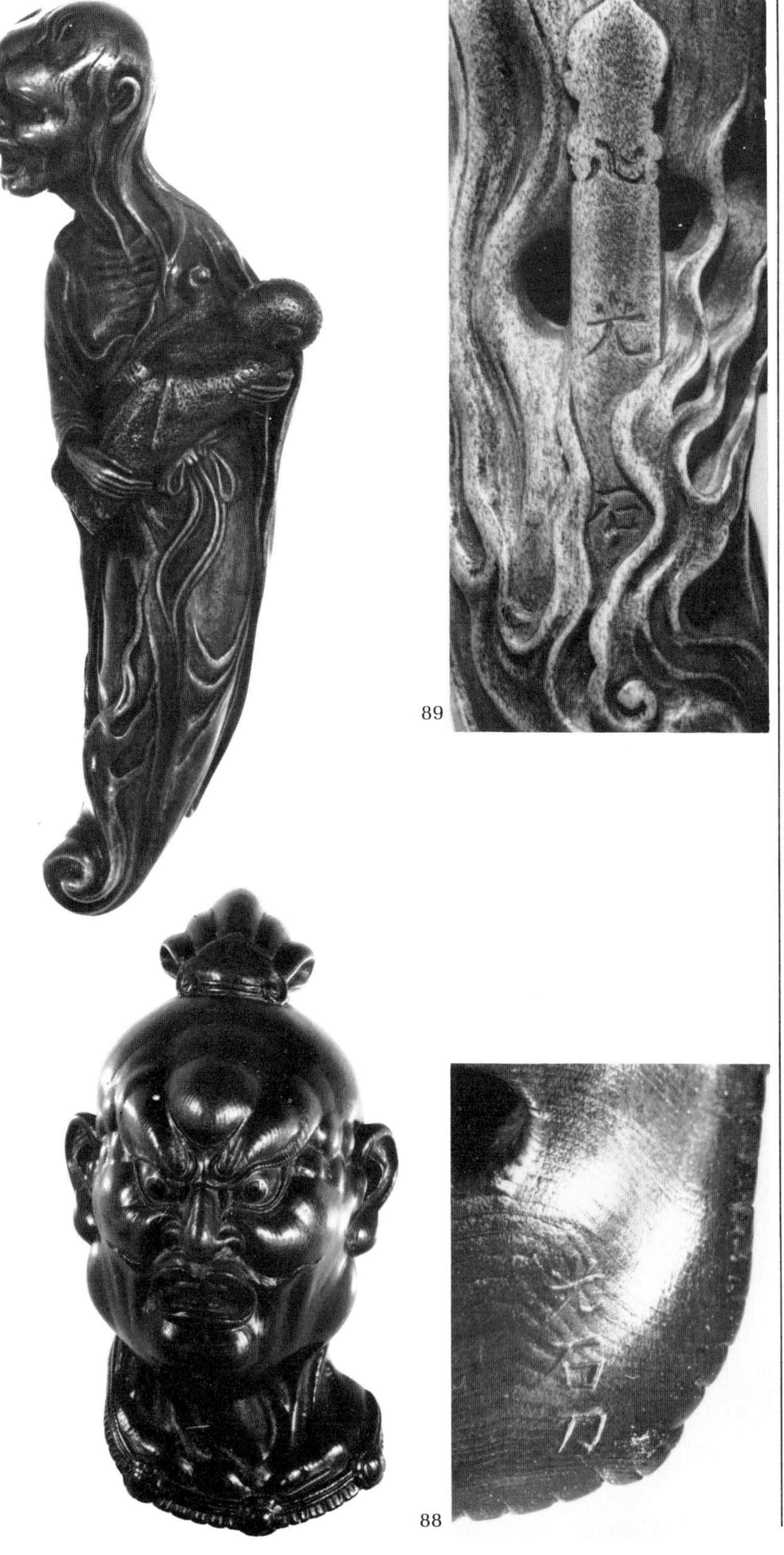
89
88

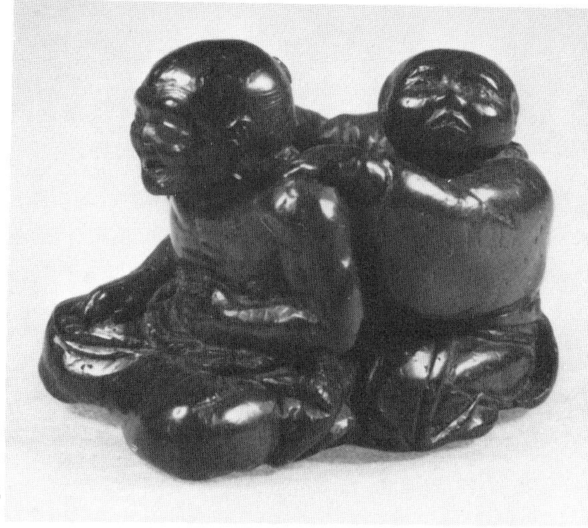

92

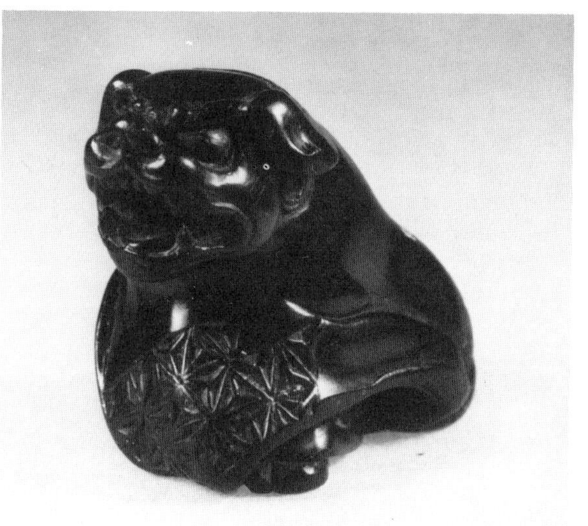

91

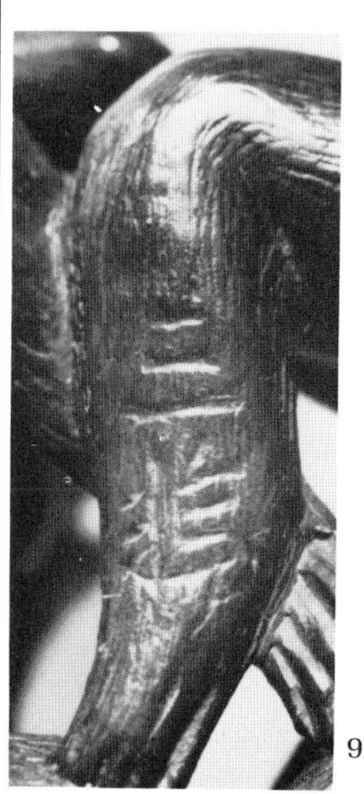

90

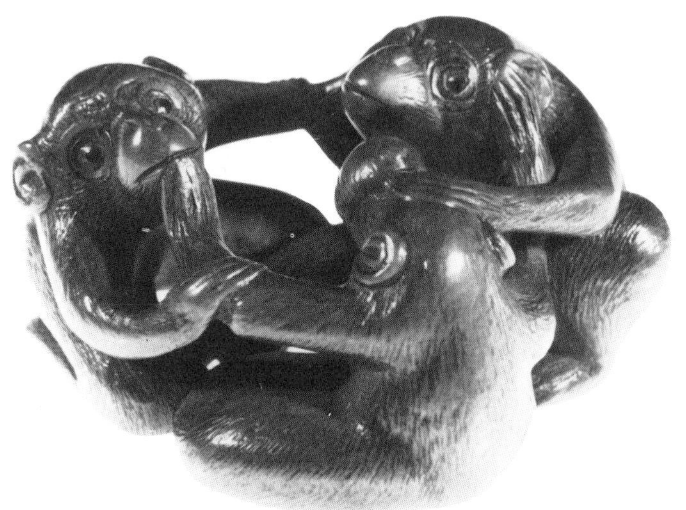

Edo (Tokyo)

90
The three monkeys encouraging each other to hear, speak and see no evil.
Wood, the eyes inlaid.
Signed Miwa on the base.
18th century.
Length 5.1cm (2in).
F.681. Franks Collection.

91
Boy doing the lion dance, the mask open to reveal his head.
Wood, the face unstained.
Signed Miwa under one foot.
Early 19th century.
Height 3.75cm ($1\frac{1}{2}$in).
F.484. Franks Collection.

92
Blind masseur at work.
Wood, the cord holes ringed with stained ivory.
Signed Miwa and with a seal (?Shin) on the base.
Late 18th century.
Length 3.25cm ($1\frac{1}{4}$in).
F.166. Franks Collection.

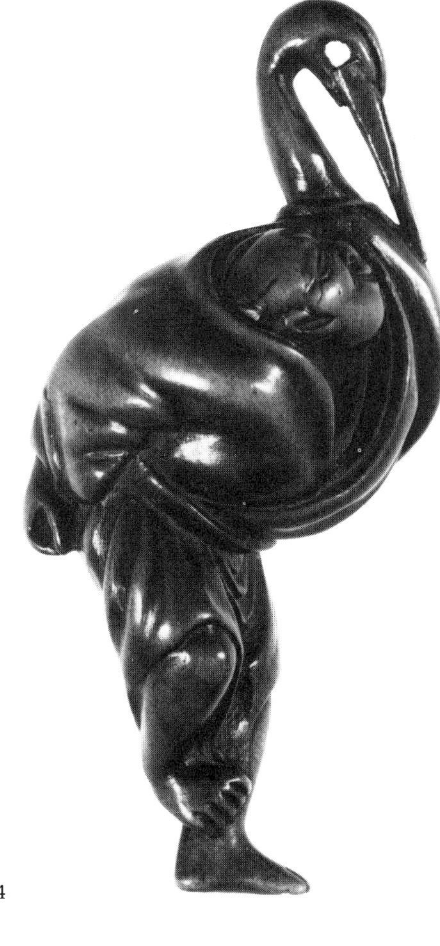

94

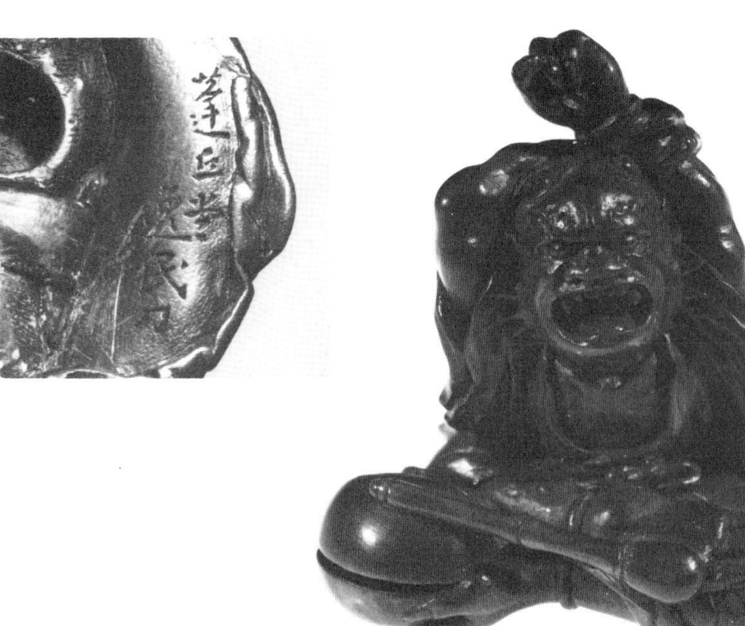

97

93
Blind masseur with client. Wood. Ivory rimmed *himotoshi*. Signed Hokuryū. 19th century. Height 3.2cm ($1\frac{1}{4}$in). F.610. Franks Collection.

94
Crane dancer, his arm raised and holding a fan, to give the silhouette of the bird. Wood. Signed Shūgetsu on the hem of the robe. 18th century. Height 6.4cm ($2\frac{1}{2}$in). 1945 10-17 571. Bequeathed by Oscar Raphael.

A very similar example, by Gessei, from the Charles A. Greenfield Collection is illustrated in R. Bushell, *Collectors' Netsuke*, p. 65, no. 80.

95
Blind man crouching and trying to lift a large stone. Wood. Signed Gessho. Late 18th–early 19th century. Height 5.1cm (2in). 1912 10-12 7. Bequeathed by Mrs H. Seymour Trower.

96
Cracked egg resting on a rock-work base, open to reveal Yoshitsune with Tengu King. Wood, a cord hole with ivory rim. Signed Shūmin with unread seal in a rectangular cartouche on the base. 19th century. Length 3.75cm ($1\frac{1}{2}$in). F.1009. Franks Collection.

97
Demon sitting and stretching, a *mokugyō* (small temple-bell) and drumstick by his knees. Wood, the eyes inlaid. Signed Hōkyūdō Itsumin Tō on the base. 19th century. Height 4.5cm ($1\frac{3}{4}$in). 1912 10-12 8. Bequeathed by Mrs H. Seymour Trower.

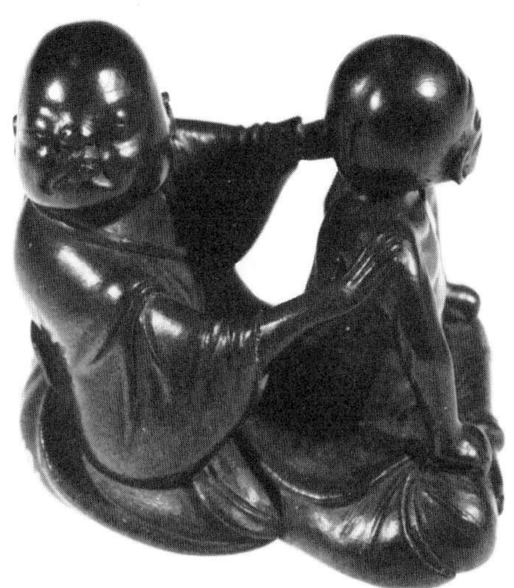

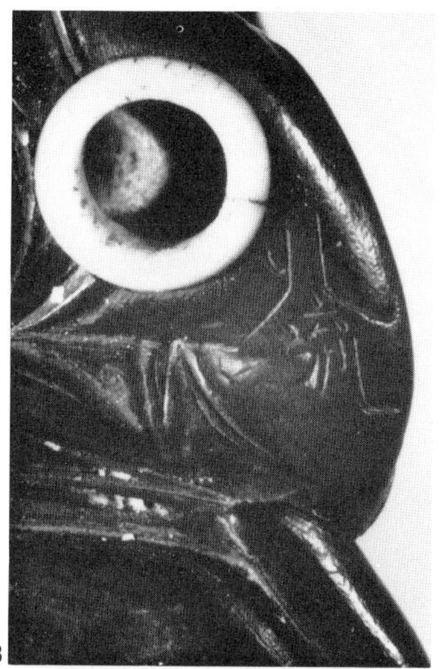

93

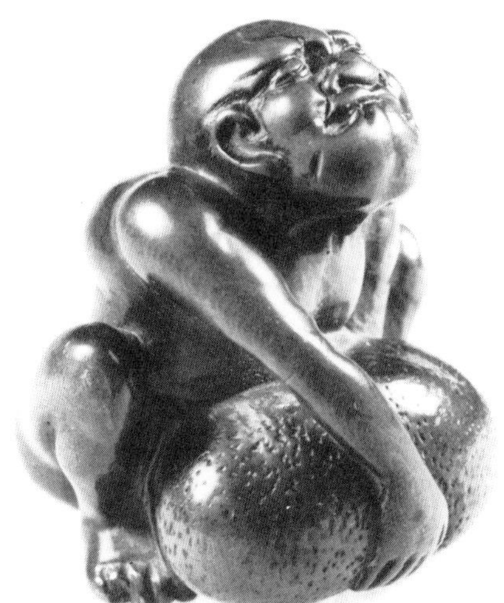

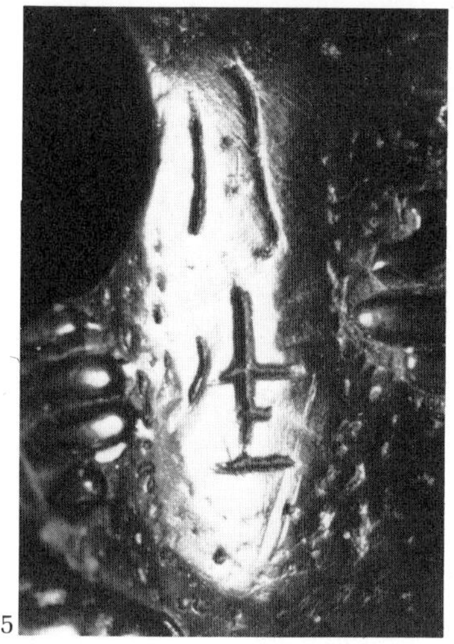

95

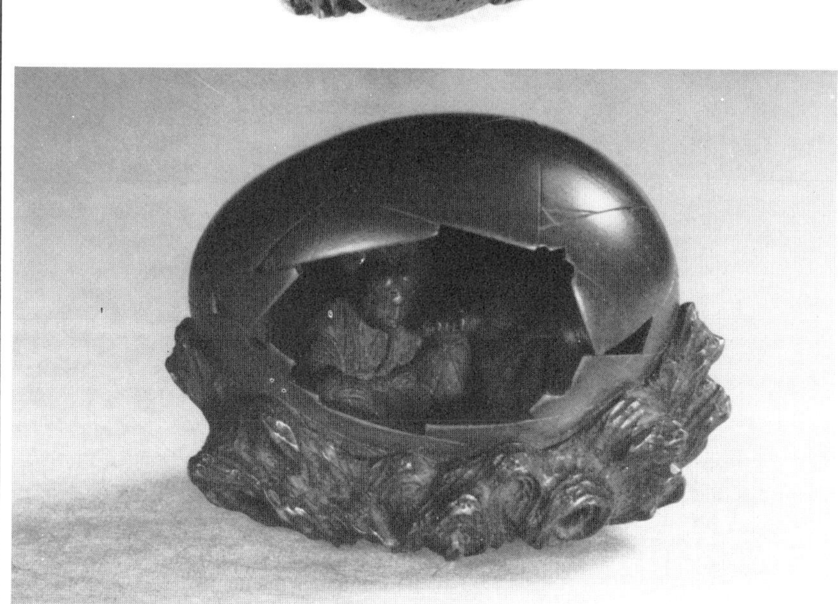

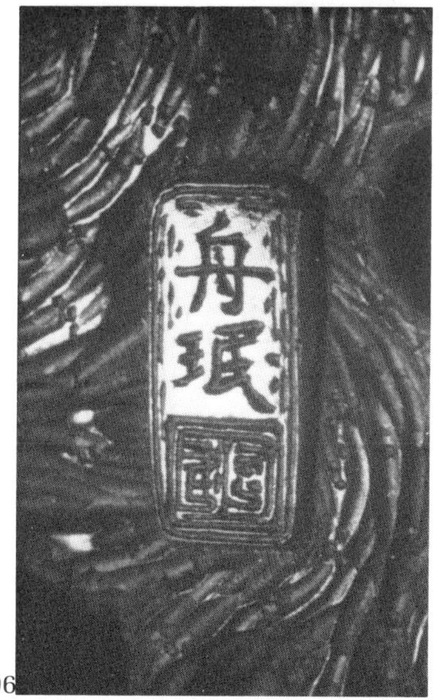

96

98
Sculptor seated by a huge head of a Buddhist Guardian King.
Wood.
Unsigned.
19th century.
Length 5.1cm (2in).
F.638. Franks Collection.

99
Shoki the Demon Queller, holding a demon by the throat.
Wood, the eyes inlaid.
Signed Minkoku in a rectangular cartouche on the back of the robe.
Late 18th century.
Height 7cm ($2\frac{3}{4}$in).
F.692. Franks Collection.

100
Square *manjū*, carved in sunk relief, with the sennin Chōkarō, holding the gourd from which his horse emerges.
Ivory. The cord-holder is detachable.
Signed Minkoku on the back.
19th century.
Length 4.25cm ($1\frac{3}{4}$in).
F.1253. Franks Collection.

101
Manjū carved in sunk relief with Fujihime holding her wisteria branch, passing a demon dressed as a priest. The natural grain of the marine ivory is left at the back.
Signed Minkoku on the back.
19th century.
Width 3.75cm ($1\frac{1}{2}$in).
F.438. Franks Collection.
Fujihime is the goddess of Mount Fuji, and of wisteria (which is also read 'Fuji' in Japanese).

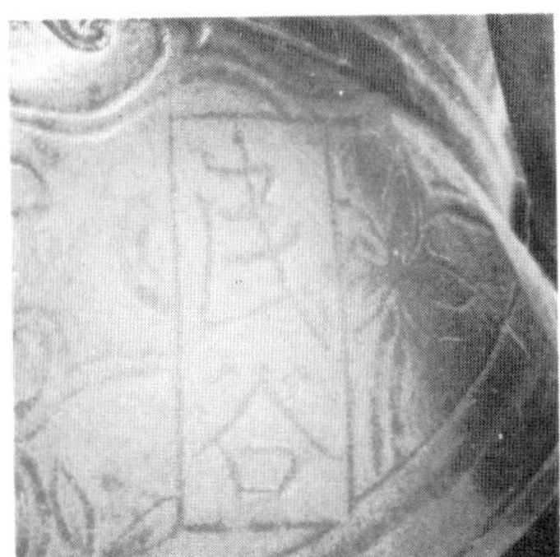

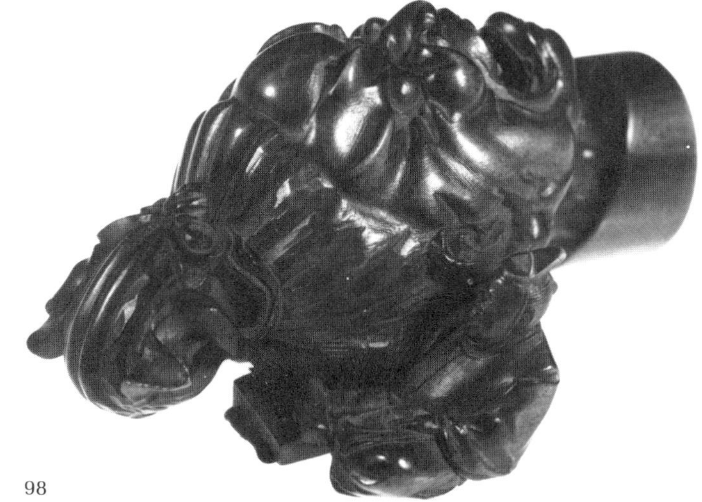

98

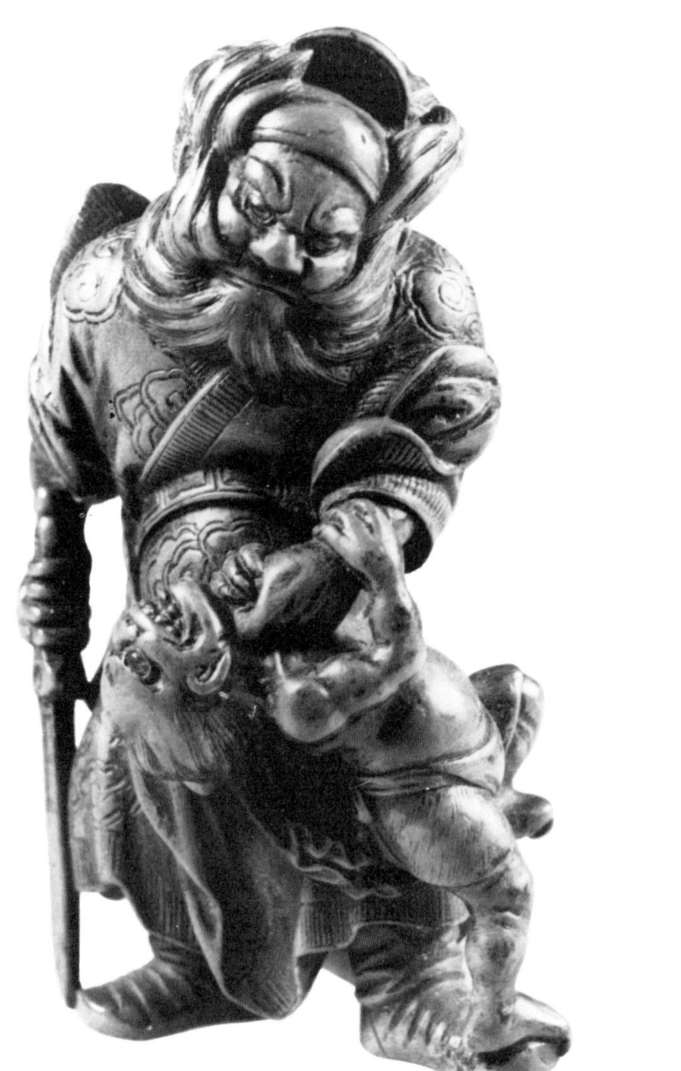

99

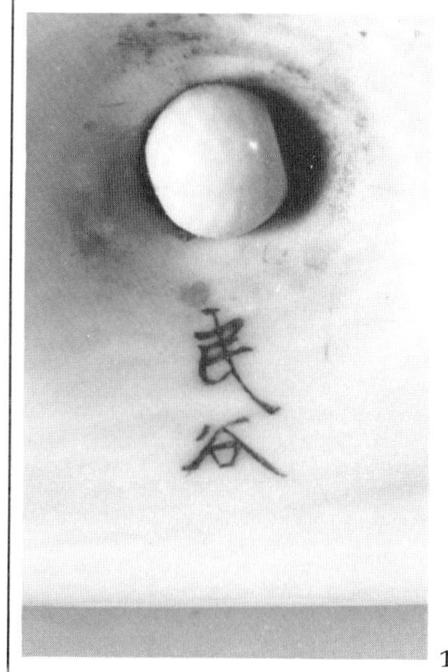

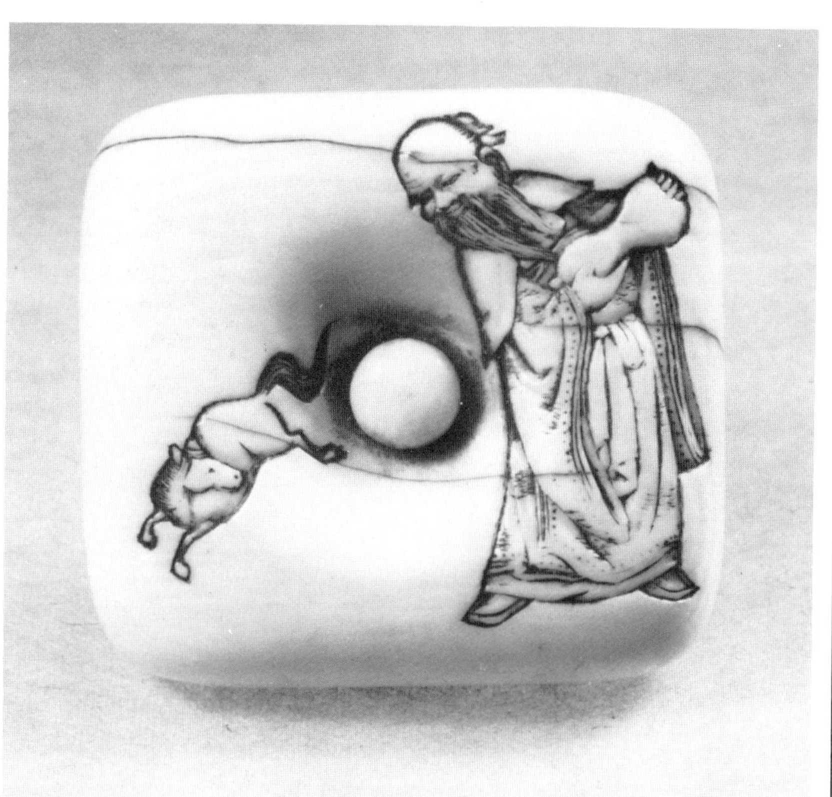

100

101

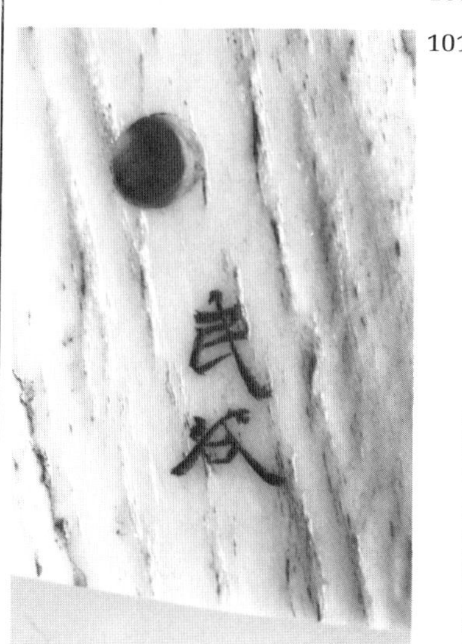

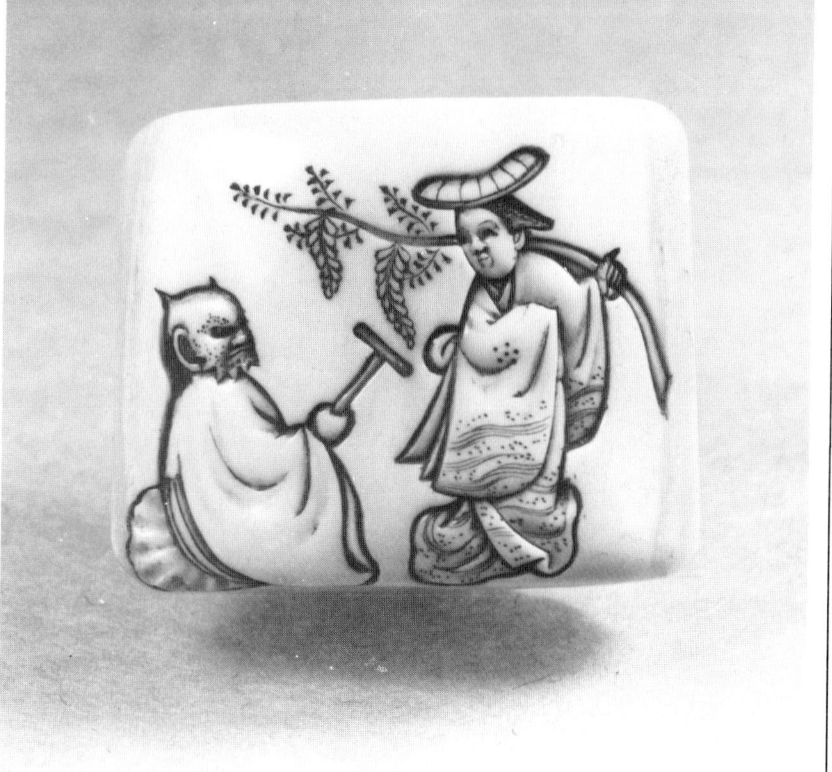

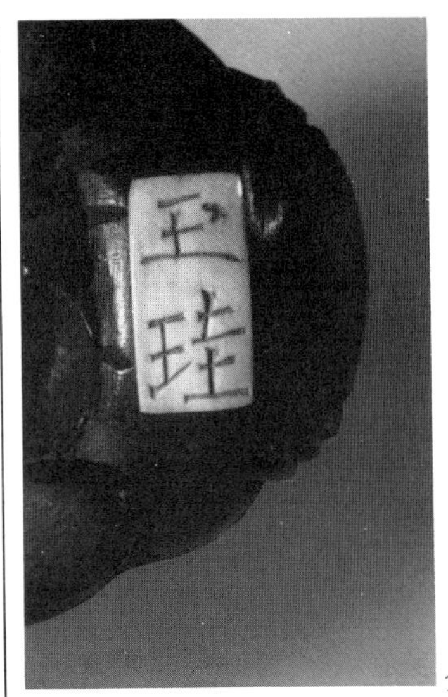

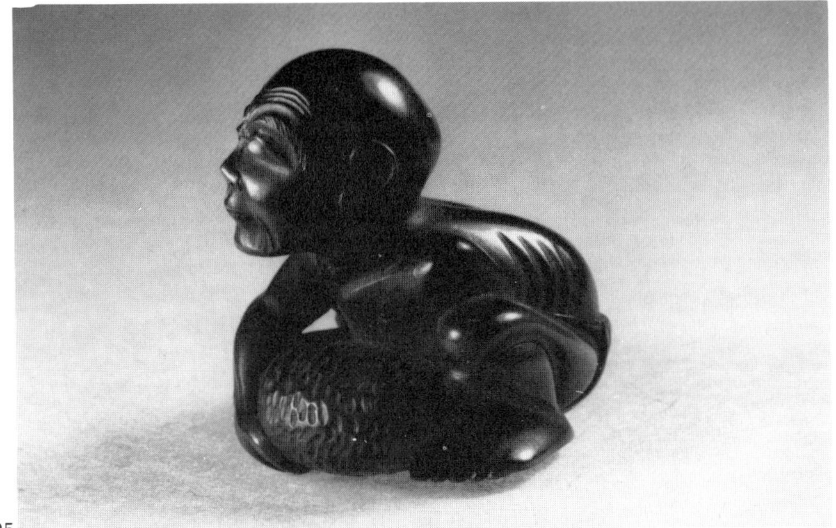

105

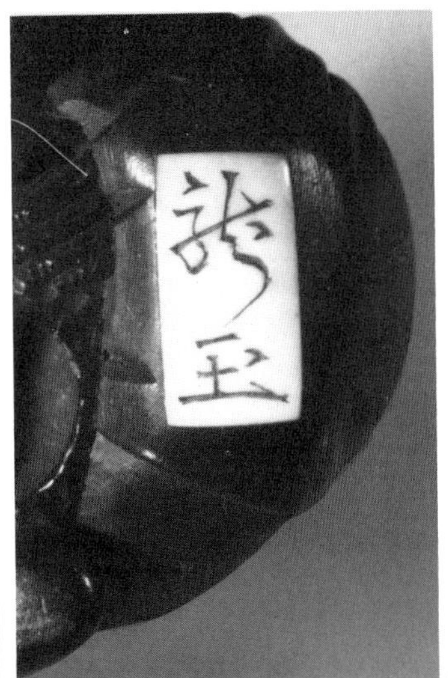

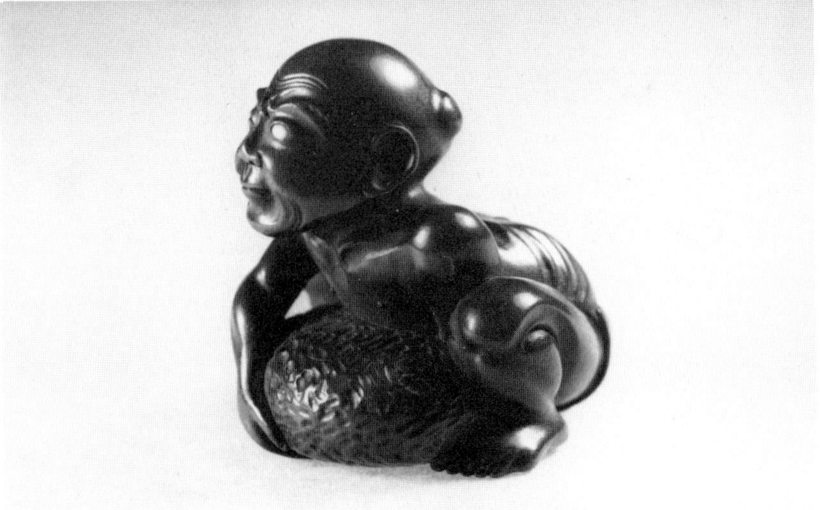

106

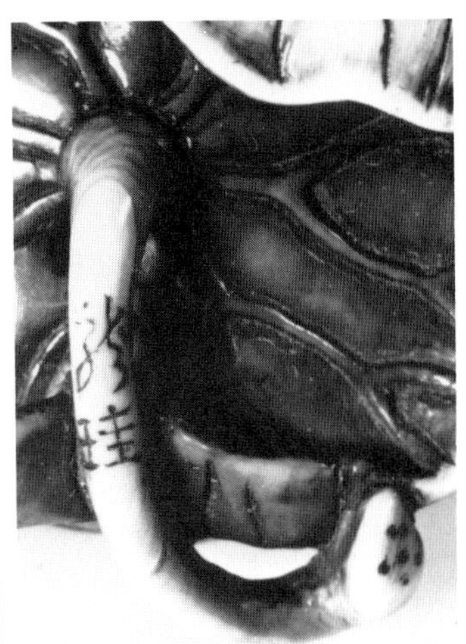

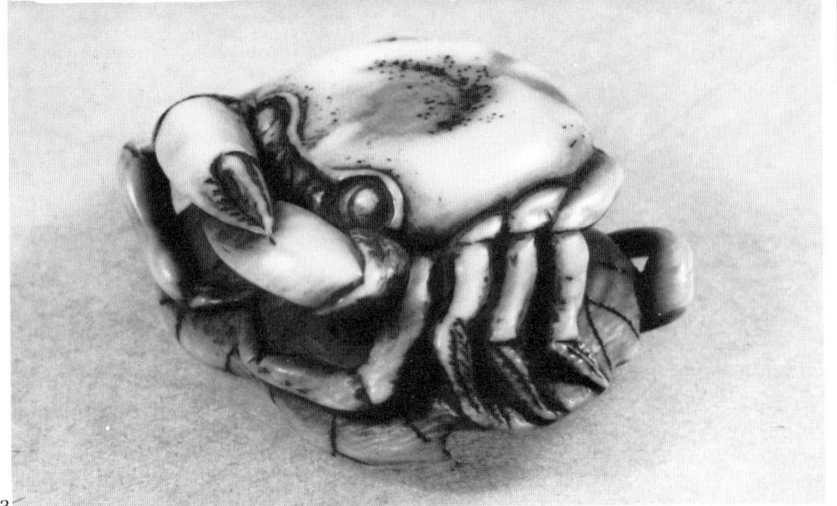

103

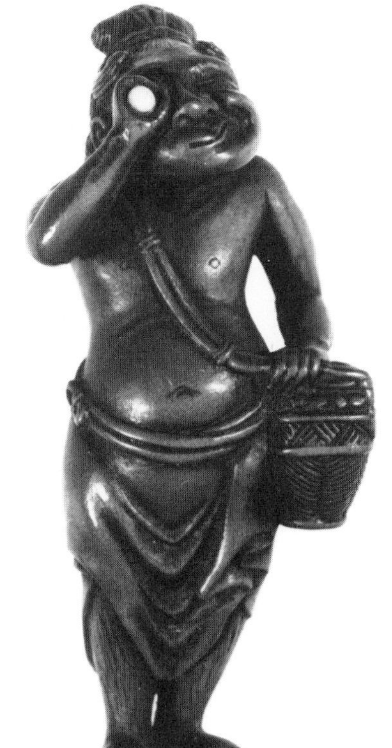

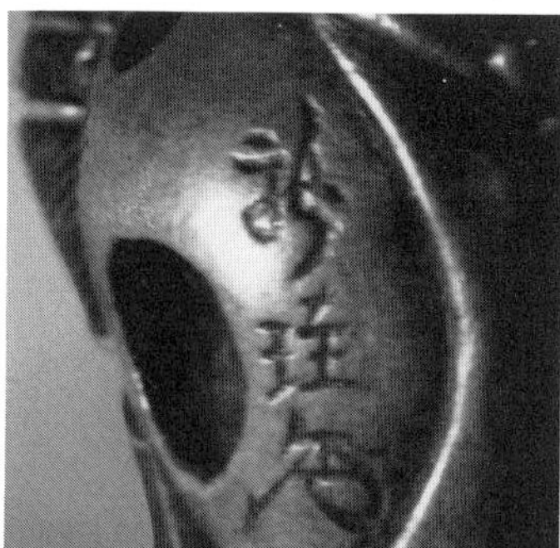

104

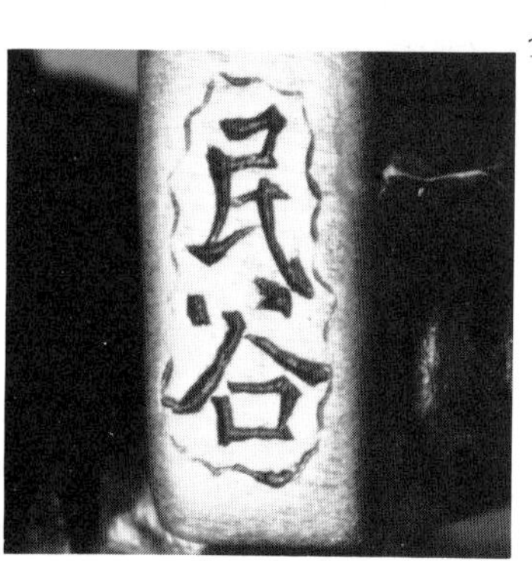

102

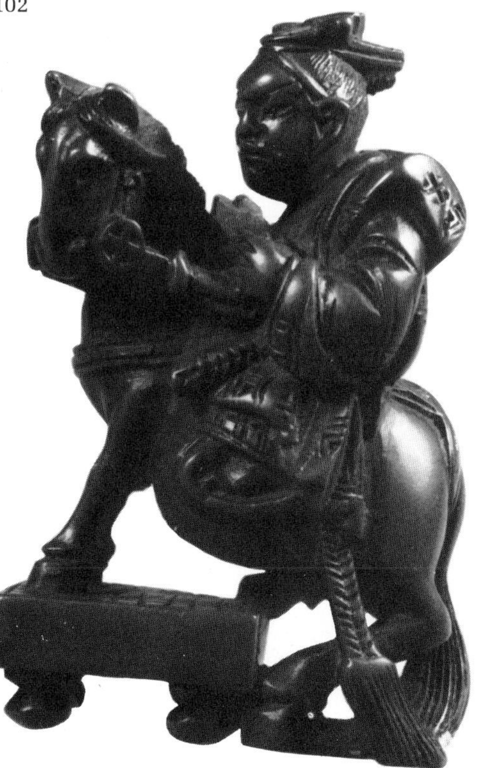

102
Oguri Hangan riding his horse onto a *go* board to show his horsemanship. Wood.
Signed Minkoku in an elongated oval cartouche on the side of the board. Probably Minkoku II.
19th century.
Height 5cm (2in).
F.1434. Franks Collection.

103
Crab on a lotus leaf, the *himotoshi* formed by the stalk.
Ivory deliberately stained.
Signed Ryūkei on bottom of the stalk.
19th century.
Width 3.75cm ($1\frac{1}{2}$in).
F.291. Franks Collection.

104
Egg-seller testing an egg.
Wood, eggs in ivory.
Signed Ryūkei with *kakihan* on back of skirt.
19th century.
Height 5.75cm ($2\frac{1}{4}$in).
F.567. Franks Collection.

105
Blind masseur trying to lift a boulder.
Wood, teeth and wall-eye inlaid in ivory.
Signed Gyokkei in a rectangular ivory cartouche on the base.
19th century.
Height 3.25cm ($1\frac{1}{4}$in).
F.159. Franks Collection.

106
Blind masseur trying to lift a boulder, similar to the preceding.
Wood, teeth and wall-eye inlaid in ivory, one cord-hole rimmed with ivory stained green.
Signed Ryūgyoku in a rectangular ivory cartouche on the base.
19th century.
Height 3.25cm ($1\frac{1}{4}$in).
F.160. Franks Collection.

107
Seated man holding a sparrow.
Ivory, deliberately stained.
Signed Sōzan on the base.
This artist is not Sōzan of the 'So' school.
19th century.
Height 3.75cm (1½in).
F.465. Franks Collection.

108
Asahina Saburō, the legendary strong-man, having a tug-of-war with two demons. Ivory.
Signed Gyokugetsu on the base.
19th century.
Length 4.5cm (1¾in).
F.863. Franks Collection.

109
Shoki the Demon Queller with a sack of demons on his back.
Wood.
Signed Jūgyoku on the base.
19th century.
Height 3.25cm (1¼in).
F.819. Franks Collection.

110
South Sea Islander on a rocky base, holding a large coral branch.
Wood and coral, ivory loin-cloth, the eyes inlaid.
Signed Jūgyoku with a *kakihan* on the base.
19th century.
Height 5cm (2in).
F.571. Franks Collection.

111
Group of dead fish.
Ivory, the eyes inlaid in mother-of-pearl.
Signed Jūgyoku on the base.
19th century.
Length 5.1cm (2in).
1945 10-17 653. Bequeathed by Oscar Raphael.

These are 'ice fish', family *Salangidae*, found on western Pacific Ocean coasts around China and Japan.

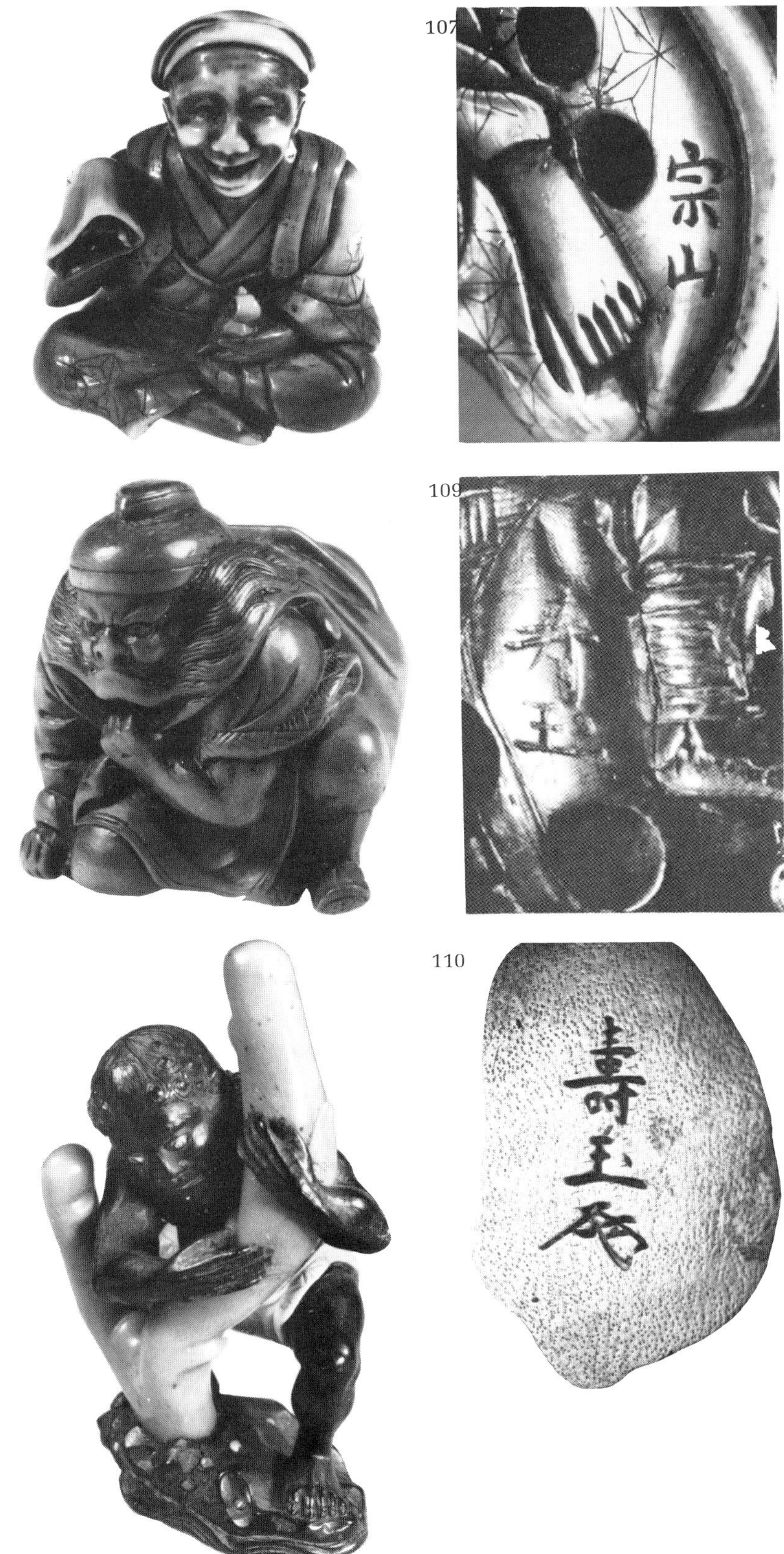

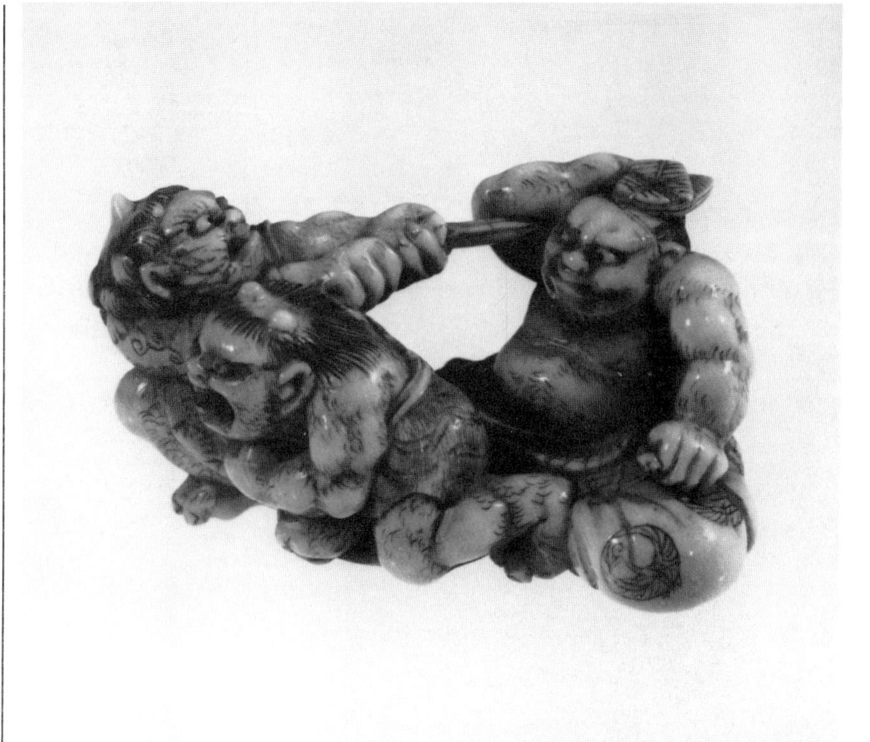

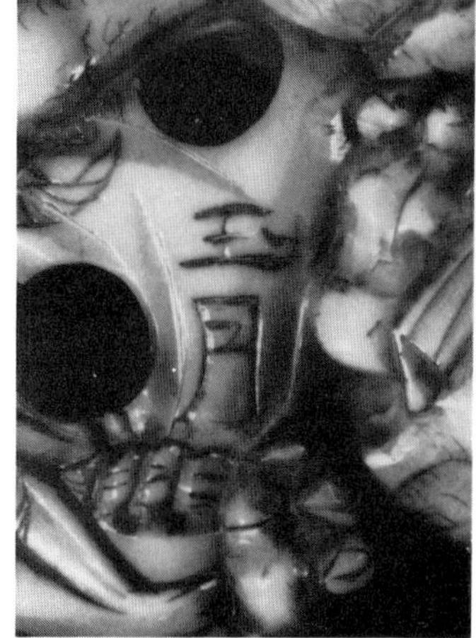

108

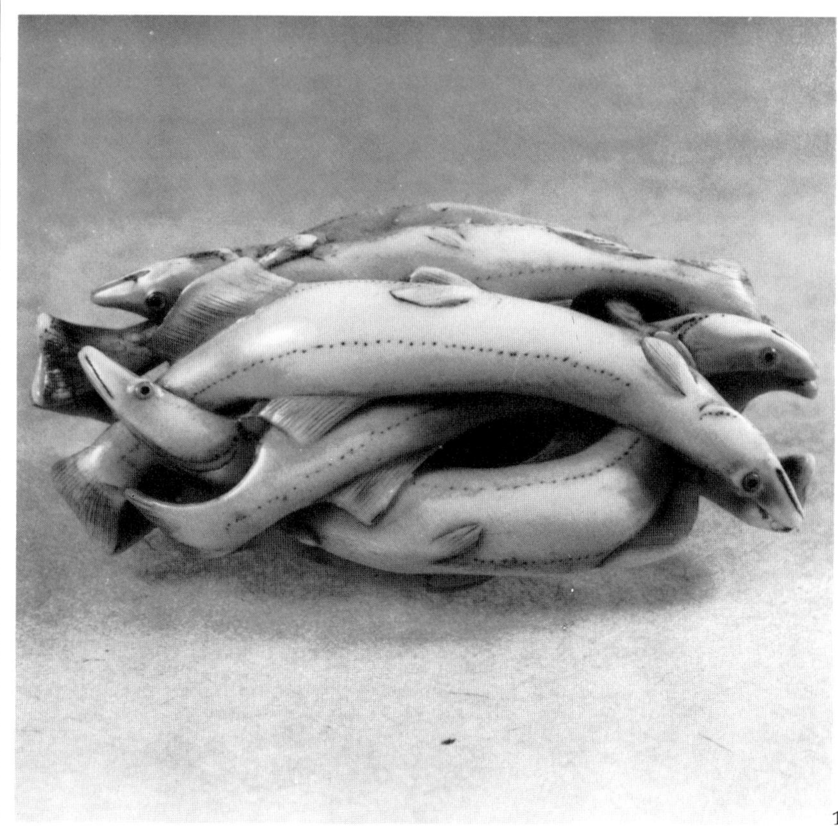

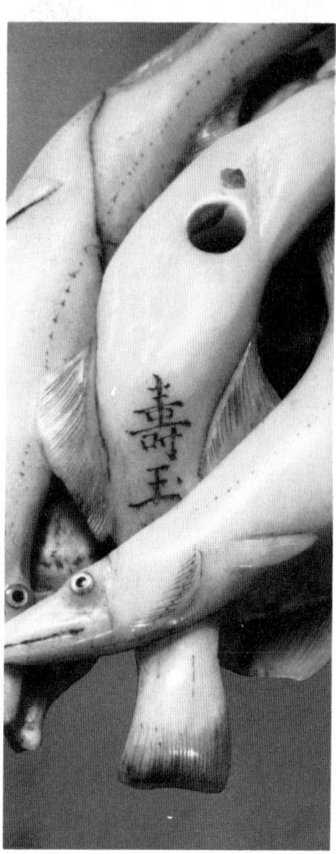

111

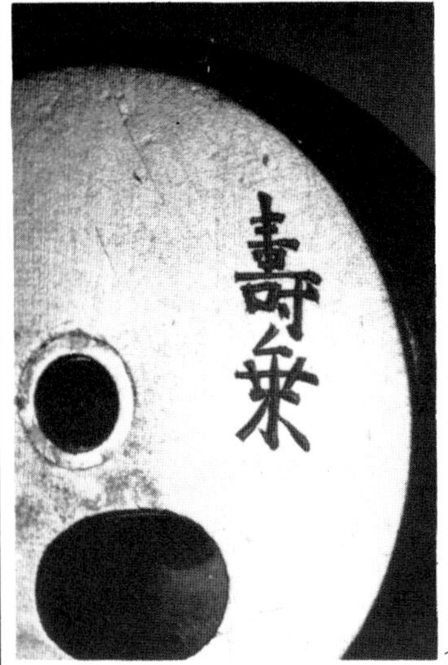

112

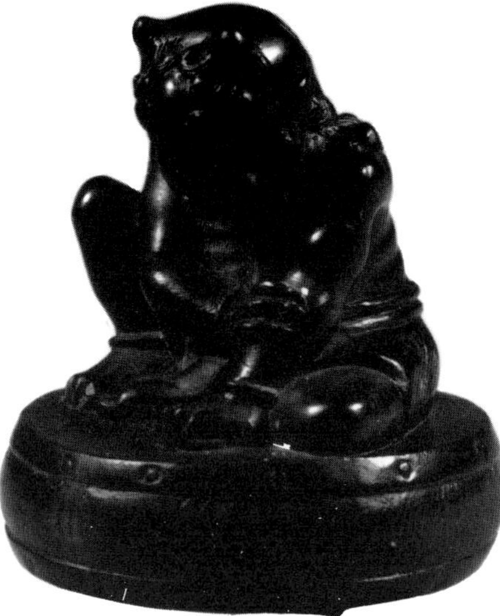

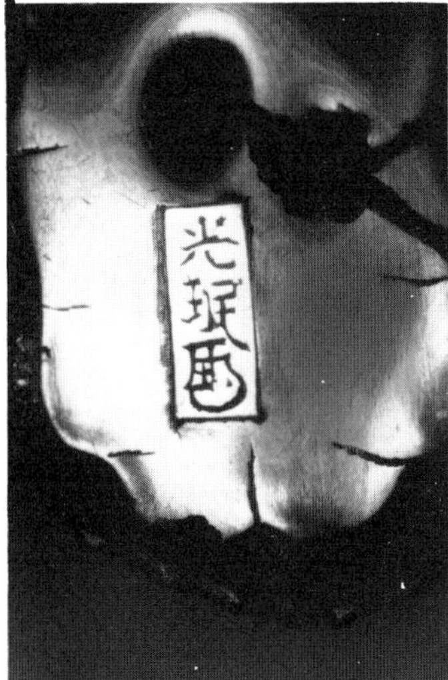

115

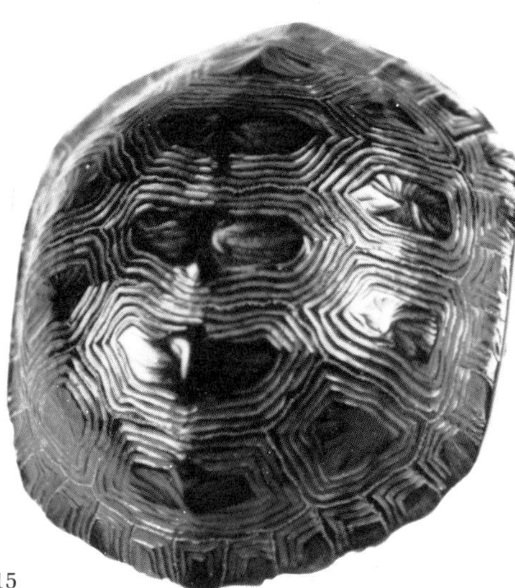

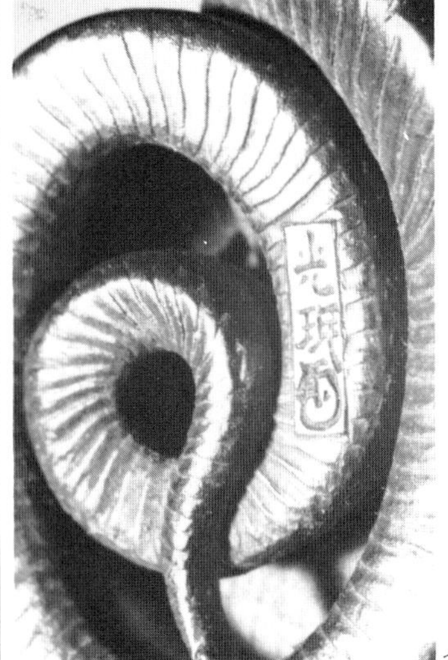

114

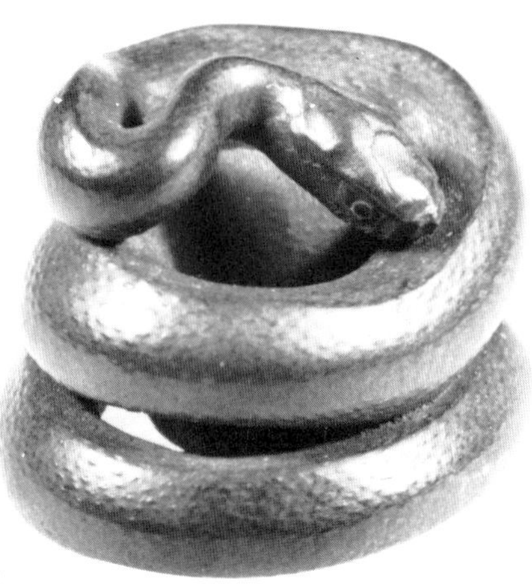

112
Raiden the thunder-god, seated on his drum.
Wood, one cord-hole rimmed with ivory stained green.
Signed Jūjō on the base.
19th century.
Height 3.75cm ($1\frac{1}{2}$in).
F.853. Franks Collection.

113
Sambasō dancer, his robes carved with good-luck symbols.
Ivory, his fan and jingle in metal.
Signed Shōunsai Joryū on the back of the robe.
19th century.
Height 3.1cm ($1\frac{1}{4}$in).
F.580. Franks Collection.

114
Coiled snake.
Wood, the eyes inlaid.
Signed Kōmin with a *kakihan* in a rectangular cartouche on the base.
19th century.
Length 3.5cm ($1\frac{1}{4}$in).
F.282. Franks Collection.

115
Tortoise.
Tortoiseshell, the eyes inlaid.
Signed Kōmin with *kakihan* on a gilt metal rectangular cartouche on the base.
19th century.
Length 3.25cm ($1\frac{1}{4}$in).
1945 10-17 616. Bequeathed by Oscar Raphael.

116
The young Yoshitsune waiting by a post of the Gojō Bridge. The hero Yoshitsune fought the giant Benkei by moonlight at this bridge in Kyoto. On the back are carved a crescent moon, Yoshitsune's fan and Benkei's halberd. Ivory.
Signed Zemin on the fan.
19th century.
Height 4.5cm ($1\frac{3}{4}$in).
F.1055. Franks Collection.

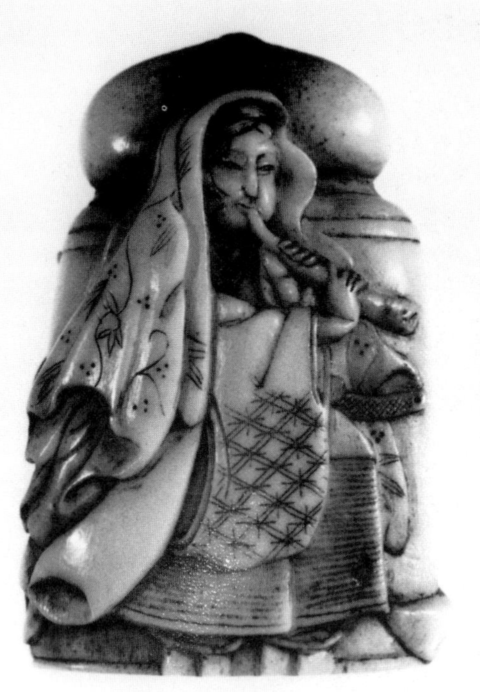

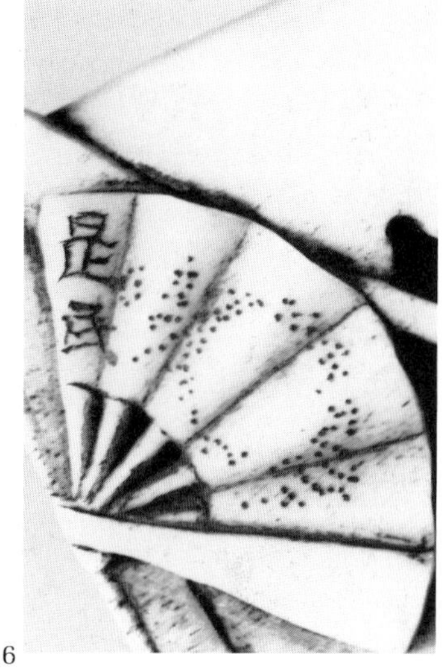

116

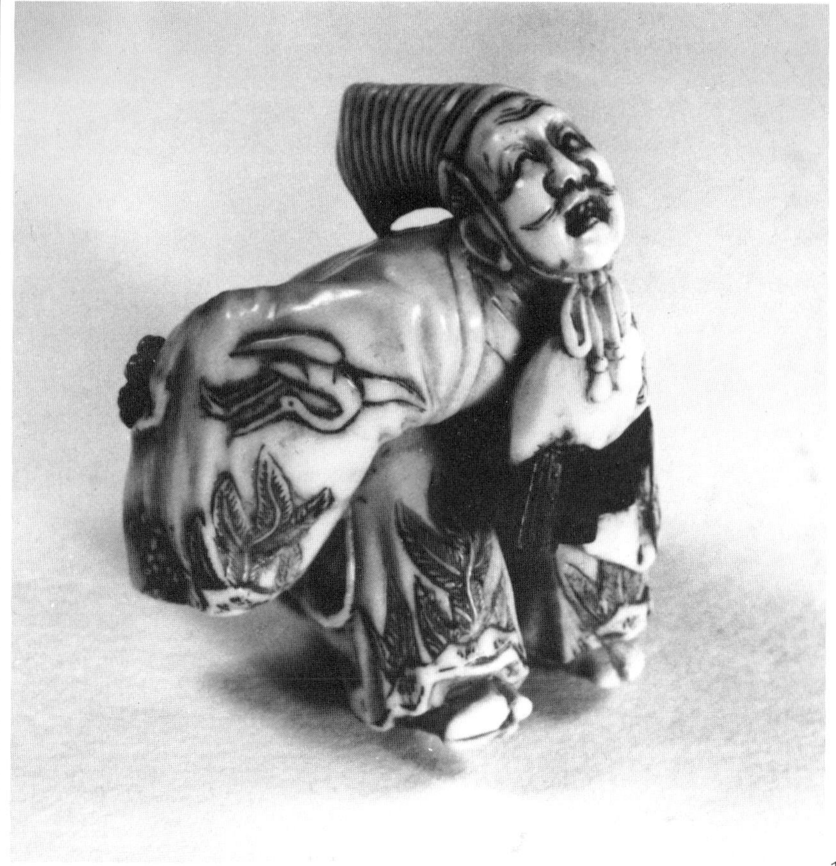

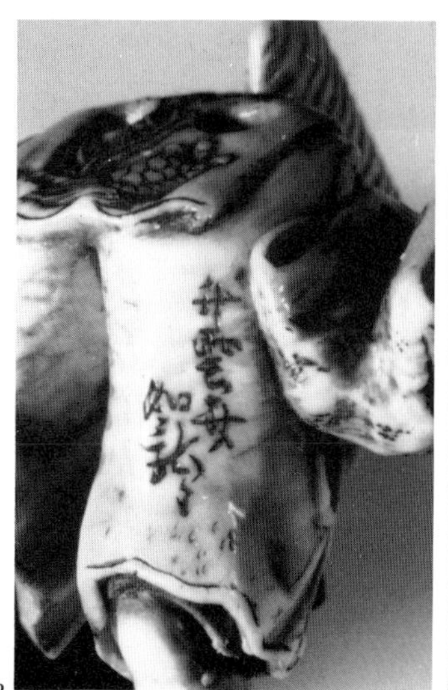

113

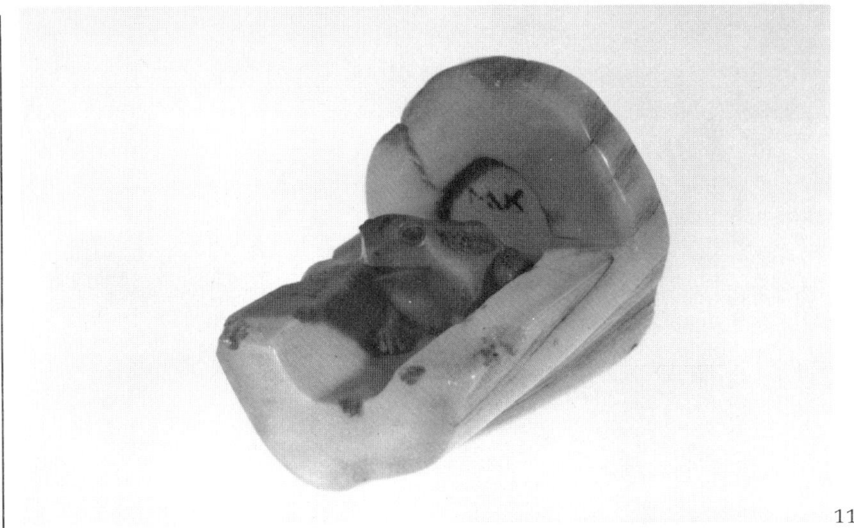

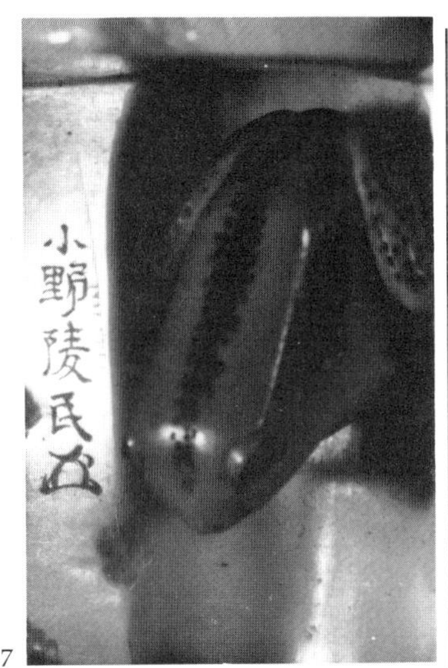

117

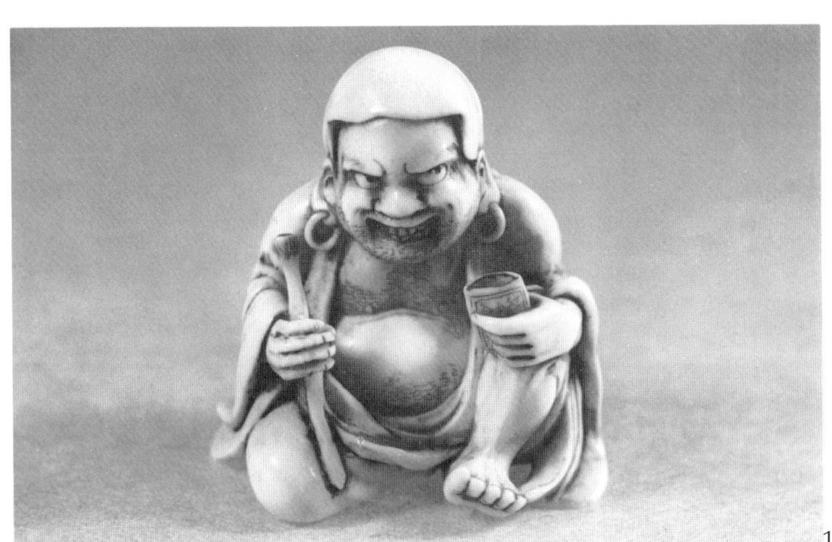

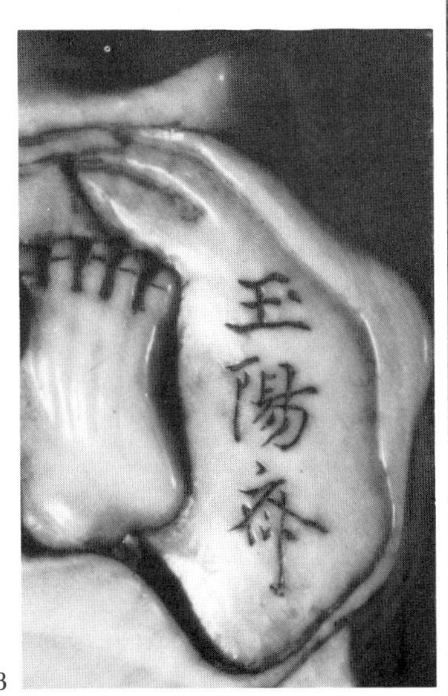

118

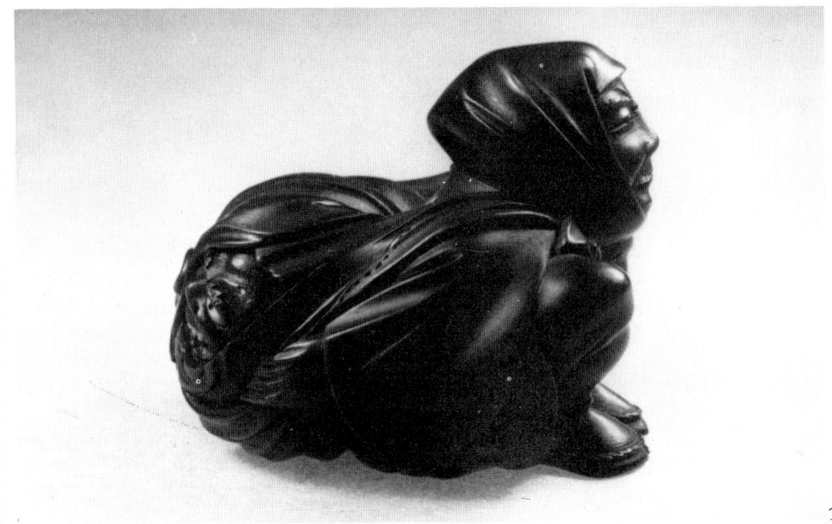

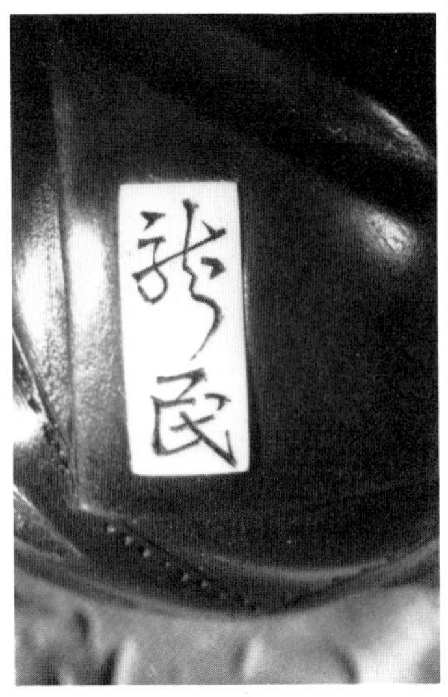

121

117
Tile-end stamped with archaistic Chinese characters, a frog eating a worm inside it. The natural grain of the marine ivory is left on the outside. The eyes are inlaid, the mouth reddened.
Signed Ono Ryōmin with a *kakihan*, on the side of the tile.
19th century.
Length 3.5cm ($1\frac{1}{2}$in).
F.277. Franks Collection.

118
Daruma seated, holding a pipe and tobacco pouch.
Ivory, the eyes inlaid.
Signed Gyokuyōsai on the base.
19th century.
Height 3.5cm ($1\frac{1}{2}$in).
F.149. Franks Collection.

119
Group of six seals of artists.
Ivory, red and black stain.
Unsigned.
19th century.
Length 3.25cm ($1\frac{1}{4}$in).
F.1117. Franks Collection.

120
Badger with distended belly, using a lotus leaf as a cloak.
Ivory.
Signed Kōgyokusai on the back.
19th century.
Height 5.1cm (2in).
F.493. Franks Collection.

121
Traveller resting, a demon peeping from his sack.
Wood, the eyes and teeth inlaid in ivory, one of the cord holes rimmed in ivory stained green.
Signed Ryūmin in an applied ivory cartouche on the sack.
19th century.
Length 3.75cm ($1\frac{1}{2}$in).
F.574. Franks Collection.

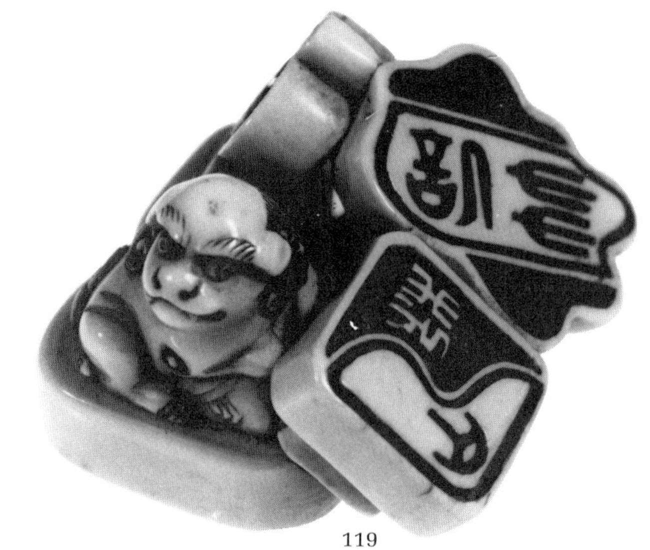

119

120

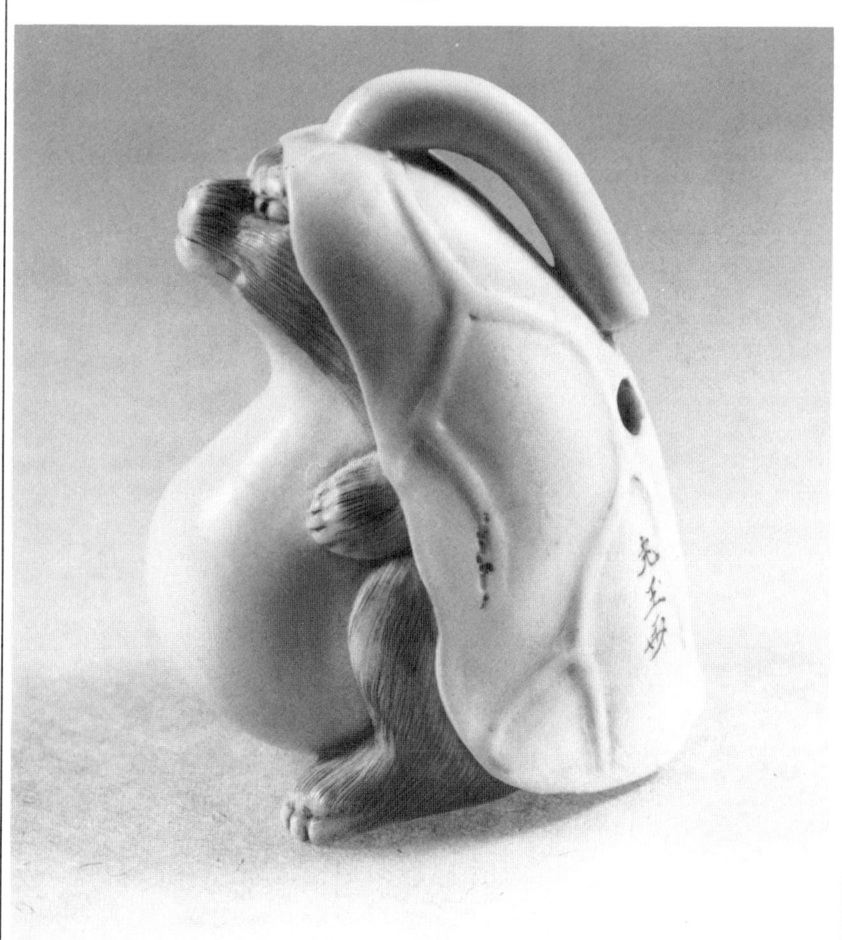

122
Inuhariko (dog-shaped papier-maché box), which opens to reveal two lovers.
Ivory, the lovers tinted.
Signed Ryūgyoku and a red *kakihan* on the base.
Length 4.5cm (1$\frac{3}{4}$in).
W.425.

123
Manjū carved in relief in *Ukiyoe* style with a girl emerging from a mosquito net, the reverse incised with a brushpot, an ink stone and a fan decorated with a poem. Ivory.
Signed Masatoshi Tō on the back (i.e. Kikugawa Masatoshi).
Early 19th century.
Diameter 4.25cm (1$\frac{3}{4}$in).
F.395. Franks Collection.

124
Manjū carved in sunk relief with *hannya* mask, the reverse with an incised maple leaf.
Ivory, the mouth reddened.
Signed Hakuunsai on the back.
19th century.
Diameter 4.25cm (1$\frac{3}{4}$in).
F.1216. Franks Collection.

125
Manjū carved in sunk relief with Endō Morito behind a waterfall, and holding a bell between his teeth. Ivory.
Signed Kōsai on the back.
19th century.
Diameter 4.25cm (1$\frac{3}{4}$in).
F.1218. Franks Collection.

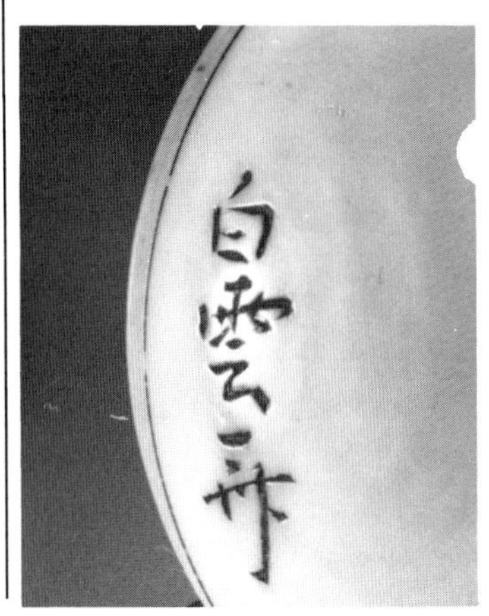

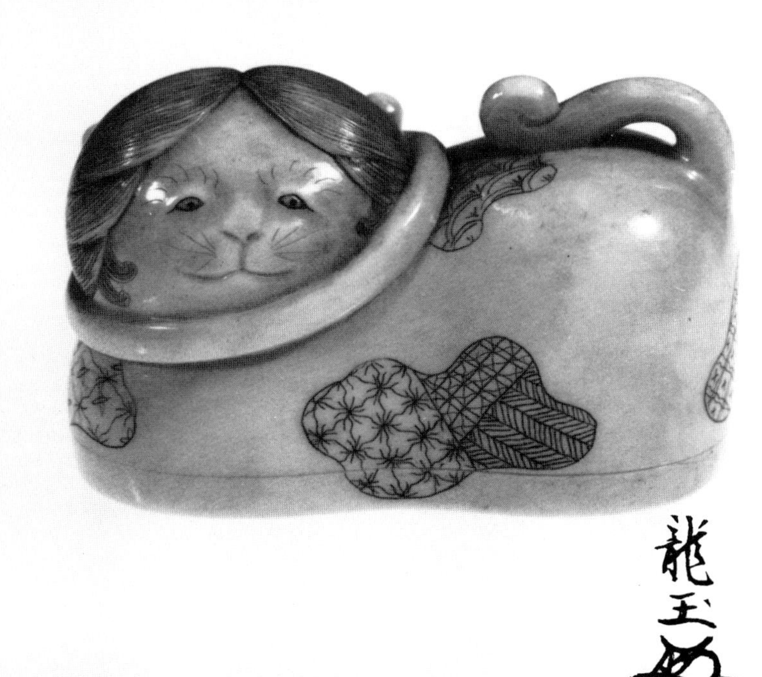

122△ 124▽

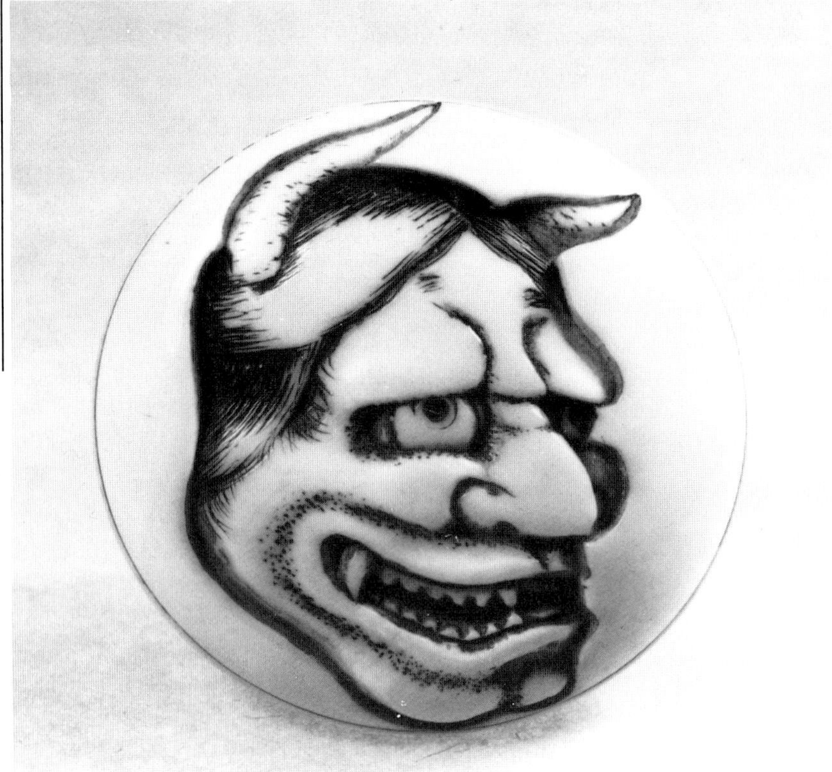

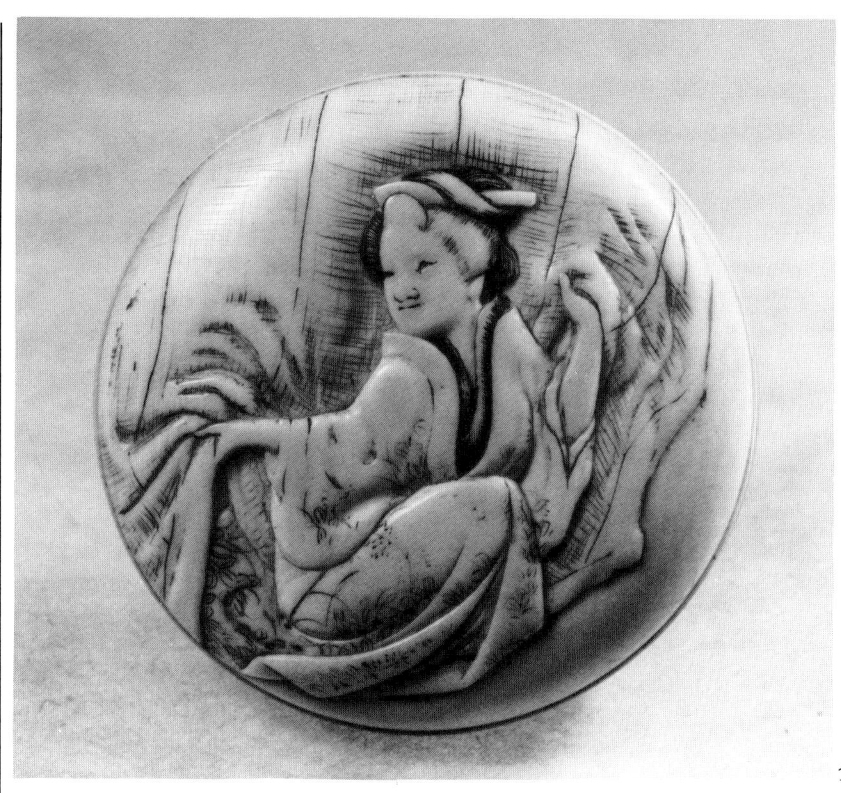

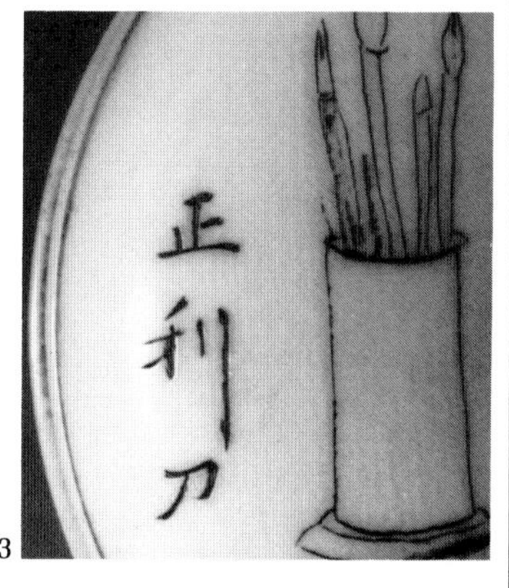

123

125

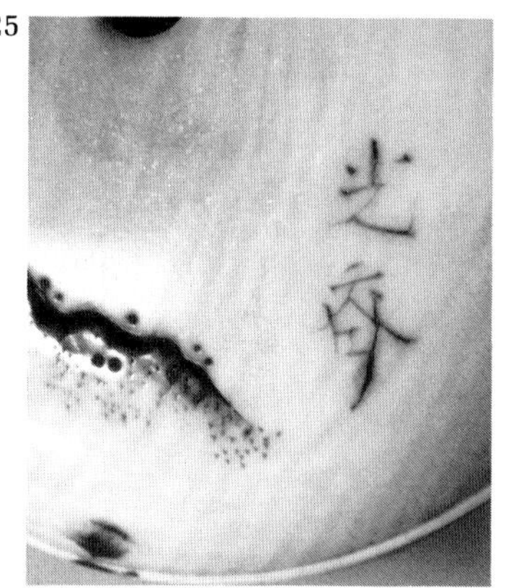

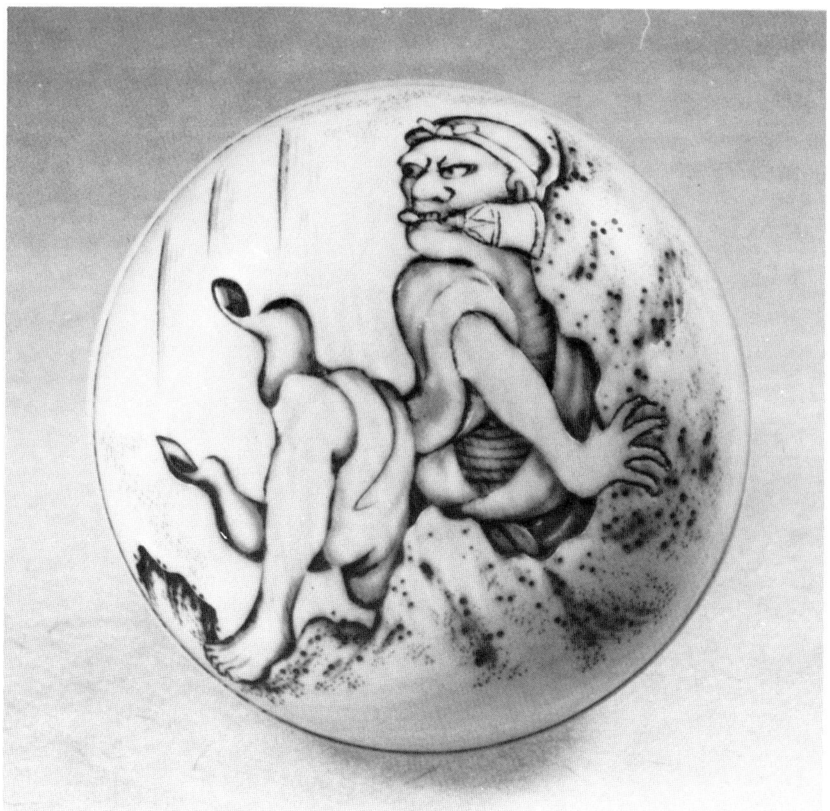

126
Manjū deeply carved with the night attack of the 47 Ronin. Ivory, metal cord-holder. Signed Kyōmin in a double-outlined oval cartouche on the side.
19th century.
Diameter 7cm ($2\frac{3}{4}$in).
1945 10-17 602. Bequeathed by Oscar Raphael.

Ex W. L. Behrens Collection, no. 1120, illustrated in the catalogue, pl. XXI. Ex Gaskell Collection. Exhibited Red Cross, London, 1915, no. 82, illustrated in the catalogue, pl. LIV. The subject illustrates the final episode of the Chūshingura story, the storming of the house of their dead master's enemy by the loyal *Ronin* (masterless samurai).

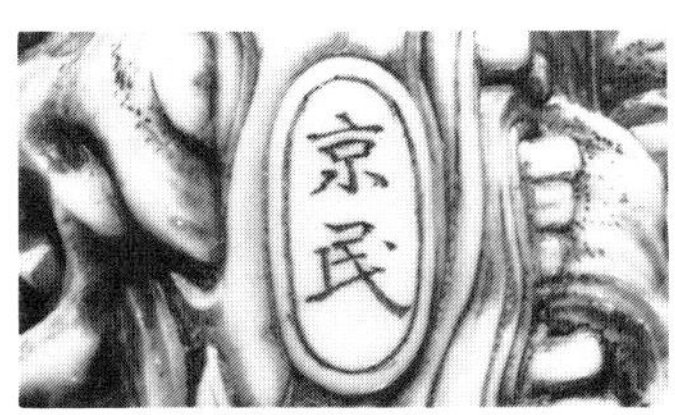

126

127
Group of sea creatures.
Ivory, the eyes inlaid with pewter.
Signed Tōun in an oval cartouche on the base.
19th century.
Length 4.25cm ($1\frac{3}{4}$in).
1945 10-17 523. Bequeathed by Oscar Raphael.

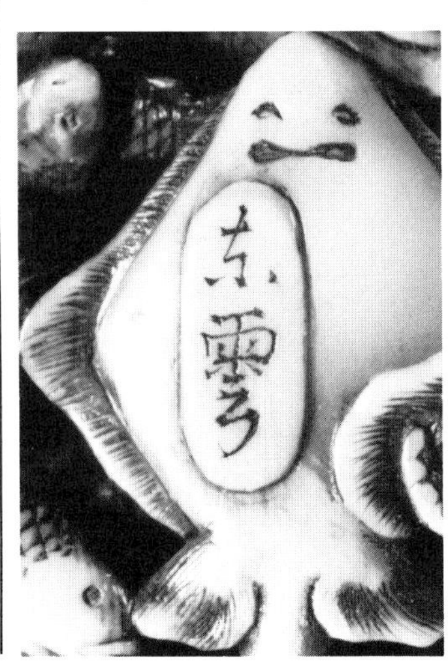

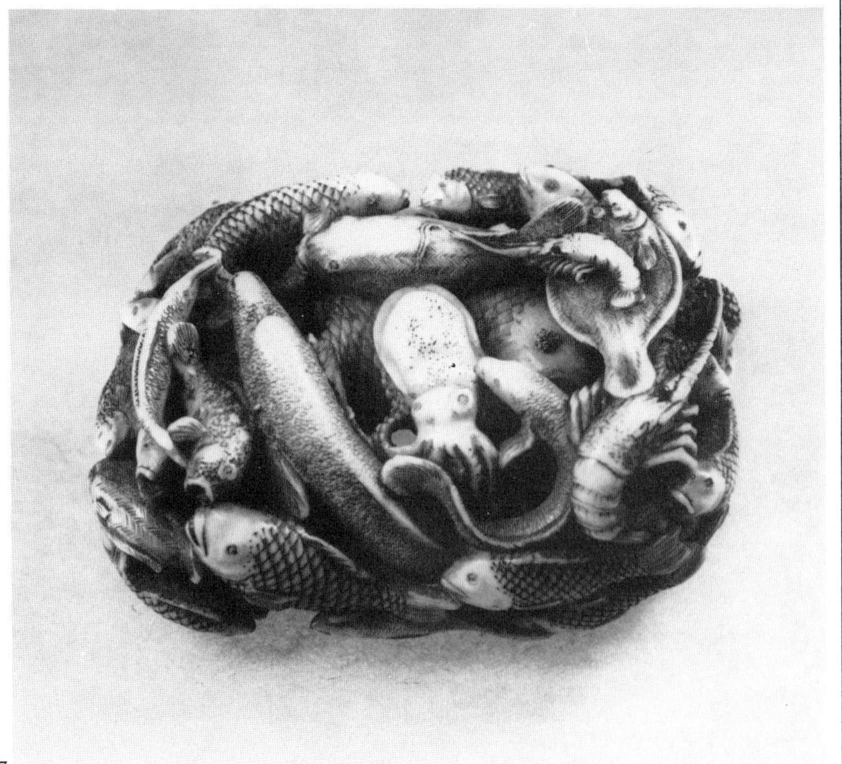

127

128
Manjū with applied monkey holding a peach.
Ivory, applied lacquer, wood, coral, and mother-of-pearl.
Signed Tōunsai in an inlaid metal cartouche on the base.
19th century.
Diameter 4.25cm (1$\frac{3}{4}$in).
F.1065. Franks Collection.

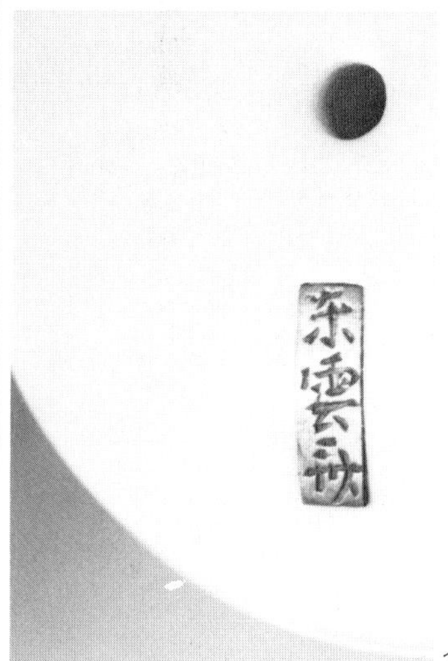

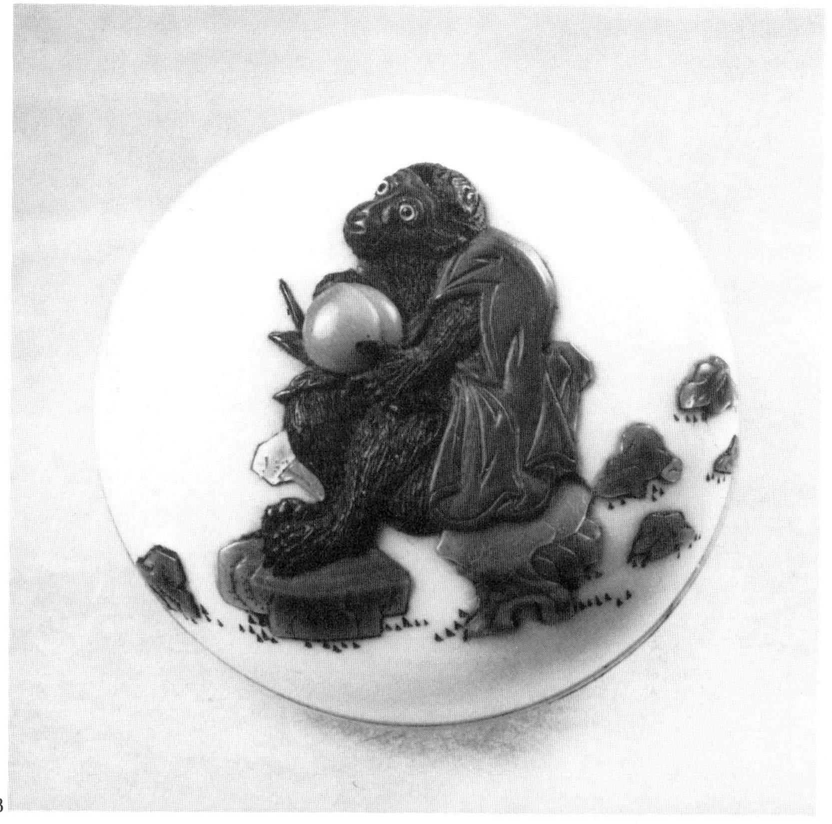

128

129
Group of eleven masks, the *himotoshi* formed by a flower-head. Ivory.
Signed Chikuyōsai Tomochika in relief-carved oval cartouche.
19th century.
Length 5.4cm (2$\frac{1}{4}$in).
1945 10-17 532. Bequeathed by Oscar Raphael.

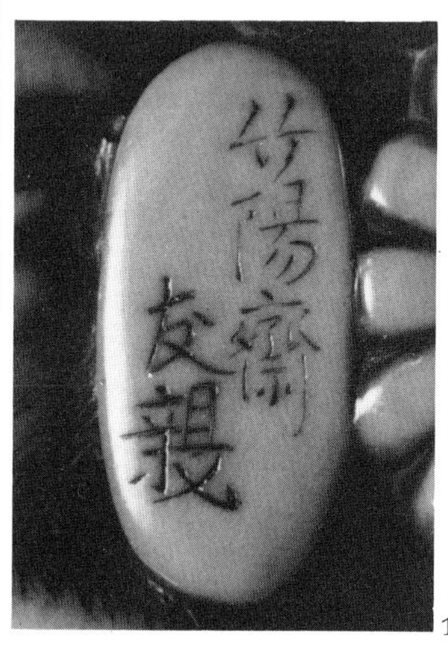

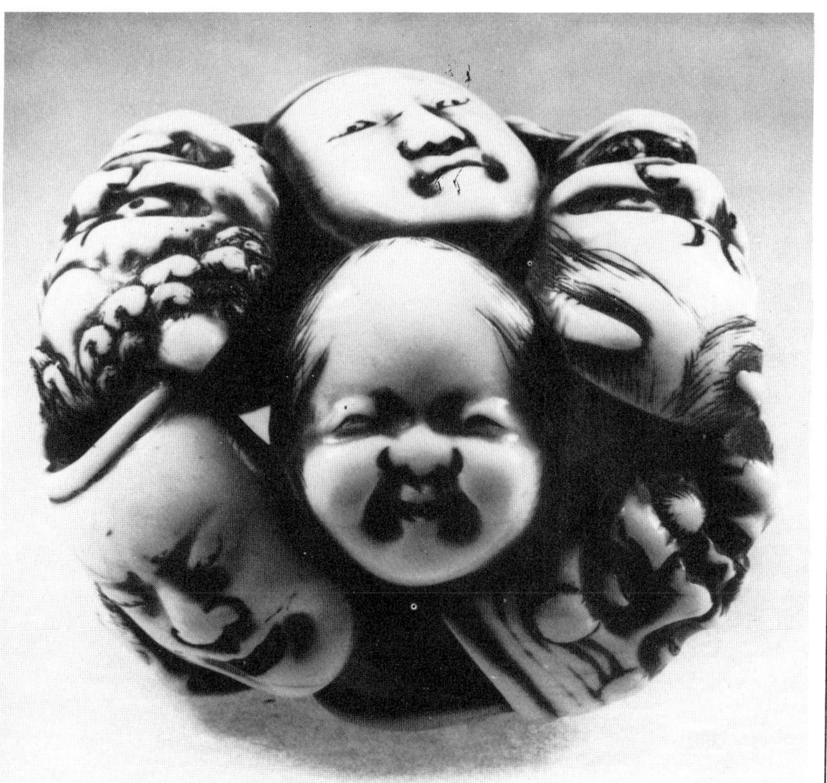

129

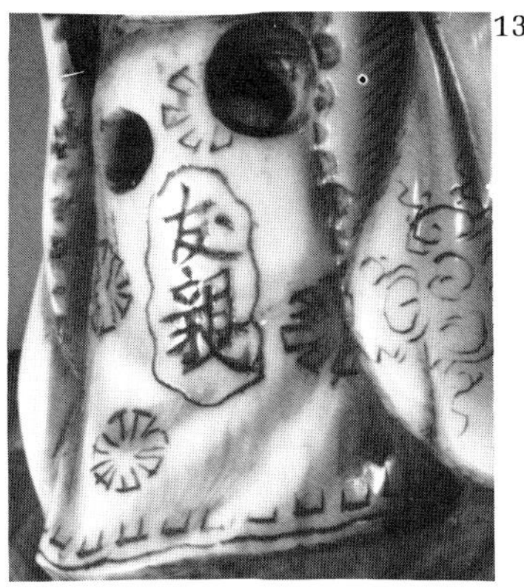

130

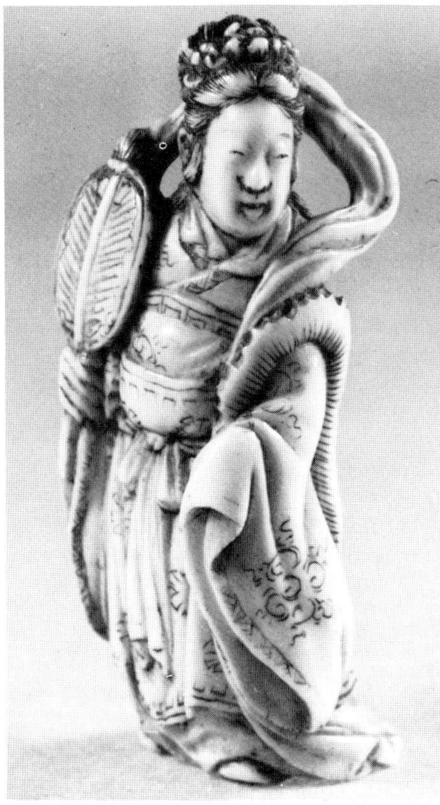

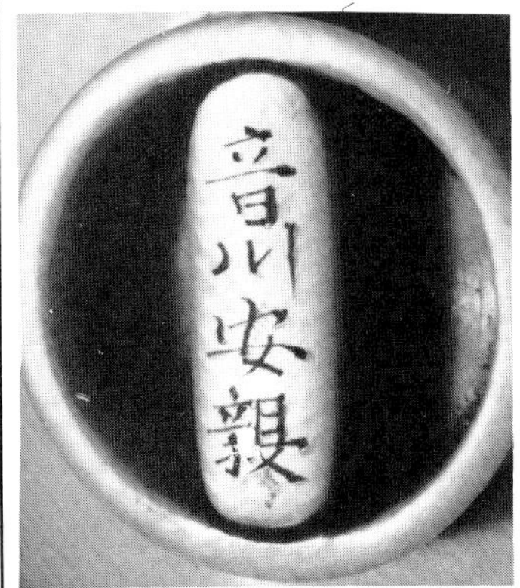

134

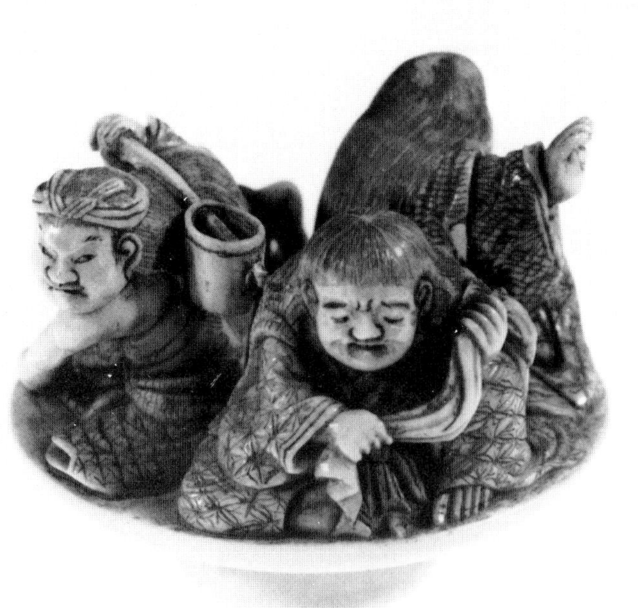

130
The goddess Benten. Ivory.
Signed Tomochika in an irregular cartouche at the back.
19th century.
Height 5.1cm (2in).
S.35.

131
Group of seven rats clambering over each other. Ivory, partly stained, their eyes inlaid.
Signed Tomochika in an irregular cartouche on the base.
19th century.
Length 4.2cm ($1\frac{3}{4}$in).
1930 12-17 81. Bequeathed by James Hilton.

132
Manjū carved in openwork with rats, Shintō prayer slips, and the mallet of the god Daikoku.
Ivory, partly stained.
Signed Chikahiro in an irregular cartouche.
19th century.
Length 4.5cm ($1\frac{3}{4}$in).
F.1227. Franks Collection.

133
Group of seven rats tumbling over each other.
Ivory, the eyes inlaid.
Signed Nobuchika in an irregular lozenge-shaped cartouche.
19th century.
Height 3.75cm ($1\frac{1}{2}$in).
F.783. Franks Collection.

134
Three *Shōjō* seated in a large saké cup. Ivory.
Signed Otogawa Yasuchika in an elongated oval cartouche in the base of the cup.
19th century.
Diameter 3.75cm ($1\frac{1}{2}$in).
F.928A. Franks Collection.

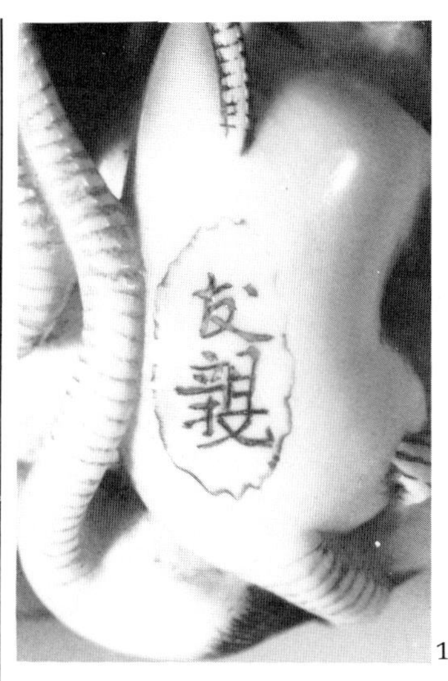

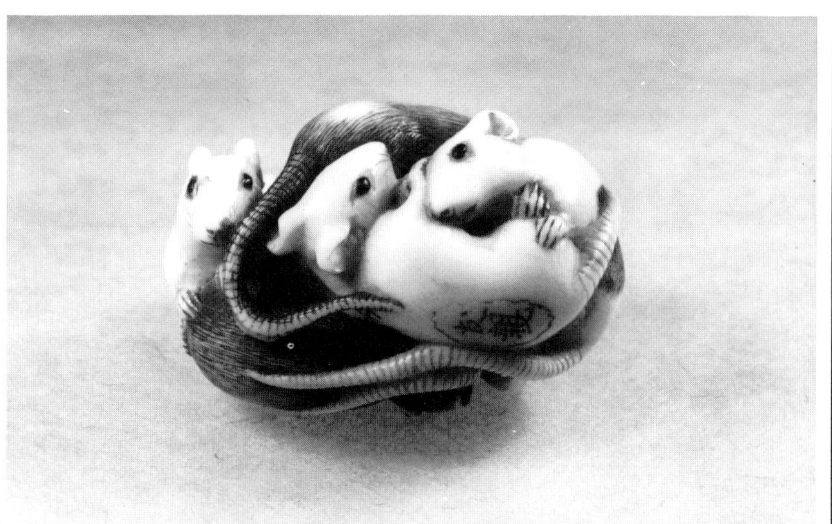

131

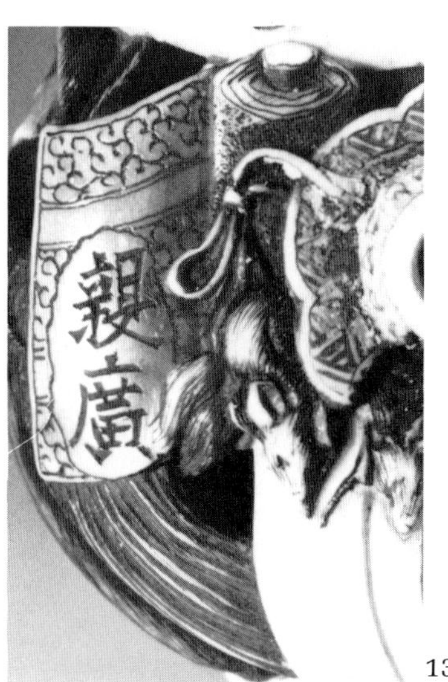

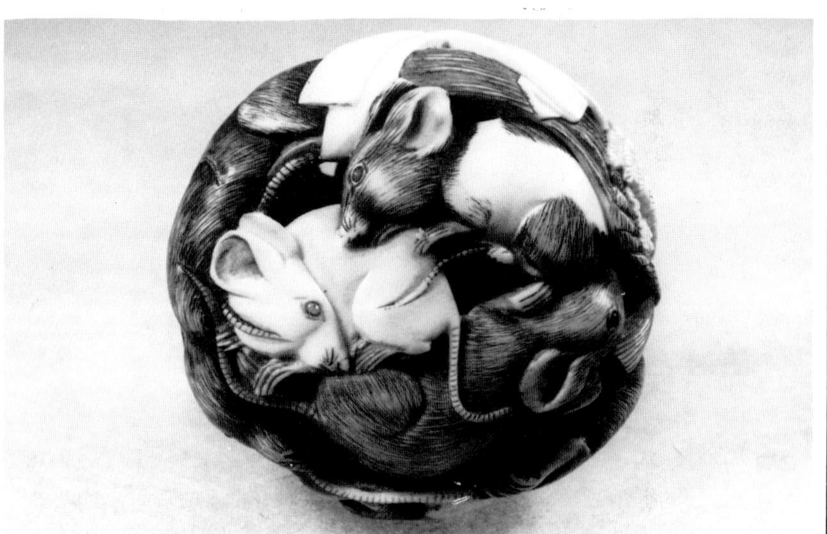

132

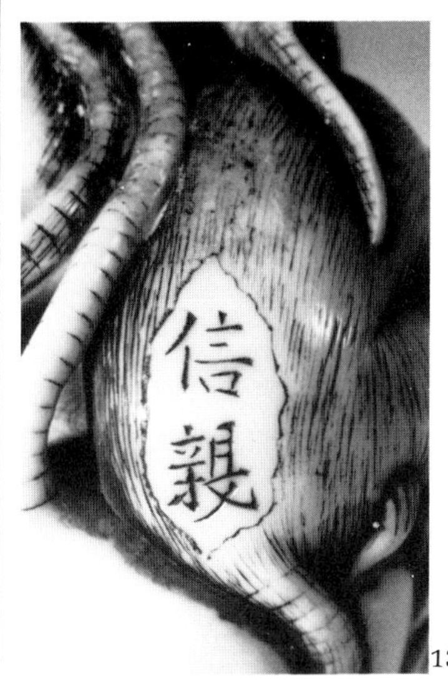

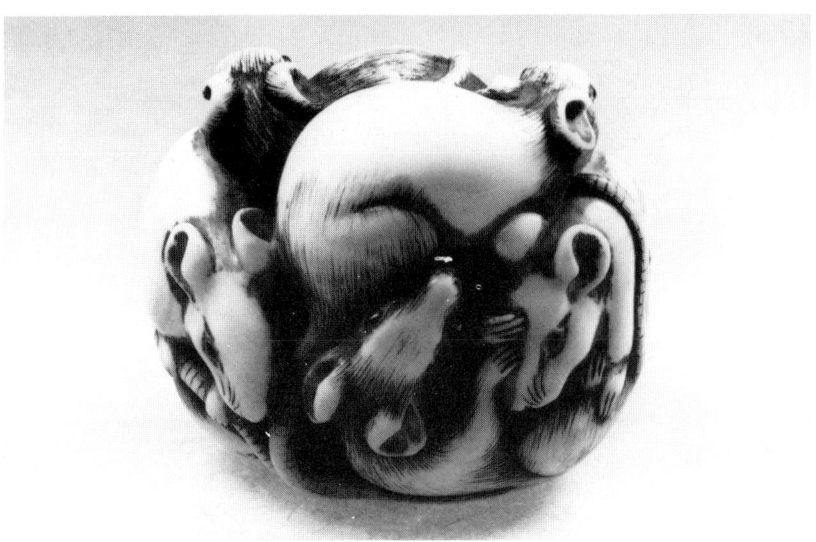

133

135
Manjū carved in *shishiaibori* (undercutting), with Endō Morito behind the waterfall, the reverse with two immortals on a cloud bank.
Ivory, with metal studs.
Signed Shunkōsai Chōgetsu in an elongated oval cartouche at the back.
19th century.
Diameter 5cm (2in).
1945 10-17 638. Bequeathed by Oscar Raphael.

The design is taken from an illustration by Katsushika Hokusai in *Ehon Sakigake*, opening 24/25 (1836).
Colour plate, page 24

136
The goddess Benten seated on the back of a dragon, a *koto* resting on her knees. Wood.
Signed Shinkeisai on the base.
19th century.
Height 5.75cm ($2\frac{1}{4}$in).
F.969. Franks Collection.

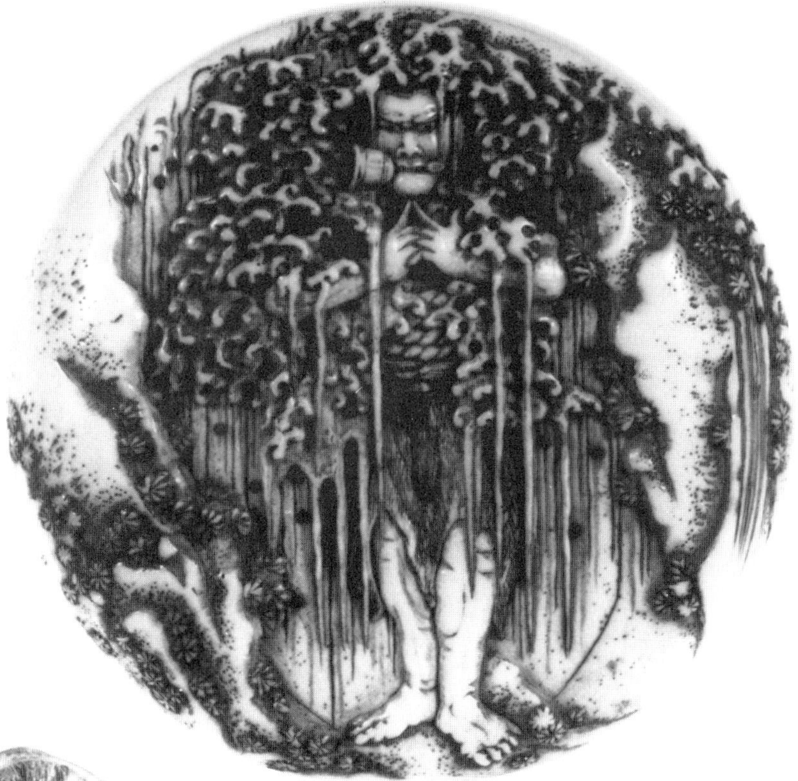

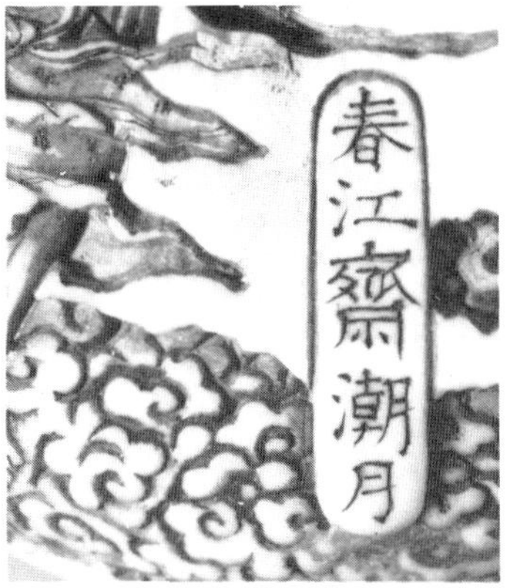

135

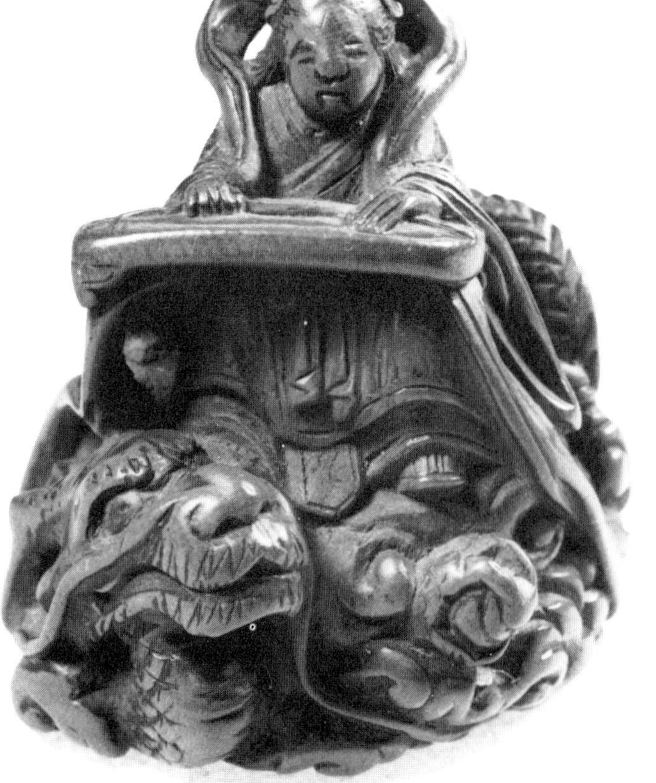

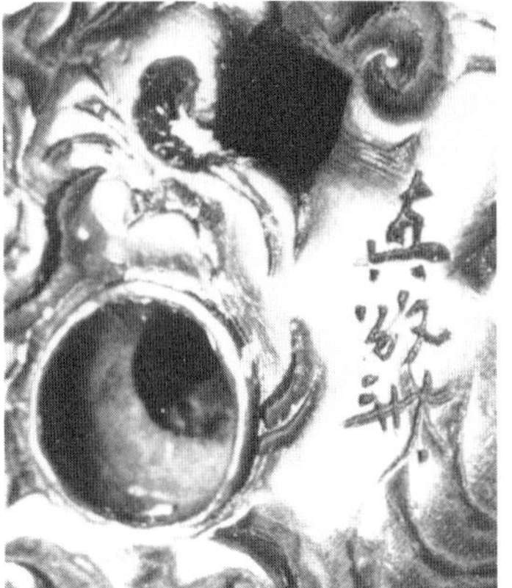

136

137
Blind masseur with client.
Wood.
Unsigned.
19th century.
Height 3.6cm (2in).
F.1063. Franks Collection.

138
Sitting South Sea Islander with a skirt of leaves. Wood.
Signed Hōjitsu in an oval ivory cartouche stained green, on the back of the skirt.
19th century.
Height 3.25cm ($1\frac{1}{4}$in).
F.1037. Franks Collection.

139
Discarded sandal on which two stag beetles are fighting watched by a smaller beetle. Wood.
Signed Hōjitsu in a rectangular cartouche on the base.
19th century.
Length 5.1cm (2in).
1953 12-17 11. Bequeathed by Mrs Helen Epstein.

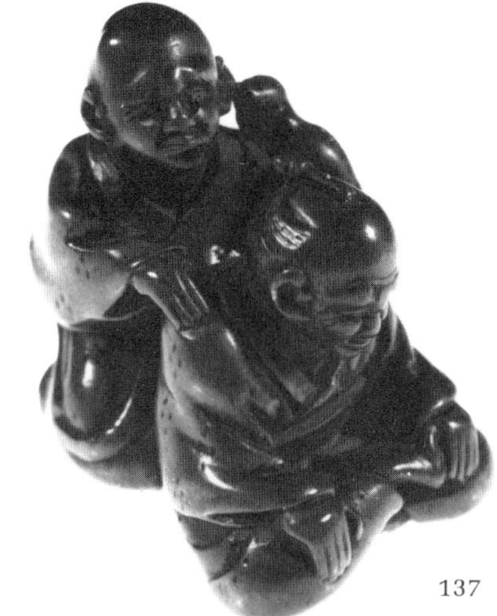

137

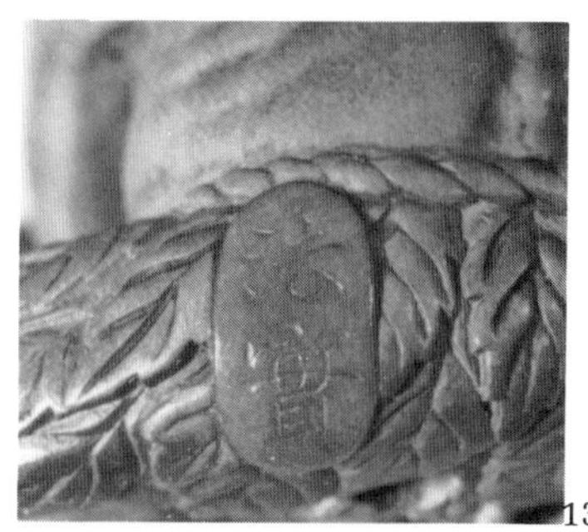

138

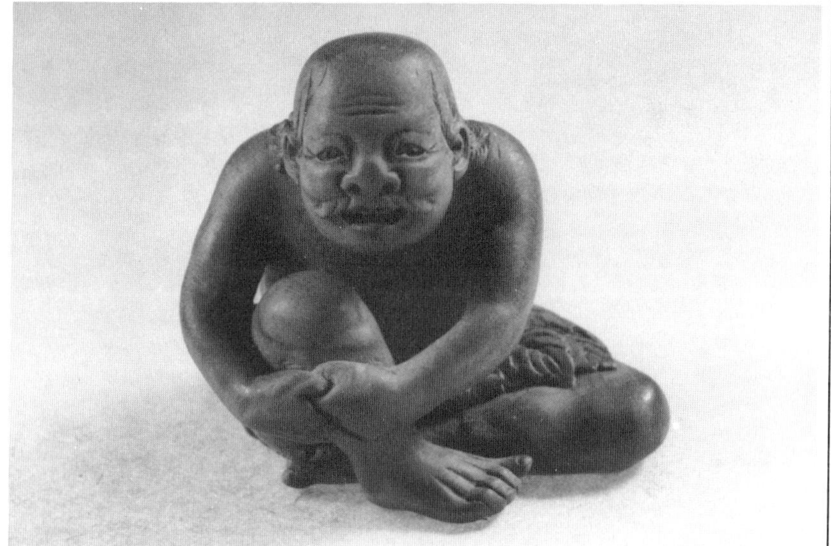

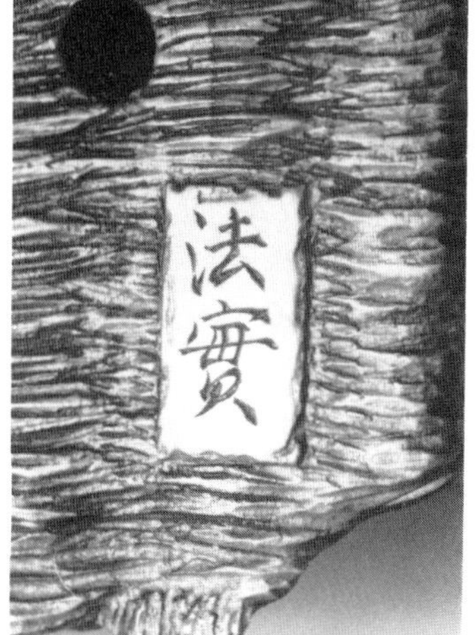

139

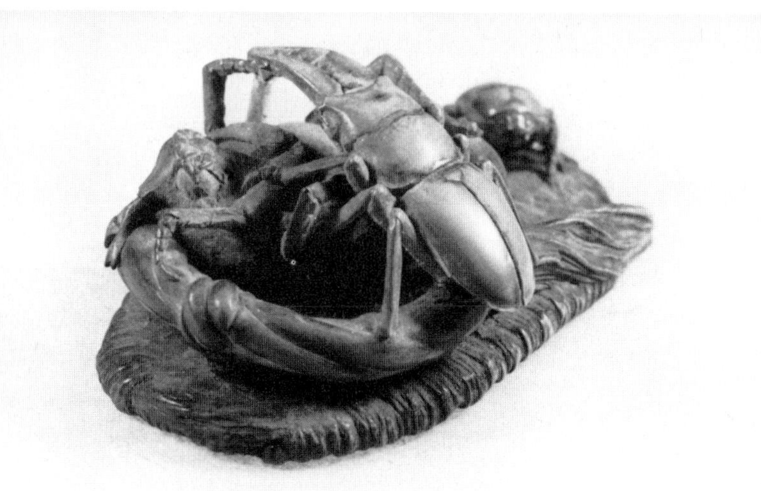

140
Saké casket tied with rope and bearing the inscription *Edo ichi* (the brand-name), with other labellings in black and red ink. Ivory, the *himotoshi* rimmed in mother-of-pearl.
Signed Hōjitsu on the side of the cask.
19th century.
Height 3.25cm ($1\frac{1}{4}$in).
1945 10–17 633. Bequeathed by Oscar Raphael.
Exhibited Red Cross, London, 1915, no. 192, pl. LI.
Colour plate, page 24

141
The Bodhisattva Kannon sitting on a lotus petal. Wood.
Signed Hōjitsu on the base.
19th century.
Length 3.5cm ($1\frac{1}{2}$in).
1945 10-17 617. Bequeathed by Oscar Raphael.

142
Two *Manzai* dancers. Wood.
Signed Hōjitsu.
19th century.
Height 4.5cm ($1\frac{3}{4}$in).
F.481. Franks Collection.

143
Child kneeling and holding a tied sack.
Ivory, partly stained red and green, with applied mother-of-pearl decoration.
Signed Ikkōsai Kōjitsu with a *kakihan* on the base.
19th century.
Length 3.75cm ($1\frac{1}{2}$in).
F.631. Franks Collection.

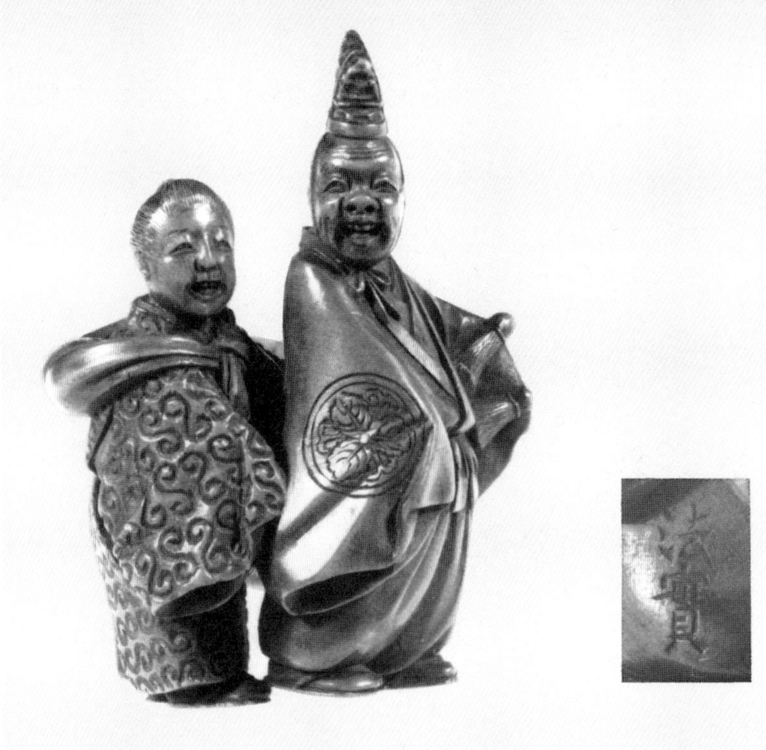

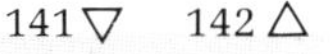

141 ▽ 142 △

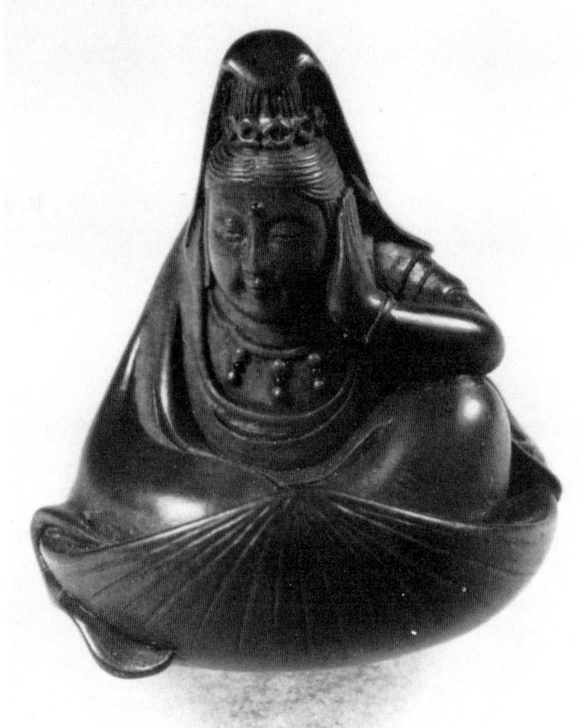

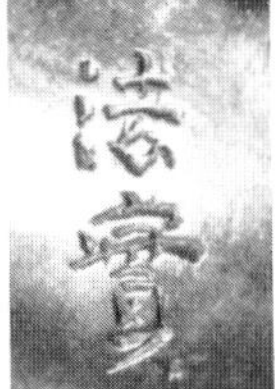

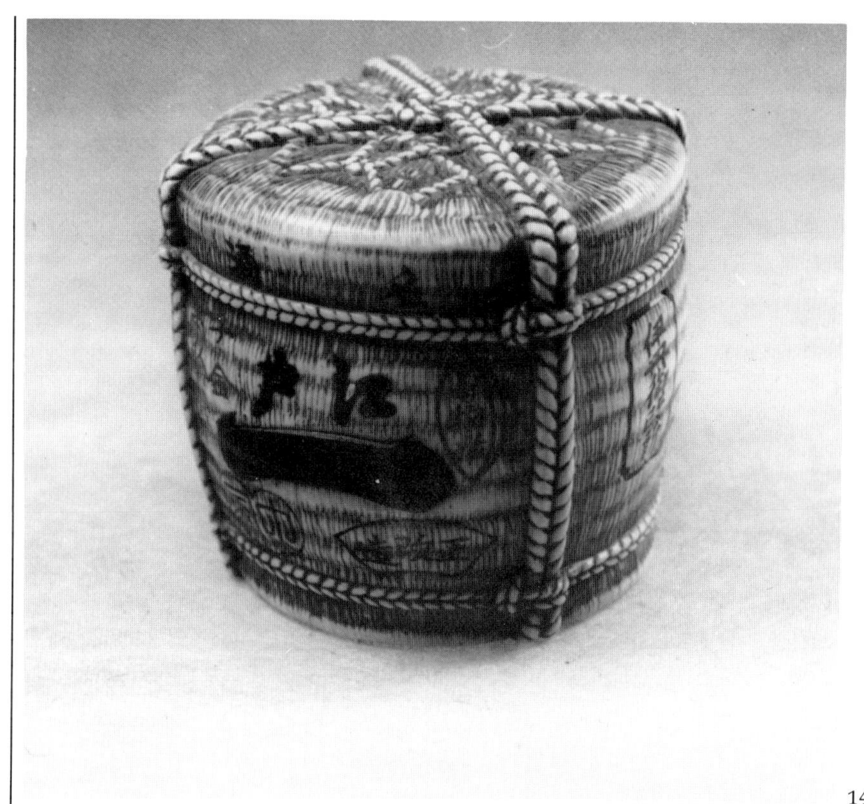

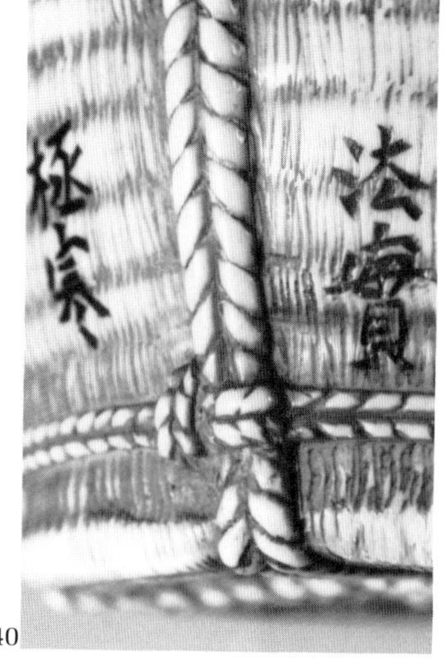

140

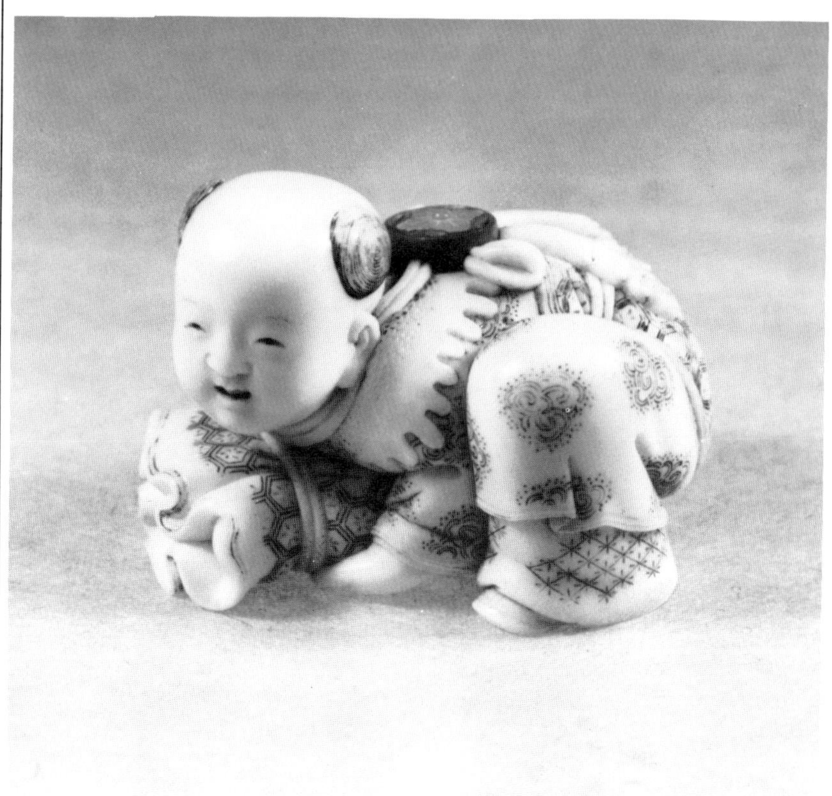

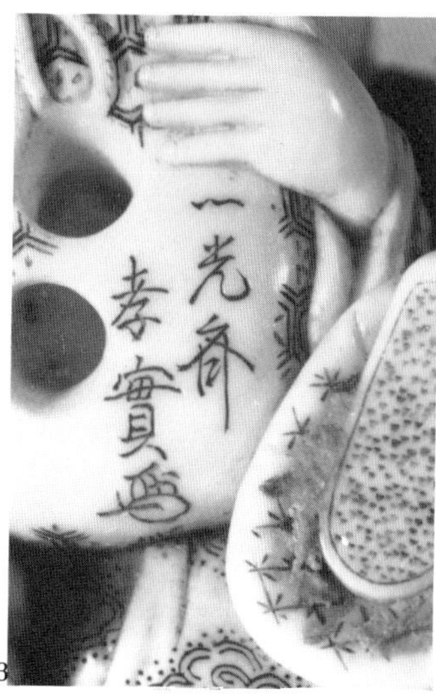

143

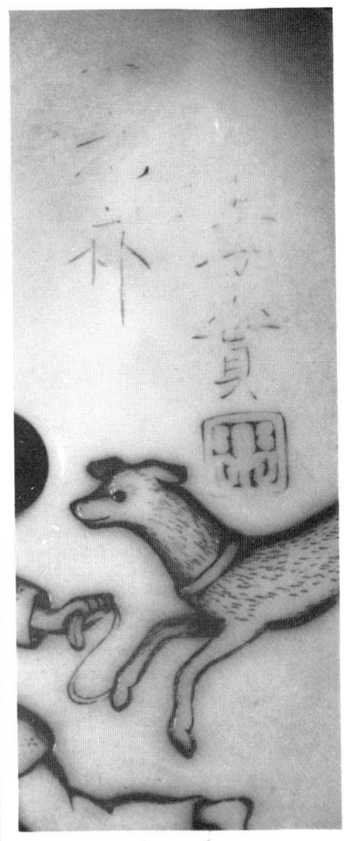
144

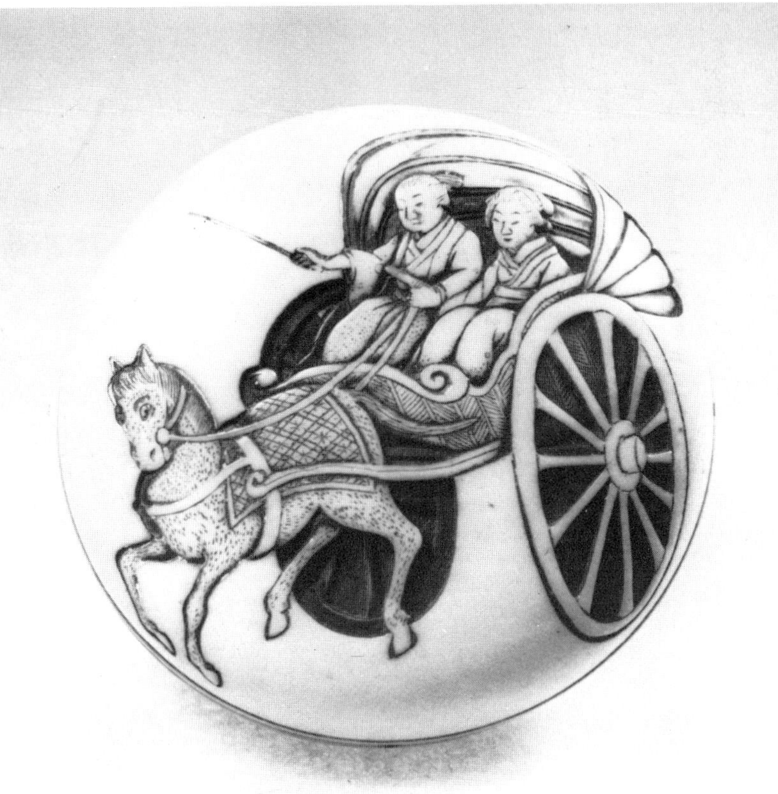

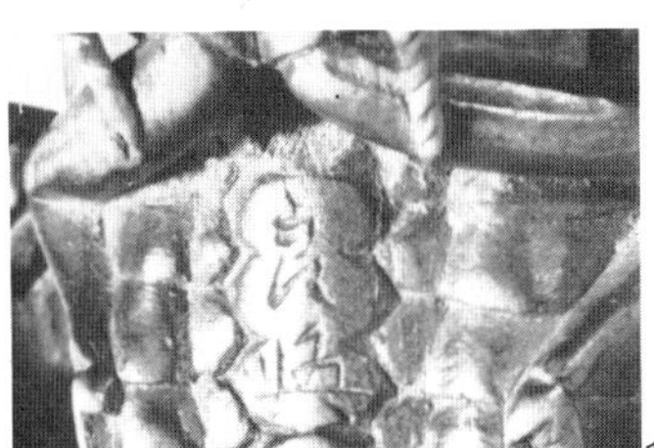
145

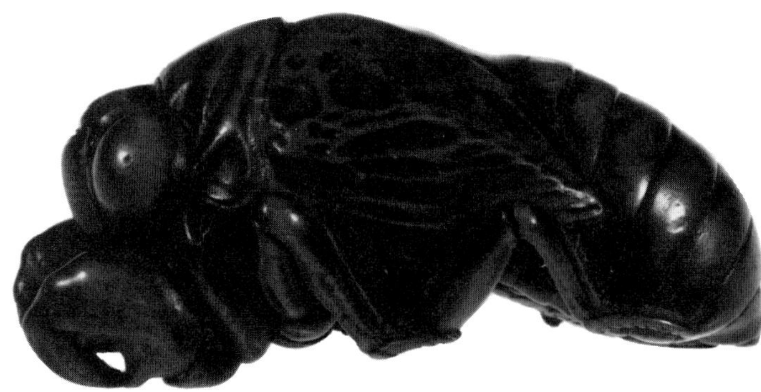

144
Manjū carved in low relief with two Japanese riding in a European style cabriolet, the reverse with a groom leading a dog. The design is probably based on a Yokohama print. Ivory.
Signed Ikkōsai Kōjitsu with unread seal on the back, both very rubbed.
19th century.
Diameter 4.25cm ($1\frac{3}{4}$in).
1945 10-17 657. Bequeathed by Oscar Raphael.
Ex W. L. Behrens Collection, no. 458.
Colour plate, page 24

145
Cicada emerging from its pupa case. Wood.
Signed Ryōshin in a treble-gourd cartouche on the base.
19th century. School of Hōjitsu.
Length 4.5cm ($1\frac{3}{4}$in).
F.108. Franks Collection.

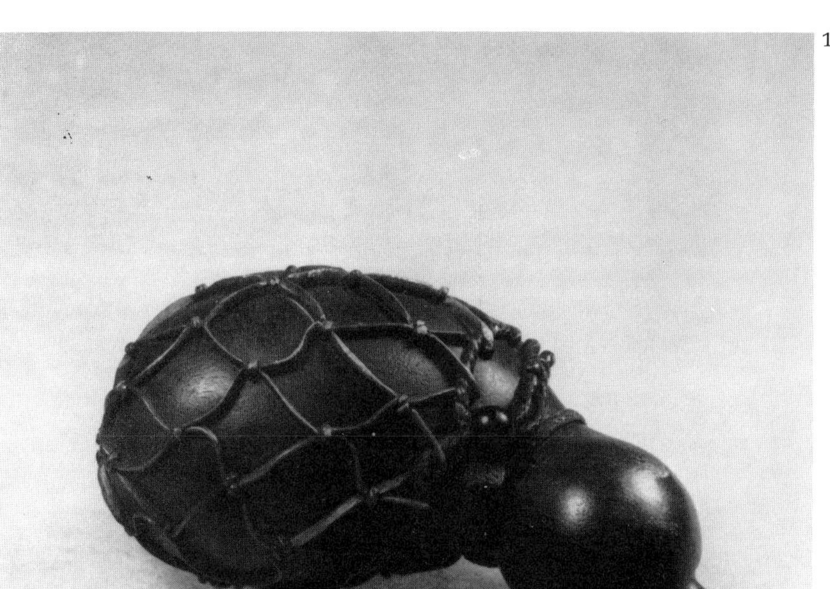

146

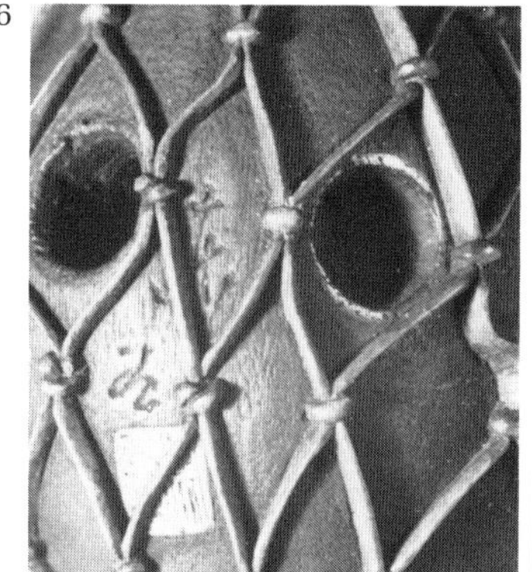

146
Gourd in a carrying net. Wood, the net and cords applied in ivory stained red, green and yellow; a metal ring at the top. The cord-holes are rimmed in ivory stained green.
Signed Tōkoku with unread gilt metal seal on the side.
19th century.
Length 4.25cm ($1\frac{3}{4}$in).
1945 10-17 580. Bequeathed by Oscar Raphael.

For an almost identical piece, *see* Bushell *Collectors' Netsuke*, p. 147, pl. 221.

147
Chestnut, one cord-hole imitating a worm-hole. Wood.
Signed Gyokusō on the base.
Late 19th–early 20th century.
Height 3cm (1in).
1945 10-17 581. Bequeathed by Oscar Raphael.

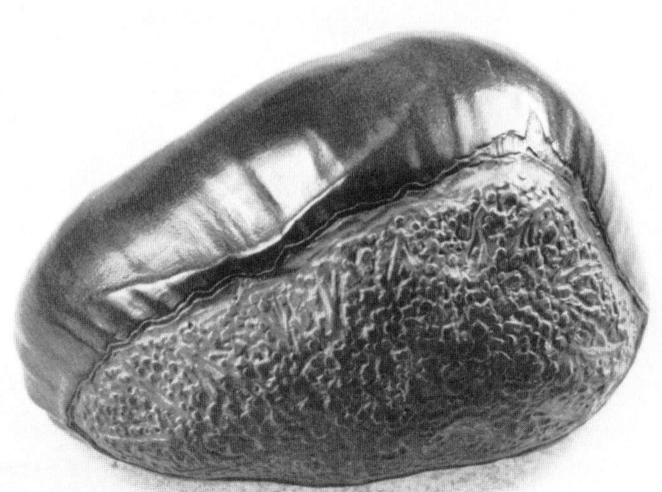

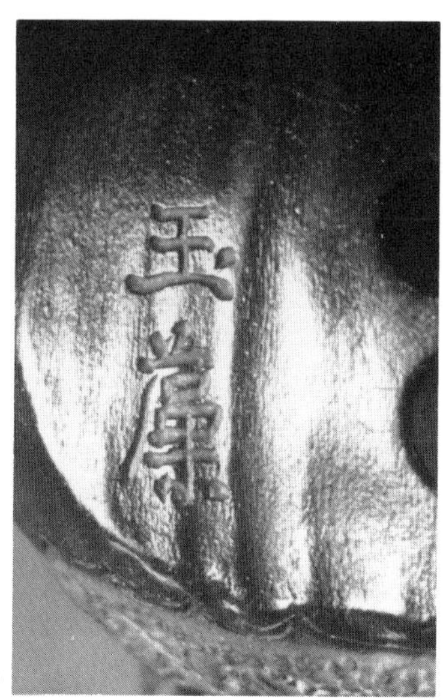

147

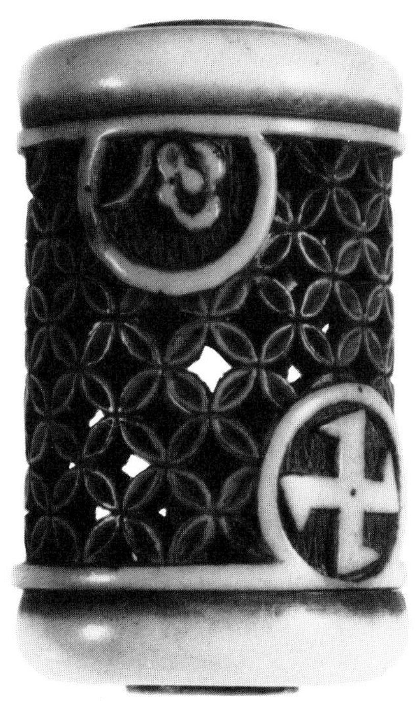

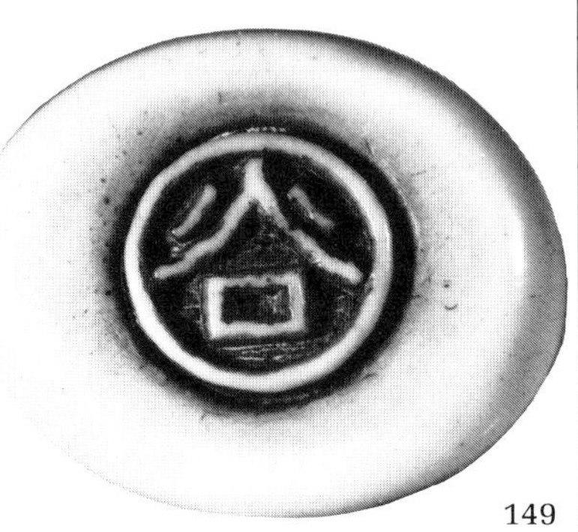

149

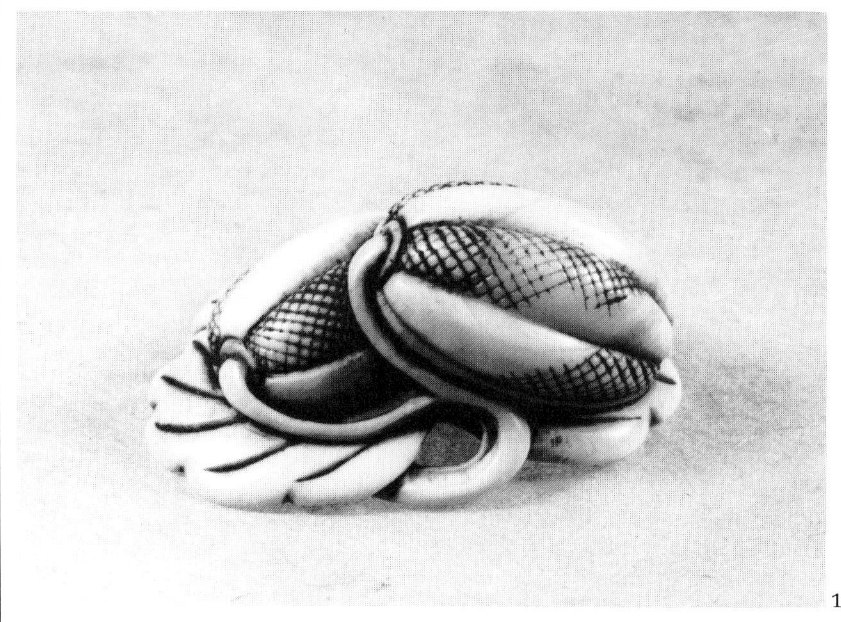

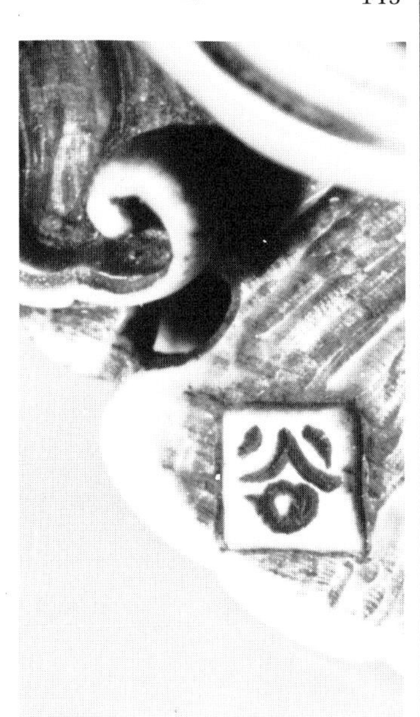

148

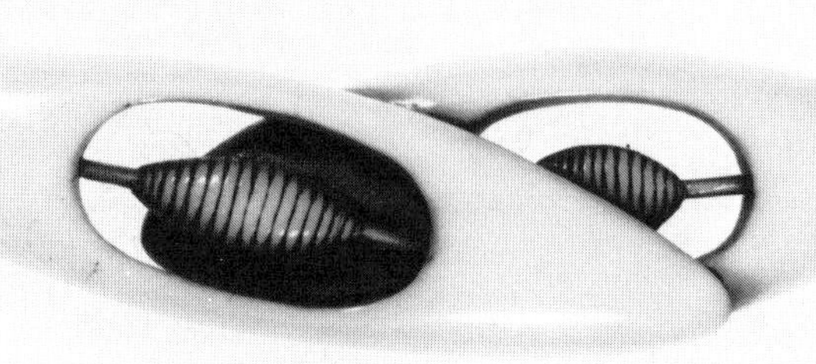

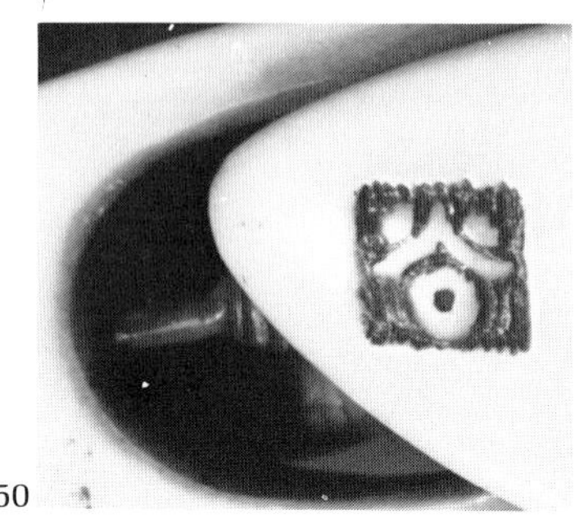

150

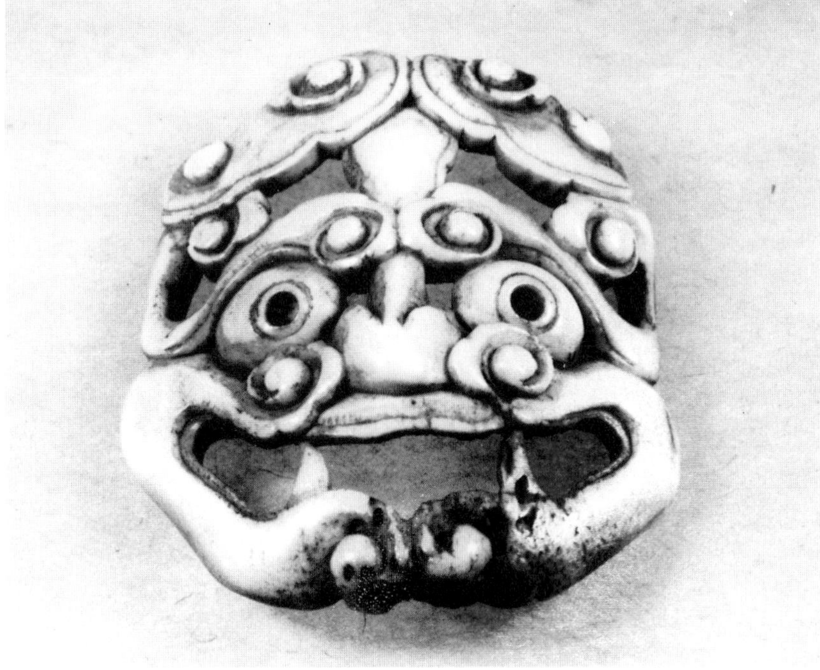

151

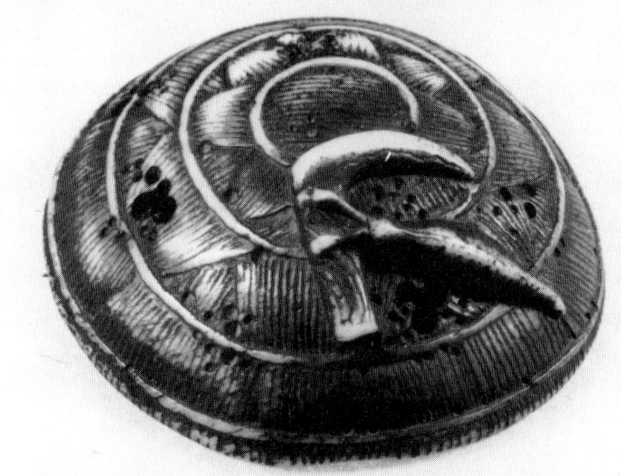

152

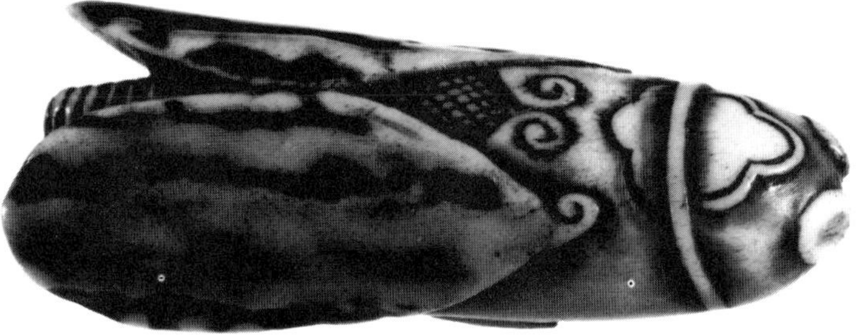

153

Asakusa District of Edo

148
Two melons on foliage. Ivory.
Signed Koku in seal form underneath (= Kokusai).
19th century.
Length 3.5cm (1¼in).
F.1110. Franks Collection.

149
Openwork cylindrical cricket-cage decorated with devices including a *manji* (swastika) in reserves. One end detaches to take the cord. Antler.
Signed Koku on the detachable end (= Kokusai).
19th century.
Height 3.75cm (1½in).
F.371. Franks Collection.

150
Two shuttles. Ivory.
Signed Koku in seal form on the base (= Kokusai).
19th century.
Length 6.75cm (2¾in).
1945 10-17 659. Bequeathed by Oscar Raphael.

Exhibited Red Cross, London, 1915, no. 18, pl. LXVII.

151
Mask of a demon. Antler.
Unsigned; school of Kokusai.
19th century.
Height 4.5cm (1¾in).
F.351. Franks Collection.
Colour plate, page 24

152
Discarded farmer's hat on which rest a sickle and a slug, a bird alarm and cord beneath. Antler.
Unsigned; school of Kokusai.
19th century.
Length 4.1cm (1½in).
F.385. Franks Collection.

153
Cicada, the surface of the wings depicted by the natural dark grain of the antler, a leaf beneath forming the *himotoshi*.
Antler.
Unsigned; school of Kokusai.
19th century.
Length 4.5cm (1¾in).
1930 12-17 96. Bequeathed by James Hilton.

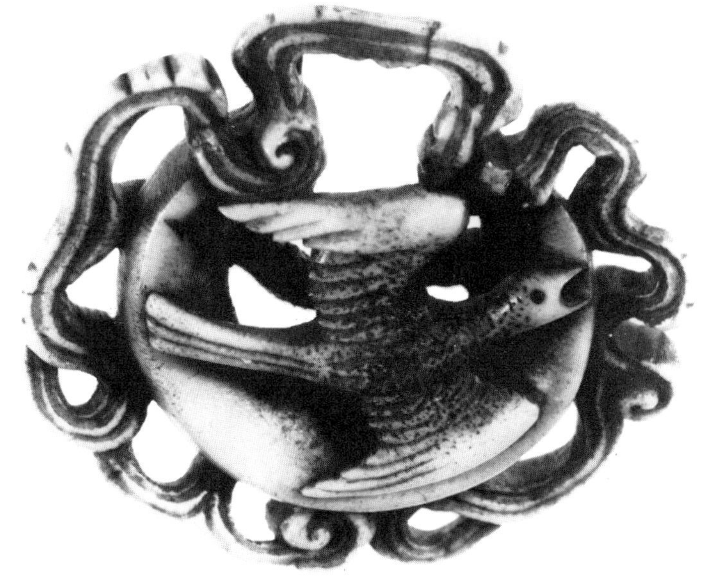

154

158△ 159▽

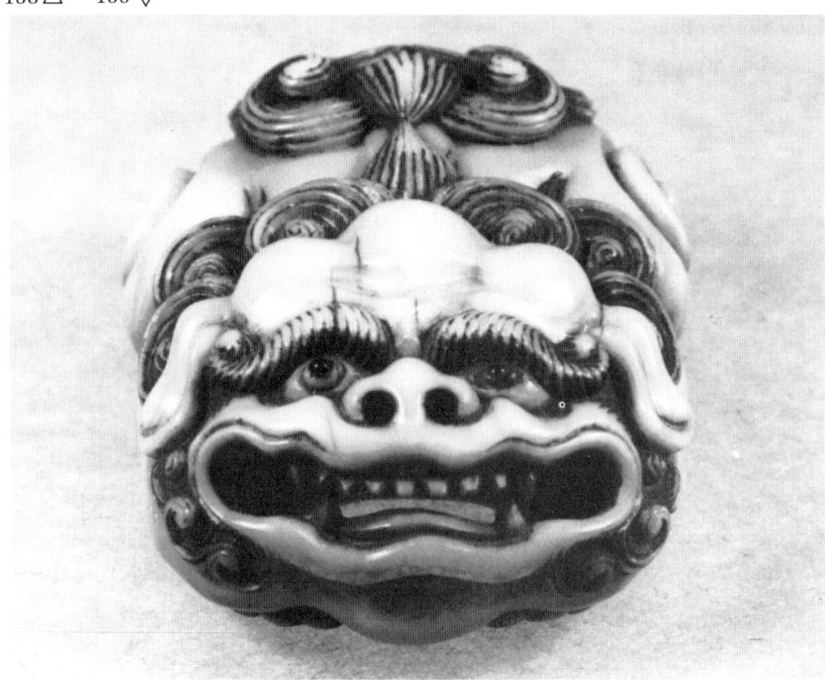

154
Bird in flight against a crescent moon, surrounded by scrolling clouds, all in openwork. Antler.
Unsigned; school of Kokusai.
19th century.
Length 4.5cm ($1\frac{3}{4}$in).
F.1154. Franks Collection.

155
Bat flying; three sacred fungi below. Antler.
Unsigned; school of Kokusai.
19th century.
Width 3.75cm ($1\frac{1}{2}$in).
F.219. Franks Collection.

156
Mokugyō (small temple bell), formed of confronting dragons holding a sacred jewel, all in openwork. Antler.
Signed Hōshunsai Masayuki and *kakihan* each side of the cord-hole.
19th century.
Length 3.75cm ($1\frac{1}{2}$in).
F.443. Franks Collection.

157
Badger as priest, a *mokugyō* (temple bell) resting on his distended scrotum. Antler.
Signed Masayuki in seal form on the base.
19th century.
Height 2.5cm (1in).
F.809. Franks Collection.

158
Elephant curled up on a round base. Antler.
Unsigned; school of Rensai.
19th century.
Diameter 2.5cm (1in).
OA+ 226.
Colour plate, page 24

159
Shishi in flattened form. Antler.
Unsigned; school of Rensai.
19th century.
Length 3.75cm ($1\frac{1}{2}$in).
F.301. Franks Collection.

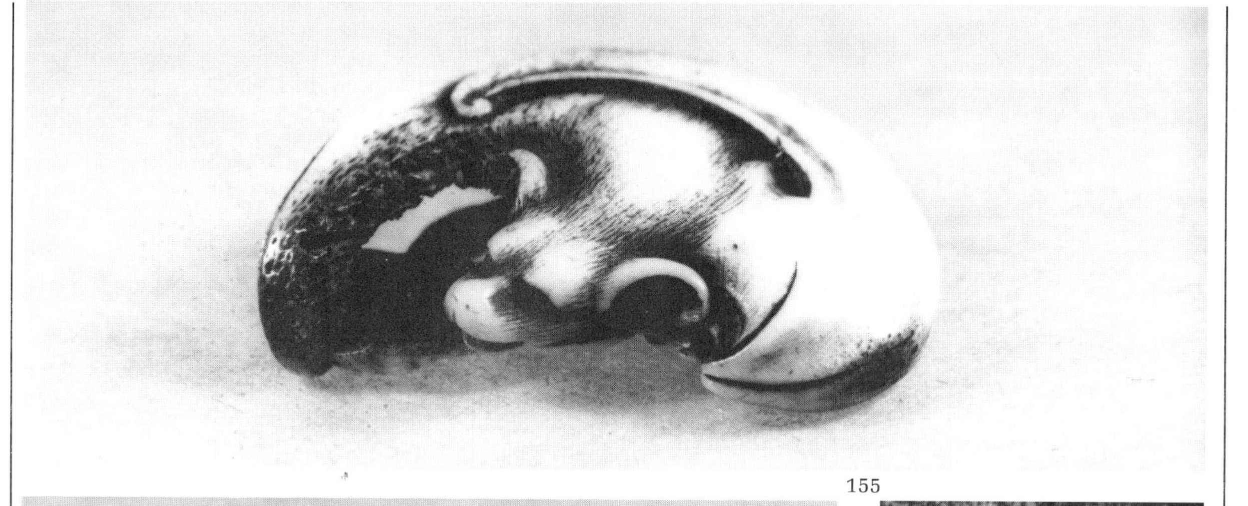

155

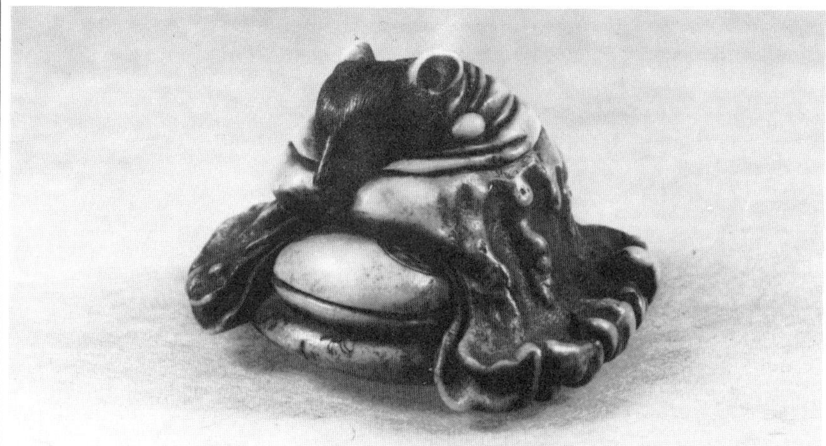

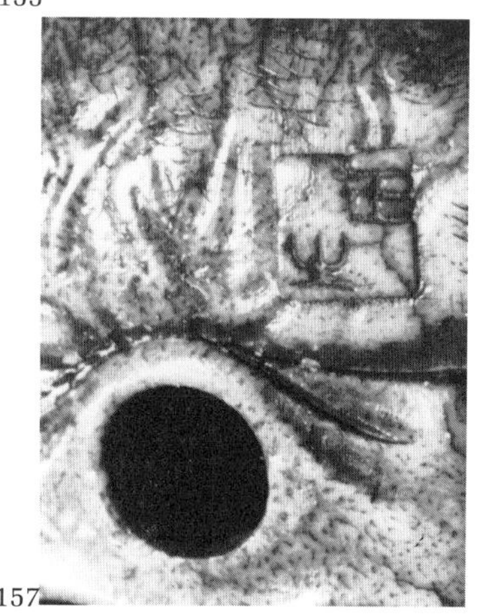

157

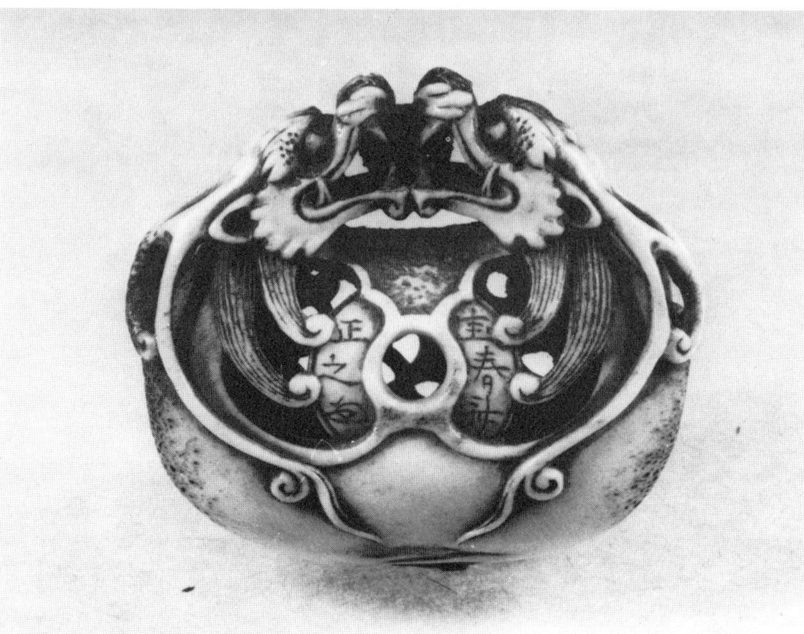

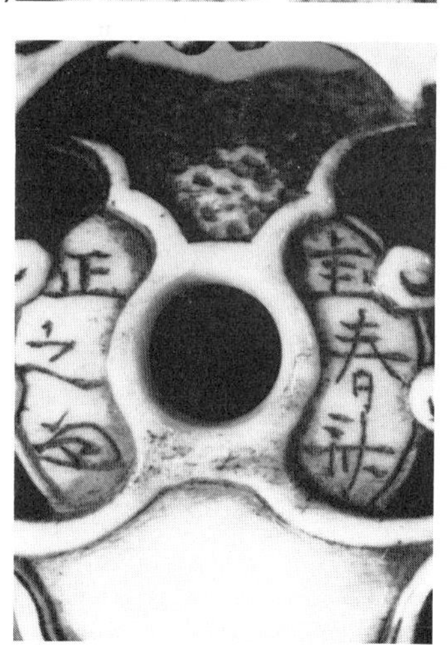

156

160
Shoe, with dragon holding a scroll twining round it, (probably a reference to a *Sennin*). Ivory.
Unsigned.
Length 4.25cm (1¾in).
F.1057. Franks Collection.

161
Sashi-netsuke in form of a sea-dragon with a single horn and a sacred jewel in its forehead. Antler, the eyes inlaid, the jewel amber.
Unsigned.
19th century.
Length 7.6cm (3in).
F.510. Franks Collection.

A *sashi-netsuke* hung simply from the sash, being hooked over it.
Colour plate, page 24

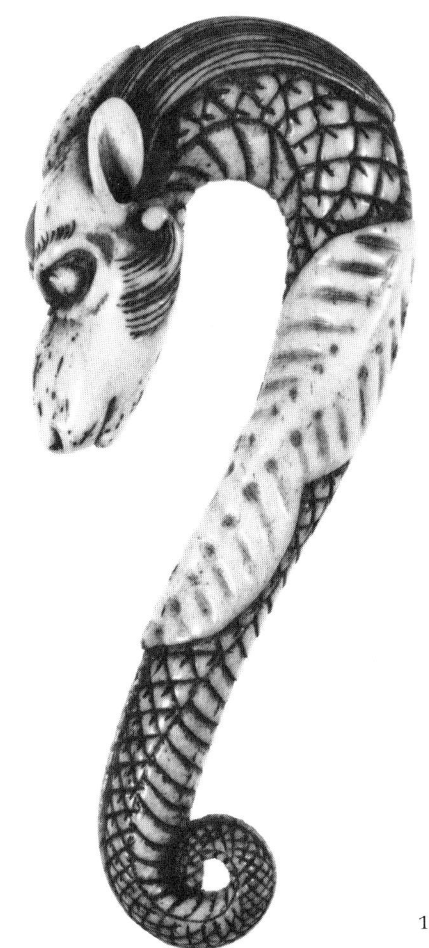

161

160

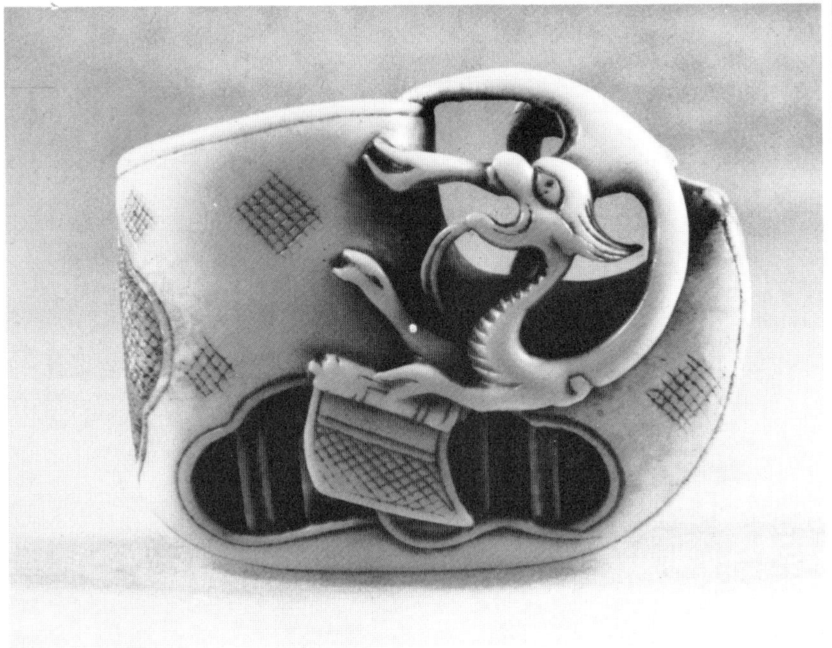

Nagoya

162
Two boars, carved with leaves on the base. Wood.
Signed Tametaka in an irregular cartouche on the base.
18th century.
Length 5.1cm (2in).
1945 10-17 645. Bequeathed by Oscar Raphael.

163
Group of seven boars, the underside carved with leaves. Wood.
Signed Tametaka in a rect-angular cartouche on the base.
18th century.
Length 5.1cm (2in).
1945 10-17 612. Bequeathed by Oscar Raphael.

164
Coiled snake. Wood.
Signed Tametaka in a rect-angular cartouche on the base.
18th century.
Width 3.5 cm (1¼in).
F.802. Franks Collection.

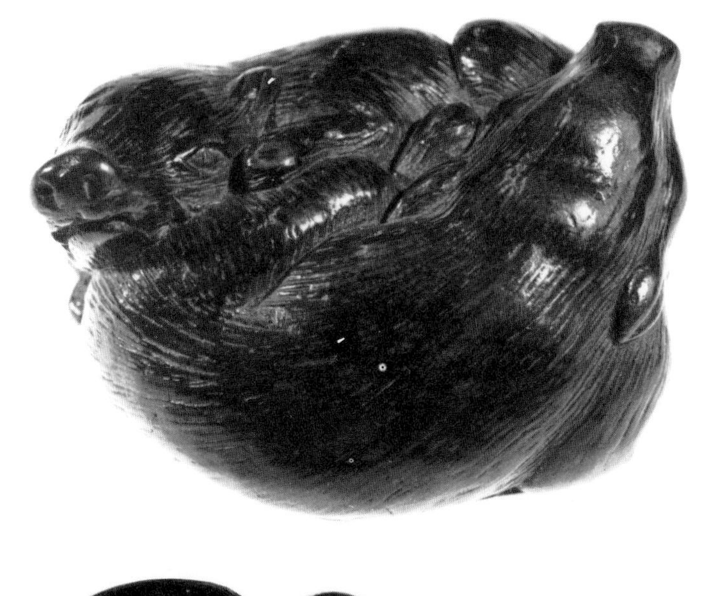

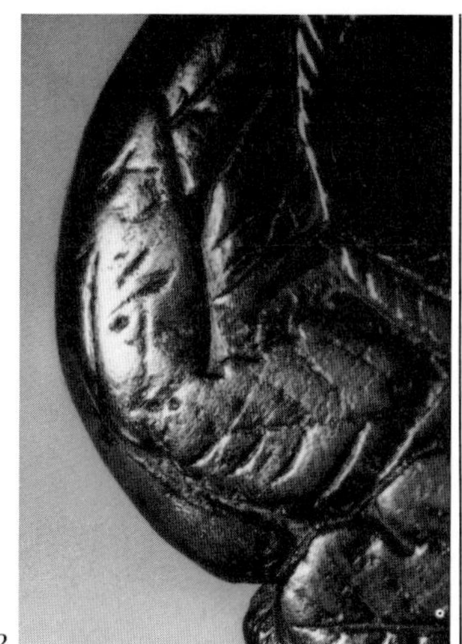

162

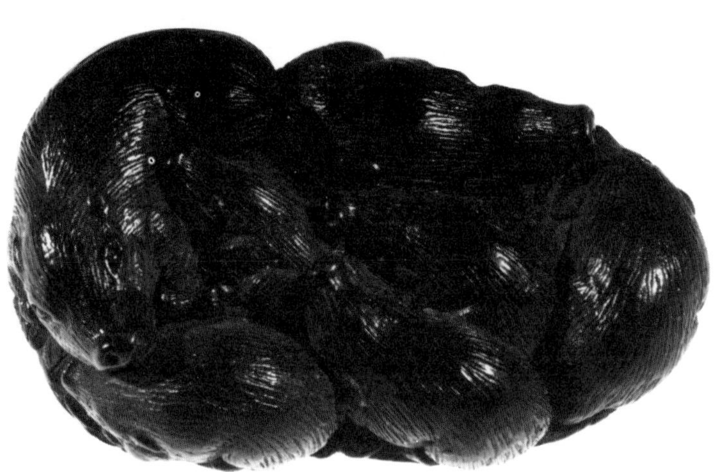

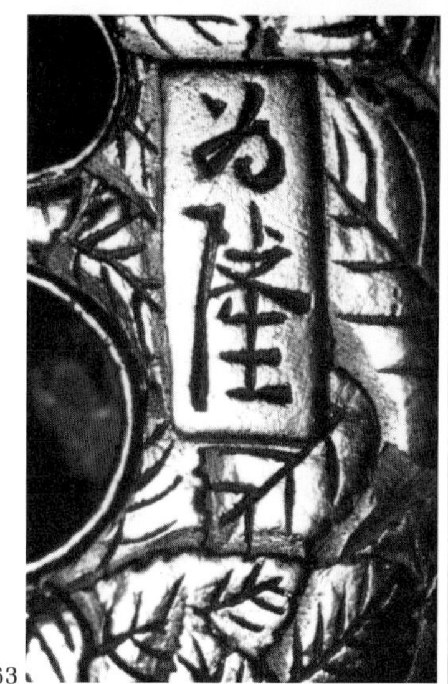

163

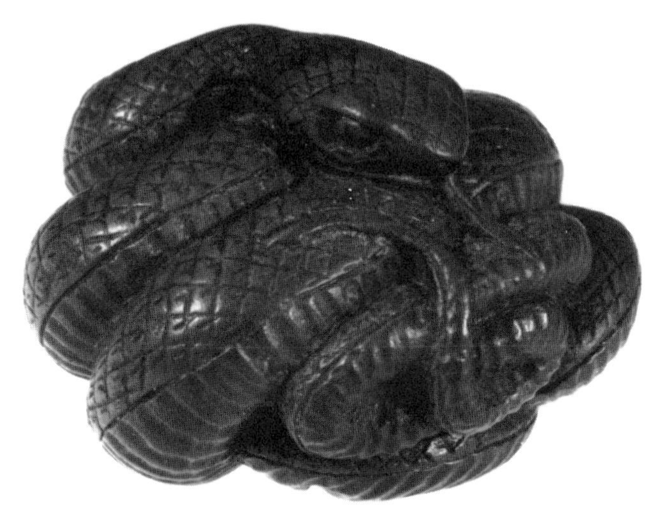

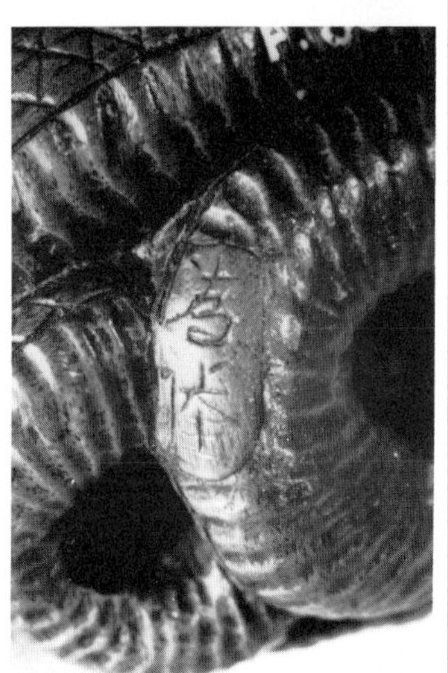

164

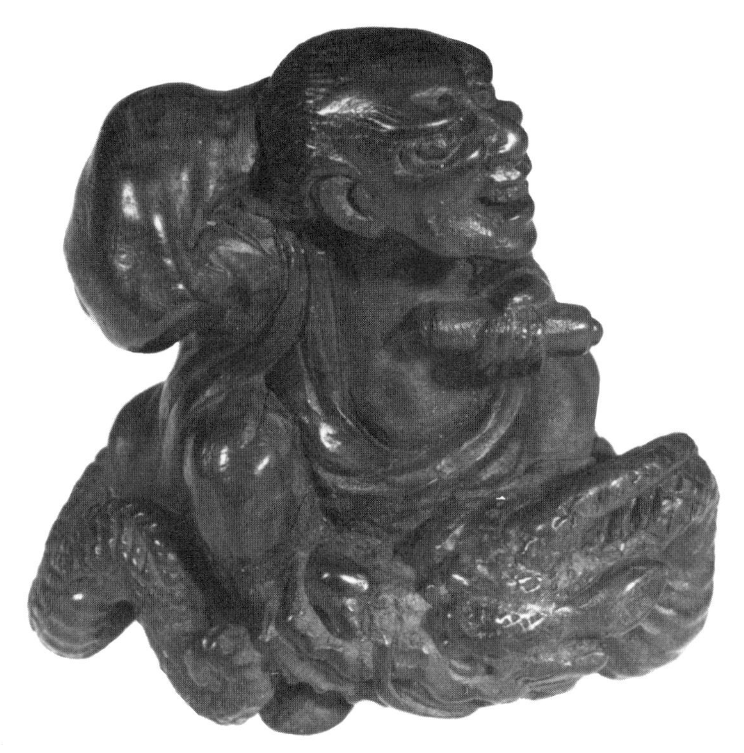

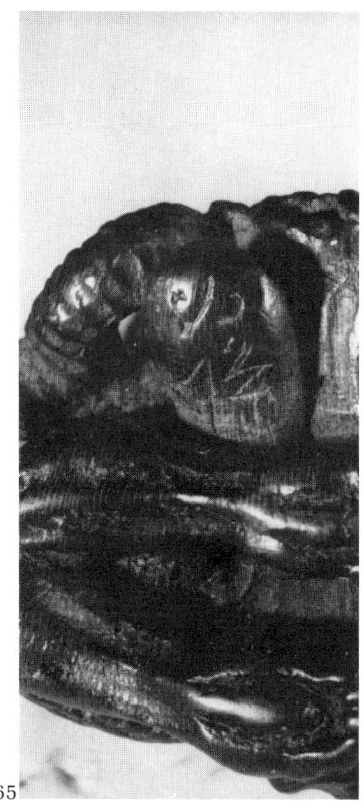

165

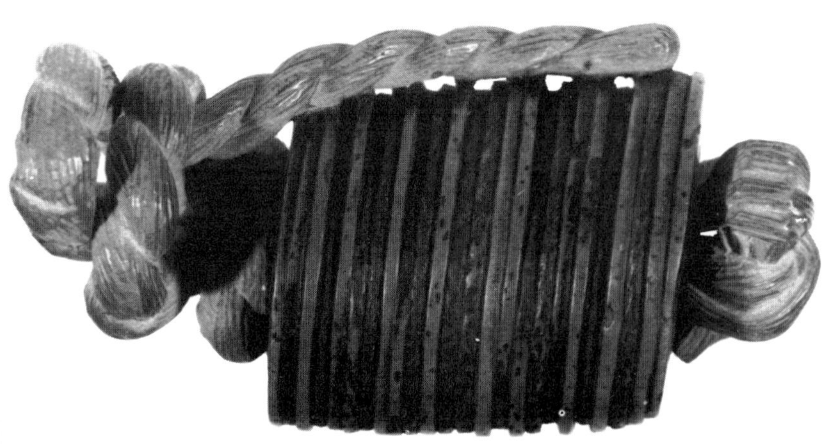

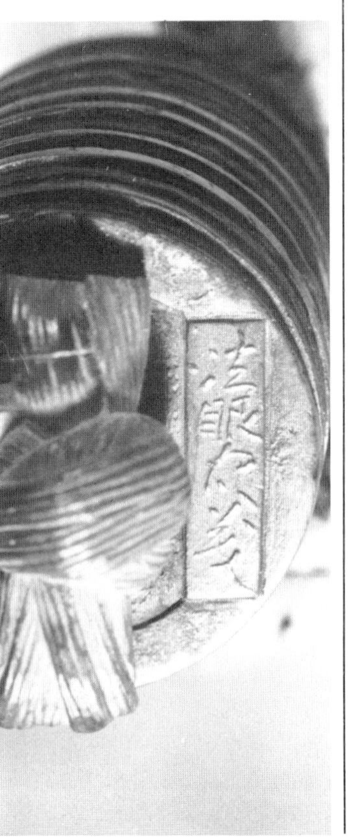

169

165
Sennin riding on a dragon and holding a scroll. Wood.
Signed Tametaka under one foot.
18th century.
Height 4.75cm (1¾in).
F.895. Franks Collection.

166
Kiyohime creeping round the bell. Wood.
Signed Chōfu Kinjō Higashi Tadatoshi on the bell-rim.
Late 18th–early 19th century.
Height 3.75cm (1½in).
F.905. Franks Collection.

167
Three Chinese boys playing hide-and-seek around a *tsuitate* screen. Wood.
Signed Tadatoshi in an elongated oval cartouche on the base.
Late 18th–early 19th century.
Height 3.25cm (1¼in).
F.128. Franks Collection.

168
Three aubergines and a pumpkin.
Wood, partly stained.
Signed Chōfu Jū Tadatoshi in two rectangular cartouches on the base.
19th century.
Width 4.25cm (1¾in).
F.324. Franks Collection.

169
Group of cash tied with a cord. Wood.
Signed Hōgen Tadayoshi in a rectangular cartouche on the bottom coin.
Early 19th century.
Height 5.1cm (2in).
F.1123. Franks Collection.

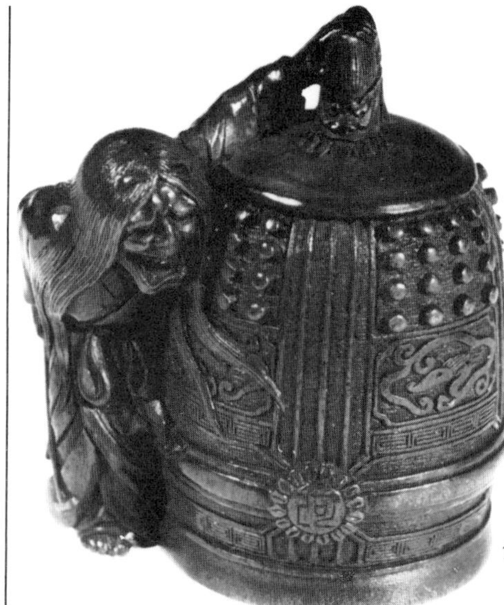

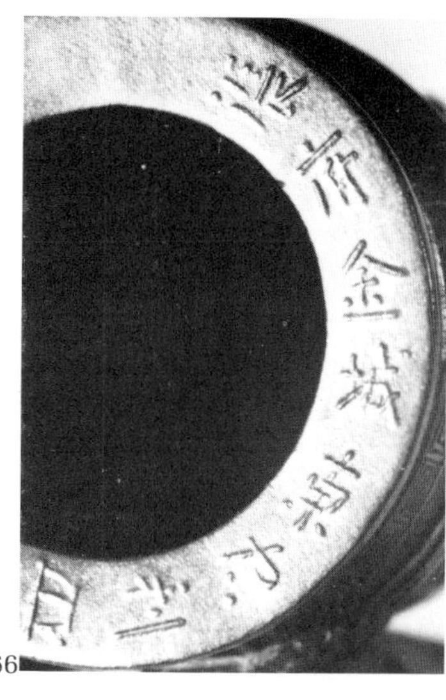

166

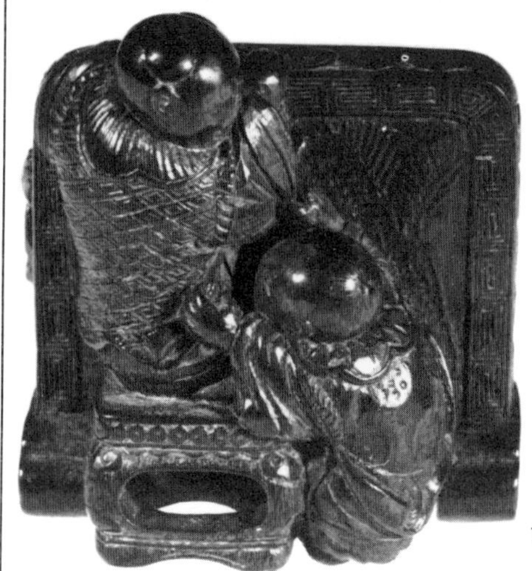

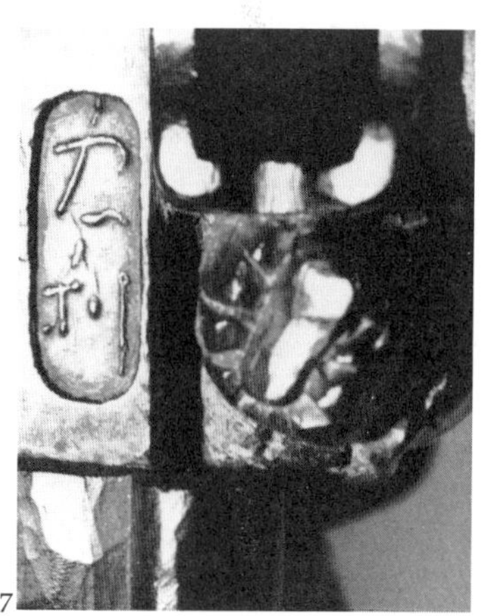

167

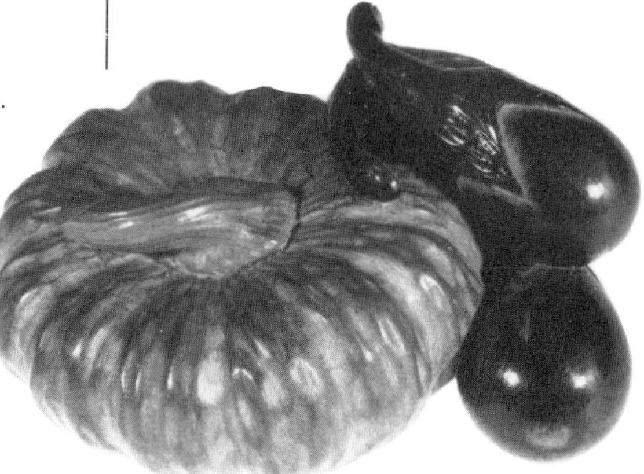

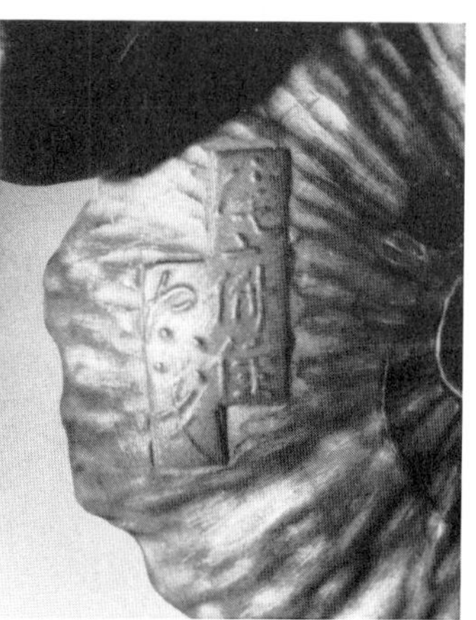

168

170
Jar with octopus in it.
Wood, some ivory incrustation.
Signed Ittan Sanjin Tō on the side.
19th century.
Height 3.75cm (1½in).
F.1079. Franks Collection.

171
Fox with hand-drum. Wood.
Signed Ittan with *kakihan* under the tail.
19th century.
Height 3.75cm (1½in).
F.245. Franks Collection.

172
Ningyō (a sort of mermaid).
Wood.
Signed Masahisa on a rectangular cartouche underneath.
19th century.
Length 3.75cm (1½in).
F.762. Franks Collection.

173
Sleeping *Shōjō*. Wood.
Unread signature in relief characters in a rectangular cartouche on the base.
19th century.
Length 3.75cm (1½in).
F.927. Franks Collection.

174
Tiger-like creature. Wood.
Signed Masanaga on the base.
19th century.
Length 4.5cm (1¾in).
F.674. Franks Collection.

175
Snail slithering down from the top of an upturned bucket.
Wood.
Signed Shigemasa on base of bucket.
19th century.
Height 4.5cm (1¾in).
1948 10-19 5. Bequeathed by H. C. Wilcox.
For a similar example *see*, *Collectors' Netsuke*, p. 89, no. 105.

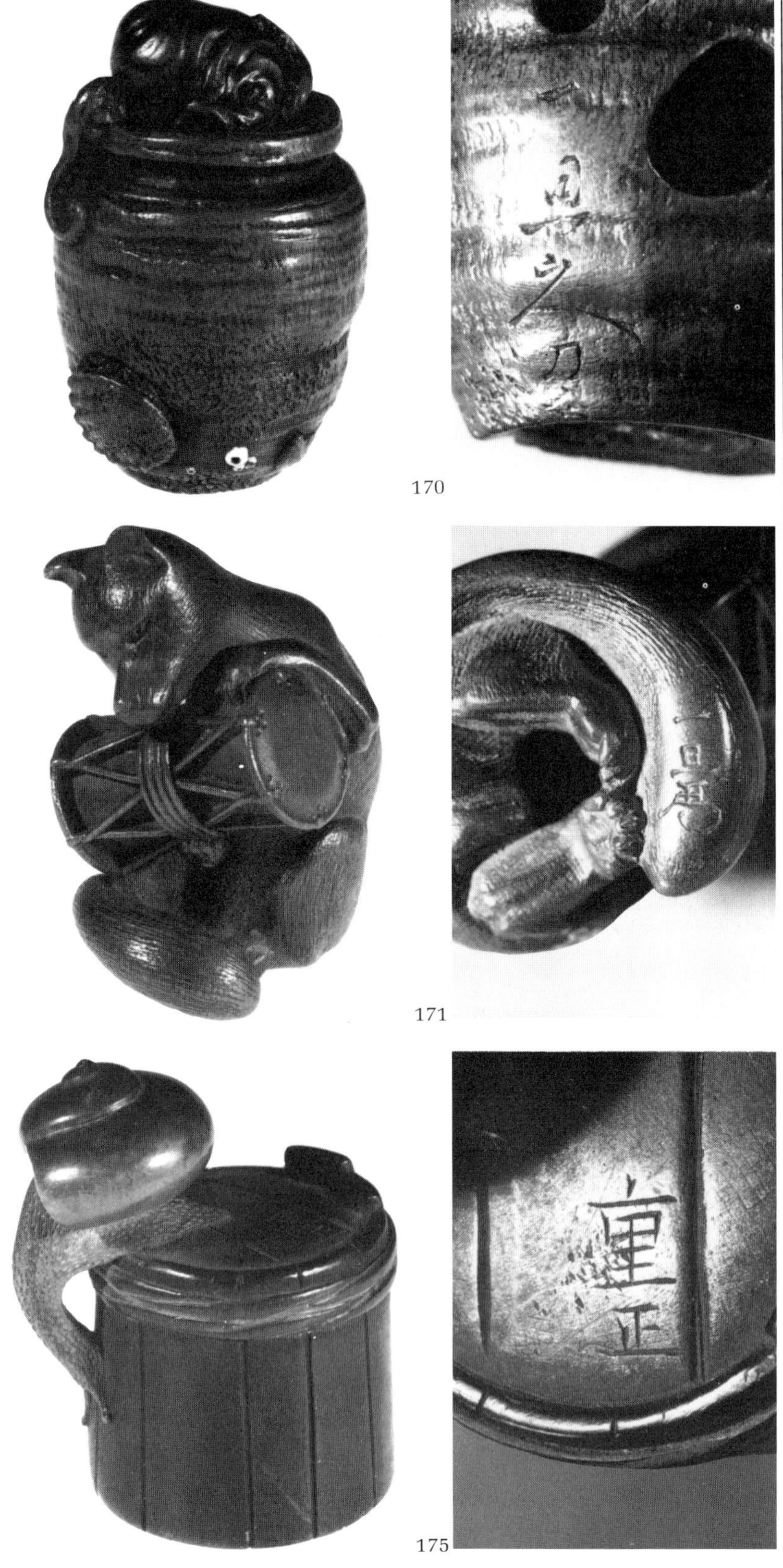
170
171
175

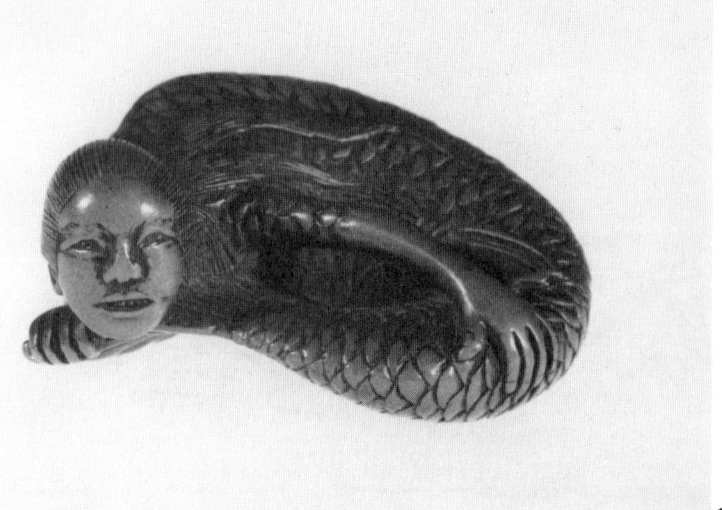

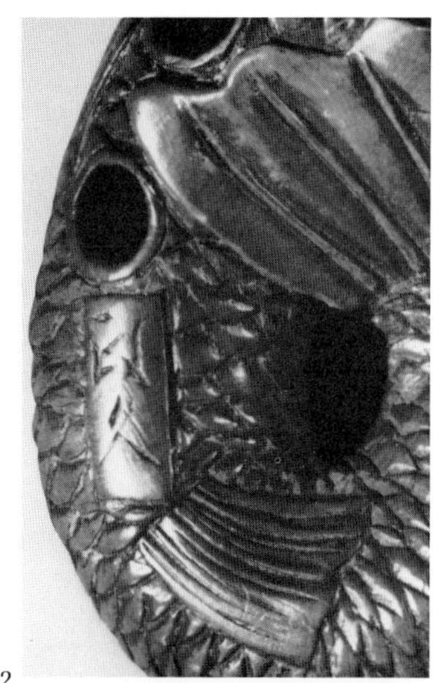

172

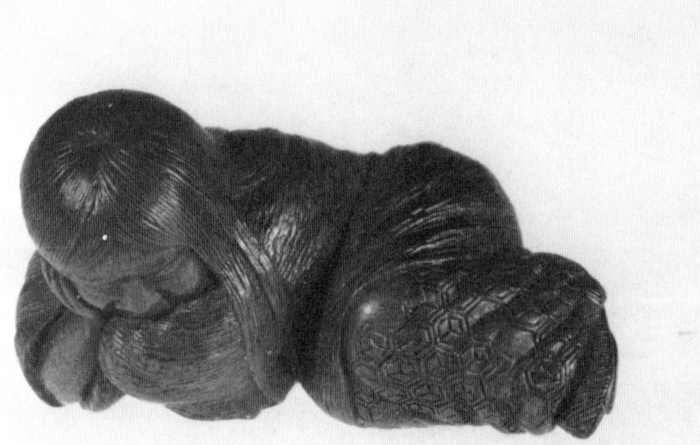

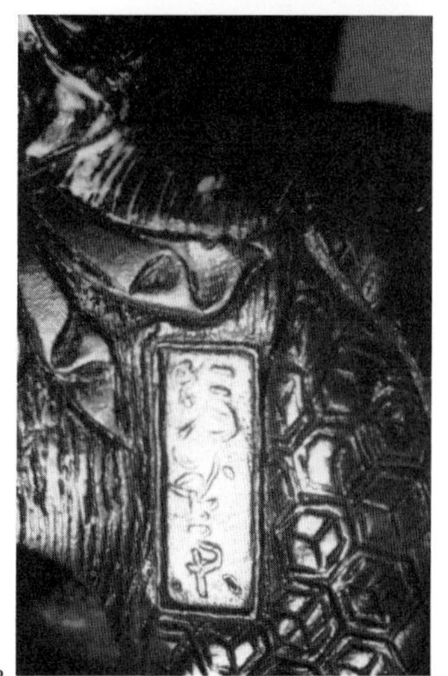

173

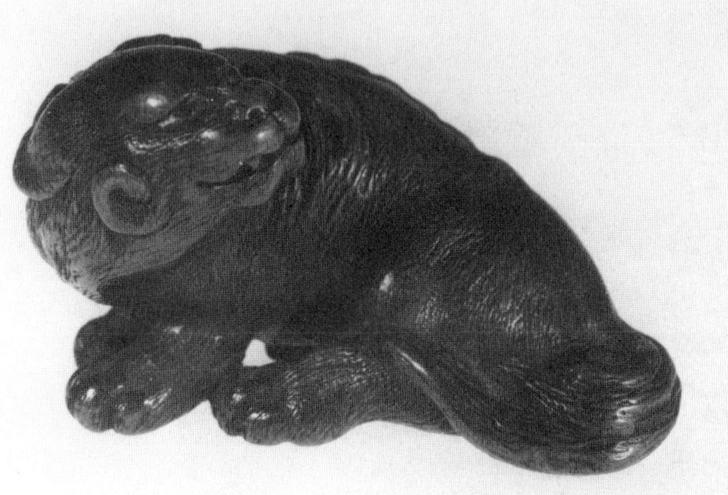

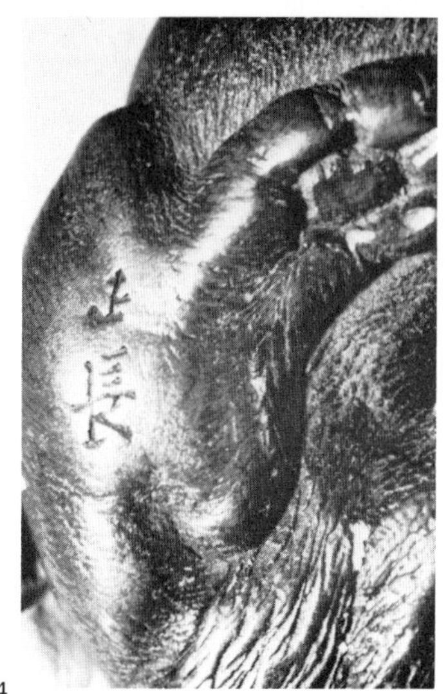

174

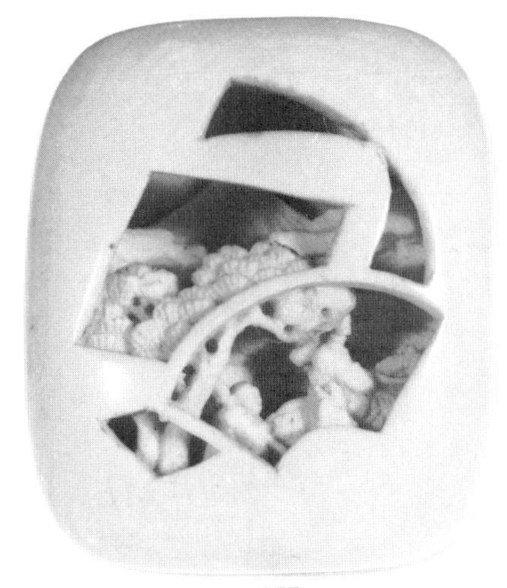

177

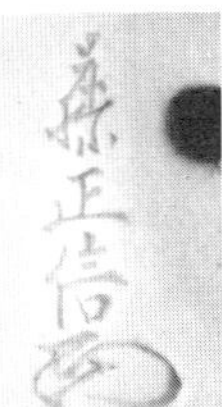

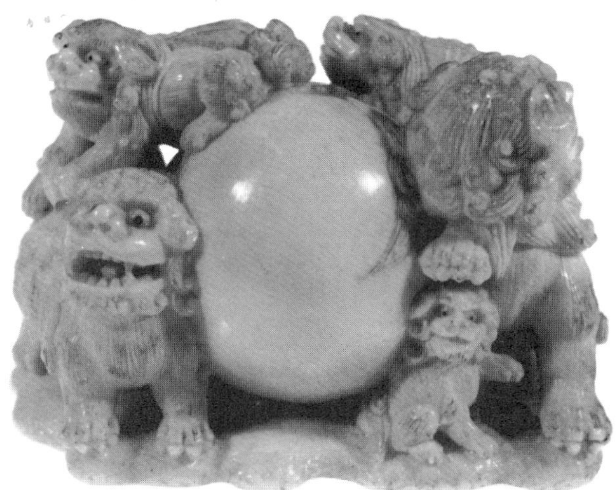

180

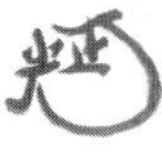

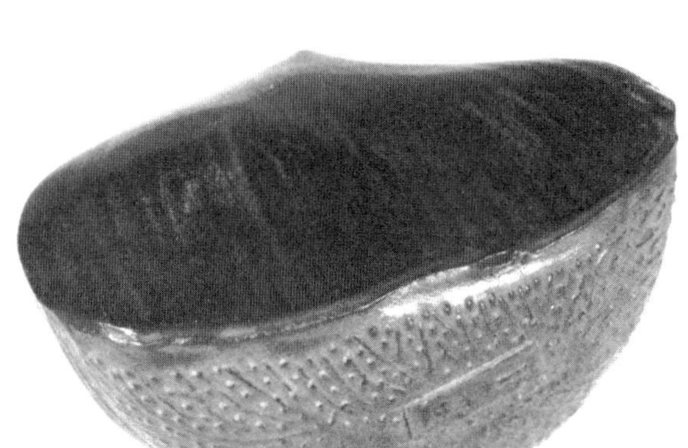

181

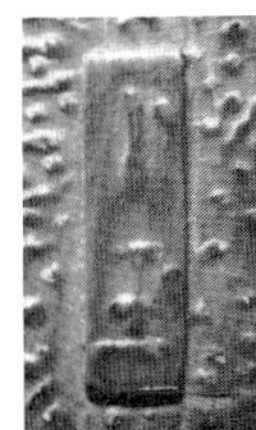

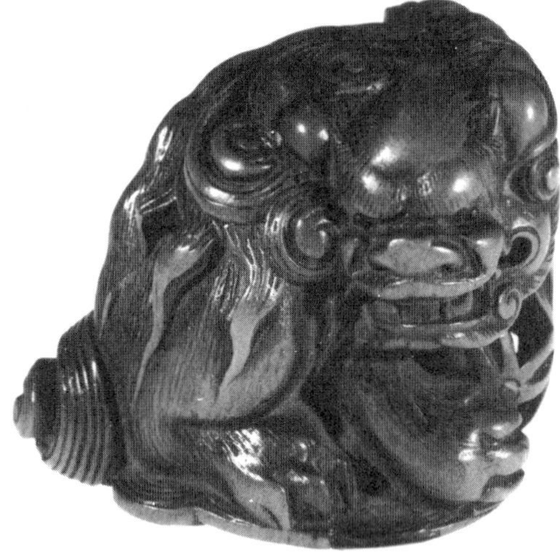

179

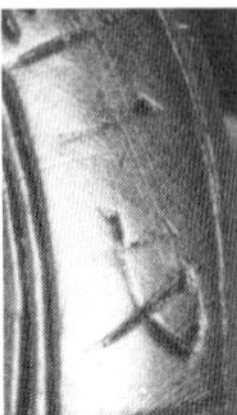

176

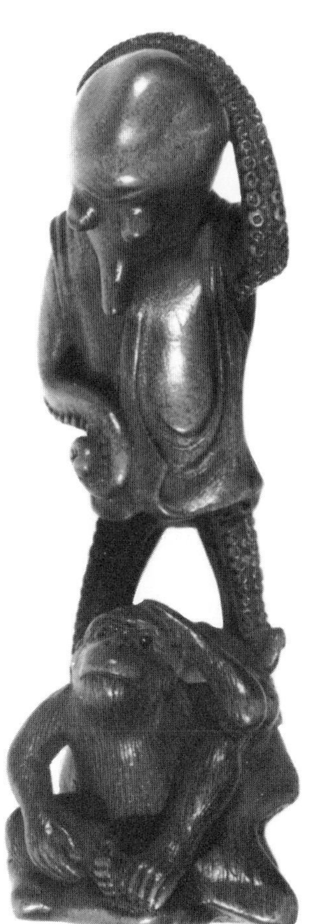

178

176
Owl perched on a branch of an oak tree.
Wood, the eyes inlaid.
Signed Sōshin under the bough.
19th century.
Height 4.25cm ($1\frac{3}{4}$in).
F.786. Franks Collection.
Colour plate, page 11

177
Manjū in box shape, the lid with fan-shaped cut-outs, revealing the exiled poet Narihira riding past Mt Fuji.
Ivory.
Signed Fuji Masanobu with *kakihan* on base.
19th century.
Length 3.25cm ($1\frac{1}{4}$in).
1930 12-17 98. Bequeathed by James Hilton.

178
Octopus-like *bakemono* looming over and imitating a monkey.
Wood, the eyes inlaid.
Signed Masakazu with *kakihan* on base.
19th century.
Height 5.75cm ($2\frac{1}{4}$in).
F.805. Franks Collection.

179
Shishi holding a brocade ball containing a free-moving ball.
Wood.
Signed Issai in a twisted rectangular cartouche on the base.
Early 19th century.
Height 3.5cm ($1\frac{1}{4}$in).
F.1094. Franks Collection.

180
Two parent *Shishi* with cubs clambering over a ball. Ivory.
Signed Masamitsu on base.
19th century.
Length 3.75cm ($1\frac{1}{2}$in).
F.1162. Franks Collection.

181
Chestnut. Wood.
Signed Bokugyoku in relief in a rectangular cartouche on the calyx.
Width 4.25cm ($1\frac{3}{4}$in).
F.311. Franks Collection.

Gifu

182
Rat.
Wood, the eyes inlaid, the teeth in ivory.
Signed Gifu Tomokazu in an elongated oval cartouche on the base.
Late 18th century.
Length 5.75cm ($2\frac{1}{4}$in).
1953 12-17 14. Bequeathed by Mrs Helen Epstein.
Colour plate, page 11

183
Demon holding Shoki the Demon Queller under a straw basket.
Wood, eyes inlaid, details in ivory.
Signed Masakazu in an oval cartouche on the base.
Mid-19th century.
Height 3.25cm ($1\frac{1}{4}$in).
F.823. Franks Collection.

184
Futen the wind-god with clouds swirling from his sack, and a drum on his back.
Wood, the eyes inlaid in ivory.
Signed Masakazu in an oval cartouche.
19th century.
Height 3.25cm ($1\frac{1}{4}$in).
F.852. Franks Collection.

185
Tortoise retracted into its shell. The central plate removes to attach the cord.
Wood, the eyes inlaid.
Unsigned.
19th century.
Length 4.5cm ($1\frac{3}{4}$in).
F.269. Franks Collection.

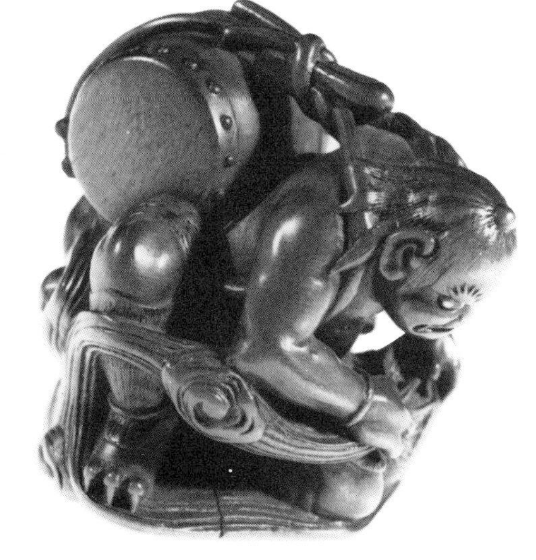

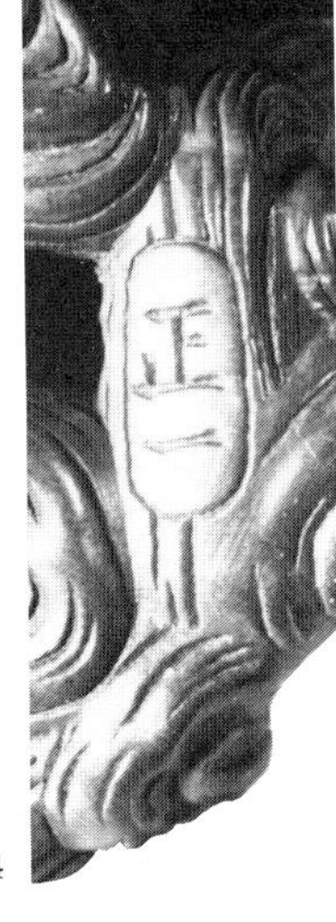

184

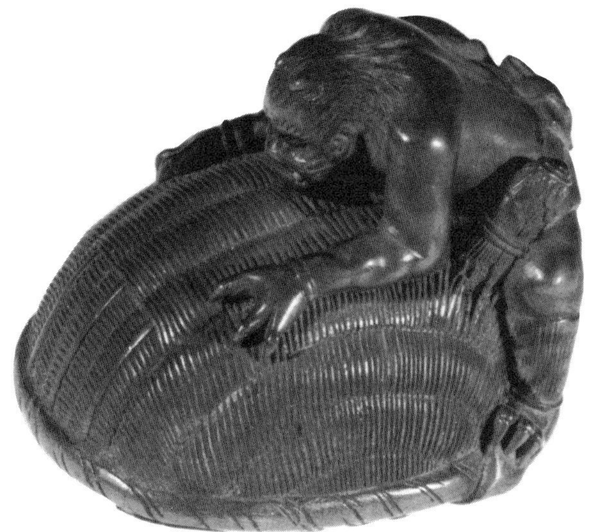

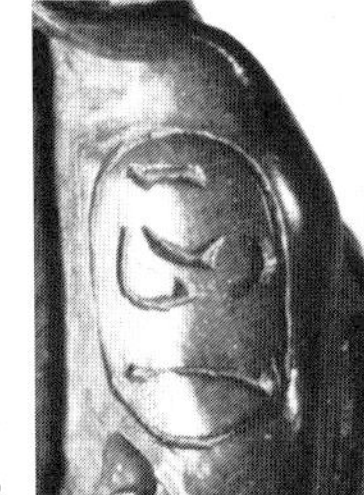

183

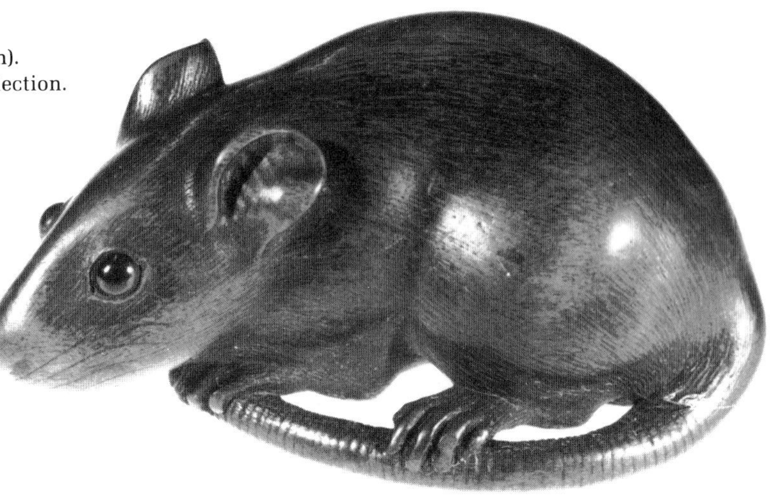

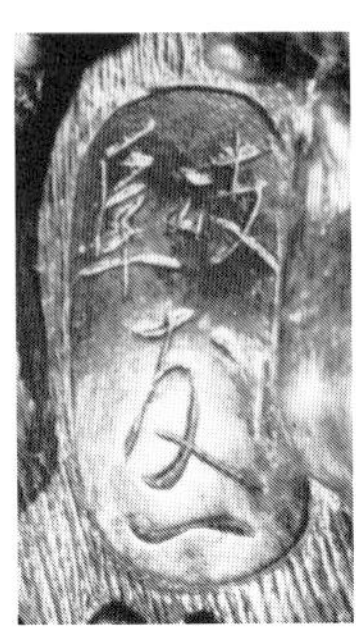

182

186
Goldfish (*Tarrasius arratus*).
Wood, the eyes inlaid in amber and ebony.
Signed Masanao on the bottom.
Early 19th century.
Length 5.5cm (2in).
F.1674. Franks Collection.
Colour plate, page 11

187
Fisherman struggling with an octopus.
Wood, one eye of the octopus inlaid.
Signed Masanao on the base.
19th century.
Height 4.25cm ($1\frac{3}{4}$in).
F.174. Franks Collection.

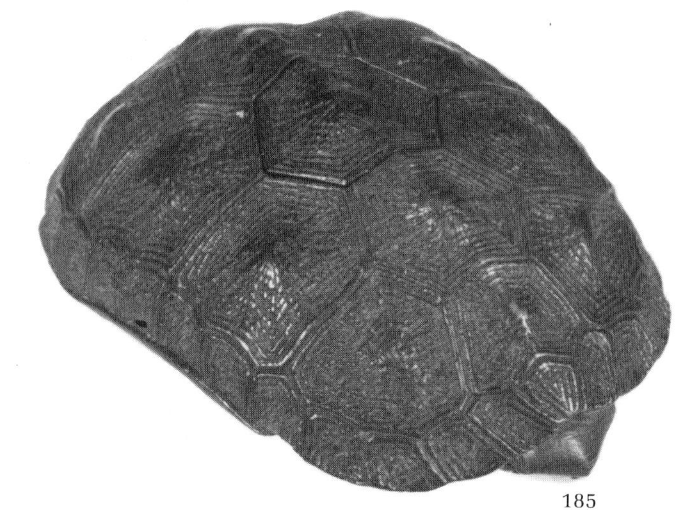

185

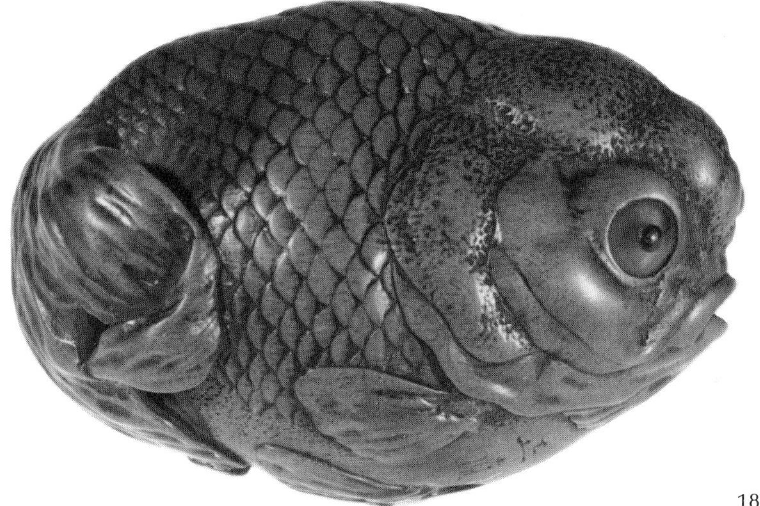

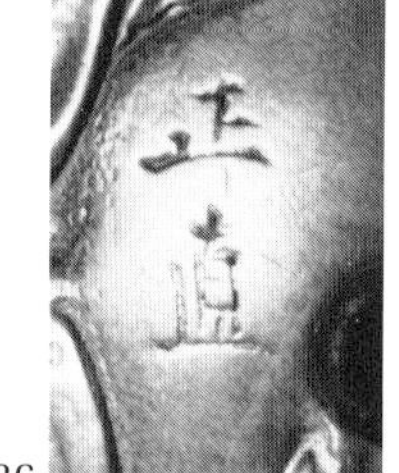

186

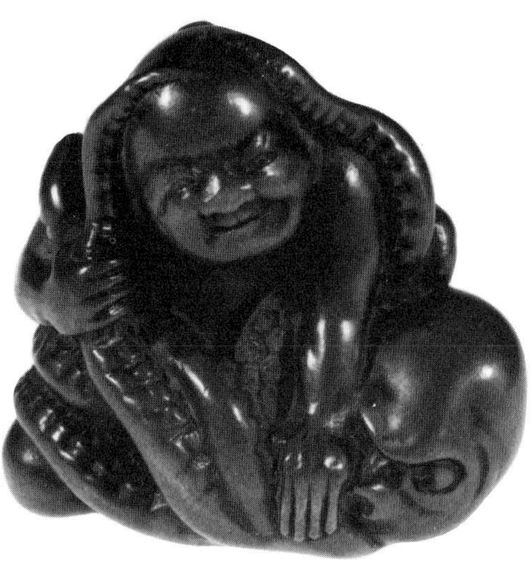

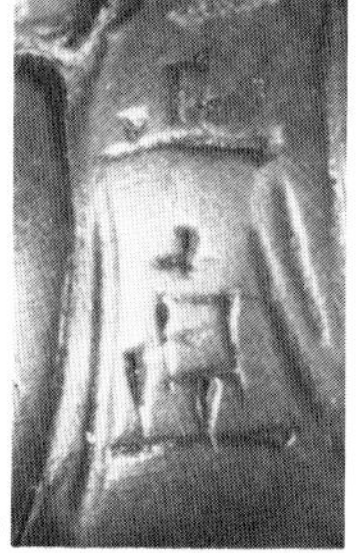

187

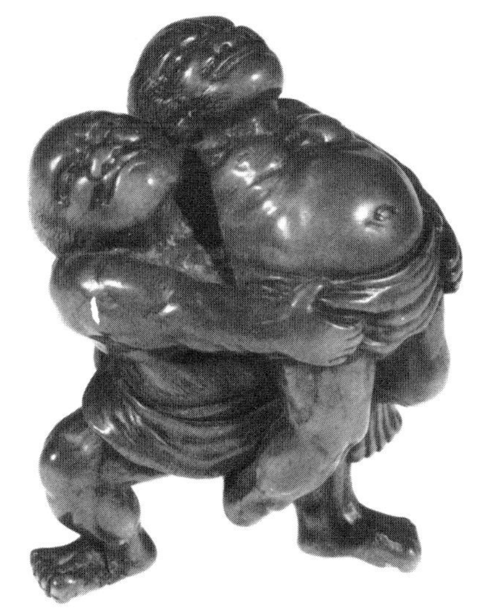

188

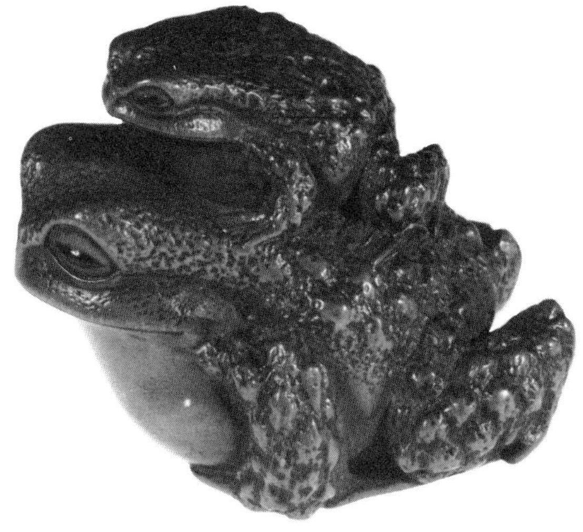

190

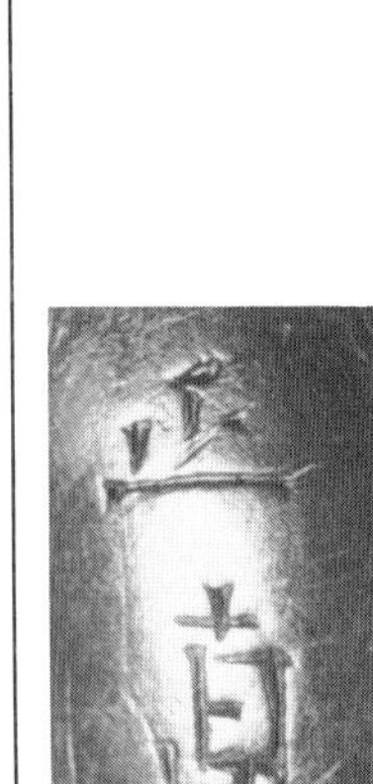

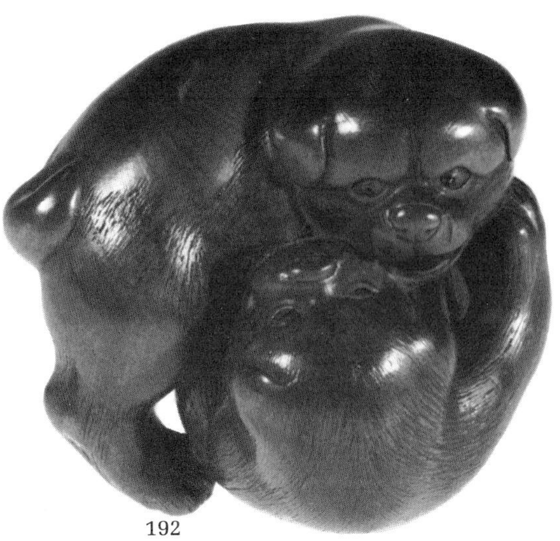

192

188
Two wrestlers, one about to use the 'Kawazu' throw.
Wood, the eyes inlaid.
Signed Masanao under one foot.
19th century.
Height 5.1cm (2in).
F.605. Franks Collection.

189
Pine cone. Wood.
Signed Masanao on the base.
19th century.
Height 3.75cm ($1\frac{1}{2}$in).
F.1109. Franks Collection.

190
Mating frogs.
Wood, the eyes inlaid.
Signed Masanao on the base.
19th century.
Length 3.75cm ($1\frac{1}{2}$in).
F.800. Franks Collection.

191
Group of sacred fungi. Wood.
Signed Masanao at the root.
19th century.
Height 5.1cm (2in).
F.1113. Franks Collection.

192
Two puppies.
Wood, the eyes inlaid.
Signed Masanao in an oval cartouche on the base.
19th century.
Height 3.75cm ($1\frac{1}{2}$in).
1930 12-17 108. Bequeathed by James Hilton.

193
Gourd, the top detachable and the *himotoshi* formed by a bar at the back. Wood.
Signed Masanao by the *himotoshi*.
19th century.
Height 7.25cm (3in).
F.1111. Franks Collection.

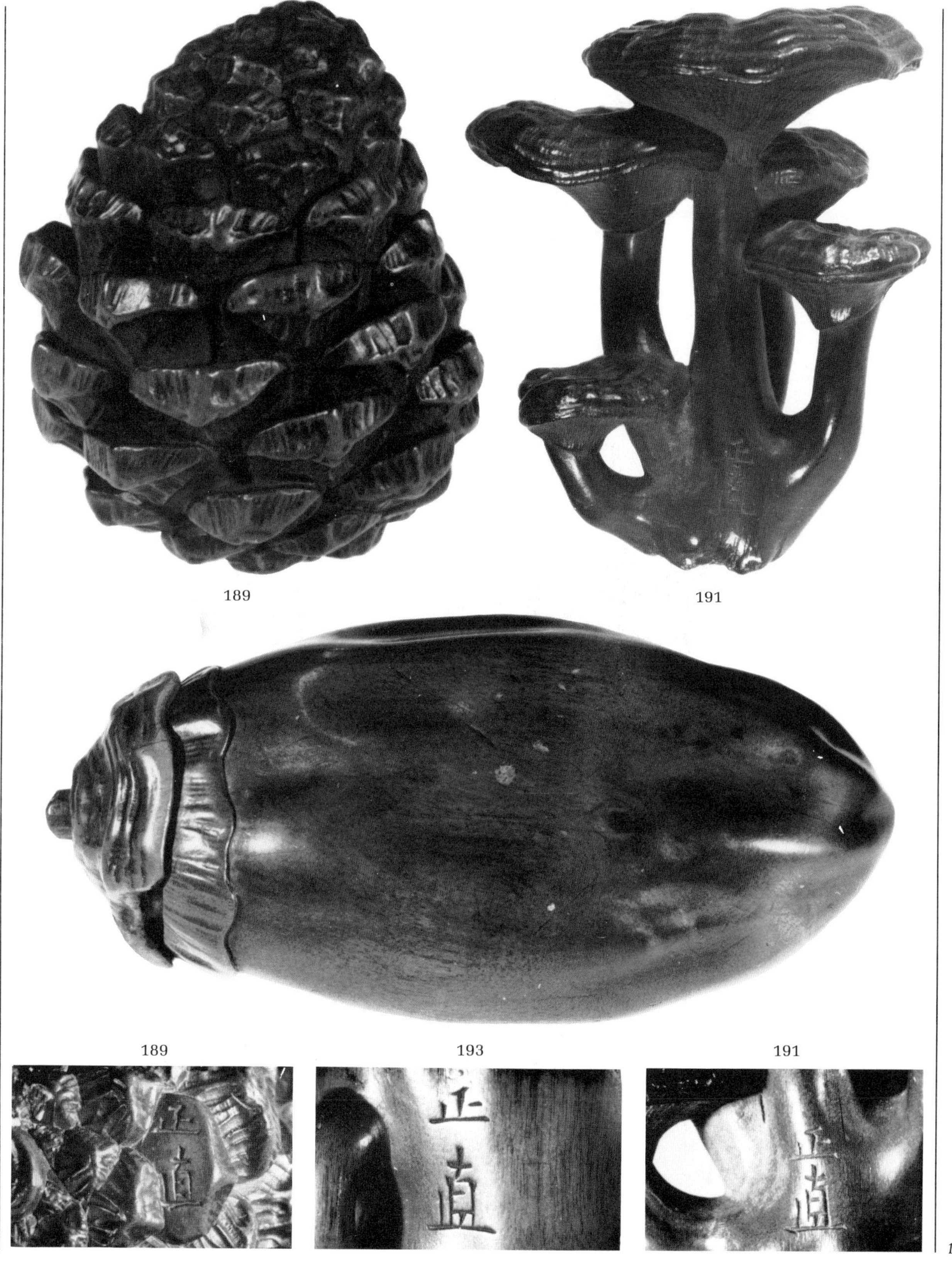

189

191

189

193

191

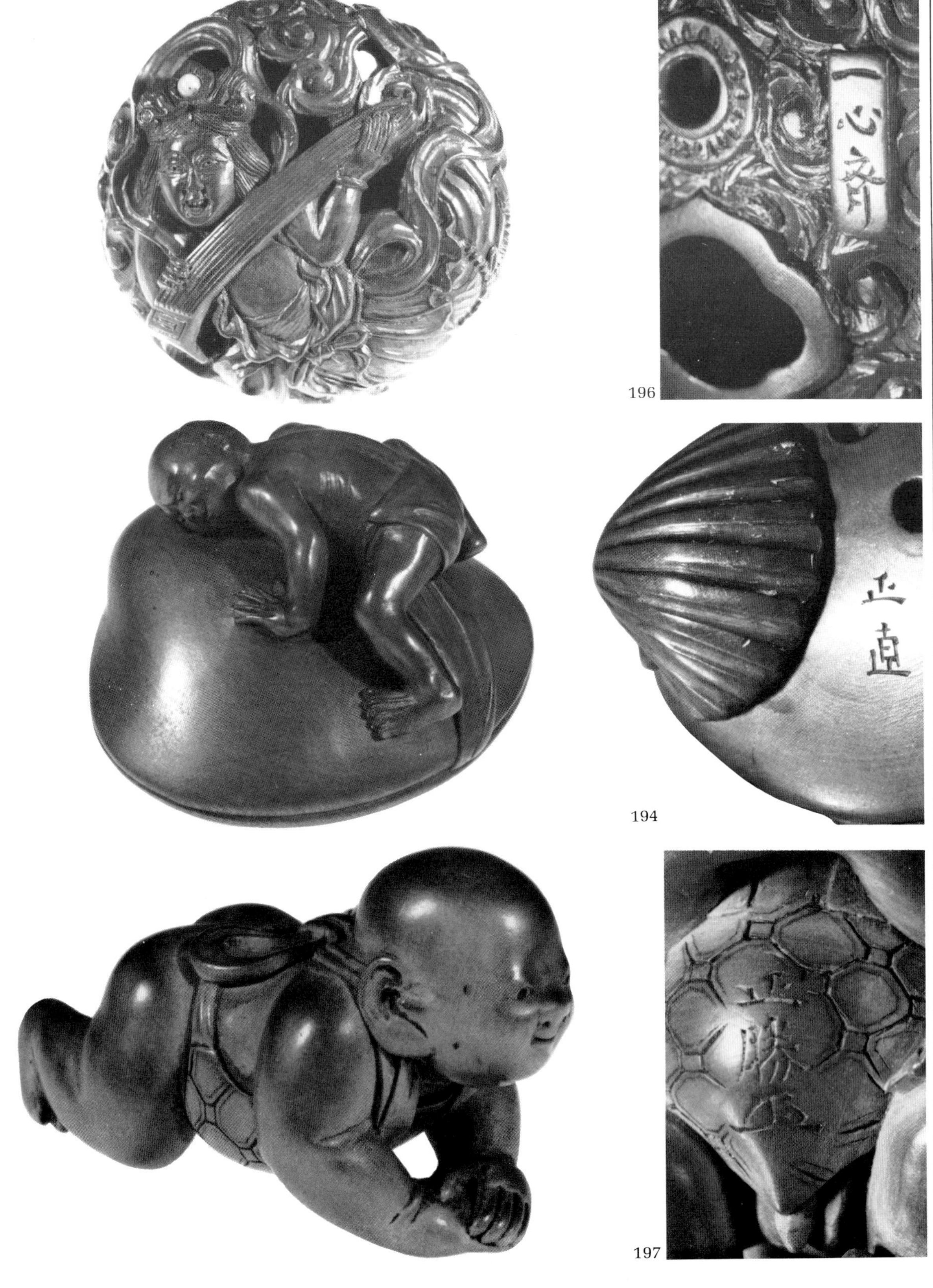

196

194

197

194
Fisherman with his loin cloth caught in a huge clam shell.
Wood.
Signed Masanao on the base.
19th century.
Height 2.75cm (1in).
F.666. Franks Collection.

195
Three turtles climbing on each other.
Wood, the eyes inlaid.
Signed Masanao on the base.
19th century.
Height 5cm (2in).
1953 12-17 13. Bequeathed by Mrs Helen Epstein.

196
Manjū decorated with an openwork *apsara* (Buddhist angel).
Wood, coral and stained ivory incrustations in the head-dress, stained ivory rim to one *himotoshi*.
Signed Ishinsai in a rectangular cartouche on the back.
19th century.
Diameter 4.2cm (1$\frac{3}{4}$in).
F.1232. Franks Collection.

197
Child crawling, wearing a tortoiseshell stomacher.
Wood, the eyes inlaid.
Signed Masakatsu with a *kakihan* underneath.
19th century.
Length 4.2cm (1$\frac{3}{4}$in).
F.145. Franks Collection.

198
Man carrying on his back a large Daruma doll.
Wood, the doll's eyes inlaid.
Signed Masakatsu with *kakihan* under one foot.
19th century.
Height 5.1cm (2in).
1953 12-17 15. Bequeathed by Mrs Helen Epstein.

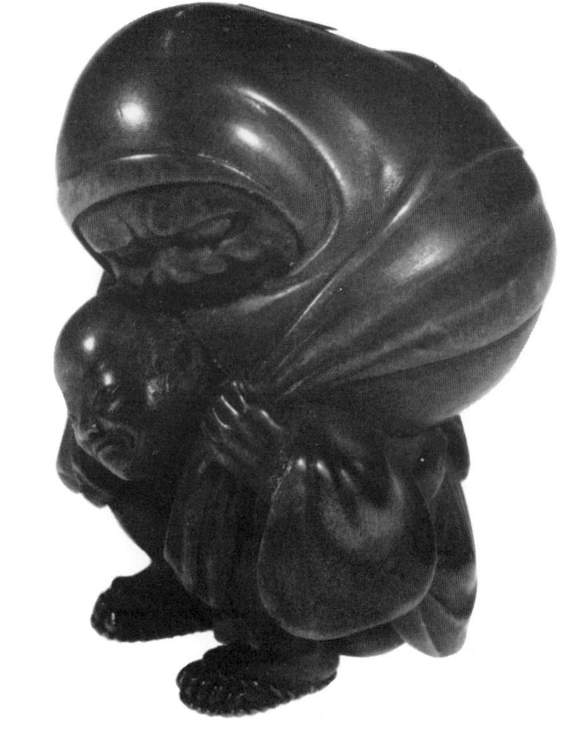

198

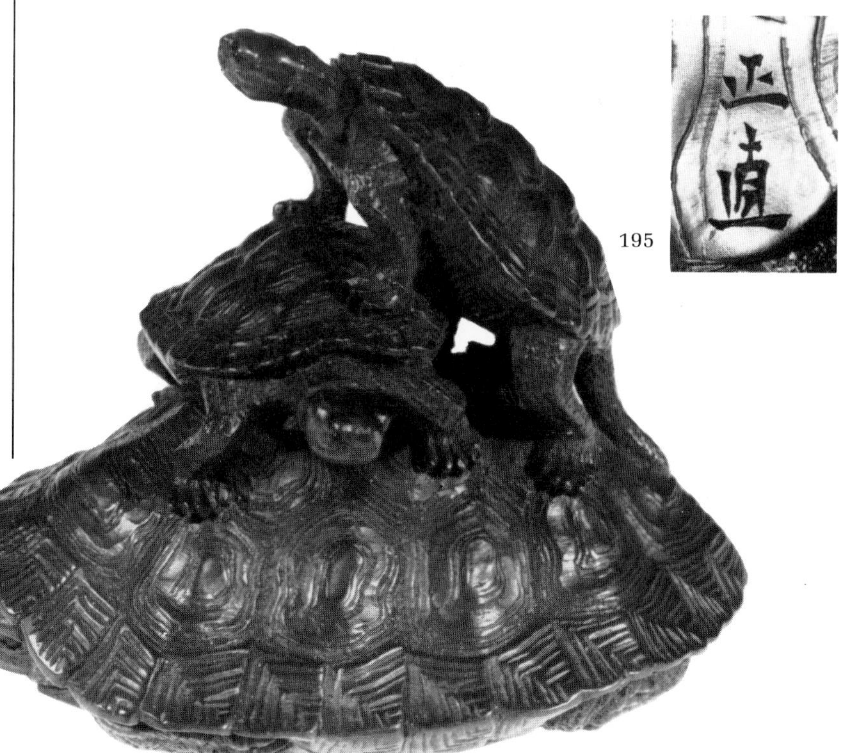

195

Tsu

199
Kiyohime coiling round the bell, through a crack of which the face of Anchin is visible.
Wood, Anchin's face tinted white.
Signed Konan Minkō on the base.
19th century.
Height 5.1cm (2in).
F.887. Franks Collection.

200
Kiyohime coiling round the bell, through a crack of which Anchin's face is visible.
Wood, details of flesh and one cord-hole rimmed in ivory.
Signed Minkō with *kakihan* on base.
Late 18th–early 19th century.
Height 3.75cm ($1\frac{1}{2}$in).
F.883. Franks Collection.

201
Tiger with a cub climbing onto its back.
Wood, the eyes inlaid and gilt.
Signed Minkō with *kakihan* on base.
Late 18th century.
Length 5.1cm (2in).
1953 12-17 12. Bequeathed by Mrs Helen Epstein.

For a similar example *see* N. K. Davey, *Netsuke*, p. 209, no. 636.
Colour plate, page 11

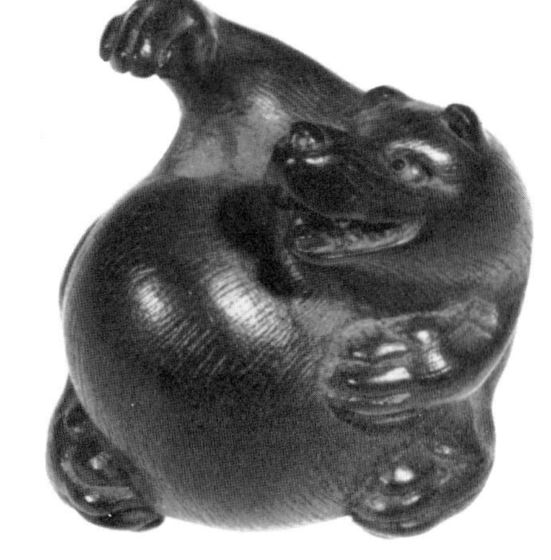

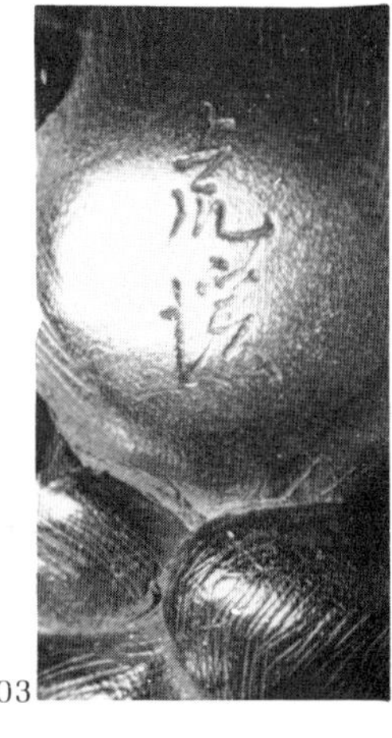

203

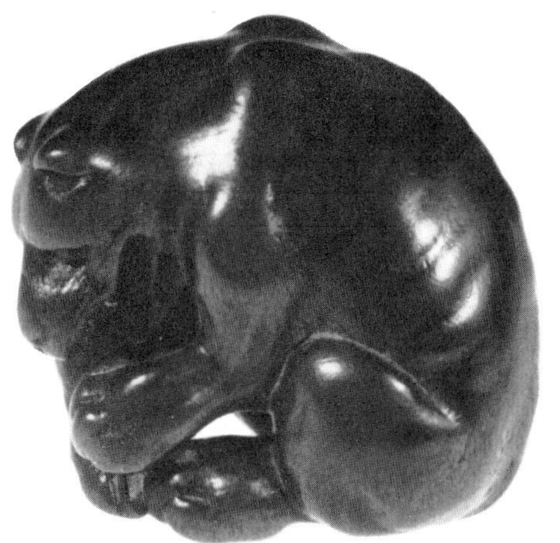

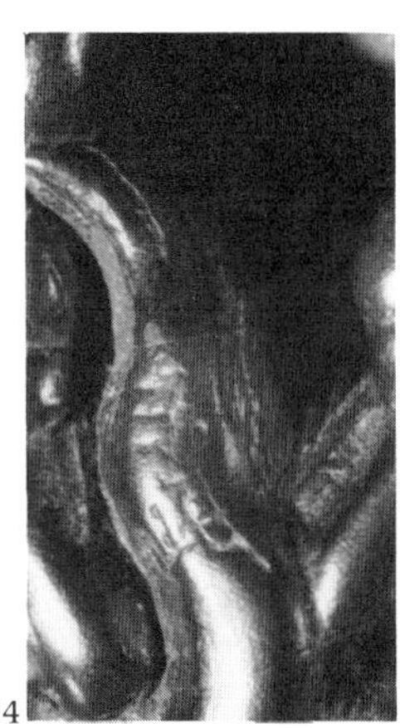

204

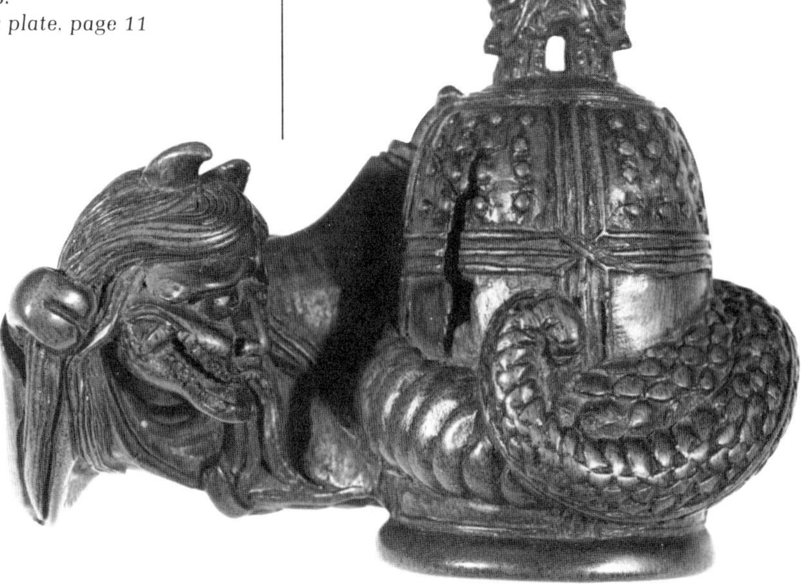

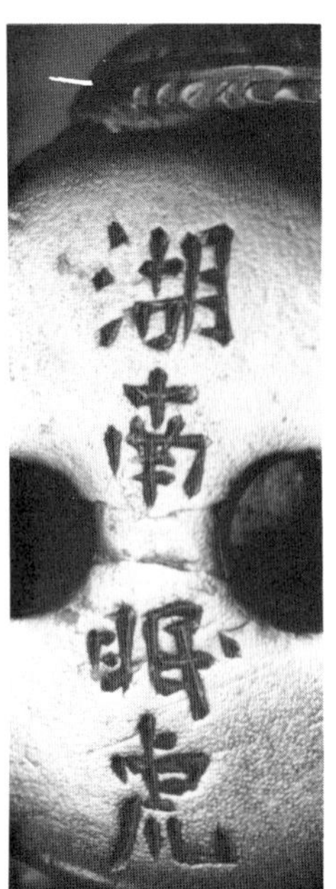

199

202
Goat.
Wood, the eyes inlaid and gilt.
Signed Minkō with *kakihan* in polished area on base.
Late 18th–early 19th century.
Length 4.5cm ($1\frac{3}{4}$in).
F.227. Franks Collection.

203
Badger beating its distended stomach.
Wood, the eyes inlaid.
Signed Kokei.
Late 18th century.
Height 3.25cm ($1\frac{1}{4}$in).
F.246. Franks Collection.

204
Wolf, eating a haunch of venison. Wood.
Signed Ranmin on the tail.
Late 18th century.
Length 3.25cm ($1\frac{1}{4}$in).
F.672. Franks Collection.

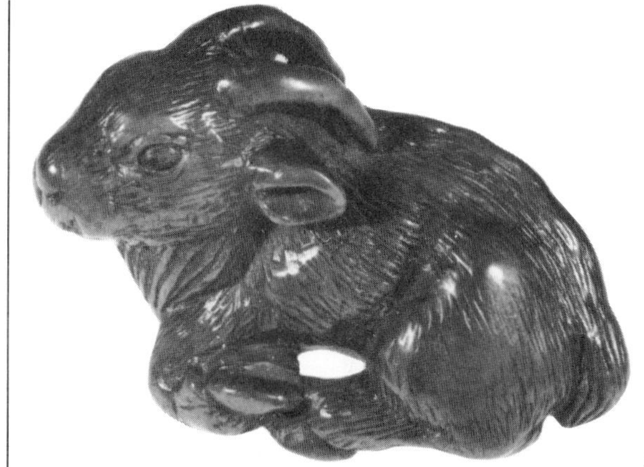

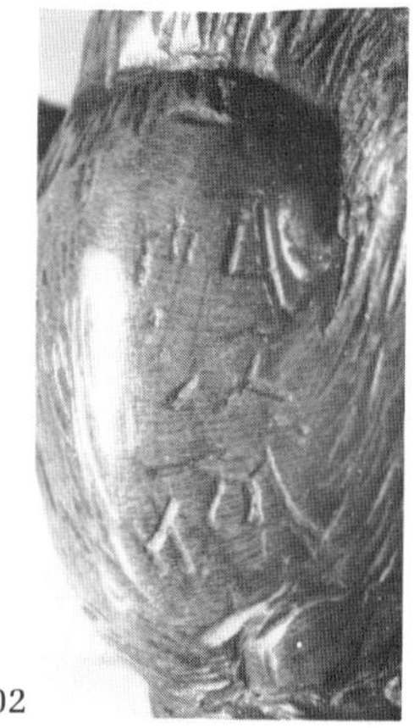

202

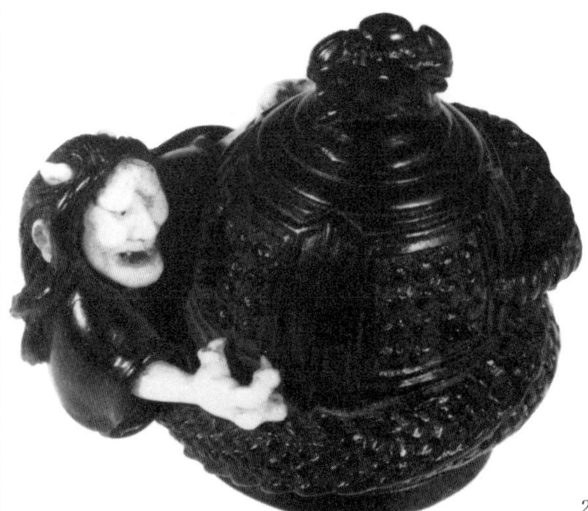

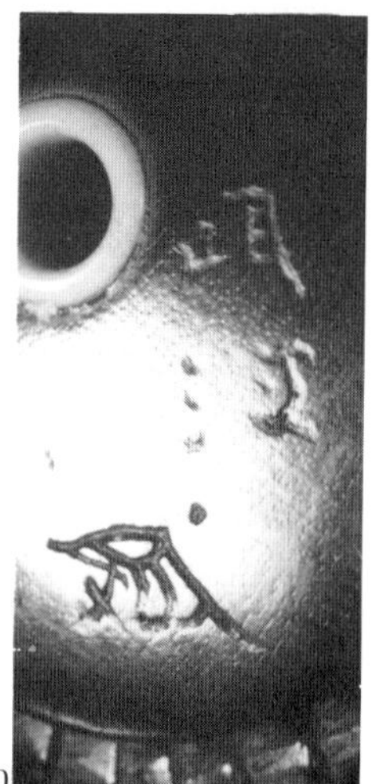

200

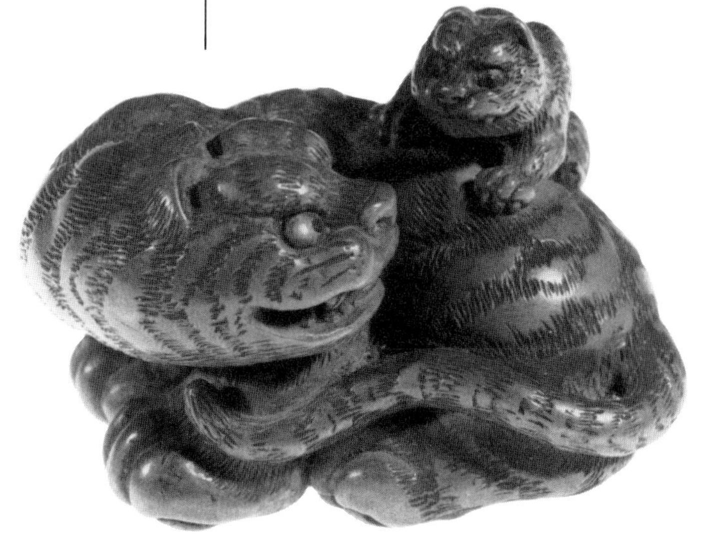

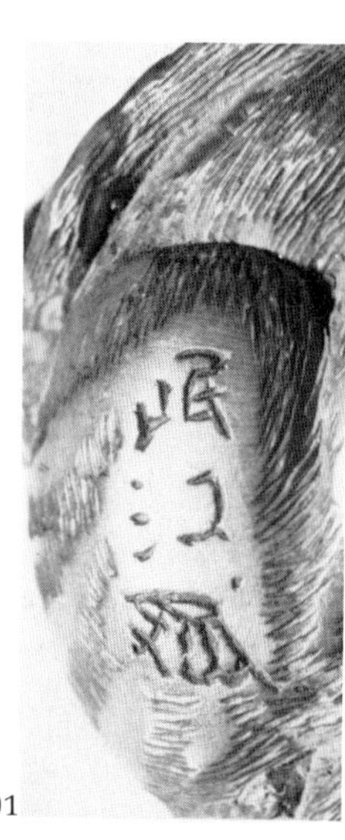

201

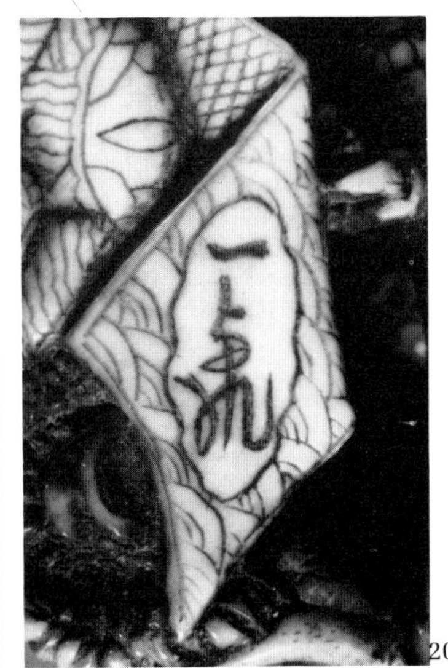
205

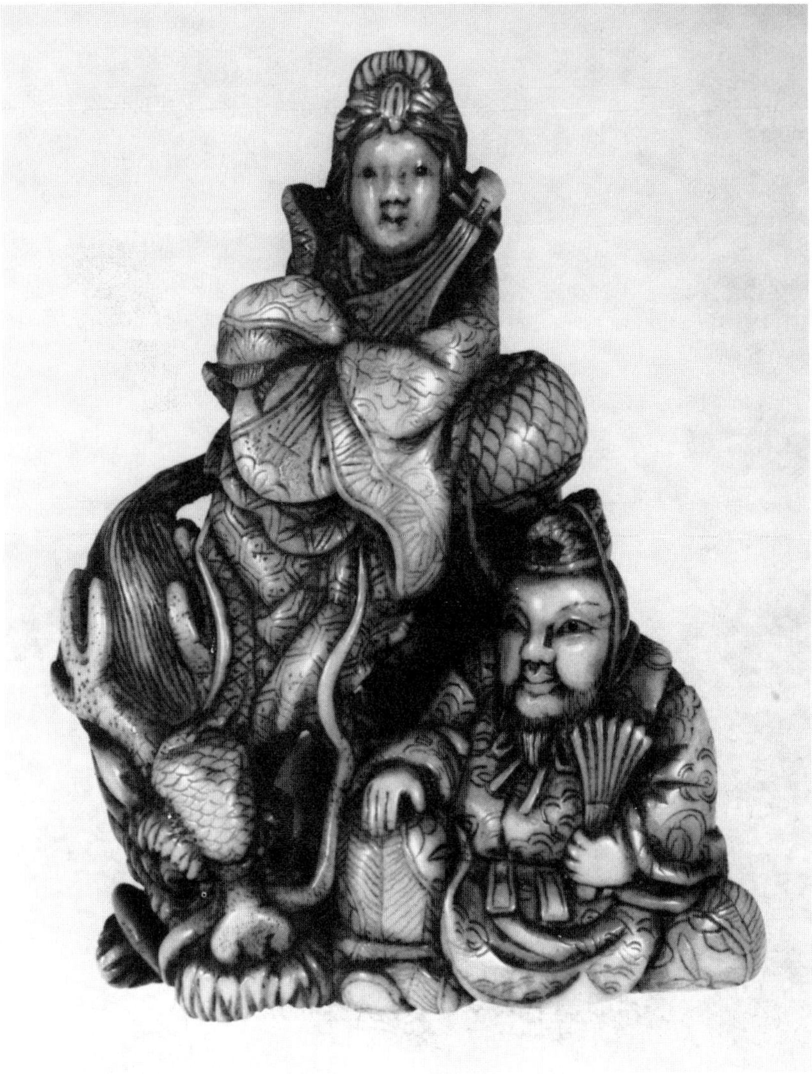

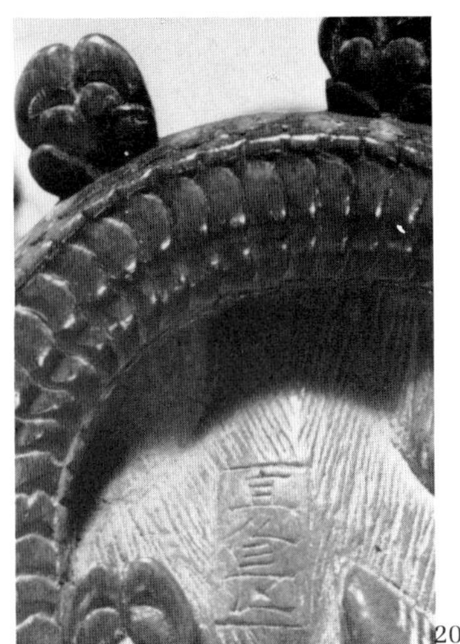
206

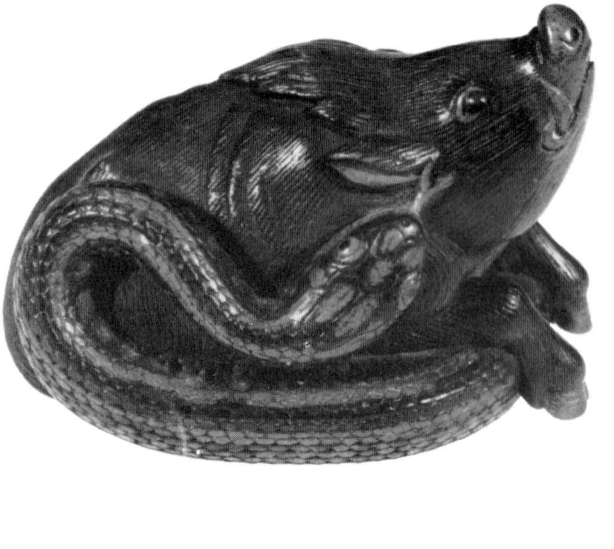

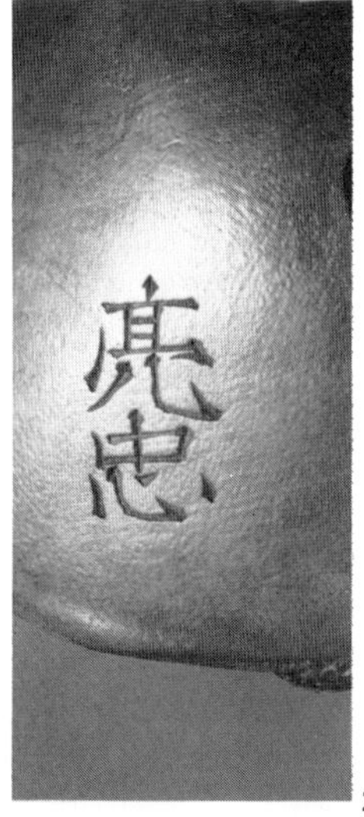

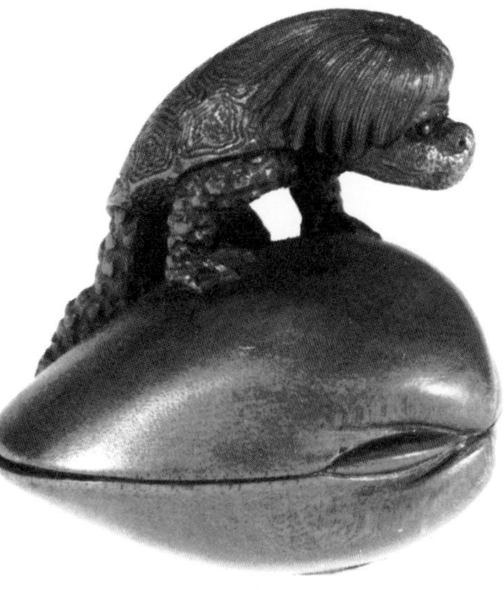

209

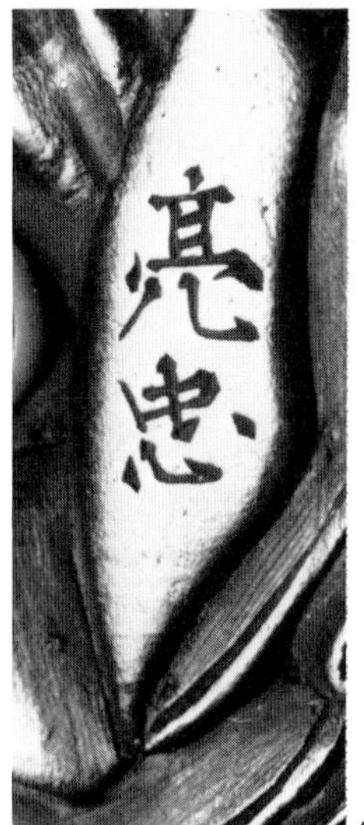

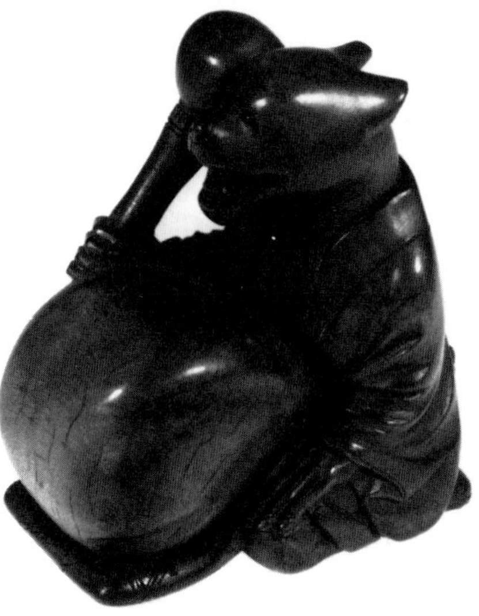

207

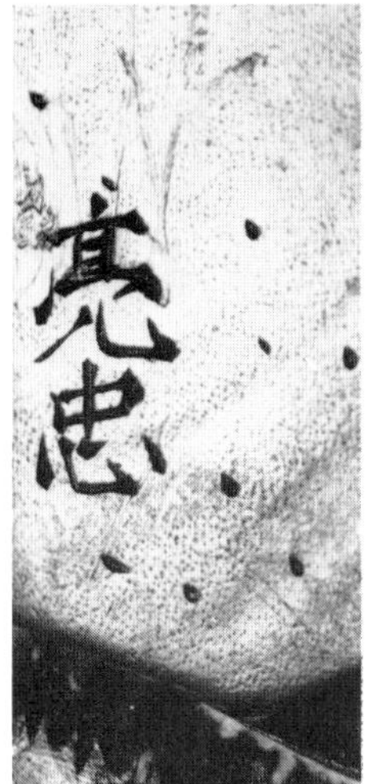

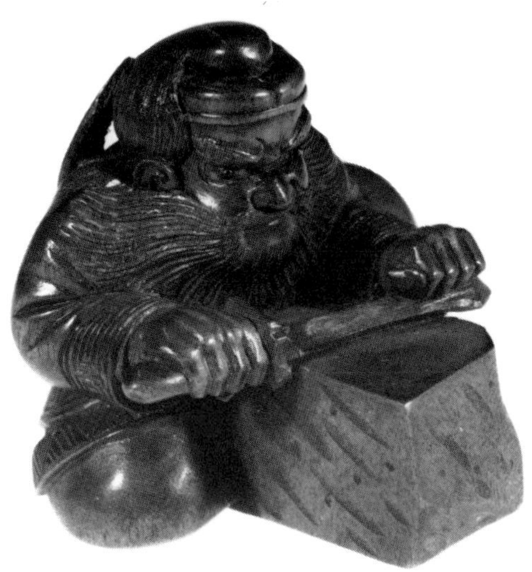

208

205
Tokimasa visiting the goddess Benten, seated on her dragon, to ask for the prosperity of his family. Ivory, the eyes inlaid.
Signed Ikko in an irregular cartouche on the base.
Late 18th–early 19th century.
Height 6.4cm ($2\frac{1}{2}$in).
1942 10-13 19. Bequeathed by Mrs Violet E. Becker.

Hida

206
Boar and snake.
Wood, the eyes inlaid.
Signed Sukenaga in a rectangular cartouche on the base.
19th century.
Length 3.75cm ($1\frac{1}{2}$in).
F.676. Franks Collection.
Colour plate, page 11

207
Badger dressed as priest, beating its distended stomach with a drum-stick.
Wood, the eyes inlaid.
Signed Suketada on base.
19th century.
Height 3.75cm ($1\frac{1}{2}$in).
F.492. Franks Collection.

208
Shoki the Demon Queller sharpening his sword on a stone.
Wood, the eyes inlaid, one cord-hole rimmed in stained ivory.
Signed Suketada on base.
19th century.
Length 3.75cm ($1\frac{1}{2}$in).
F.820. Franks Collection.

209
Kappa climbing over a clam, one hind foot caught in it.
Wood, the eyes inlaid, one cord-hole rimmed in ivory.
Signed Suketada on the base.
19th century.
Length 4.5cm ($1\frac{3}{4}$in).
F.754. Franks Collection.

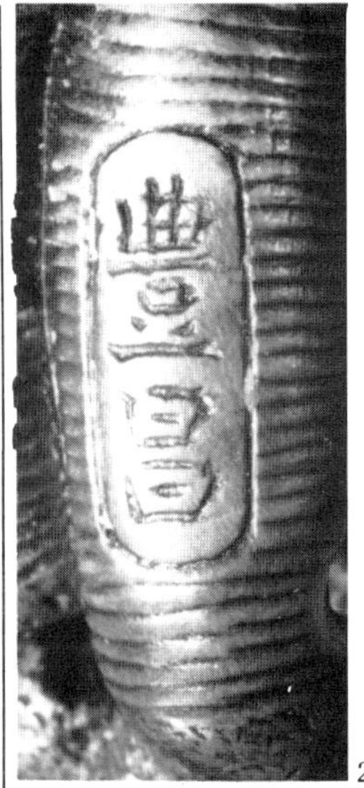

212

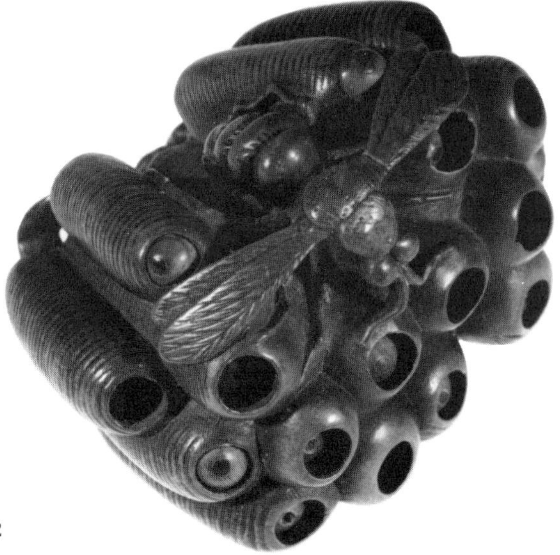

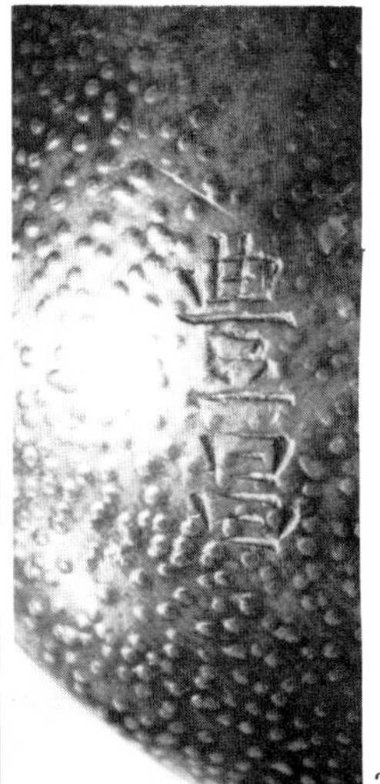

211

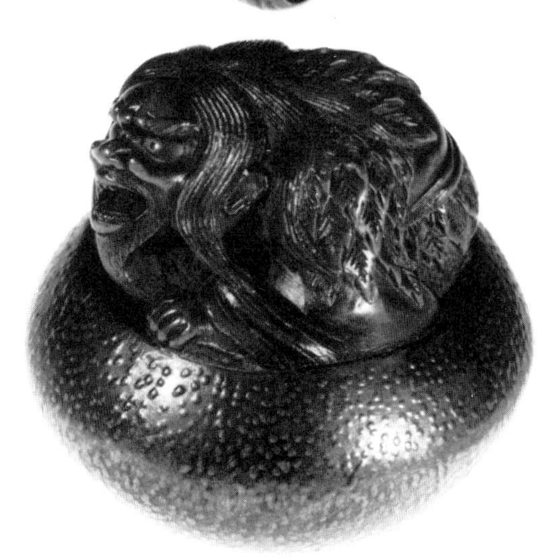

Tamba

210
Dragon emerging from an egg.
Wood, the eyes inlaid in horn.
Signed Hachijū-sai Toyomasa (Eighty-year-old Toyomasa) on the base.
Early 19th century.
Length 4.5cm ($1\frac{3}{4}$in).
F.1091. Franks Collection.

211
Kokō Sennin in the begging bowl in which he would spend the night.
Wood, the eyes inlaid in horn.
Signed Toyomasa on the base.
Early 19th century.
Height 4.25cm ($1\frac{3}{4}$in).
F.900. Franks Collection.

212
Wasp on a nest, the larvae free-moving. Wood.
Signed Toyomasa in an elongated oval cartouche on one cell.
Early 19th century.
Height 3.75cm ($1\frac{1}{2}$in).
F.1084. Franks Collection.

Exhibited Red Cross, London, 1915, no. 40. Illustrated in the catalogue, pl. XLVIII.

For an almost identical example *see* R. Bushell, *The Netsuke Handbook of Ueda Reikichi*, p. 91, pl. 86.
Colour plate, page 11

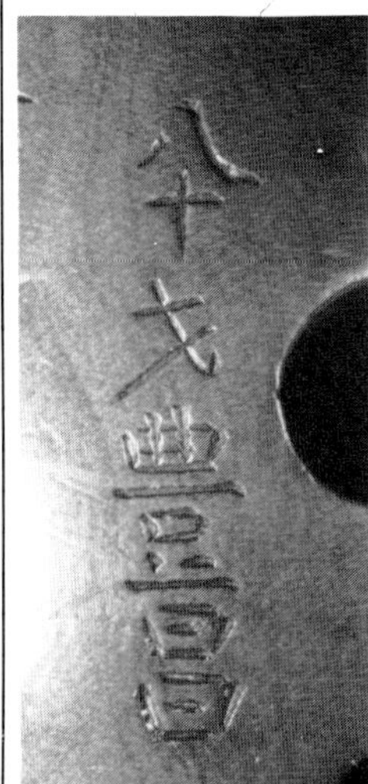

210

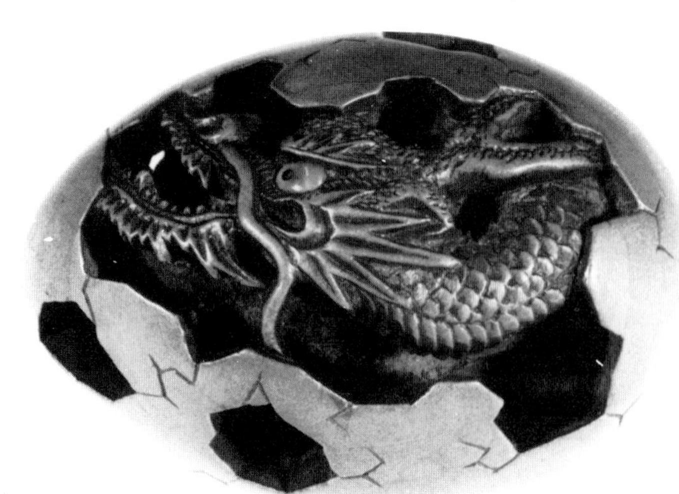

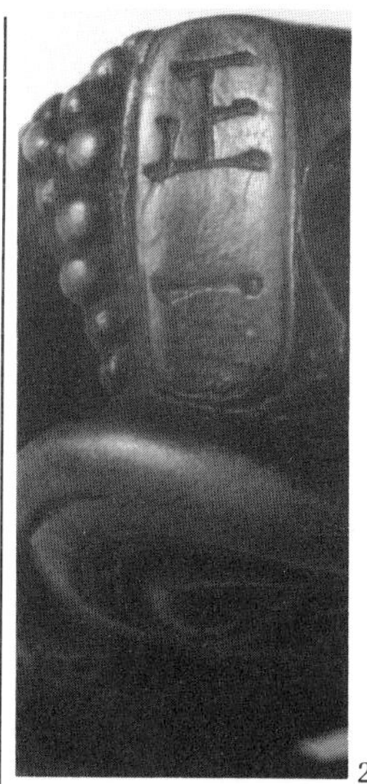

214

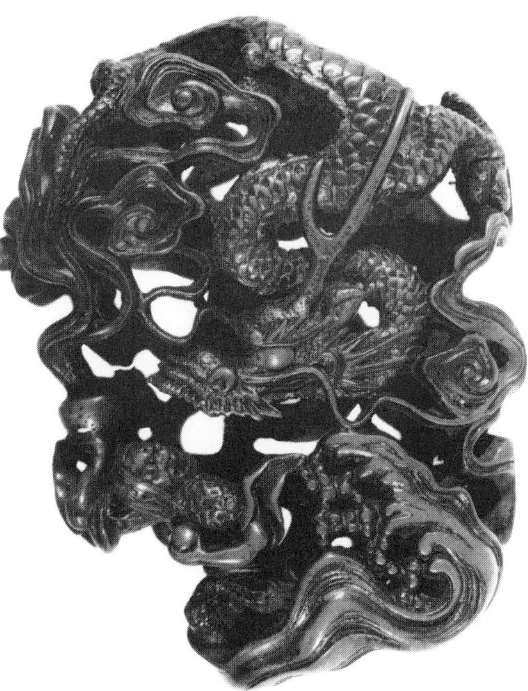

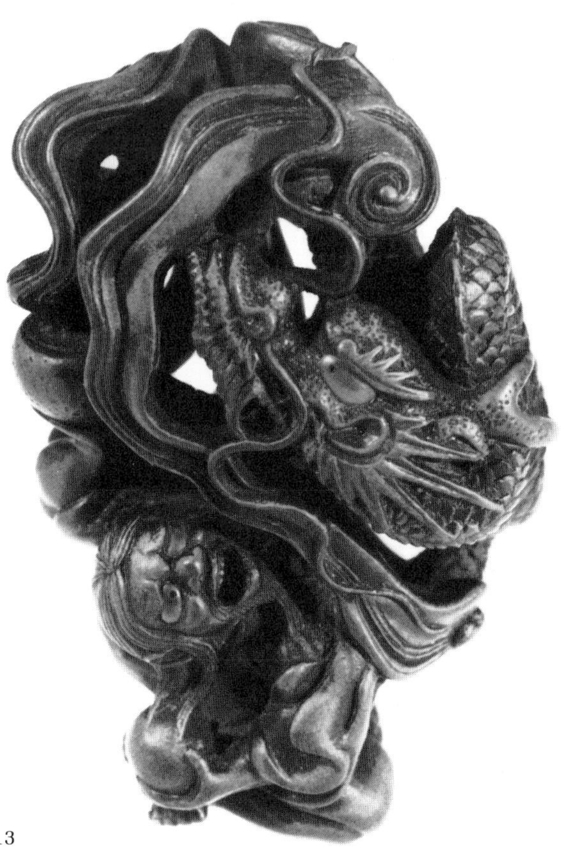

213

213
Handaka Sonja with a dragon among clouds issuing from his alms bowl.
Wood, the eyes inlaid in horn.
Signed Toyomasa on the base.
Early 19th century.
Height 5cm (2in).
1912 10-12 13. Given by Mrs H. Seymour Trower.

214
Handaka Sonja with a dragon issuing from his begging bowl.
Wood, the eyes inlaid in horn.
Signed Masakazu in an elongated oval cartouche on the base.
Early 19th century.
Height 5.1cm (2in).
F.54. Franks Collection.

The signature on this piece was probably added at a later date.

215
Boar tusk, carved in relief with a squirrel among grape vines, the squirrel's eyes inlaid.
Unsigned.
Late 18th century.
Length 7cm (2¾in).
F.258. Franks Collection.
Colour plate, page 24

216
Frog on a folded lotus leaf.
Wood.
Unsigned, style of Mitani Gohō
Late 18th century.
Length 8.1cm (3¼in).
F.801. Franks Collection.

217
Mushrooms with ants crawling through holes.
Bamboo, ebony and horn. Ants in various metals, including oxidized pewter.
Inscribed Ōjū Tō ('carved to order') and with *kakihan* of Gambun on the base.
19th century.
Width 3.75cm (1½in).
1945 10-17 669. Bequeathed by Oscar Raphael.
Exhibited Red Cross, London, 1915, no. 182, pl. XLVIII.

218
Pod with two free-moving beans inside, several ants crawling over it.
Umimatsu (sea-pine), ants in metal, ivory on beans.
Unsigned, style of Gambun.
19th century.
Length 10.75cm (4¼in).
1945 10-17 662. Bequeathed by Oscar Raphael.

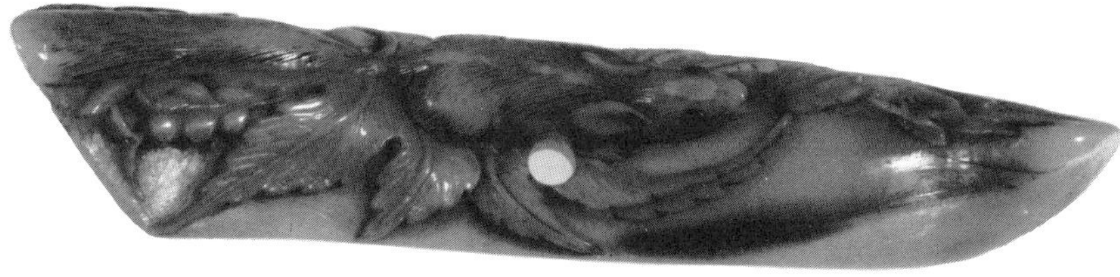
215

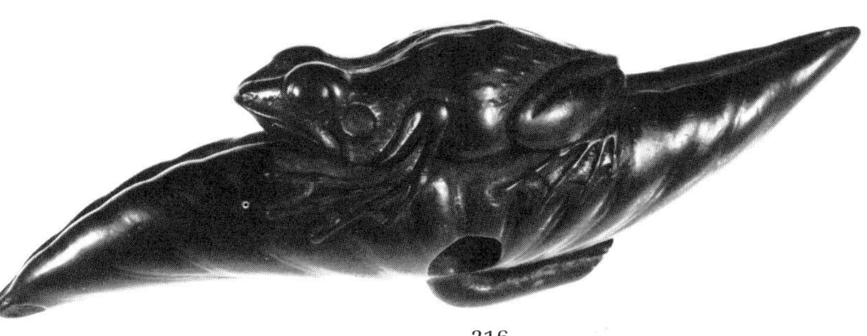
216

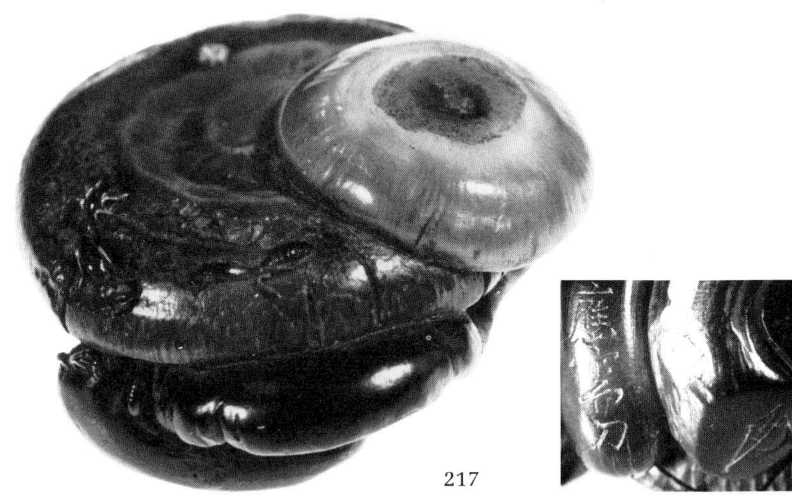
217

218
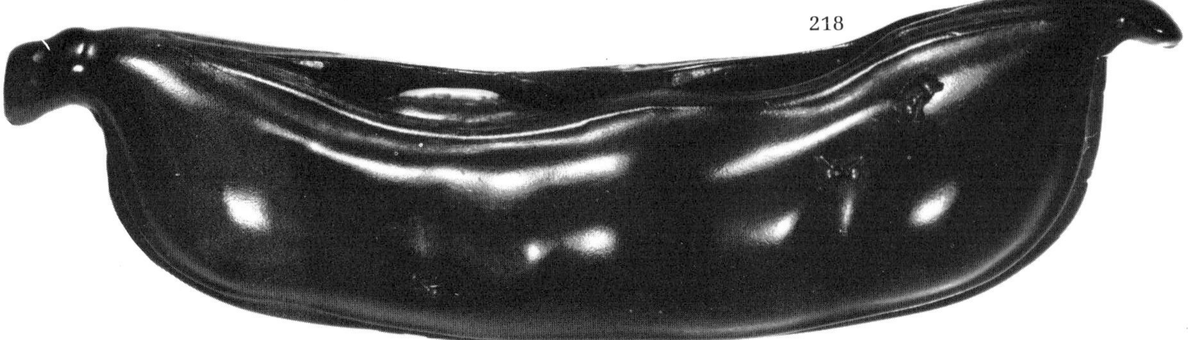

Hakata

219
Boy playing a flute while riding on the back of an ox, the whole set on an oval base. Ivory, the eyes inlaid.
Signed Otoman on the base.
19th century.
Height 3.25cm ($1\frac{1}{4}$in).
F.663. Franks Collection.

The boy on his ox is a common symbol in the teaching of Zen Buddhism.

Kaga

220
Snail. Ivory.
Signed on the underside Kashū Komatsu Jū ('living in Komatsu in Kaga Province'), on a rectangular cartouche, and Tameoto in a hexagonal cartouche with a *kakihan*.
Late 18th century.
Width 3.75cm ($1\frac{1}{2}$in).
F.1156. Franks Collection.

Echizen

221
Rectangular *manjū*, carved in sunk relief with a *kappa* holding a cucumber on wave ground. Ivory.
Signed Setsusai (Sessai) on the back.
Late 19th century.
Length 4.4cm ($1\frac{3}{4}$in).
F.1256. Franks Collection.

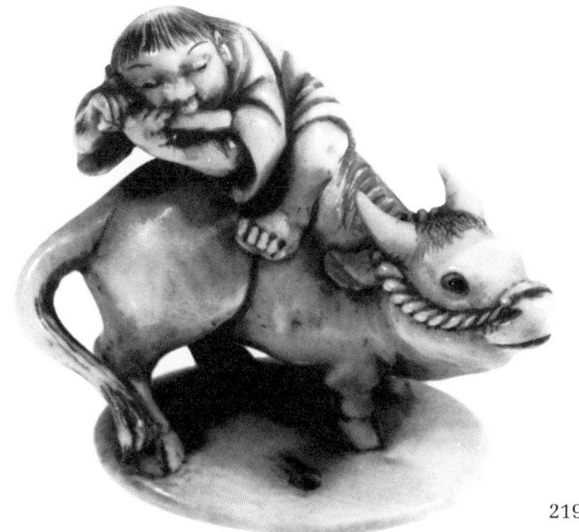
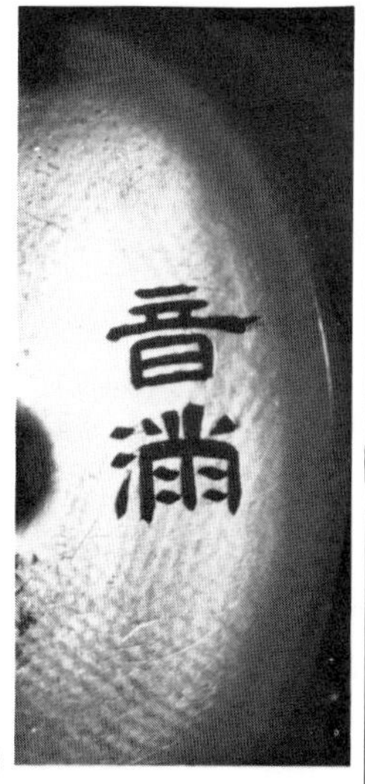

219

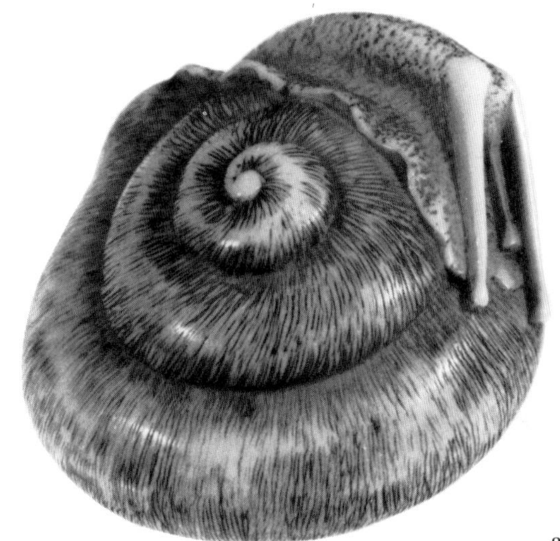
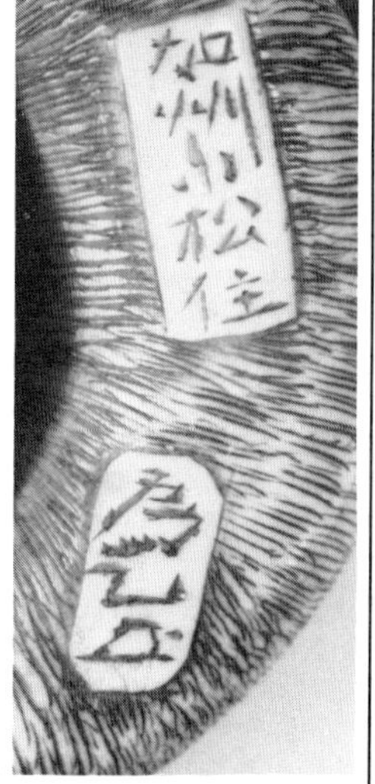

220

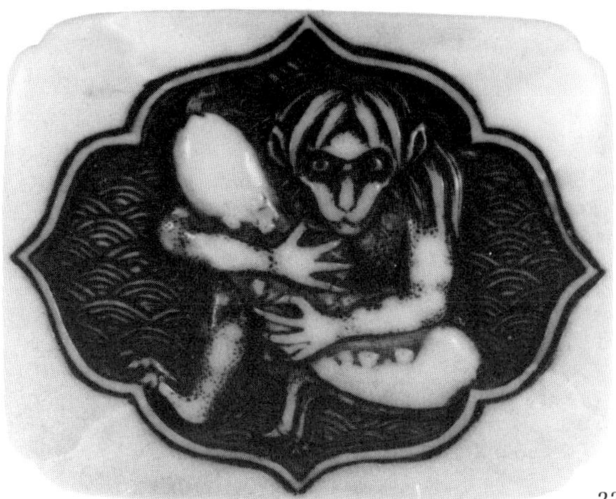
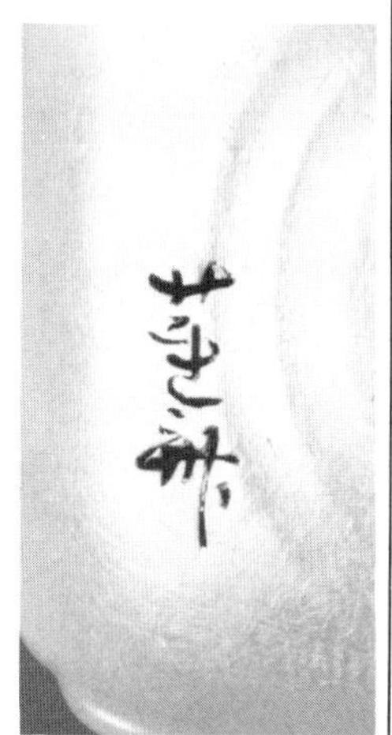
221

Wakayama

222
A *rōnin* (masterless samurai), crouching in ambush, his sword half drawn. Wood.
Unsigned, attributable to Ogasawara Issai.
18th century.
Length 5.4cm (2in).
1945 10-17 643. Bequeathed by Oscar Raphael.

For a similar example in whaletooth, *see* R. Bushell, *The Netsuke Handbook of Ueda Reikichi*, p. 88, no. 80.

223
Mermaid holding a sacred jewel. Ivory.
Signed Natsuki in an elongated oval cartouche on the base.
19th century.
Length 3.75cm ($1\frac{1}{2}$in).

For a similar example by Issai, *see* N. K. Davey, *Netsuke*, p. 268, no. 823.

224
Mermaid with her child, holding a bowl with a free-moving ball in it. Ivory.
Unsigned, probably school of Ogasawara Issai.
Late 18th century.
Length 5.1cm (2in).
F.760. Franks Collection.

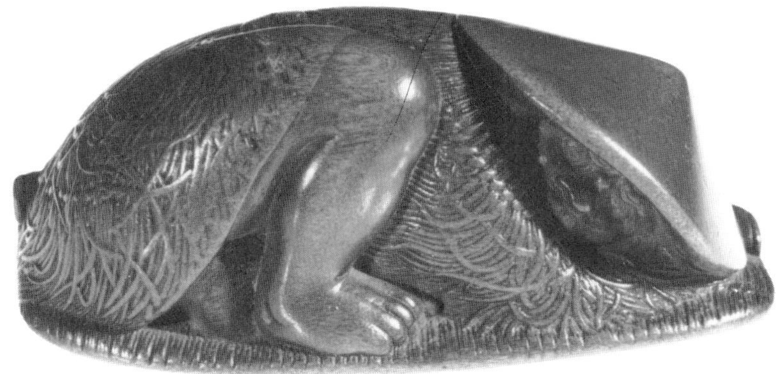

222

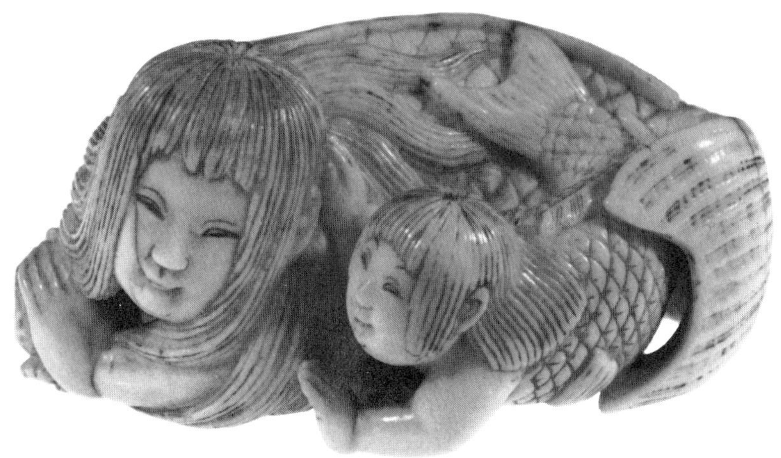

224

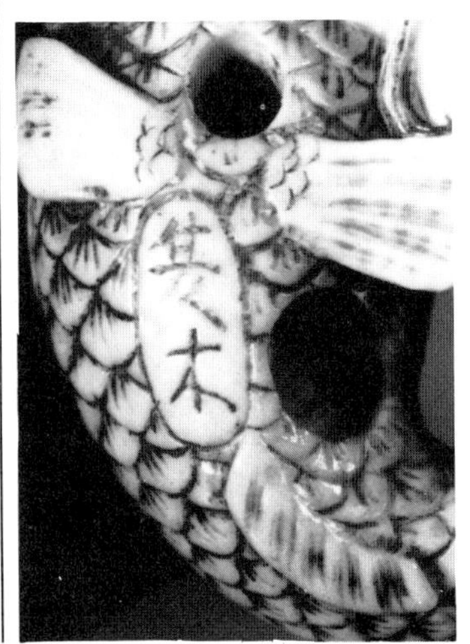

223

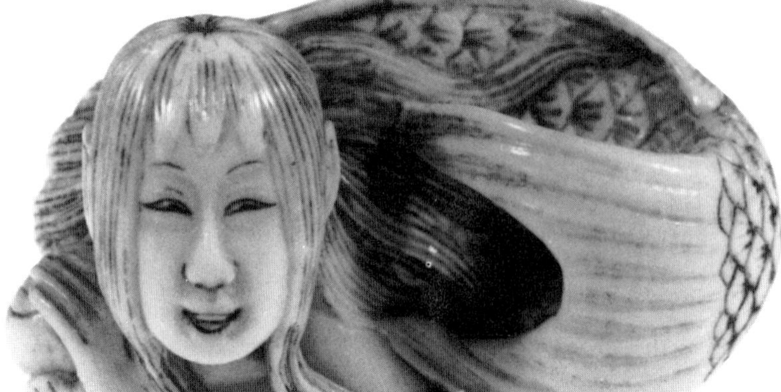

Iwashiro

225
Rat holding a bean-pod.
Wood, the eyes inlaid.
Signed Sari in an irregular cartouche under the pod.
Late 18th century.
Length 4.2cm ($1\frac{3}{4}$in).
F.257. Franks Collection.

226
Urashima on a giant tortoise.
Wood.
Signed Hidari Issan on the base.
Early 19th century.
Length 5.5cm (2in).
F.601. Franks Collection.
Urashima travelled to the realm of the dragon-king on a sacred tortoise.

227
Snail emerging from its shell.
Wood.
Signed Hidari Issan with *kakihan* read Uma on the base.
Early 19th century.
Length 3.75cm ($1\frac{1}{2}$in).
1953 12-17 16. Bequeathed by Mrs Helen Epstein.

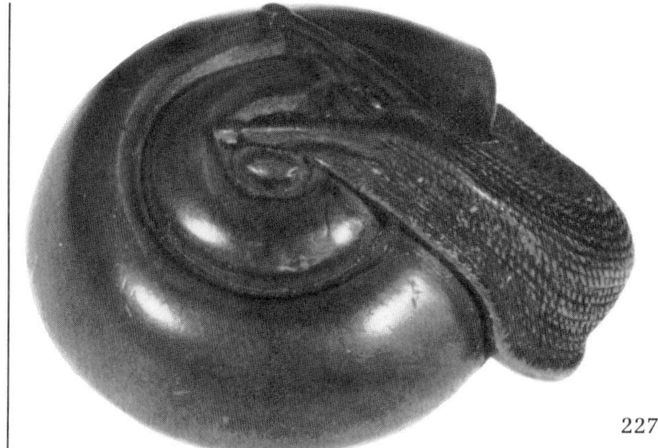
227
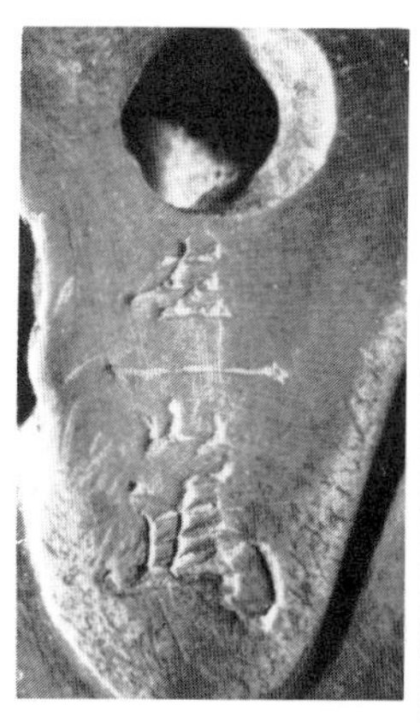

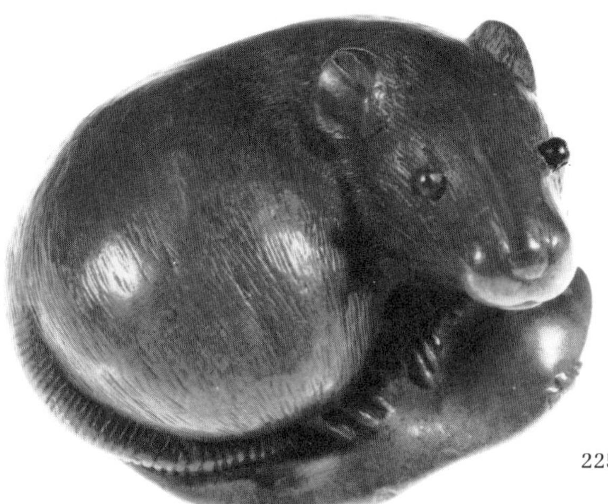
225
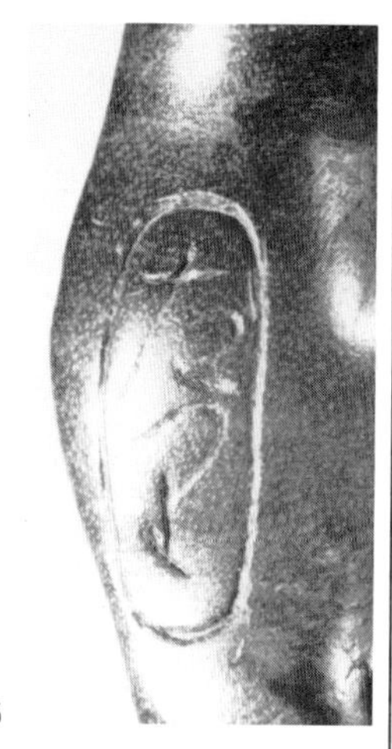

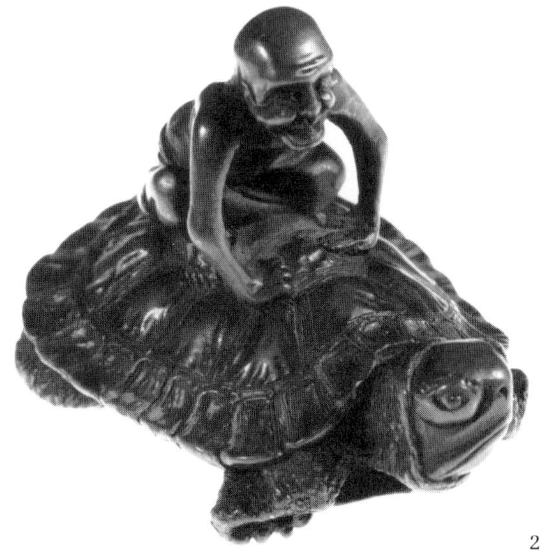
226
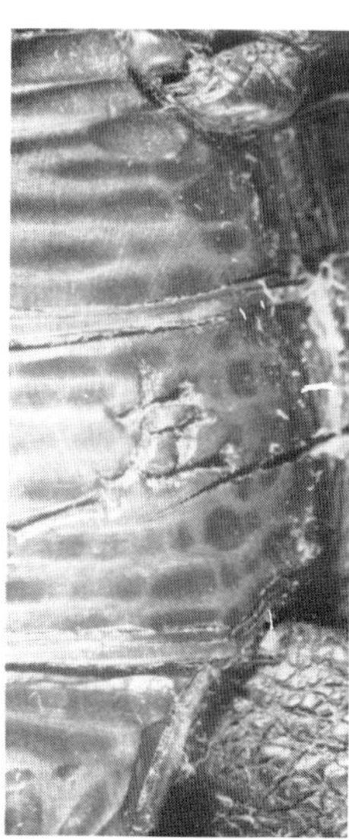

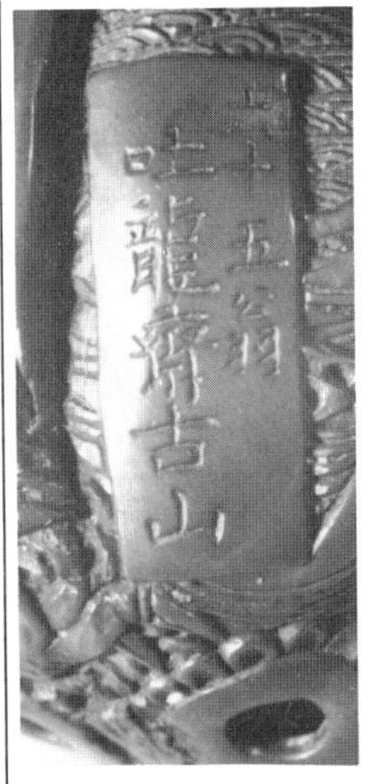

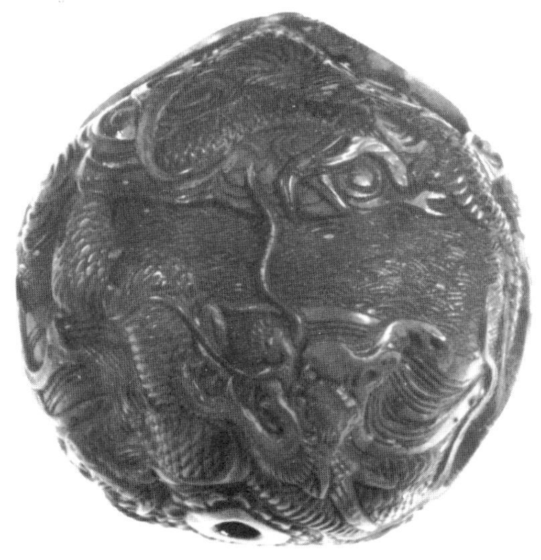

228

228
A natural nut carved in relief with a dragon.
Applied metal studs.
Signed Rokujū-go Ō Toryūsai Kozan ('the 65-year old man Toryūsai Kozan') on a rectangular cartouche.
19th century.
Length 3.1cm (1¼in).
F.535. Franks Collection.

Izumi

229
Manjū engraved with the names of the Tōkaidō and Kisokaidō posting-stations, and accounts of their distances. Ivory.
Signed Nanka Tō.
19th century.
Diameter 3.4cm (1¼in).
1945 10-17 654. Bequeathed by Oscar Raphael.

The Tōkaidō and Kisokaidō were the coastal and inland routes between Tokyo and Kyoto. The posting-stations along them (53 and 69 respectively), formed the subjects for prints, paintings, and lacquer, as well as netsuke.

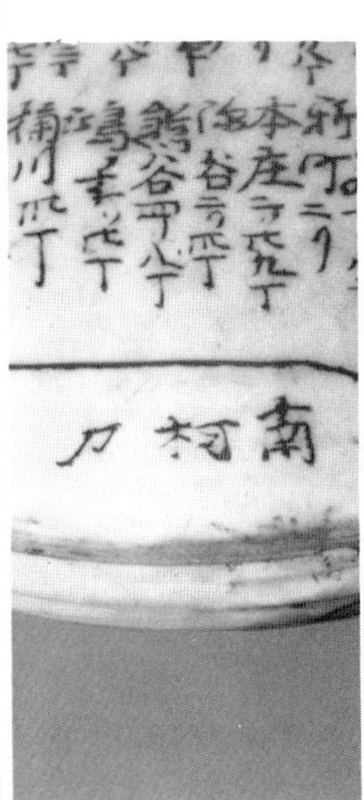

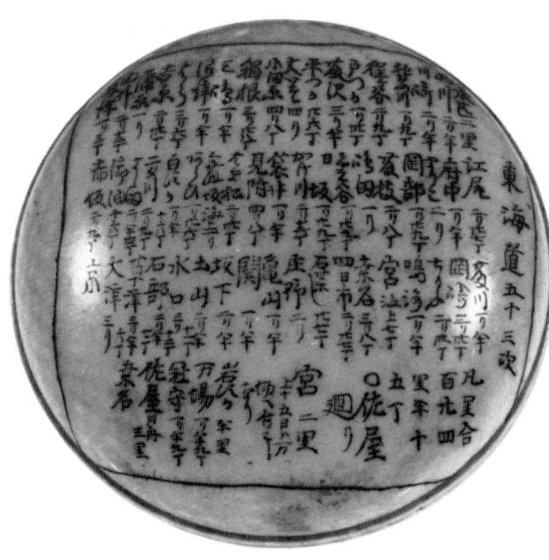

229

Artists of Unknown Origin

230
Kanyū stroking his beard. Ivory.
Signed Atokama in seal-script at base of robe.
Late 18th century.
Height 8cm (3in).
1912 10-12 16. Given by Mrs H. Seymour Trower.

For a similar example, *see* N. K. Davey, *Netsuke*, p. 284, no. 863.
Colour plate, page 13

231
Kanyū stroking his beard. Wood.
Signed Atokama in seal-script at base of robe.
Late 18th century.
Height 7.6cm (3in).
F.691. Franks Collection.

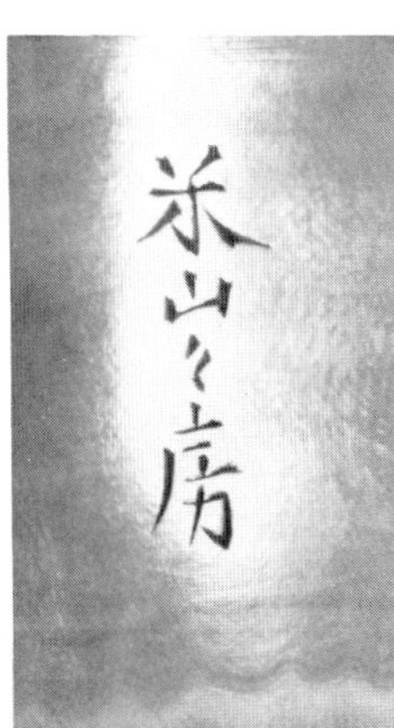

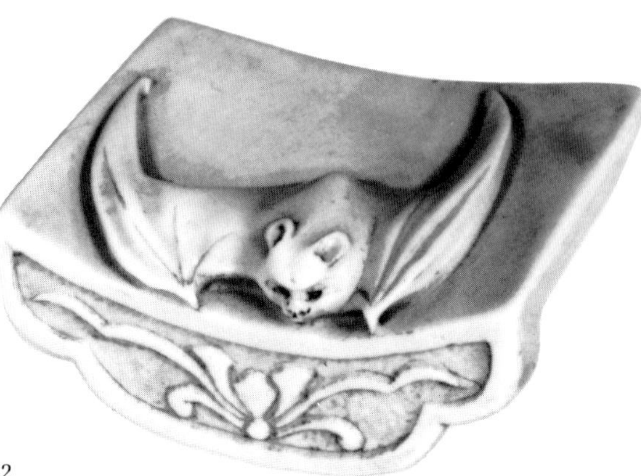

232

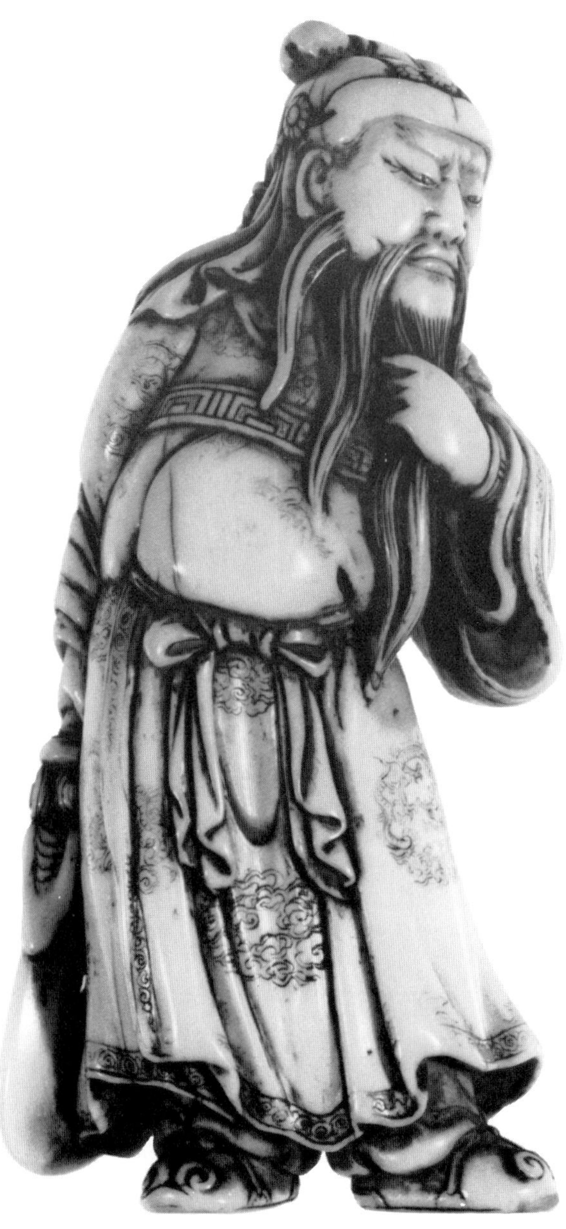

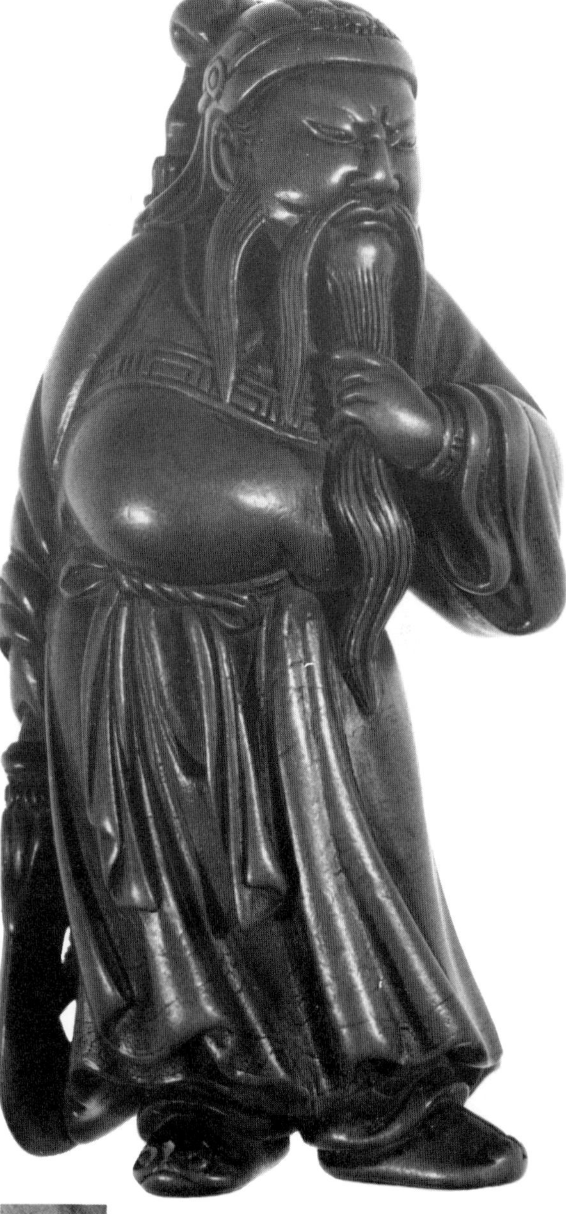

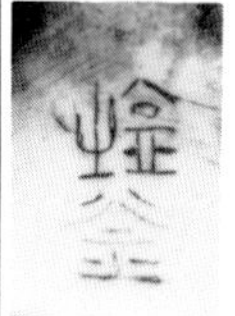

230

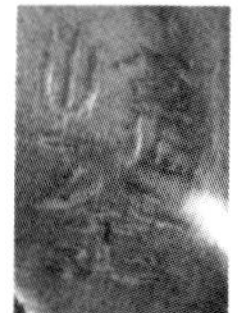

231

232
Bat resting on the end of a roof tile. Ivory.
Signed Beizan Sanbō on the back.
19th century.
Length 3.25cm ($1\frac{1}{4}$in).
F.1067. Franks Collection.

233
Okame.
Wood, ivory face.
Signed Hidemasa on back.
Early 19th century.
Height 13.25cm (5¼in).
F.602. Franks Collection.

234
Troop of monkeys in and around a spreading pine tree. Wood.
Signed Hidemasa in an elongated oval cartouche on the base.
19th century.
Length 5.1cm (2in).
1945 10-17 667. Bequeathed by Oscar Raphael.
Ex W. L. Behrens collection, no. 1614, illustrated in the catalogue, pl. XXIX.

235
Seated figure of a priest and boy with the tea kettle that turned into a badger. Ivory.
Signed Hirotada on base.
19th century.
Height 3.75cm (1½in).
F.1019. Franks Collection.

236
Handaka Sonja holding aloft his begging-bowl from which issues a one-horned dragon. Wood.
Signed Yoshinaga under one foot.
18th century.
Height 8.25cm (3¼in).
1945 10-17 585. Bequeathed by Oscar Raphael.

237
Fisherman struggling with an octopus. Wood.
Signed Hōen on a rectangular cartouche on the base.
19th century.
Height 3.75cm (1½in).
F.175. Franks Collection.

238
Cockerel, hen and chick, Ivory.
Signed Ichijō Saku in an irregular cartouche on the back.
Late 18th century.
Length 6.4cm (2½in).
F.262. Franks Collection.

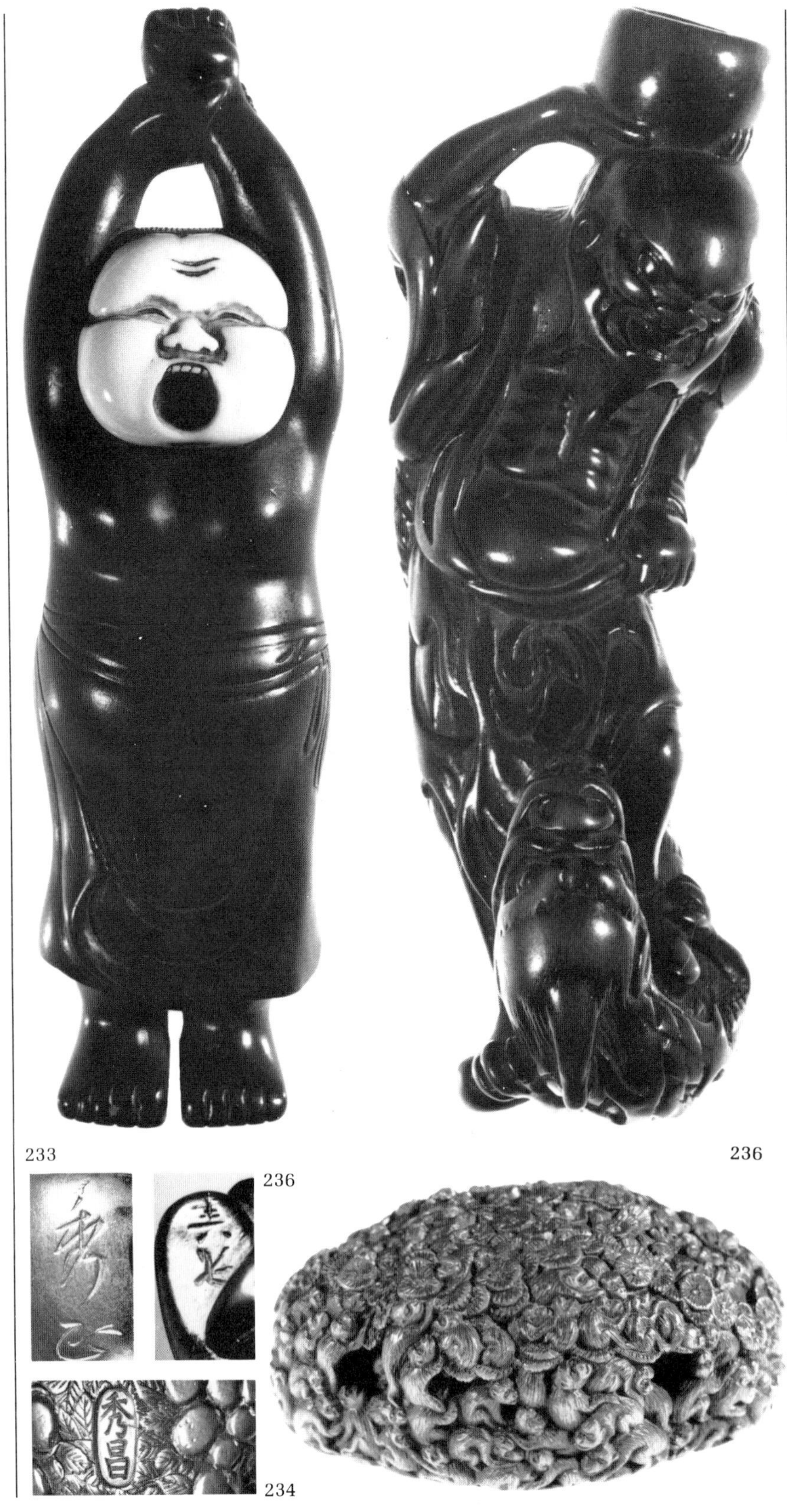
233 236 236 234

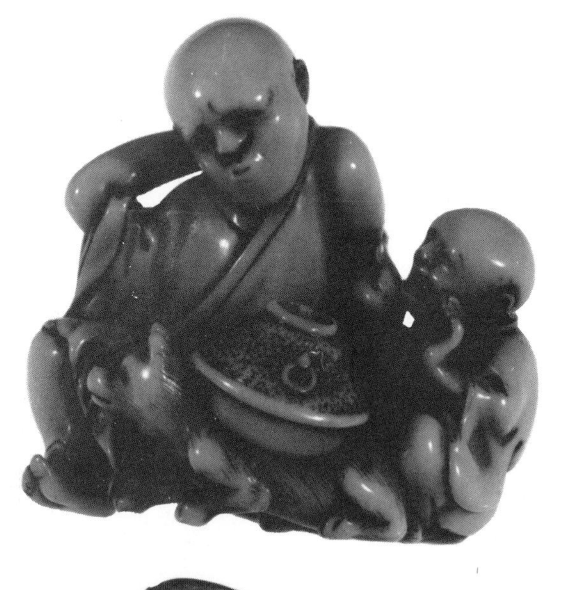

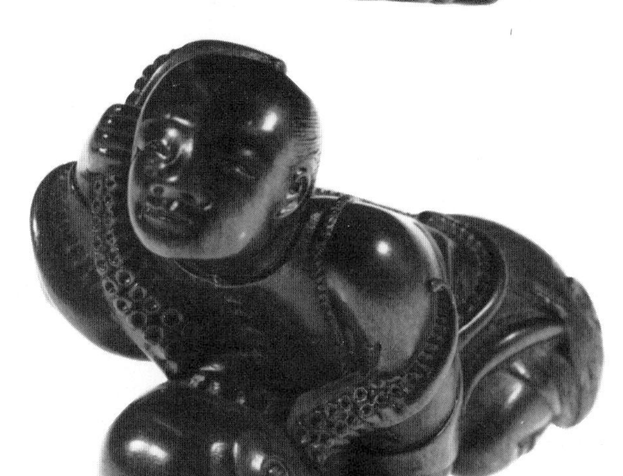

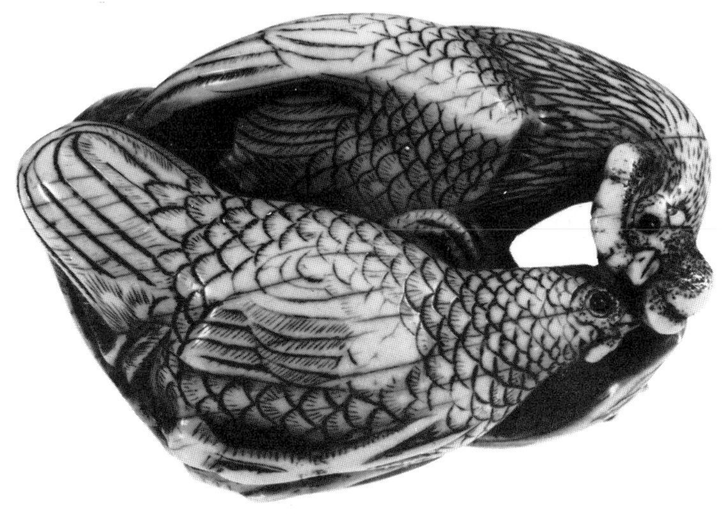

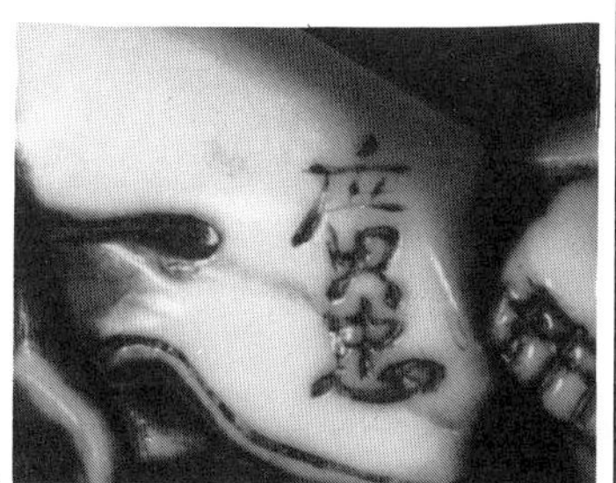

235

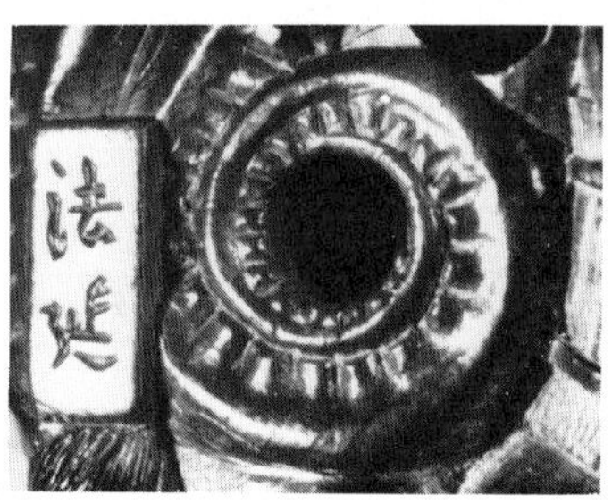

237

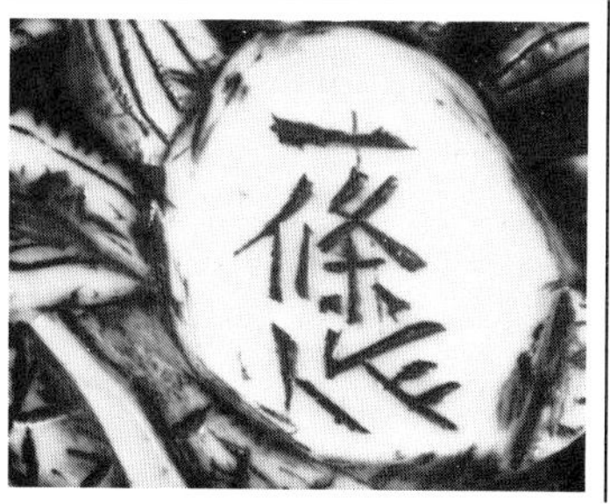

238

239
Seated *Kappa*.
Wood, the eyes inlaid.
Signed Kitamasa or Hokushō in seal-script on the back.
Late 18th century.
Height 5.1cm (2in).
F.747. Franks Collection.

240
The popular god Ebisu on his carp in the river, handing his mallet to Daikoku, who is crossing the bridge on a rat.
Ivory.
Signed Masatami or Seimin with *kakihan* on the base.
19th century.
Height 3.5cm ($1\frac{1}{2}$in).
F.726. Franks Collection.

The subject is a parody of the story of the Chinese general Chōryō, who rescued the shoe of an old traveller from the river.

241
Group of the Twelve Animals of the Zodiac.
Wood, the eyes inlaid.
Signed Masatoshi in a rectangular cartouche on the base.
19th century.
Length 3.75cm ($1\frac{1}{2}$in).
1945 10-17 652. Bequeathed by Oscar Raphael.

242
Manjū carved in relief with a view of Lake Konmei (in China).
Ivory.
Signed on the back (a) Hokkyō Okada Gyokuzan Naotomo Zenga ('Complete drawing by the *Hokkyō* [a Buddhist rank] Okada Gyokuzan Naotomo') with seals Gyoku and San
(b) Konmei-ko (Lake Konmei)
(c) Matsumoto Chikuga Masakichi Saikoku ('Finely carved by Matsumoto Chikuga Masakichi') with seals Chiku and Ga.
19th century.
Diameter 4.8cm (2in).
F.1230. Franks Collection.

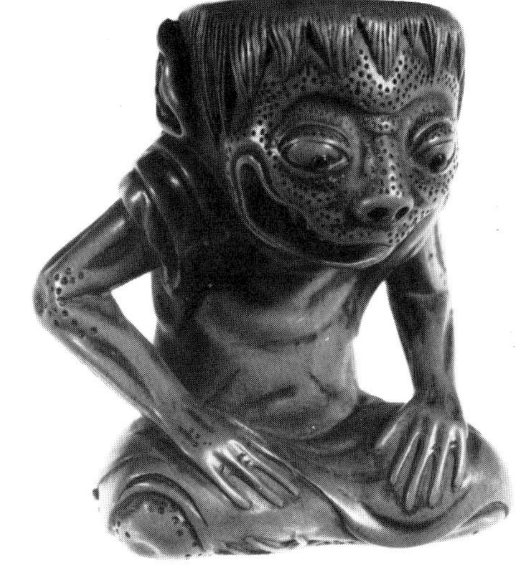

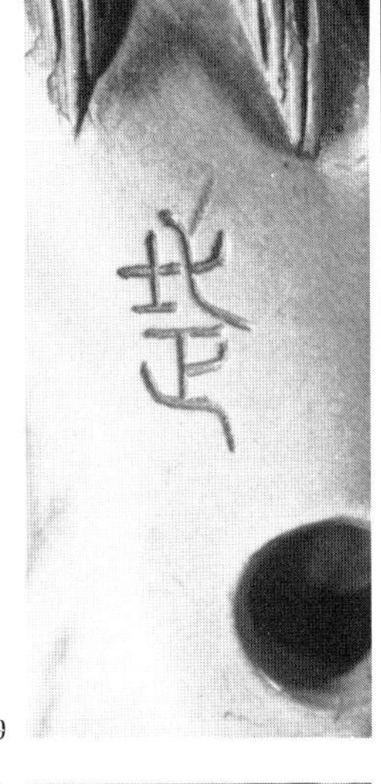

239

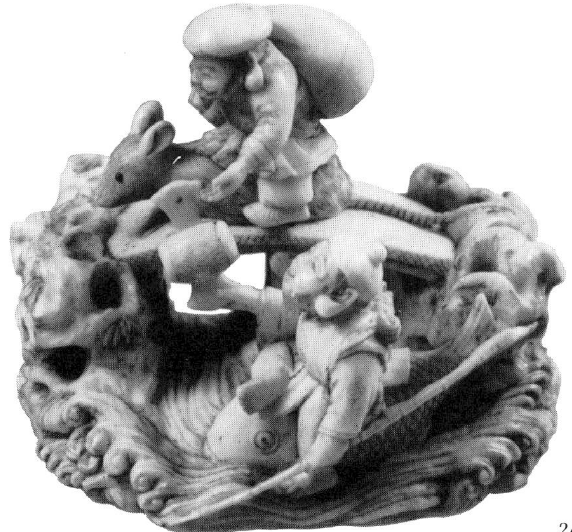

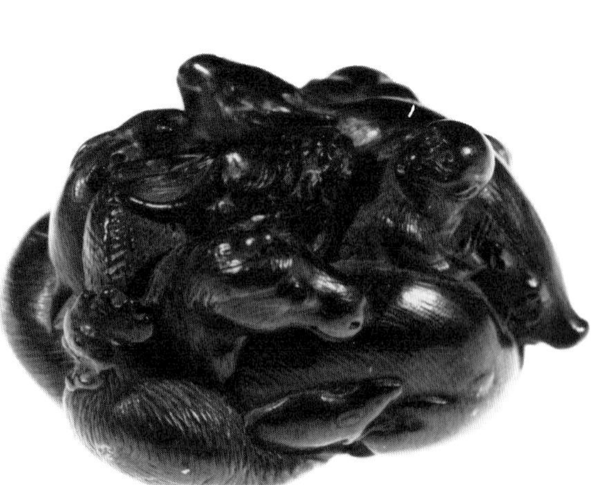

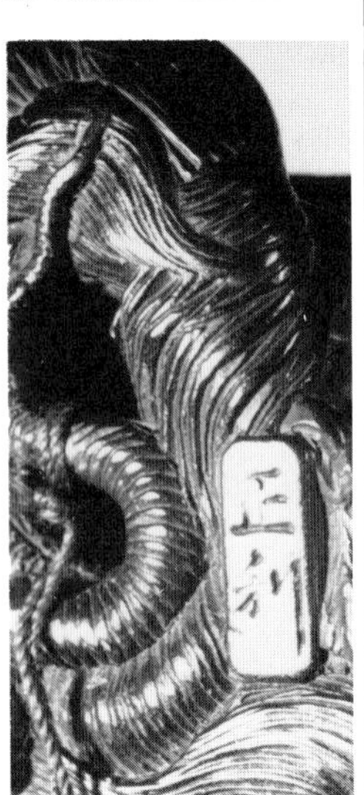

240

241

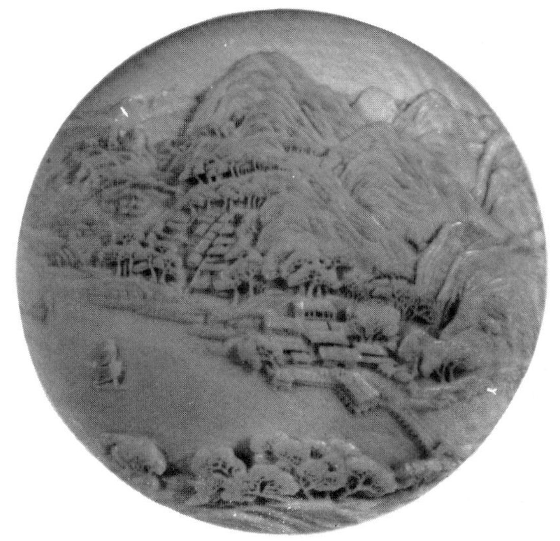

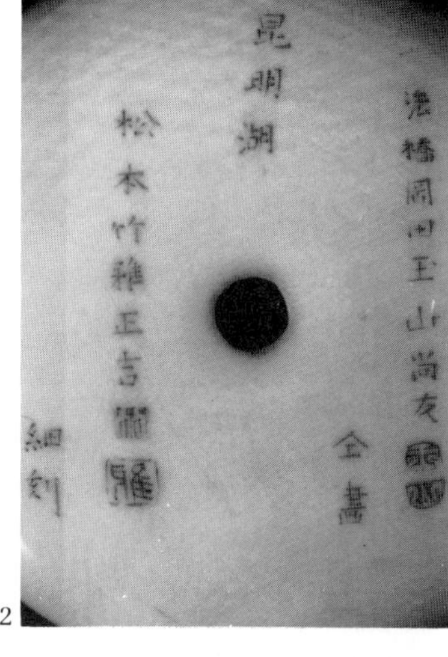

242

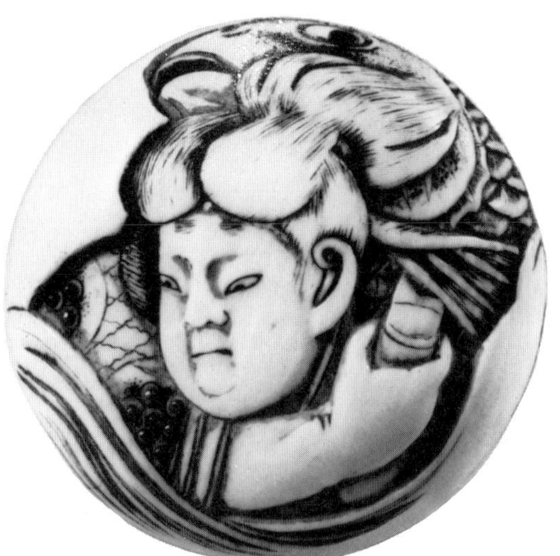

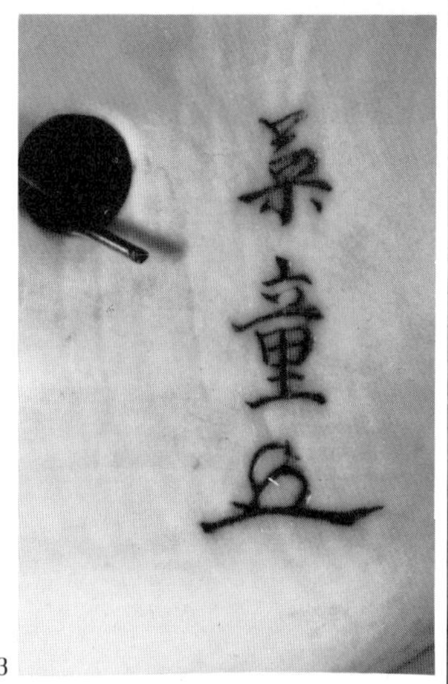

243

243
Manjū carved in low relief with the young Benkei wrestling with the giant carp.
Ivory, the carp's mouth stained.
Metal studs.
Signed Randō with *kakihan* on the back.
19th century.
Diameter 4.25cm ($1\frac{3}{4}$in).
F.409. Franks Collection.

244
Two dragons pursuing the flaming jewel. Ivory.
Signed Seikanshi with *kakihan* on base.
19th century.
Width 4.5cm ($1\frac{3}{4}$in).
OA + 24.

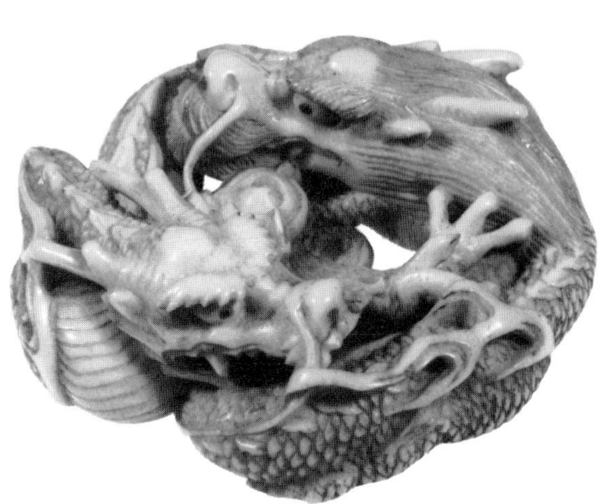

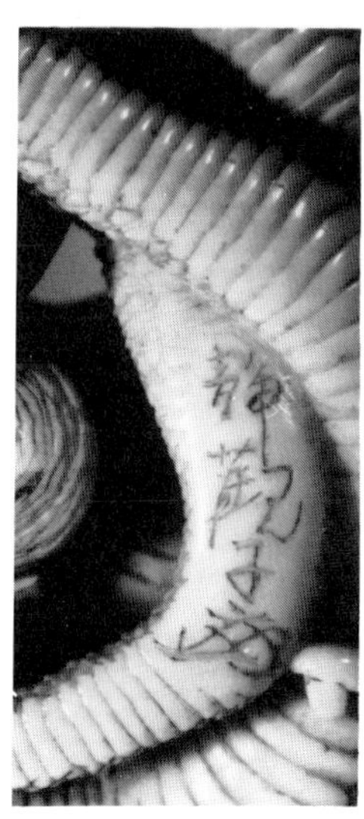

244

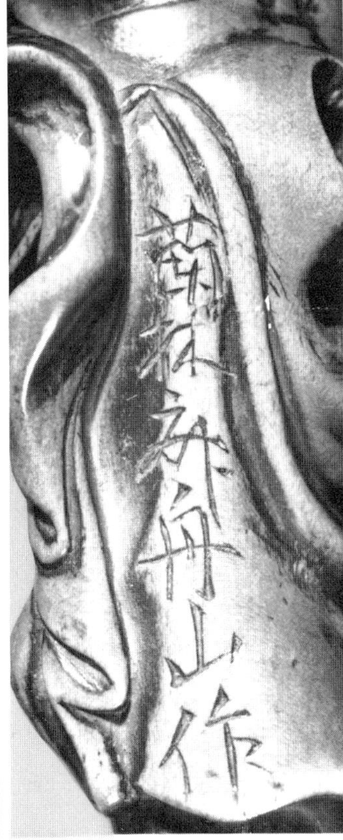

249

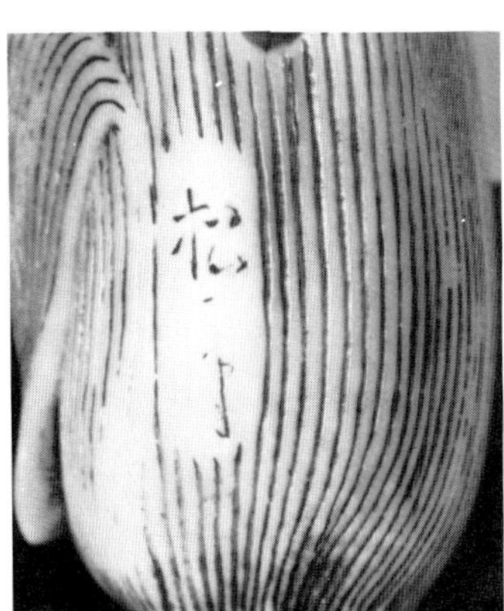

246

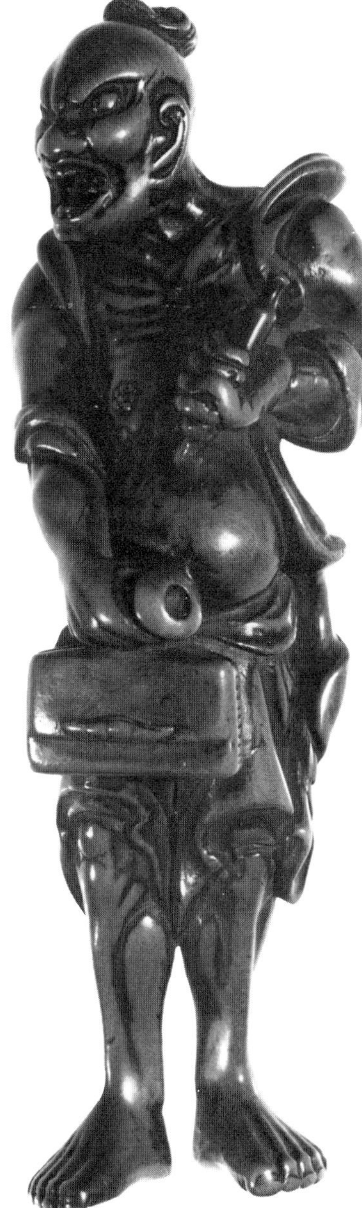

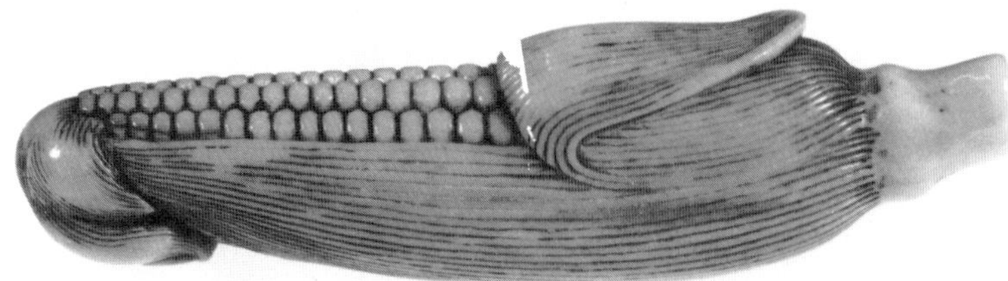

245
Manjū with applied figures of the popular gods Daikoku and Ebisu as Manzai dancers.
Ivory, applied stained ivory, mother-of-pearl and lacquer.
Signed Shibayama Saku ('made by Shibayama') in an ornate mother-of-pearl cartouche on the back.
19th century.
Diameter 3.2cm ($1\frac{1}{4}$in).
F.1066. Franks Collection.

246
Corn cob. Ivory.
Signed Shōgetsu in an irregular cartouche on the side.
19th century.
Length 6.4cm ($2\frac{1}{2}$in).
F.1106. Franks Collection.

247
Coiled dragon, holding the sacred jewel in its claw. Wood.
Signed Shōtō in an inlaid ivory cartouche on the base.
19th century.
Width 3.5cm ($1\frac{1}{4}$in).
F.296. Franks Collection.

248
The severed head of Nitta no Yoshisada.
Wood, the blood in red lacquer.
Signed Ōe Shunzō on back of head.
19th century.
Height 4.5cm ($1\frac{3}{4}$in).
F.1051. Franks Collection.

Nitta no Yoshisada was a fourteenth century general who eventually cut off his own head after being mortally wounded.

249
Buddhist Guardian King holding a tobacco pouch and a pipe.
Wood.
Signed Ranrinsai Shūzan Saku on the back.
Early 19th century.
1945 10-17 648. Bequeathed by Oscar Raphael.

Exhibited Red Cross, London, 1915, no. 5, pl. XLVI.

The tobacco pouch is held by an ashtray netsuke.

Colour plate. Frontispiece

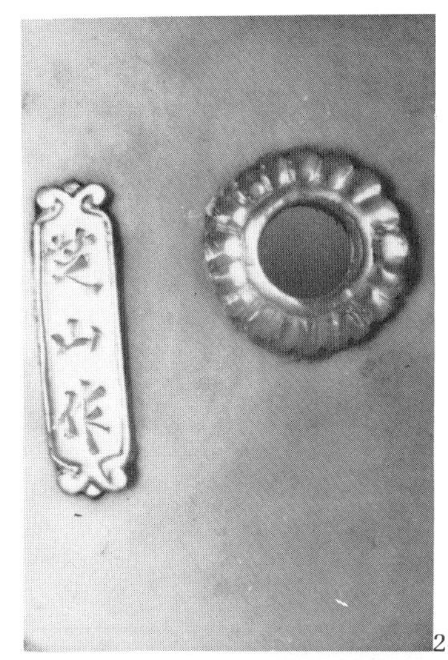

245

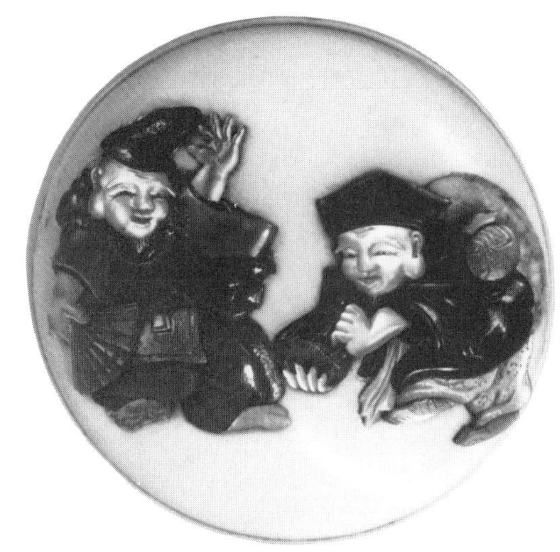

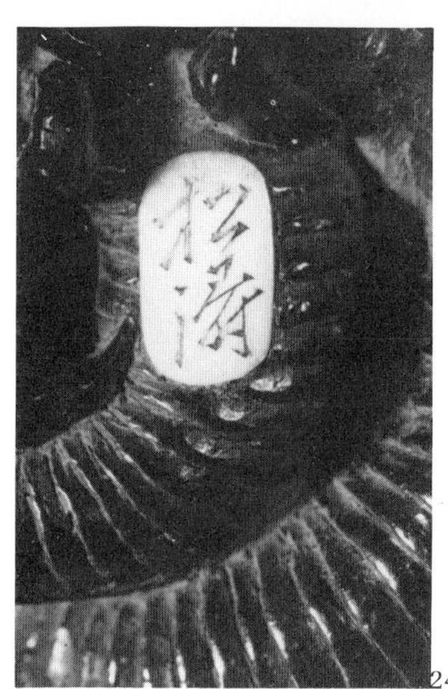

247

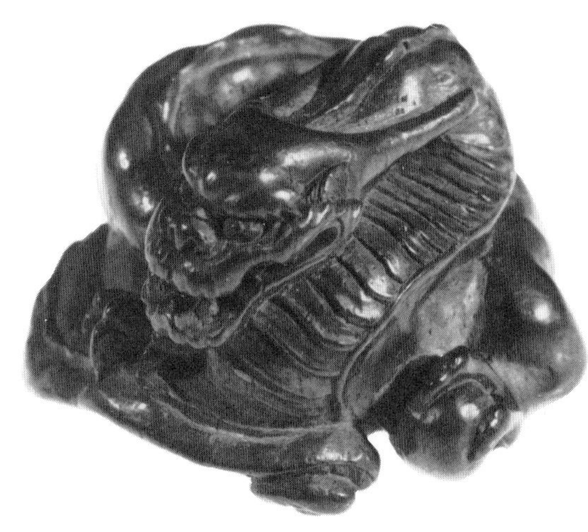

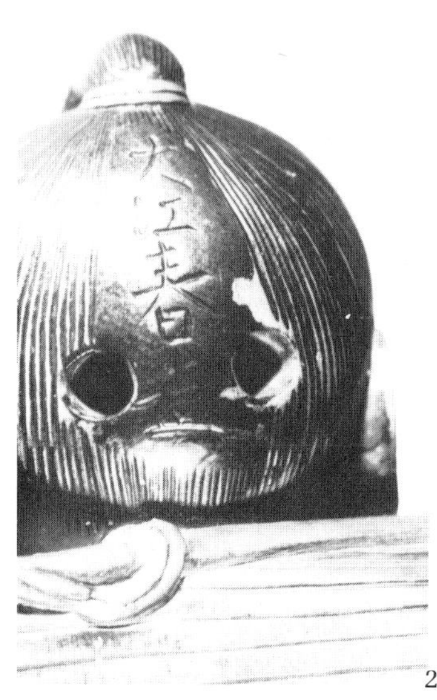

248

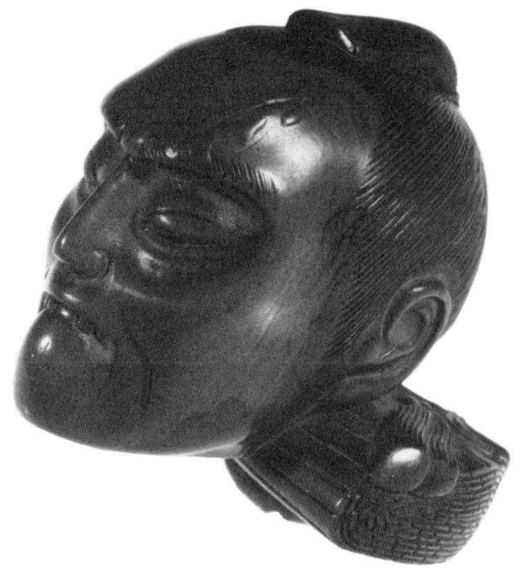

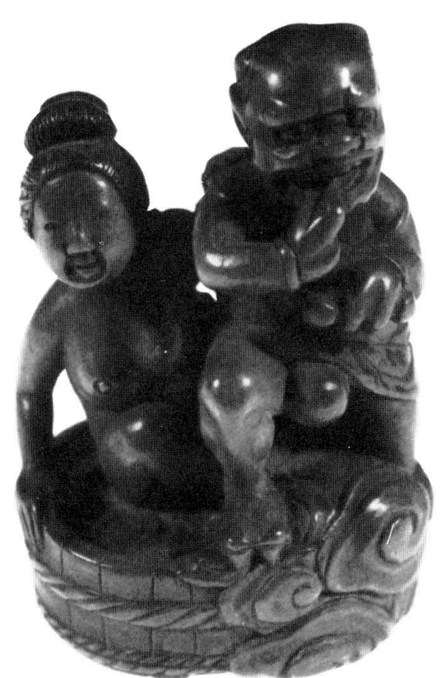

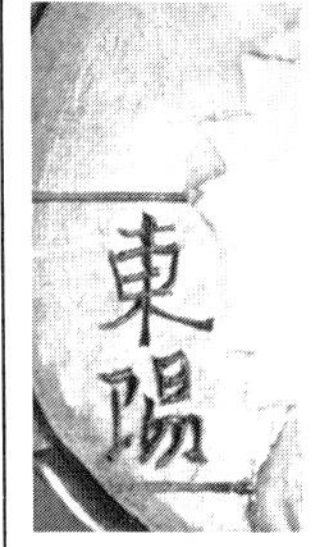

252

251

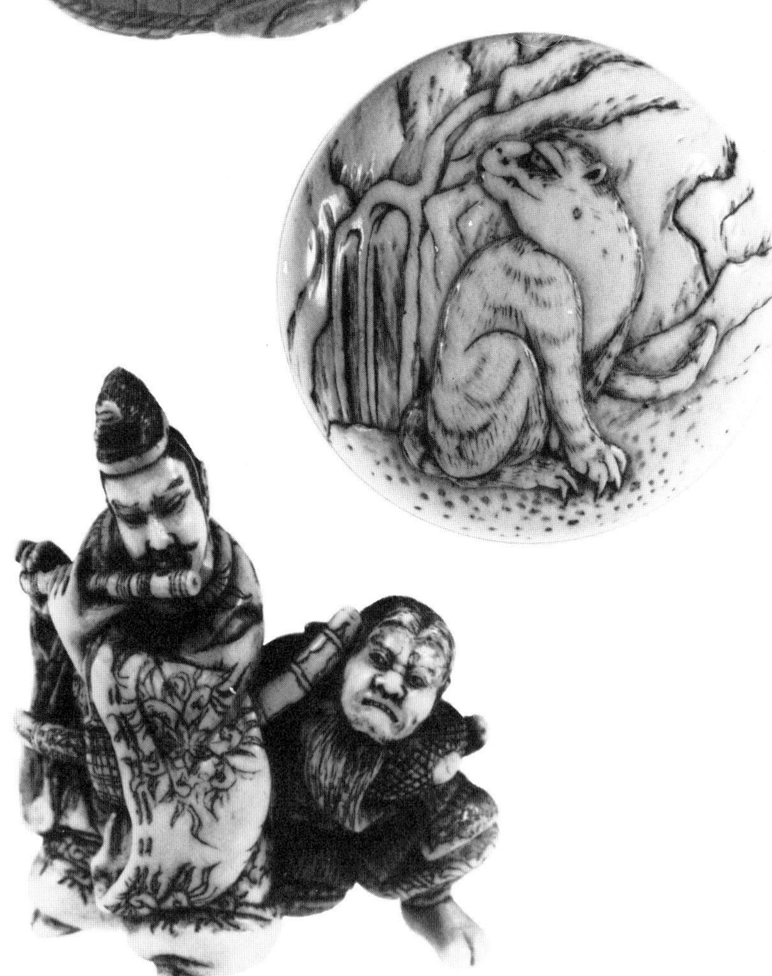

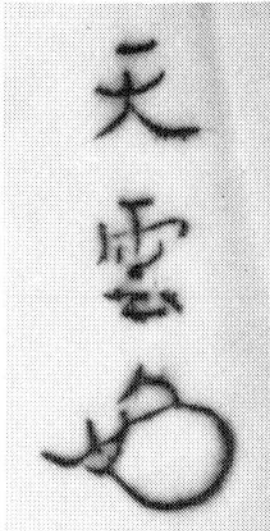

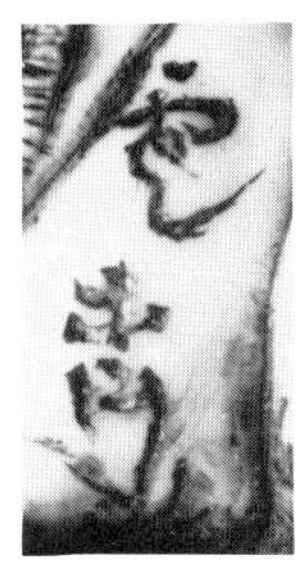

254

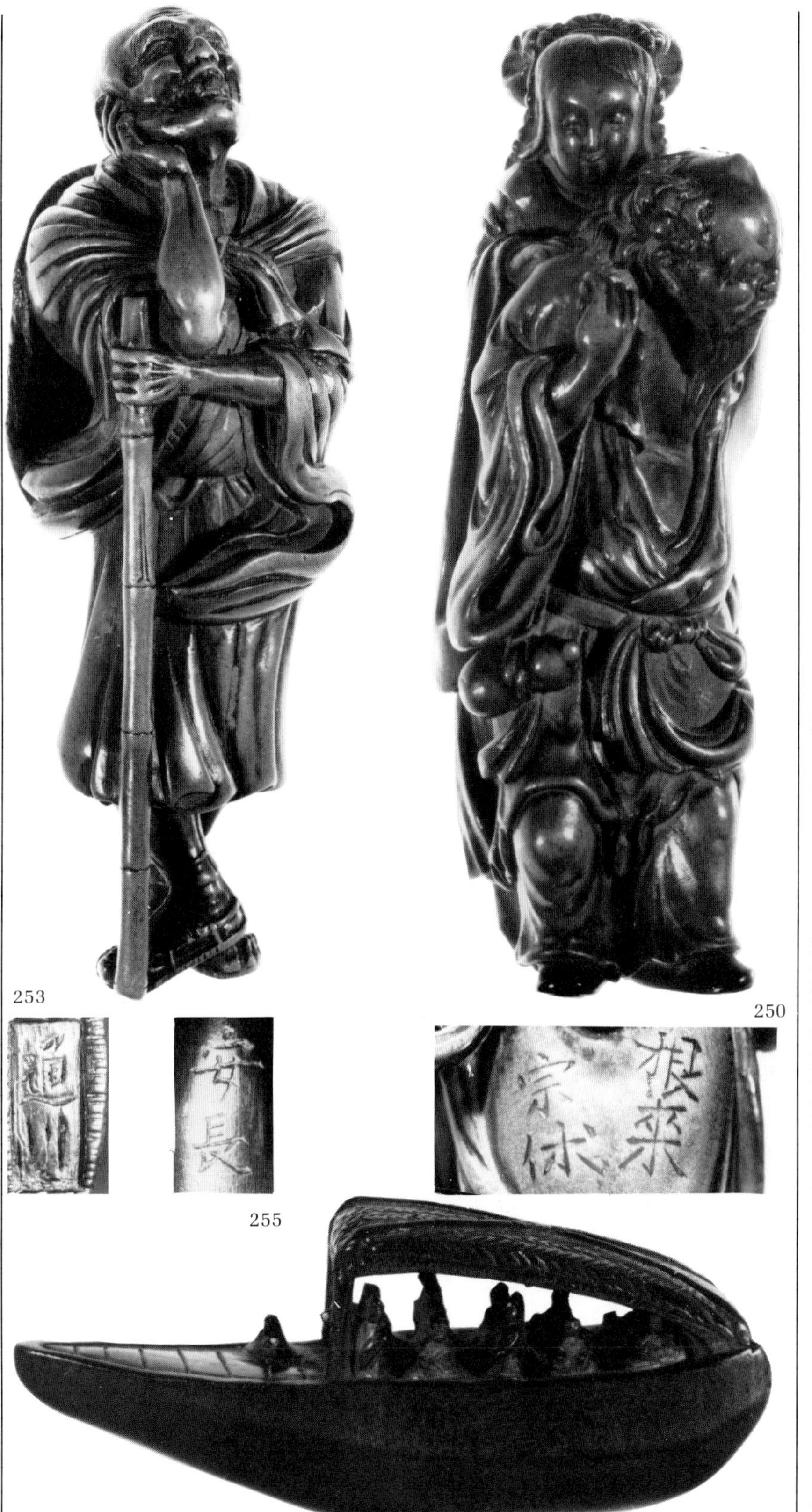
253 250 255

250
Ikkaku Sennin carrying the Indian princess on his back. Wood, the eyes inlaid.
Signed Negi Sōkyū on the back.
18th century.
Height 7cm (2¾in).
1945 10-17 664. Bequeathed by Oscar Raphael.

251
Manjū carved in relief with a tiger seated by a waterfall. Ivory.
Signed Tenun with *kakihan* on the back.
19th century.
Diameter 4.5cm (1¾in).
F.400. Franks Collection.

252
Woman joined in the bath-tub by a lasciviously inclined *Raijin* (thunder-god). Wood.
Signed Tōyō on the base.
Height 4.5cm (1¾in).
W.419.

253
Travelling priest. Wood.
Signed Tsūsen in a rectangular cartouche under one foot.
18th century.
Height 9.5cm (3¾in).
1945 10-17 646. Bequeathed by Oscar Raphael.

254
Kidomaru who, charmed by the music of his brother Yoshimasa's flute, is diverted from his attempt at fratricide.
Ivory. Signed Unsei on the base.
19th century.
Height 4.5cm (1¾in).
F.949. Franks Collection.

255
River-barge with bamboo awning. Wood.
Signed Yasunaga on bottom.
19th century.
Length 6.75cm (2¾in).
F.629. Franks Collection.

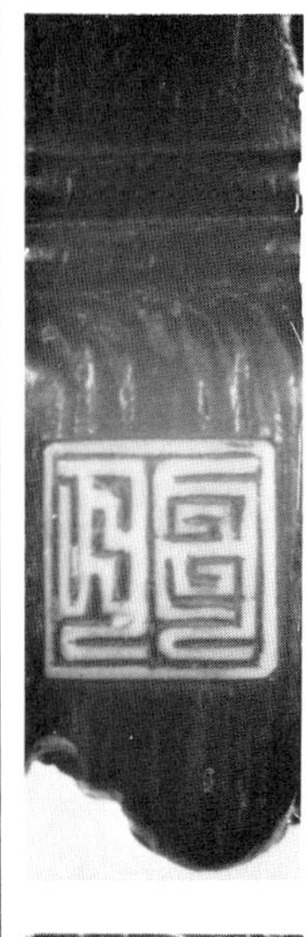

258

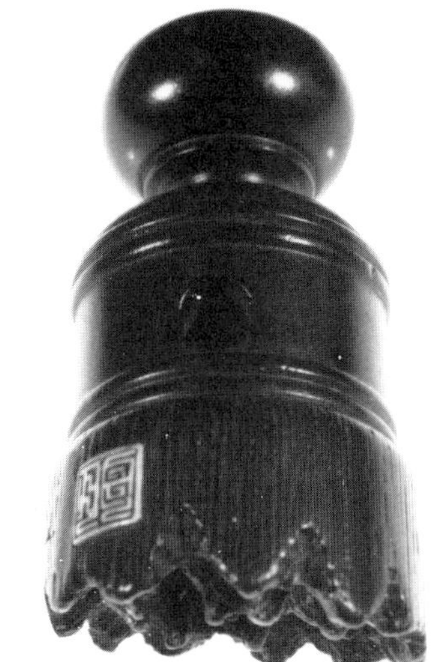

256

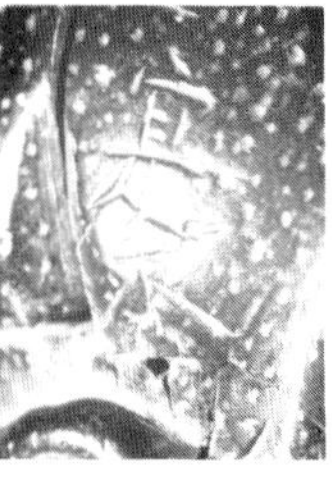

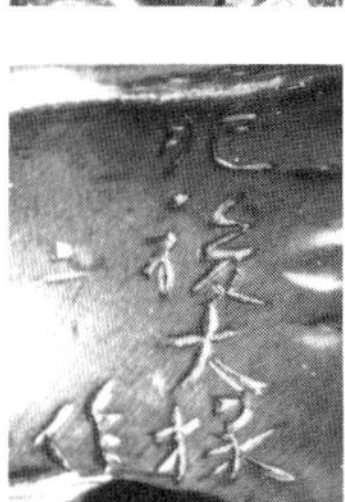

257

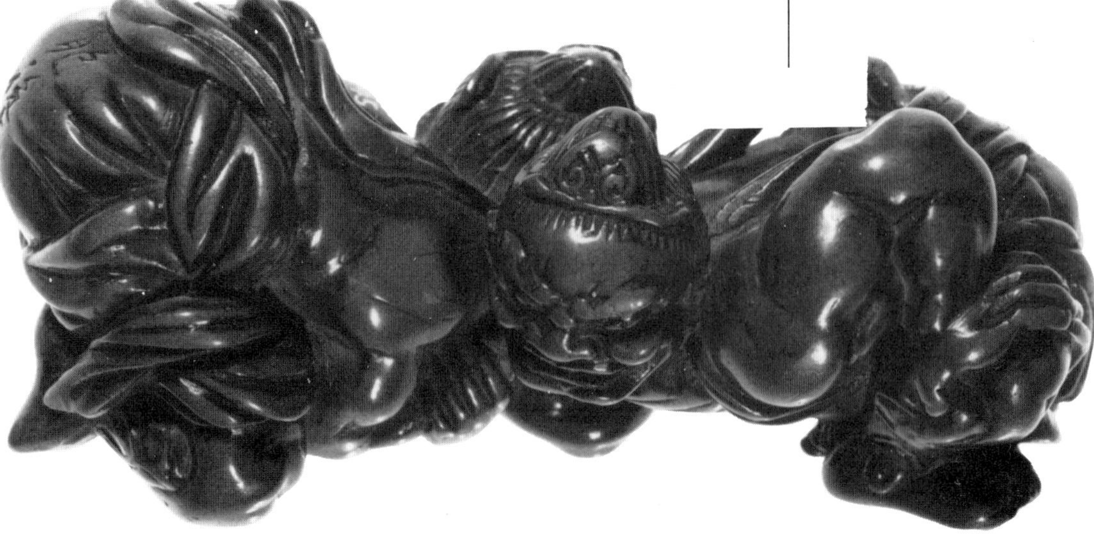

256
Orange which opens to reveal two *Sennin* playing the game of *go*.
Wood, the figures of stained ivory.
Signed Natsuki by the *himotoshi*.
Width 3.75cm ($1\frac{1}{2}$in).
OA + 540.

257
Two Buddhist Guardians hand-wrestling. Wood.
Signed Higo Daijō Saku ('Made by an honorary official of Higo Province') on one Guardian's behind.
18th century.
Length 7.5cm (3in).
1945 10-17 524. Bequeathed by Oscar Raphael.

258
Broken-off bridge post. Wood.
Signed ?Hōgetsu in an ivory seal.
19th century.
Height 5.75cm ($2\frac{1}{4}$in).
F.1054. Franks Collection.

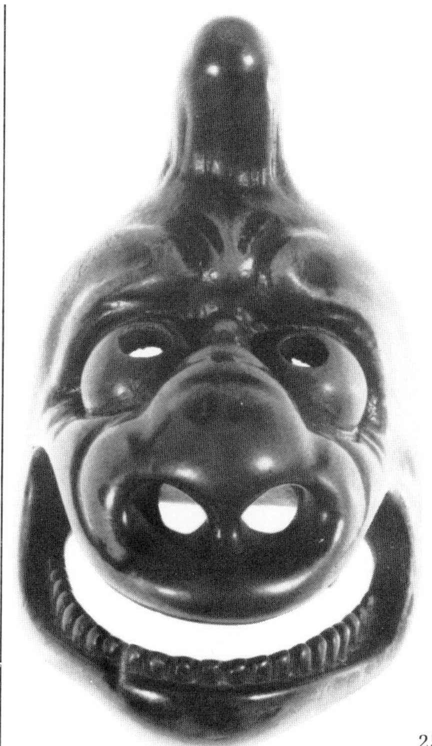

259

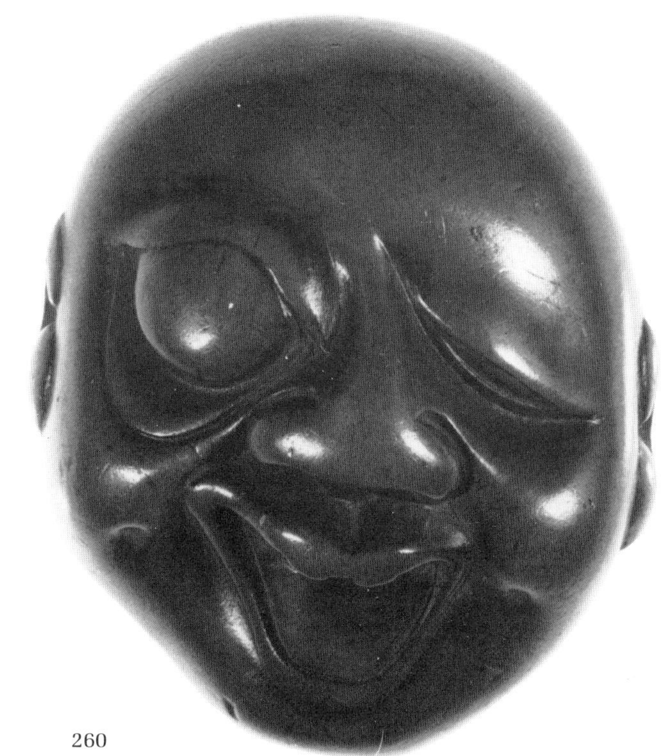

260

Mask Netsuke

259
Bugaku mask of a single-horned beast.
Wood, traces of pigment.
Unsigned.
Height 5.75cm ($2\frac{1}{4}$in).
Early 19th century.
1945 10-17 621. Bequeathed by Oscar Raphael.

Bugaku was a court entertainment of music and dance.

260
Mask of a blind man with a wall eye.
Wood, the tongue lacquered red.
Unsigned.
18th century.
Height 5.7cm ($2\frac{1}{4}$in).
1945 10-17 542. Bequeathed by Oscar Raphael.
Colour plate, page 23

261
Kyōgen (comic drama) mask of the sort called *Hyottoko*. Wood.
Signed Garaku on the back.
18th century.
Height 3.75cm ($1\frac{1}{4}$in).
F.357. Franks Collection.

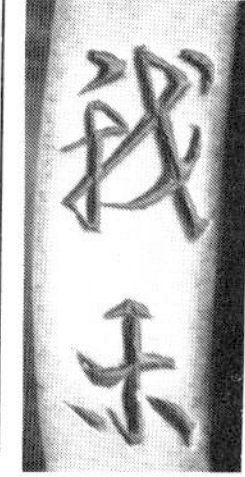

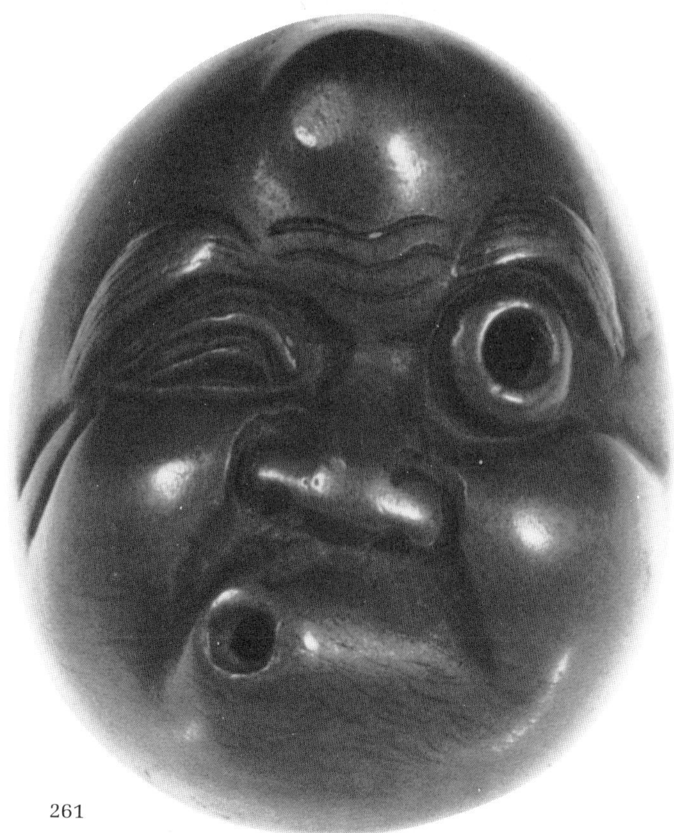

261

262
Mask of a *tengu*.
Wood, the pupils inlaid.
Signed Yūga Saku.
Late 18th century.
Height 3.3cm (1½in).
1945 10-17 578. Bequeathed by Oscar Raphael.

263
Mask of a *tengu* as a *yamabushi* (mountain priest). Wood.
False signature of Rantei.
18th century.
Height 3.75cm (1½in).
F.356. Franks Collection.

264
Mask of Hannya.
Lacquered wood, the eyes in glass over gold and black pigment.
Unsigned.
Late 18th–early 19th century.
Height 5.1cm (2in).
1945 10-17 627. Bequeathed by Oscar Raphael.
Colour plate, page 23

265
Mask of Jō (type of an old man).
Wood.
Signed Deme Uman and Tenka Ichi on the back.
Early 19th century.
Height 4.6cm (2in).
F.1135. Franks Collection.

266
Mask of a female *Shōjō*. Wood.
Signed Shūmin with *kakihan* on the back.
19th century.
Height 5.3cm (2in).
F.1185. Franks Collection.

267
Nō mask of a young woman.
Wood.
Signed Tomotoshi on the back.
19th century.
Height 6.7cm (2¾in).
1945 10-17 583. Bequeathed by Oscar Raphael.
Colour plate, page 23

268
A mask of Okame winking.
Wood, one eye of silver and black lacquer.
Signed Sekkō (Setsukō).
19th century.
Height 5.5cm (2¼in).
F.1133. Franks Collection.

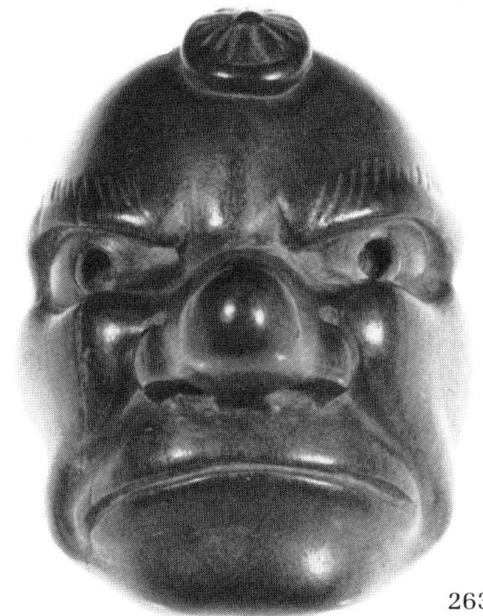
263

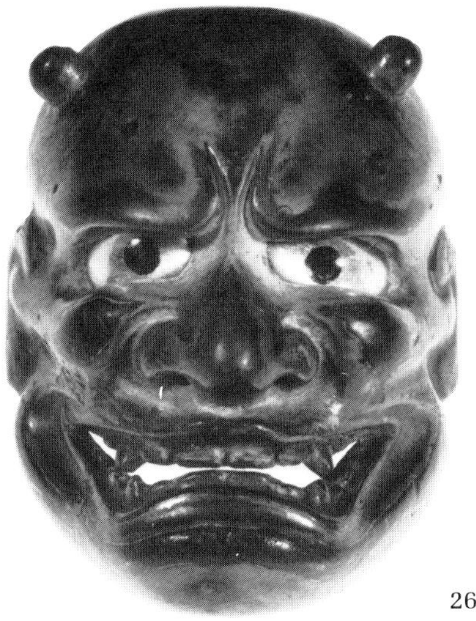
264

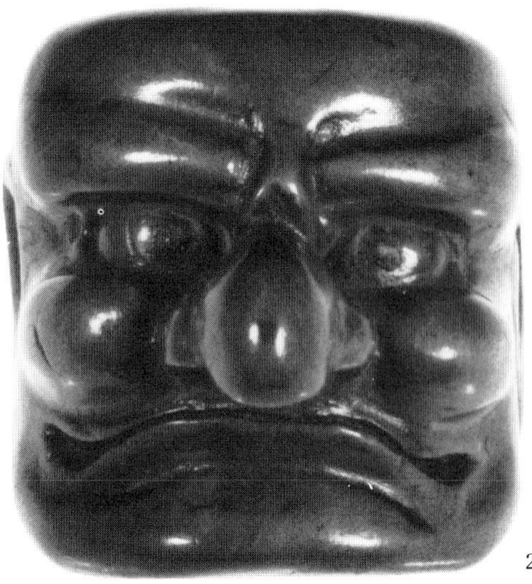
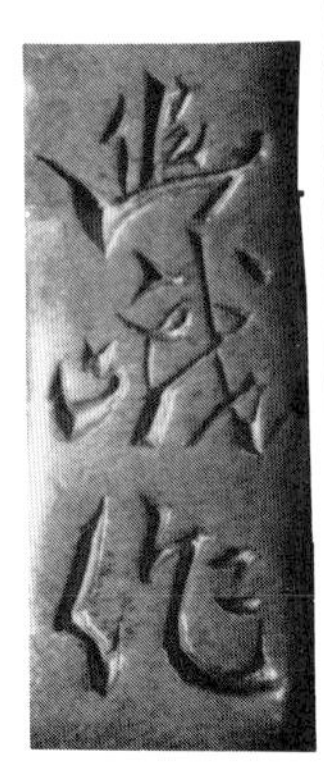
262

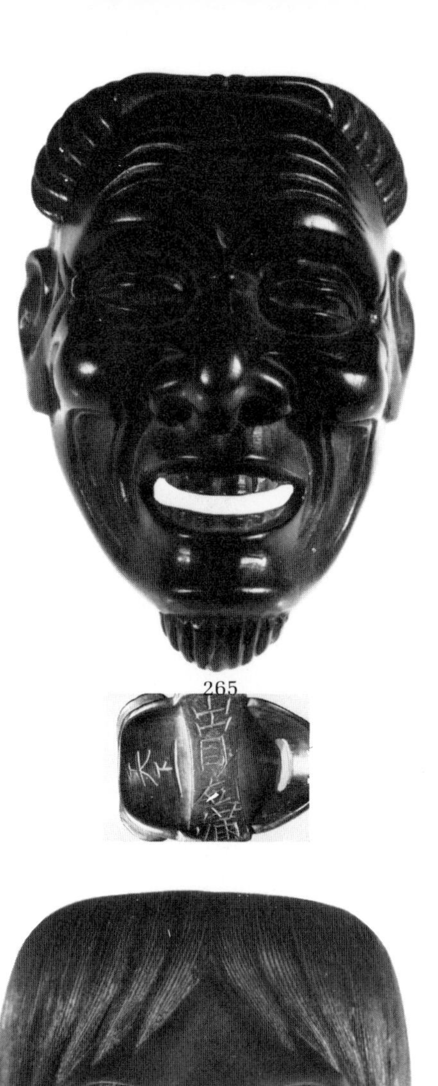

265

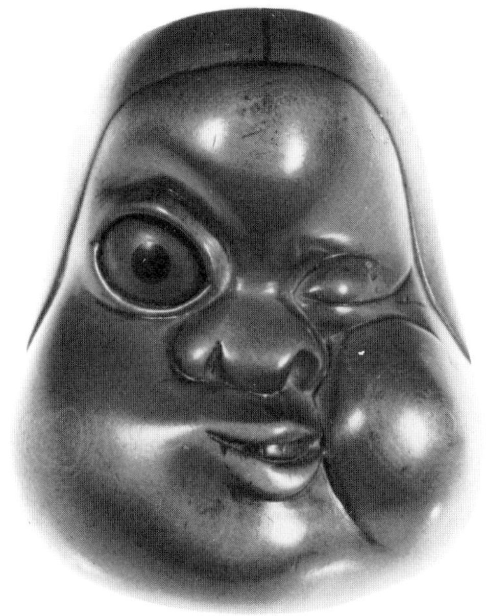

268

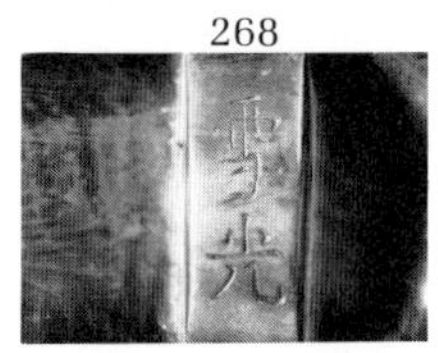

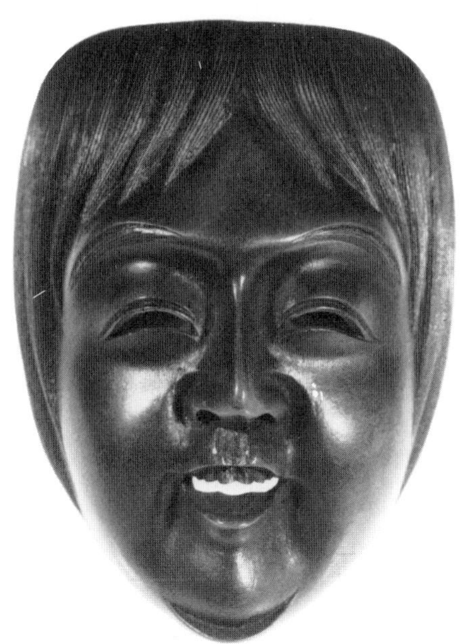

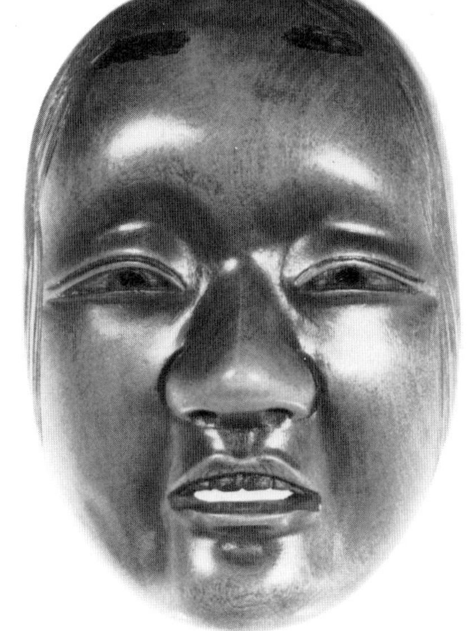

266

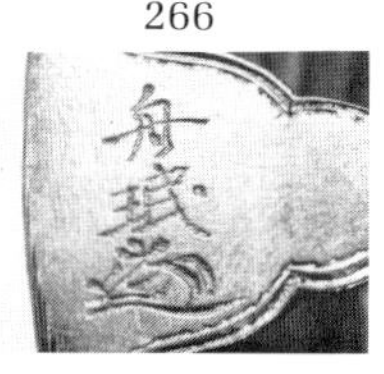

267

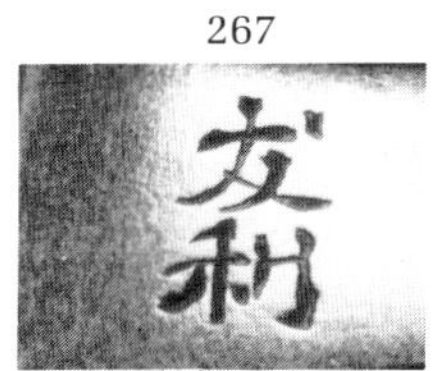

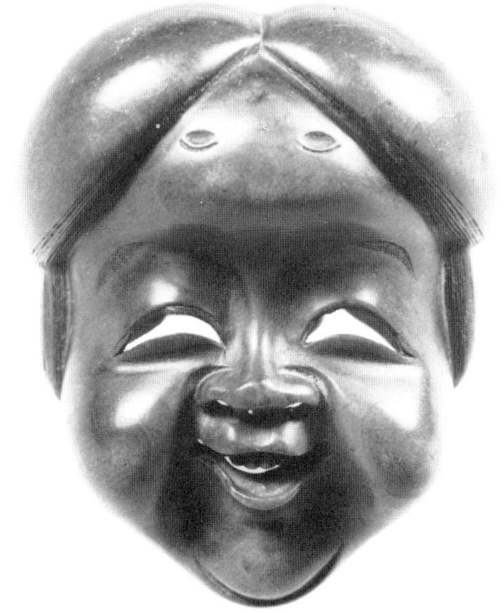

272

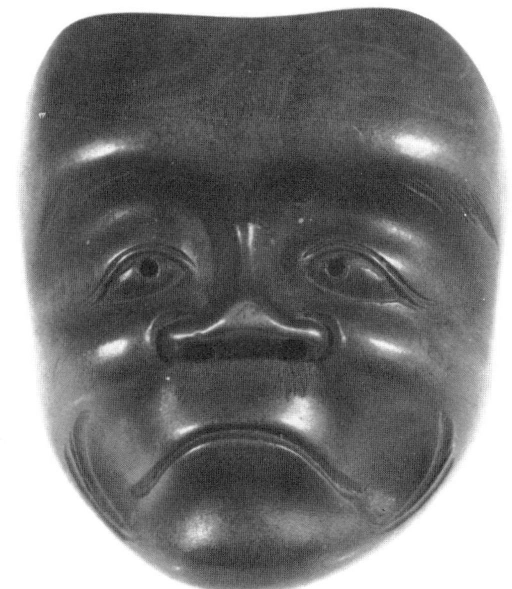

274

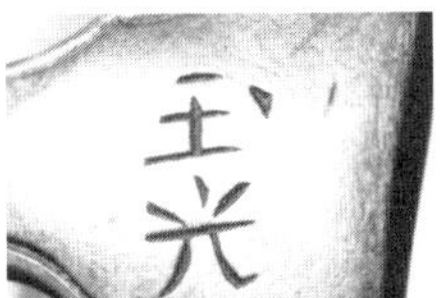

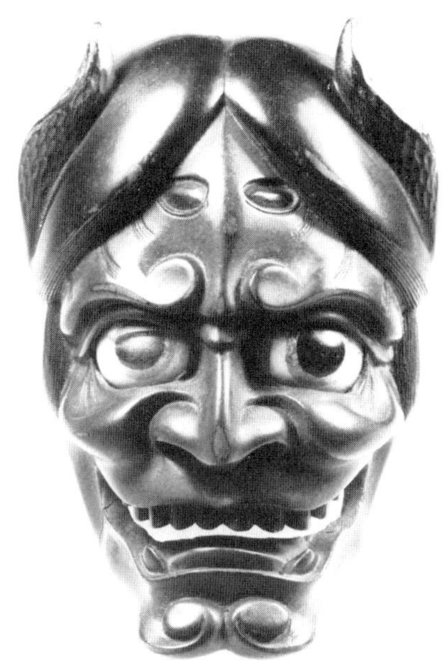

271

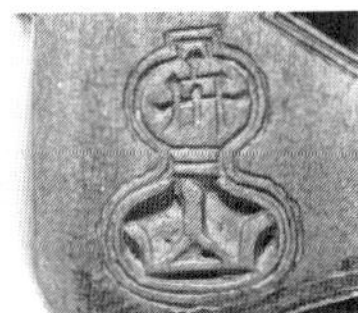

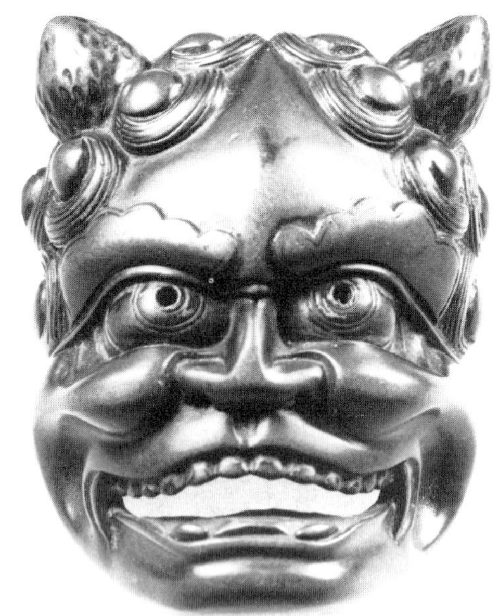

273

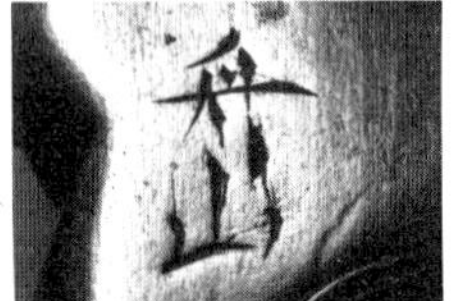

269
A three-quarter mask of a *Rakan*, a rosary and fly-whisk forming the *himotoshi* at the back. Wood.
Unsigned.
19th century.
Height 4.5cm ($1\frac{3}{4}$in).
1945 10-17 626. Bequeathed by Oscar Raphael.
Illustrated in *Legends in Japanese Art*, by Henri L. Joly, opp. p. 216.
Colour plate, page 23

270
Mask of a *bakemono*.
Wood, the pupils inlaid.
Signed Masakatsu on the back.
19th century.
Height 5.2cm (2in).
F.1183. Franks Collection.

271
Mask of Hannya.
Lacquered wood, the eyes inlaid in glass over pigment.
Signed Shūzan in a seal-type double-gourd on the back.
19th century.
Height 8.25cm ($3\frac{1}{4}$in).
F.1449. Franks Collection.

272
A mask of Okame. Wood.
Sealed Shūzan on the back.
19th century.
Height 6.25cm ($2\frac{1}{2}$in).
F.1448. Franks Collection.

273
Mask of an *oni* (demon). Wood, partly gilt and lacquered.
Signed Shūzan on the back.
19th century.
Height 7.75cm (3in).
F.1447. Franks Collection.

274
Comic mask.
Signed Gyokkō on the back.
19th century.
Height 3.75cm ($1\frac{1}{2}$in).
F.359. Franks Collection.

275
Mask of an old man. Ivory.
Unsigned.
19th century.
Height 3.25cm ($1\frac{1}{4}$in).
F.1196. Franks Collection.

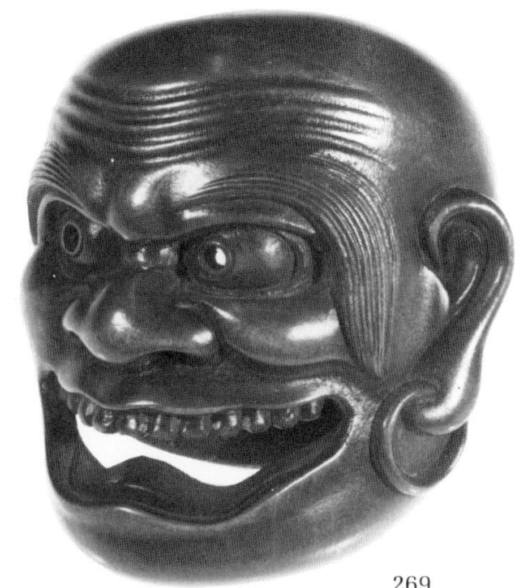
269

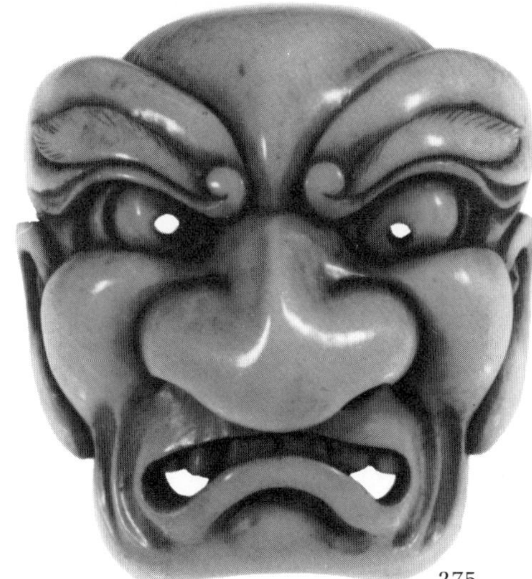
275

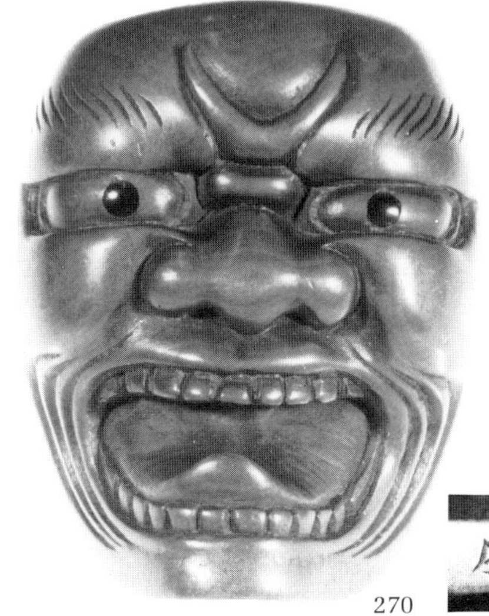
270

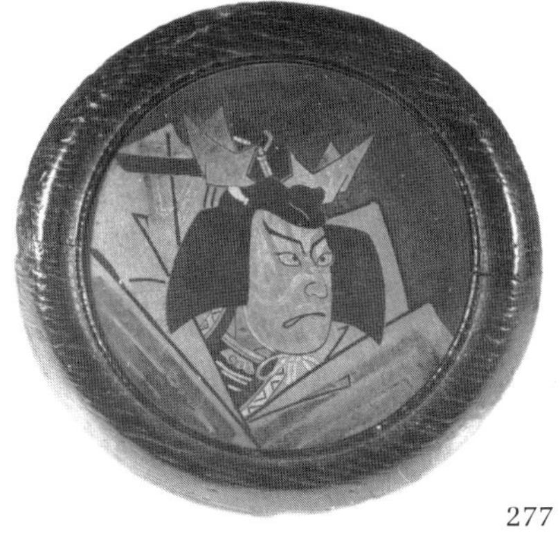
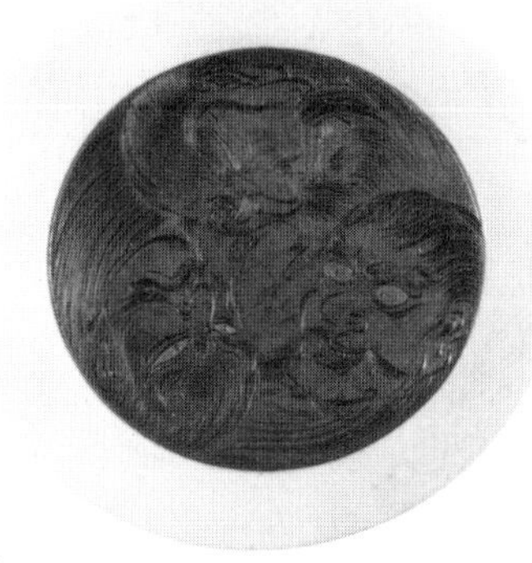

277 278

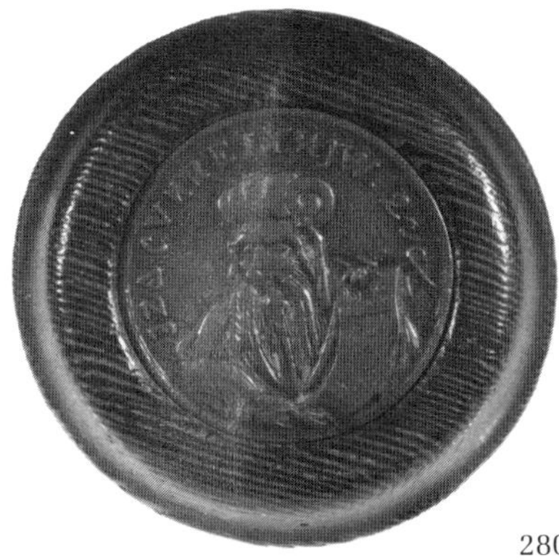
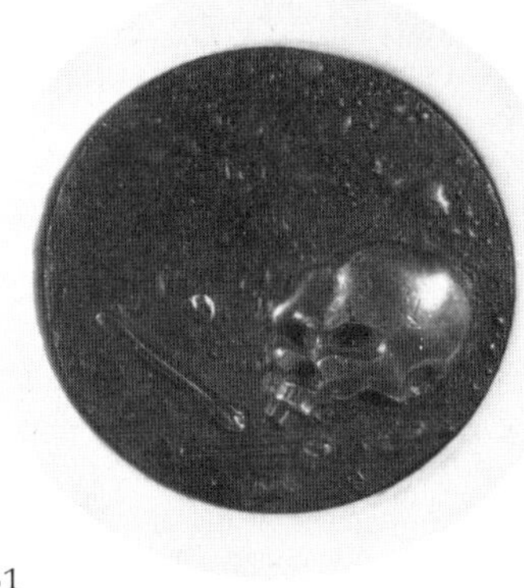

280 281

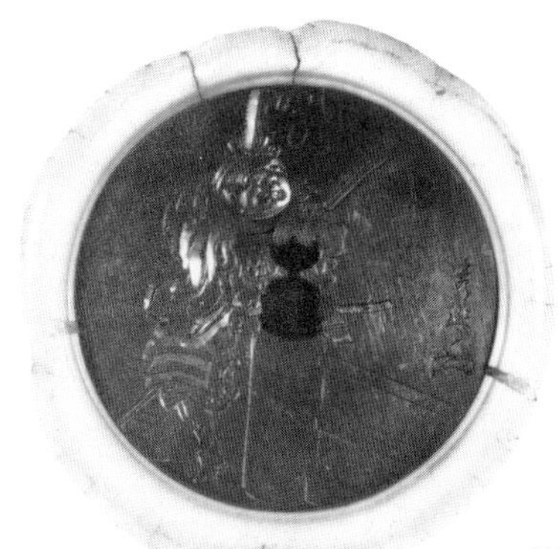
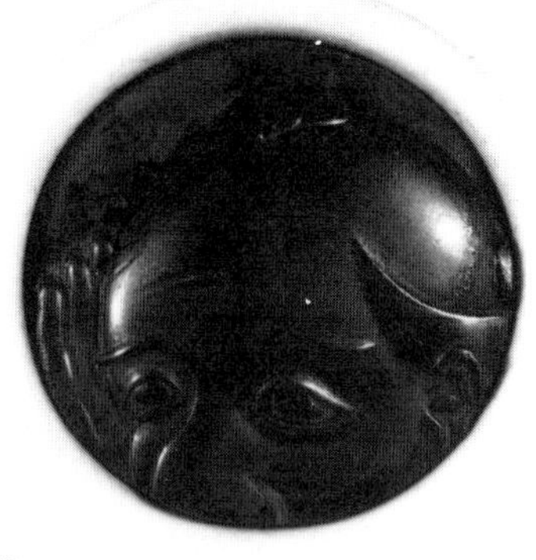

276 279

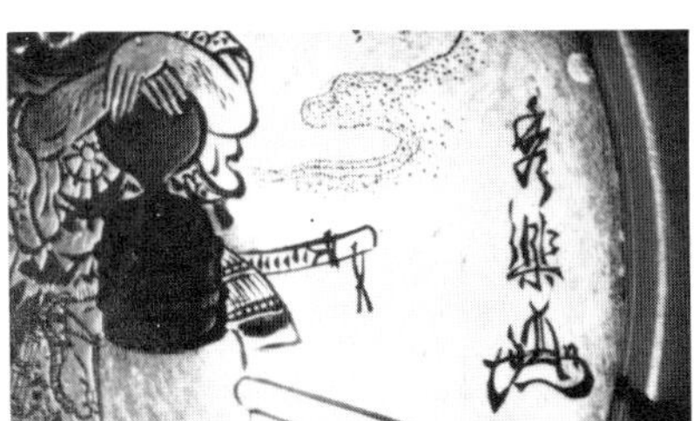
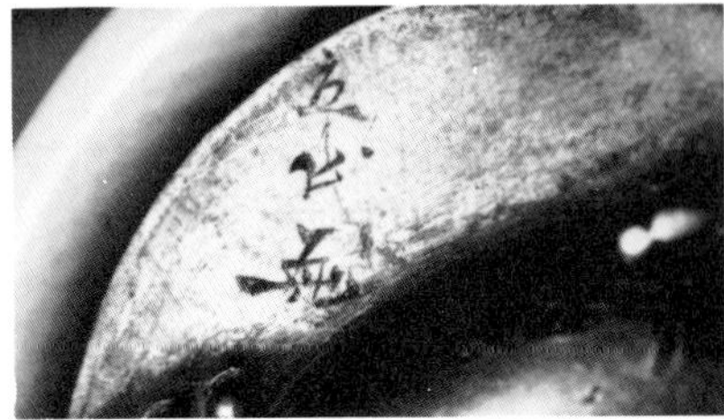

Kagamibuta

276
Kagamibuta. The gilt-metal plate depicting Benkei by the Gojō Bridge in engraved line, with *shakudō* and copper overlays. The case in narwhal tooth, carved with a chrysanthemum. The plate signed Shūraku with a *kakihan*.
19th century.
Diameter 4.2cm (2in).
1945 10-17 555. Bequeathed by Oscar Raphael.

277
Kagamibuta, the metal plate depicting in inlays of copper, silver, gold and *shakudō* the actor Danjūrō in a scene from the Kabuki play *Shibaraku*.
Wooden case with ivory rimmed cord-hole.
Signed on the back of the plate Masaaki, sealed the same in gold, and with a double-gourd seal in gold Kyū-Daime ('9th Generation', probably referring to the Danjūrō family).
Diameter 4.5cm ($1\frac{3}{4}$in).
1945 10-17 630. Bequeathed by Oscar Raphael.

Ex W. L. Behrens Collection, no. 1000, illus. pl. XX. Exhibited Red Cross, London, 1915, no. 13, illus. in the catalogue, pl. XLVI.

278
Kagamibuta, the metal plate engraved with the heads of the Three Generals of the Han Dynasty, their eyes inlaid in gold.
Ivory case.
Signed ? Ienaga with *kakihan* in centre of plate.
19th century.
Diameter 3.7cm ($1\frac{3}{4}$in).
1945 10-17 656. Bequeathed by Oscar Raphael.

Exhibited Red Cross, London, 1915, no. 196, illus. in the catalogue, pl. LI.

279
Kagamibuta, the metal plate decorated in relief with a fly resting on the top of a man's shaved head.
Ivory case.
Signed Nao . . . and *kakihan* on edge of plate.
19th century.
Diameter 4.2cm (1¾in).
F.1294. Franks Collection.

280
Kagamibuta, the copper plate in the form of a coin with the Immortal Gomō and meaningless Roman letters in relief, the case in wood.
Unsigned.
19th century.
Diameter 4.5cm (1¾in).
F.1306. Franks Collection.

281
Kagamibuta, the metal plate decorated in relief overlay with a skull and bones.
Ivory case.
Unsigned.
19th century.
Diameter 4.2cm (1¾in).
1945 10-17 554. Bequeathed by Oscar Raphael.

Unsigned: Wood

282
Sennin with a gnarled staff and a gourd at his waist.
Wood, with traces of pigment.
Unsigned.
18th century.
Height 10.2cm (4in).
F.102. Franks Collection.

283
Gama Sennin with his toad climbing onto his head.
Wood, eyes inlaid.
Unsigned.
18th century.
Height 10.2cm (4in).
1945 10-17 615. Bequeathed by Oscar Raphael.

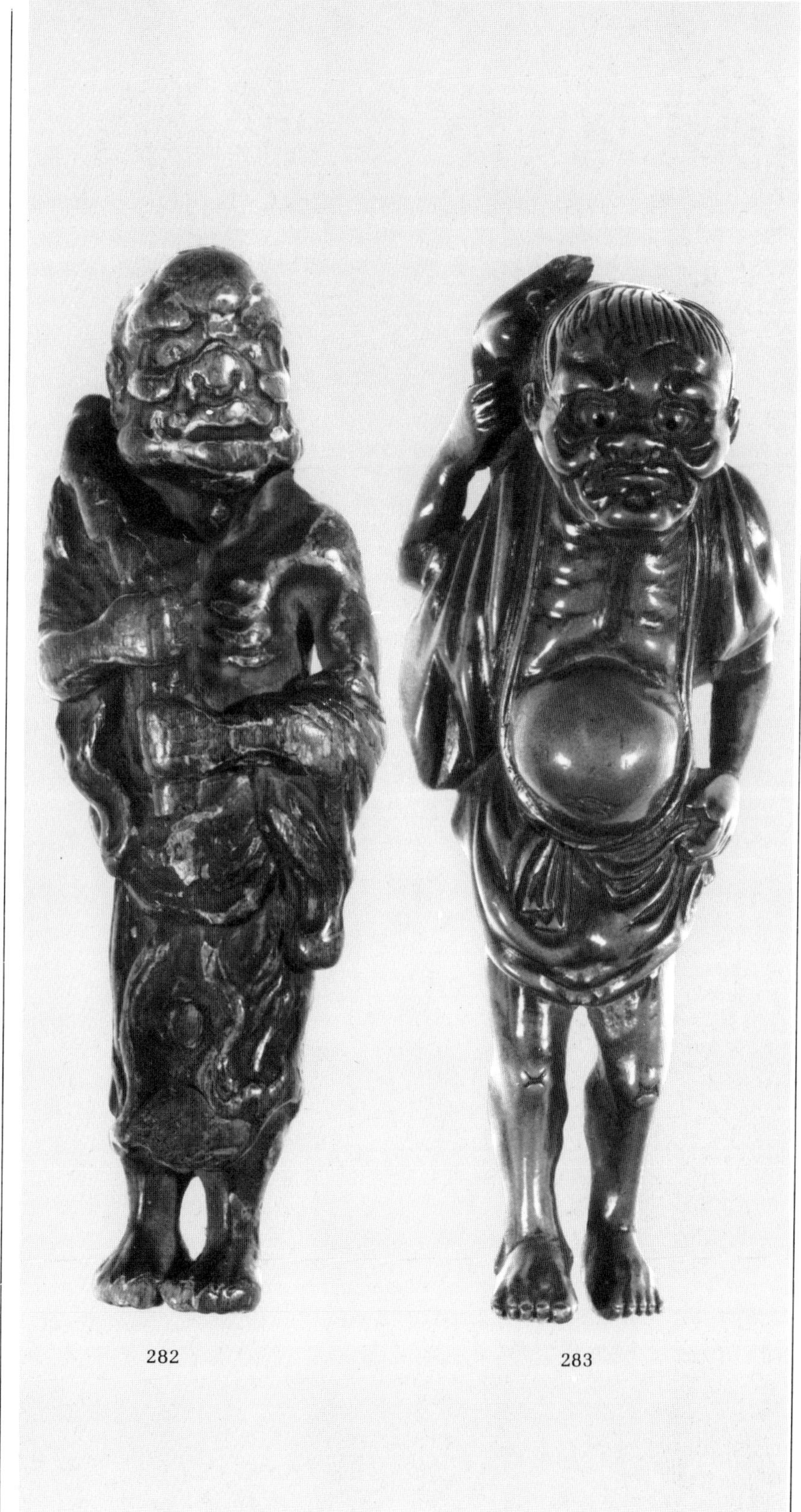

282 283

284
Sennin wearing a large hat on his back. Ebony.
Unsigned.
18th century.
Height 10.8cm (4¼in).
1945 10-17 573. Bequeathed by Oscar Raphael.

285
Shoki with an *oni* (demon) sitting on his shoulders. Wood.
Unsigned.
18th century.
Height 12.1cm (4¾in).
1945 10-17 531. Bequeathed by Oscar Raphael.

286
Shoki holding an *oni* (demon) by its jaw. Wood.
Unsigned.
18th century.
Height 5.8cm (2¼in).
1945 10-17 619. Bequeathed by Oscar Raphael.

287
Shoki grasping an *oni* (demon) by the arm. Wood.
Unsigned.
18th century.
Height 11.5cm (4½in).
1945 10-17 622. Bequeathed by Oscar Raphael.

288
Oni (demon) lying on his side. Wood.
Unsigned.
18th century.
Height 9.8cm (4in).
1945 10-17 649. Bequeathed by Oscar Raphael.

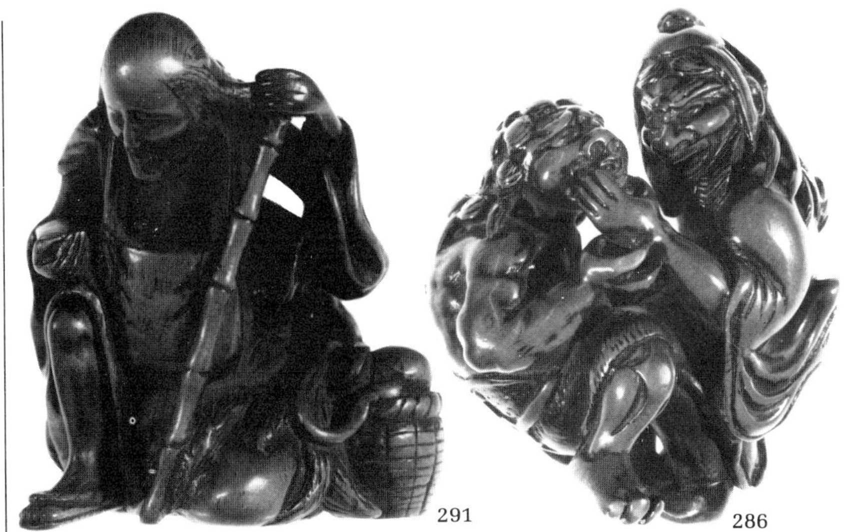

291 286

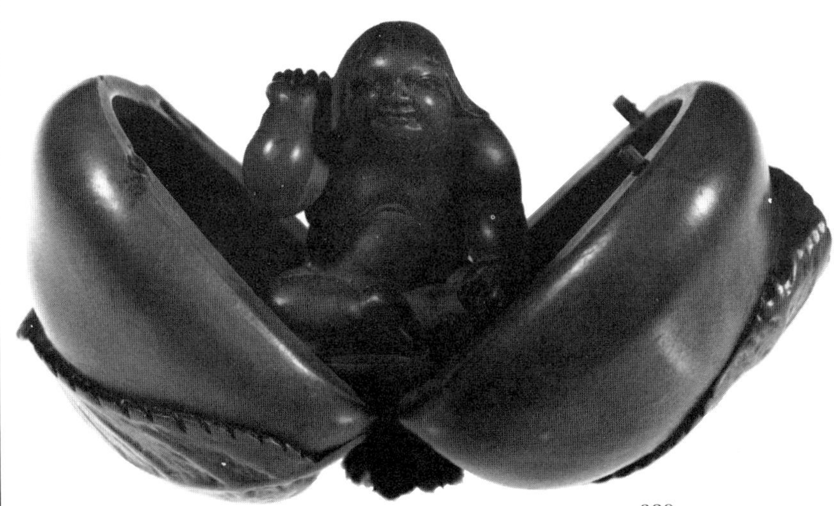

290

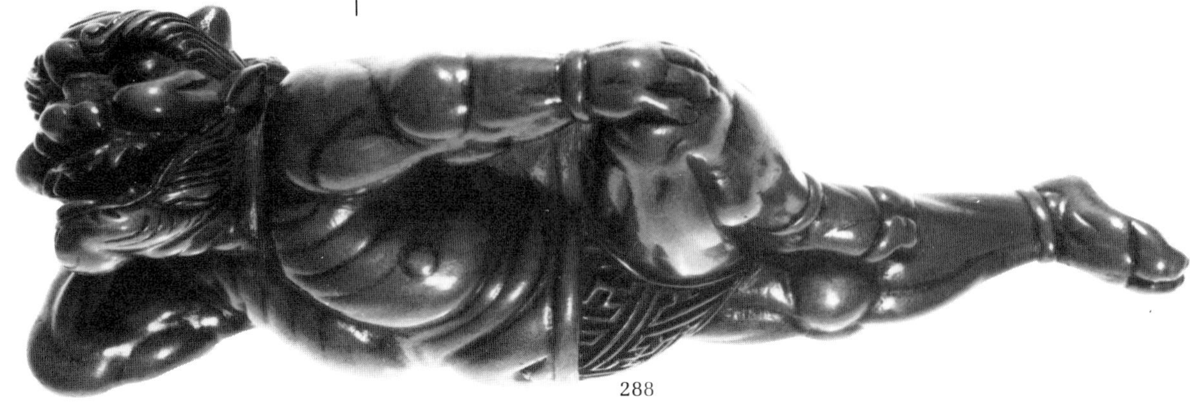

288

289
An *oni* (demon) with a cloth draped over his head and back. Wood, eyes inlaid in mother-of-pearl, the cloth lacquered in red and gold.
Unsigned.
Early 19th century.
Height 8.9cm (3½in).
F.733. Franks Collection.

290
Peach which opens to reveal Momotarō. Wood.
Unsigned.
19th century.
Height 3.75cm (1½in).
F.1040. Franks Collection.

291
The poetess Ono no Komachi in her aged destitution. Wood.
Unsigned.
19th century.
Height 4.5cm (1¾in).
F.1017. Franks Collection.

292
The Bodhisattva Kannon preparing to breastfeed a puppy. Wood.
Unsigned.
18th century.
Height 10.5cm (4in).
F.744. Franks Collection.

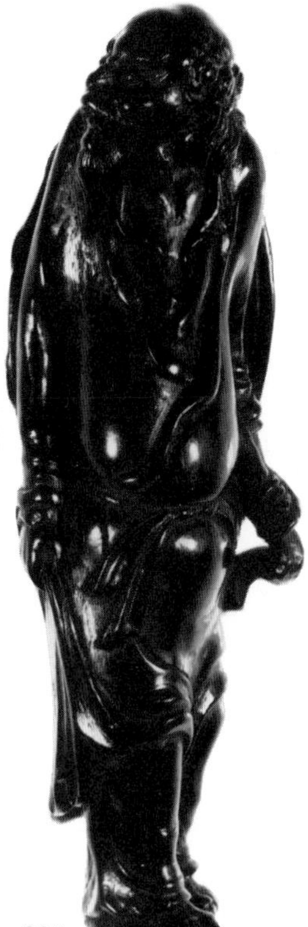

284

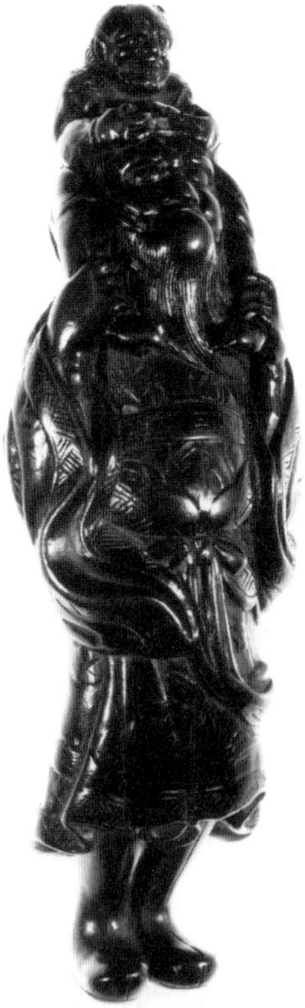

285

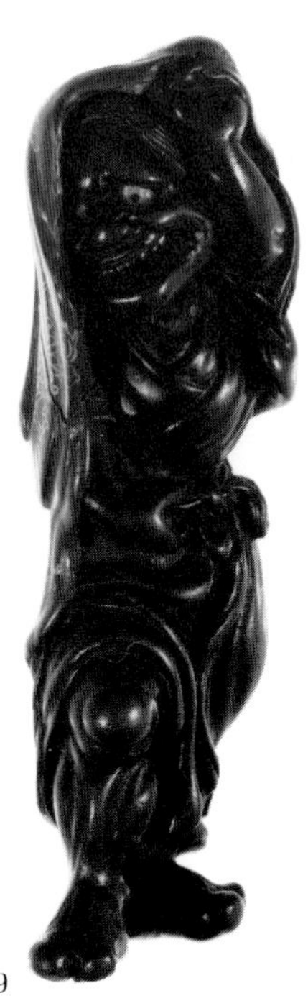
289

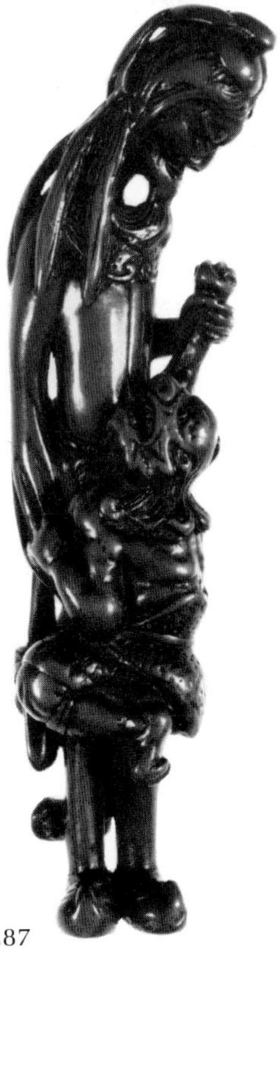

287

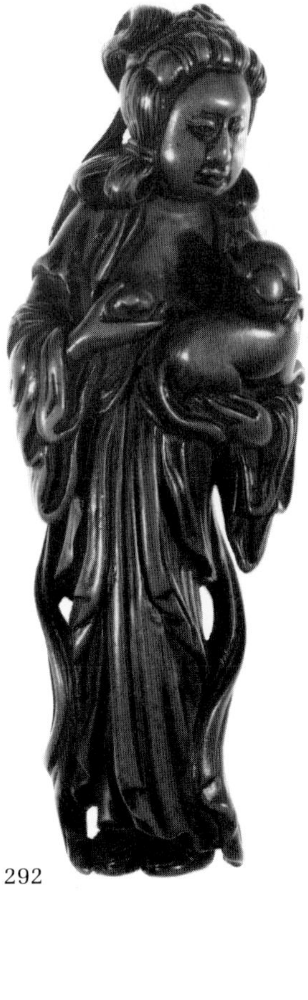

292

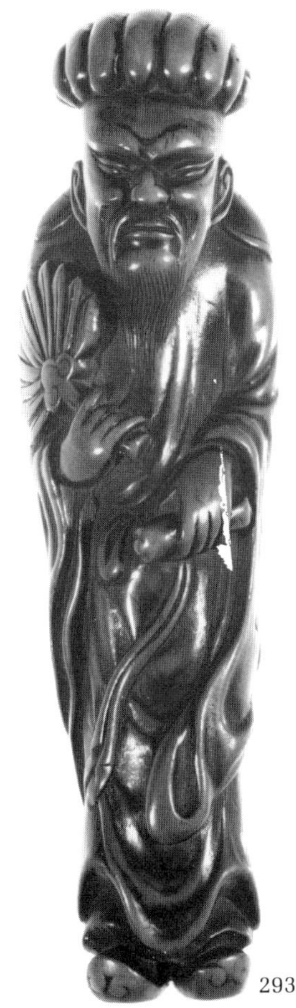
293

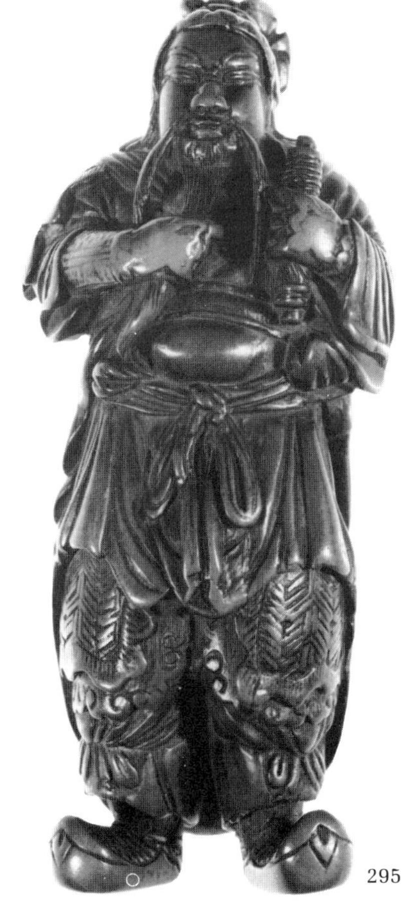
295

293
Chinese Immortal, probably Gomō, holding a feather fan and a scroll. Wood.
Unsigned.
18th century.
Height 11.8cm ($4\frac{3}{4}$in).
1945 10-17 647. Bequeathed by Oscar Raphael.

294
Hotei sitting on his sack, pulled by two small boys. Wood.
Unsigned.
18th century.
Length 8cm ($3\frac{1}{2}$in).
1945 10-17 650. Bequeathed by Oscar Raphael.

295
Kanyū stroking his beard, and holding a scroll. Wood.
Unsigned.
18th century.
Height 10.2cm (4in).
F.689. Franks Collection.

296
Ryūjin, the dragon king, with the sacred jewel. Wood.
Unsigned.
18th century.
Height 9.5cm ($3\frac{3}{4}$in).
F.732. Franks Collection.

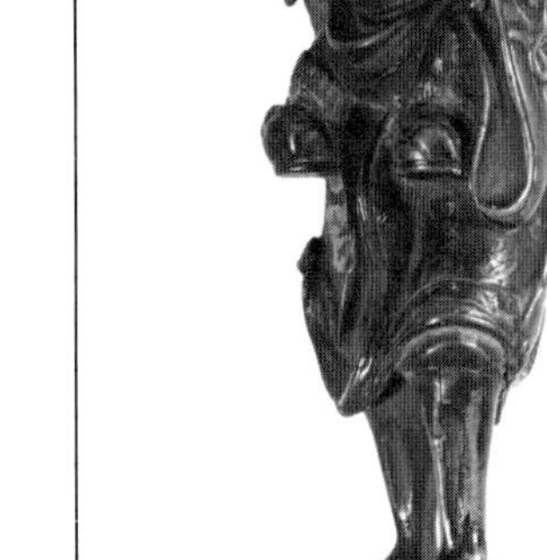
298

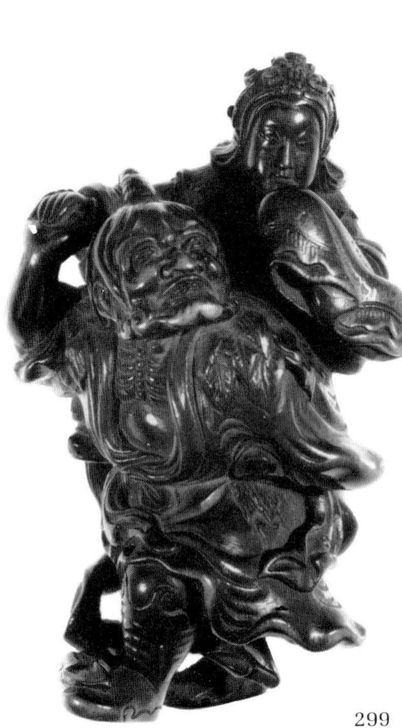
299

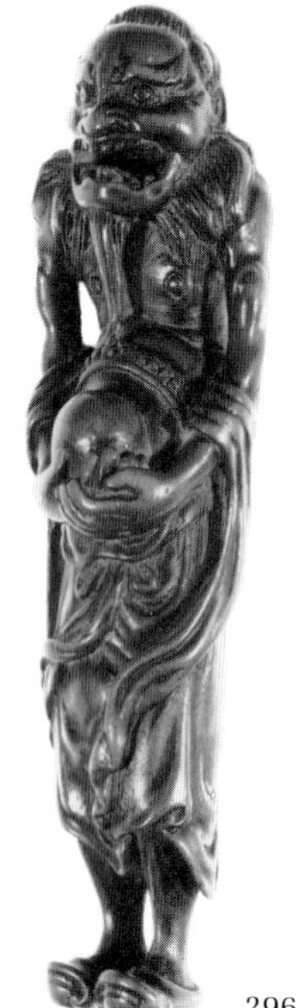
296

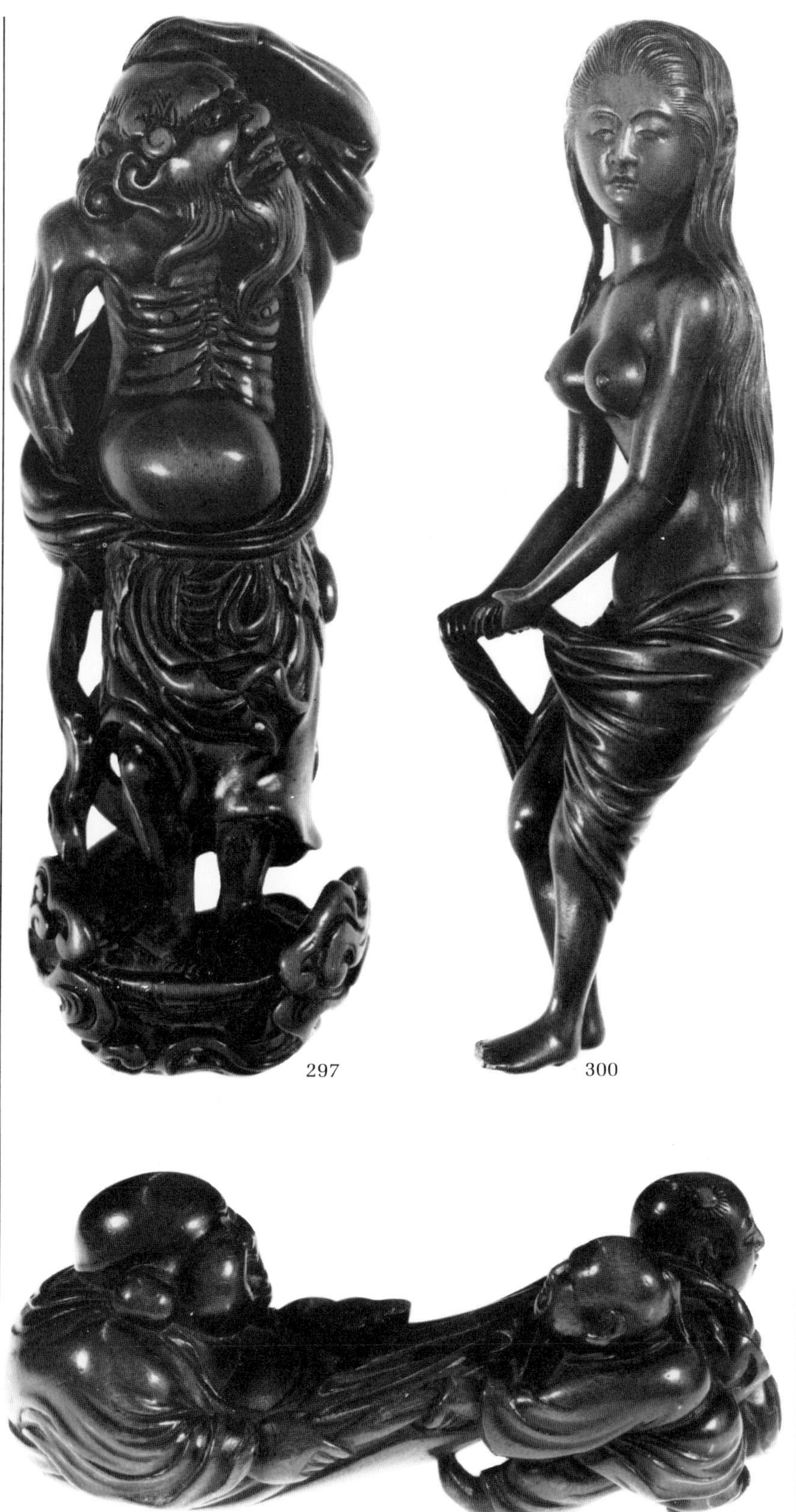

297 300

294

297
The *sennin* Chinnan crossing a river on his hat. Wood.
Unsigned.
18th century.
Height 9.5cm (3¾in).
1945 10-17 535. Bequeathed by Oscar Raphael.
Exhibited Red Cross, London, 1915, no. 2, and illustrated in the catalogue, pl. XLVI.

298
Ikkaku Sennin carrying the beautiful princess.
Wood, painted in red, green and gold.
Unsigned.
Late 18th–early 19th century.
Height 11.5cm (4½in).
F.63. Franks Collection.

299
Ikkaku Sennin carrying the beautiful princess. Wood.
Unsigned.
19th century.
Length 8cm (3in).
1956 10-19 7. Bequeathed by Mrs M. Macrae White.

300
Awabi fisher-girl. Wood.
Unsigned.
Late 19th–early 20th century.
Height 11.4cm (4½in).
1945 10-17 673. Bequeathed by Oscar Raphael.

301
Man catching his testicles in a loin-cloth. Wood.
Unsigned.
18th century.
Height 11.5cm (4½in).
1945 10-17 671. Bequeathed by Oscar Raphael.
Colour plate, page 14

302
South Sea Islander in a loin cloth, bent back as if tied by the hands. Wood.
Unsigned; attributed to Miwa I of Edo.
18th century.
Height 12.1cm (4¾in).
F.569. Franks Collection.

303
Dutchman doing the *bekkakō* gesture and holding a cockerel. Wood.
Unsigned.
18th century.
Height 12.75cm (5in).
1945 10-17 586. Bequeathed by Oscar Raphael.
Colour plate, page 14

304
Sennin holding a cockerel. Wood.
Unsigned.
18th century.
Height 11.2cm (4¼in).
1945 10-17 623. Bequeathed by Oscar Raphael.

305
Foreigner, probably a Chinaman, wearing a tall hat and holding a cockerel. Wood.
Unsigned.
18th century.
Height 10cm (4in).
1945 10-17 620. Bequeathed by Oscar Raphael.

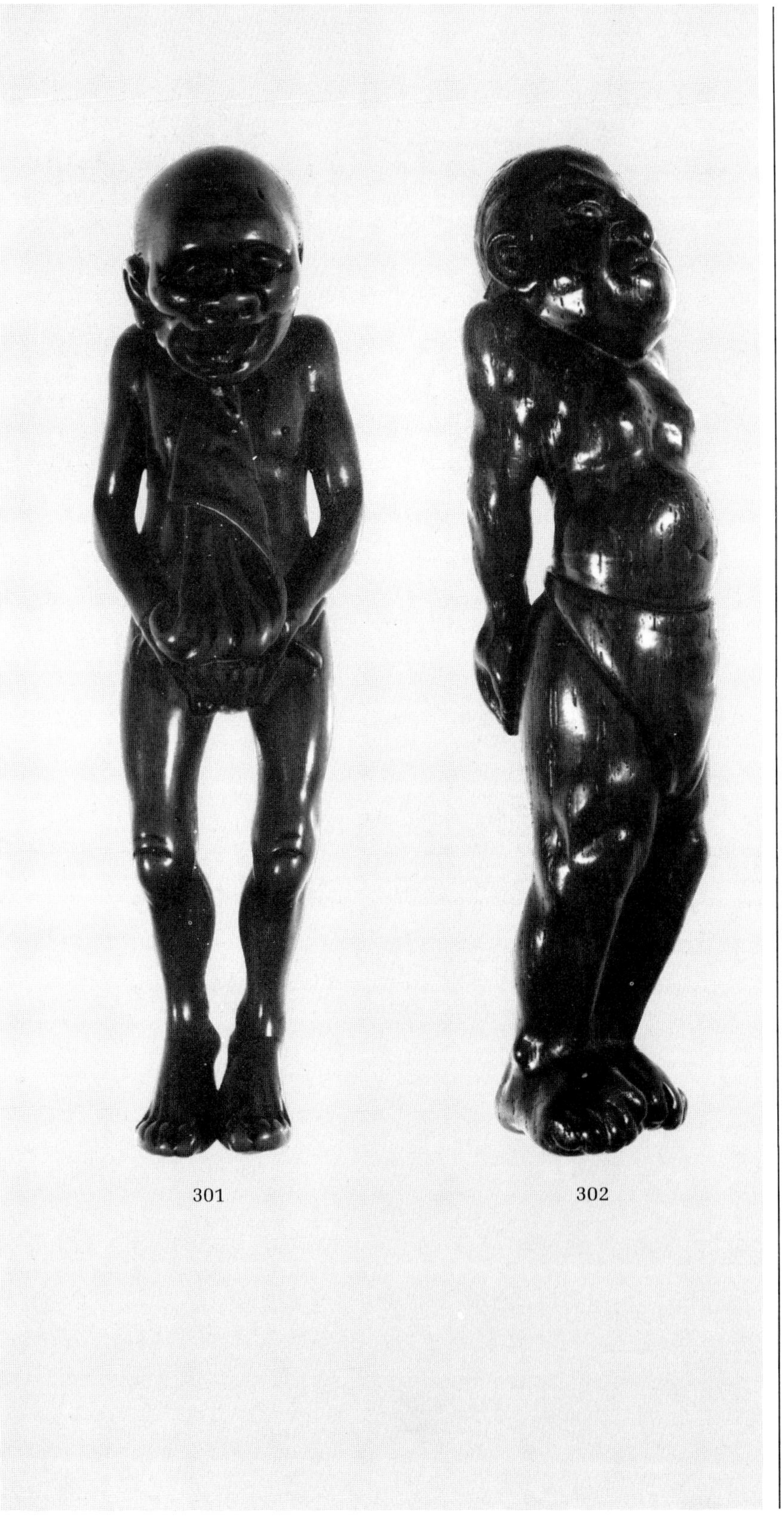
301 302

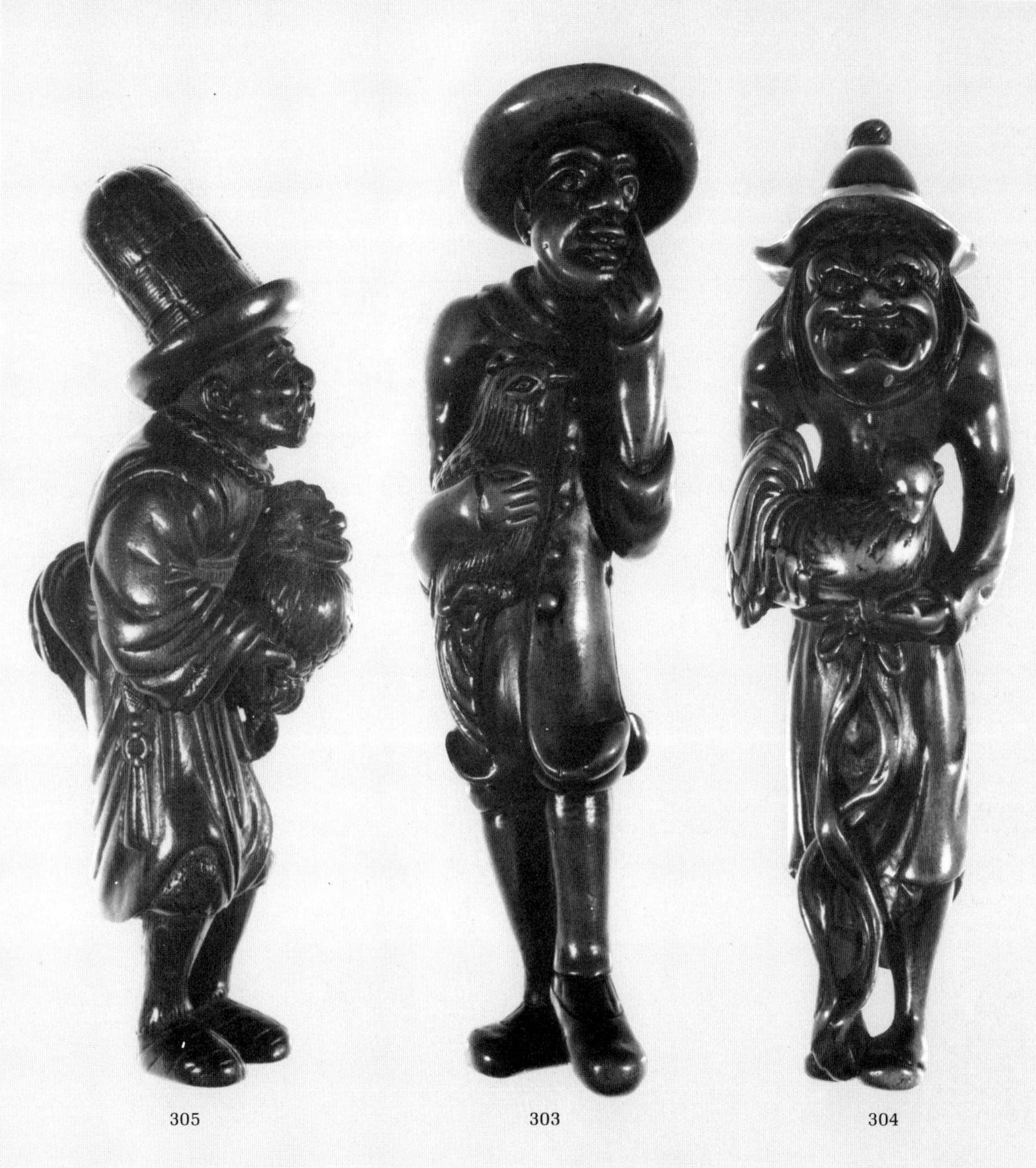

305 303 304

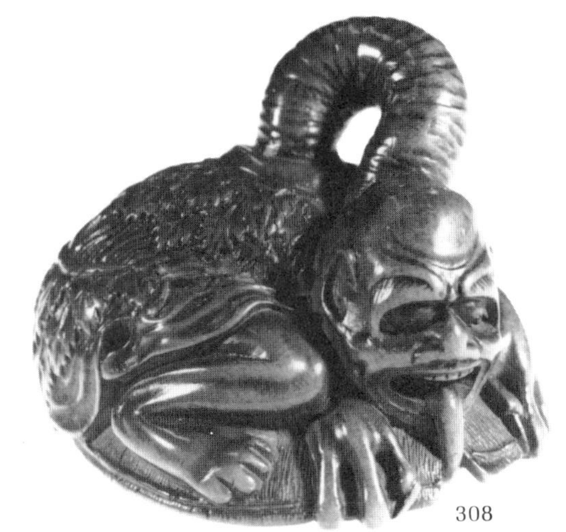
308

306
Large ghost rising above a terrified man.
Wood, the eyes inlaid.
Unsigned.
18th century.
Height 10.2cm (4in).
1912 10-12 2. Given by Mrs H. Seymour Trower.

307
Huge *bakemono* rising behind a blind man.
Wood, the ghost's eyes inlaid in brass.
Unsigned.
18th century.
Height 9.25cm ($3\frac{3}{4}$in).
F.756. Franks Collection.

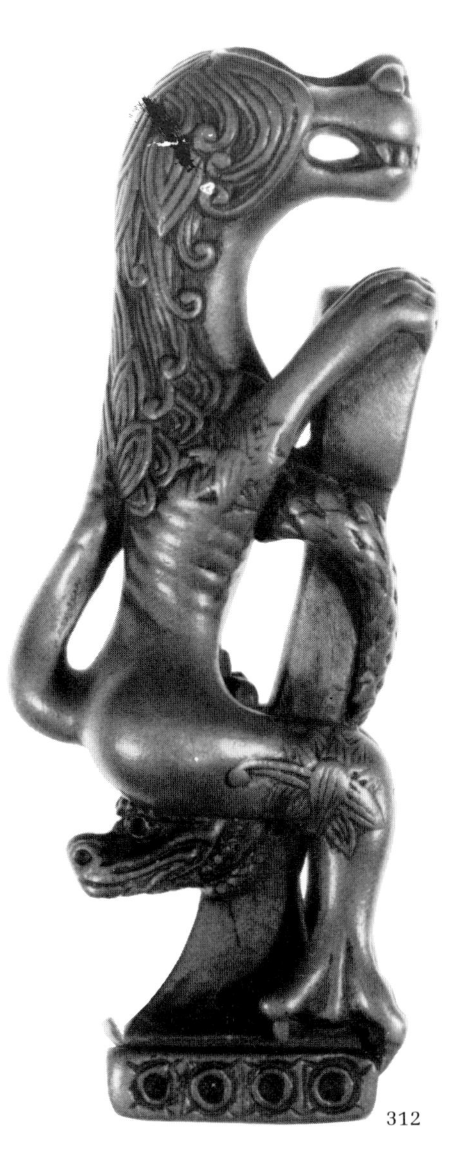
312

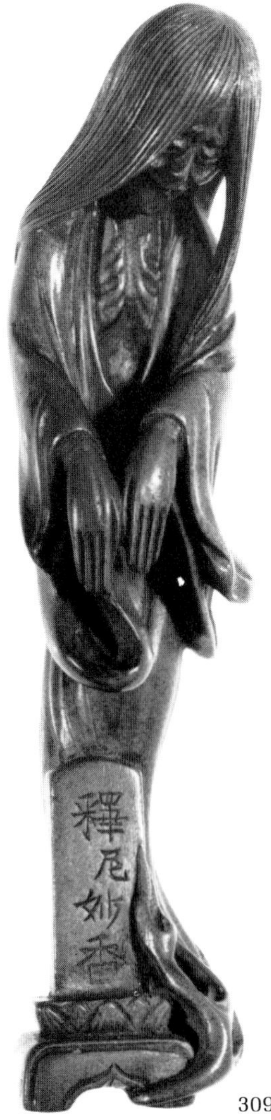

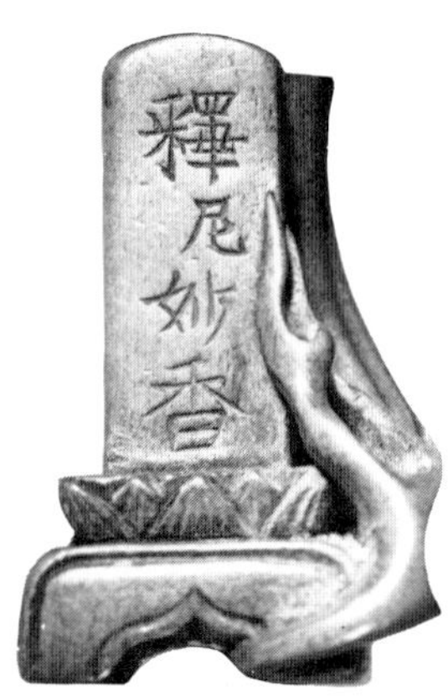

309

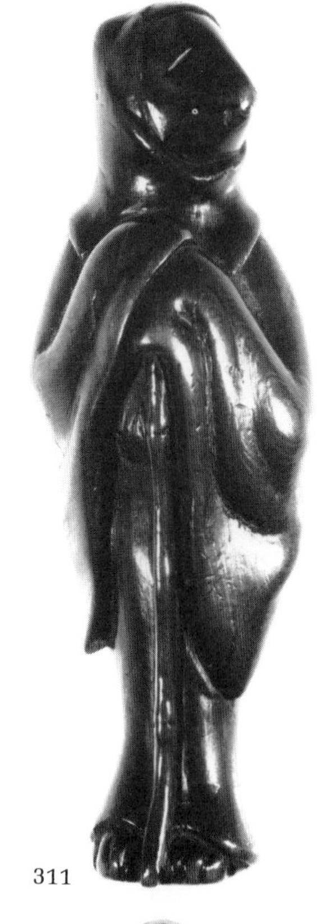

311

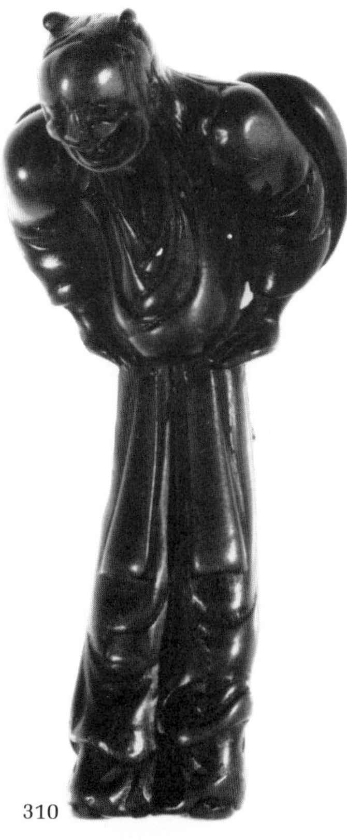

310

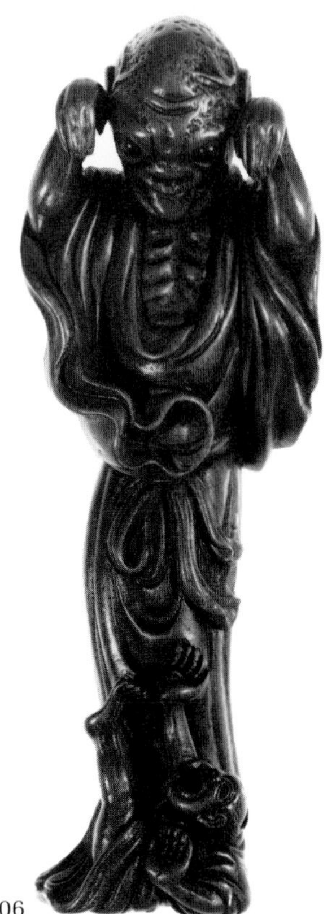

306

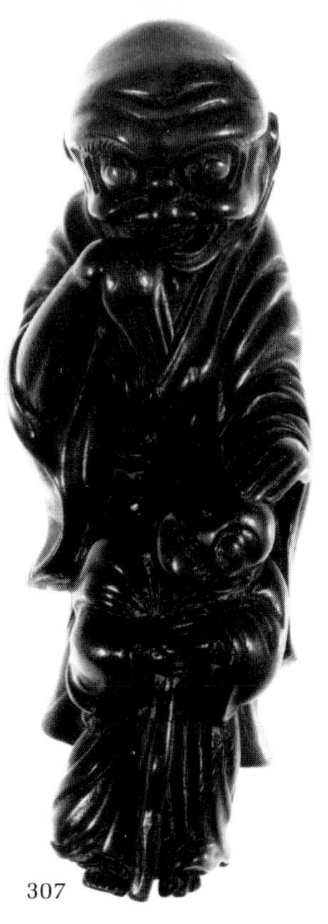

307

308
Long-necked *bakemono* crouching over a peasant's hat, under which are carved in half-relief a fence, a scarecrow and a bird-alarm.
Wood, the eyes inlaid.
Unsigned.
19th century.
Length 3.7cm (1½in).
1945 10-17 651. Bequeathed by Oscar Raphael.

309
Ghost of a woman rising from a gravestone, inscribed Shaka Ji Myōkō ('The Buddha's Nun Myōkō'). Wood.
Unsigned.
19th century.
Height 9.4cm (3¾in).
1912 10-12 5. Given by Mrs H. Seymour Trower.

310
Hannya (woman turning to a demon). Wood.
Unsigned.
18th century.
Height 6.75cm (2¾in).
1945 10-17 543. Bequeathed by Oscar Raphael.

311
Fox priest. Wood.
Unsigned.
18th century.
Height 10.8cm (4½in).
1945 10-17 576.
Bequeathed by Oscar Raphael.

For a similar example in ivory, *see* N. K. Davey, *Netsuke*, p. 318, no. 972.

312
Seal in the form of a heraldic lion resting on an ornamental dragon-seat raised on a seal base. Wood.
The seal carved Raku.
Unsigned.
18th century.
Height 8.25cm (3¼in).
F.1105. Franks Collection.

For a similar example in ivory, *see* N. K. Davey, *Netsuke*, p. 319, no. 977.

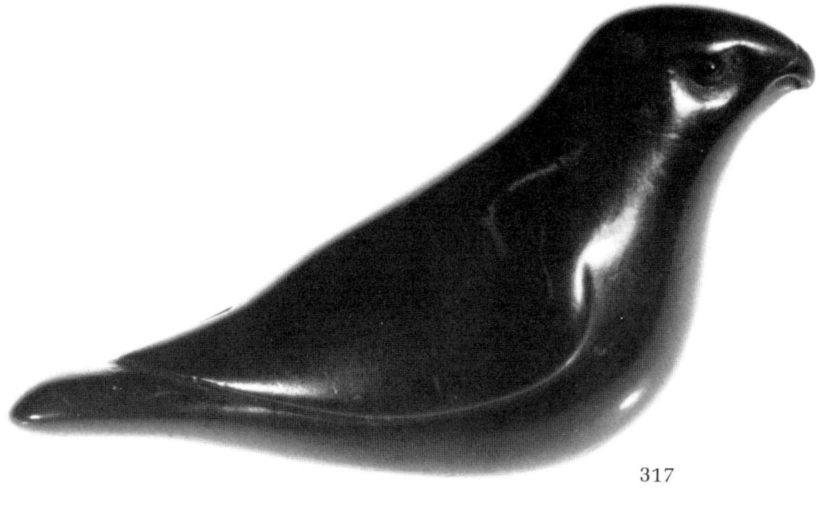

317

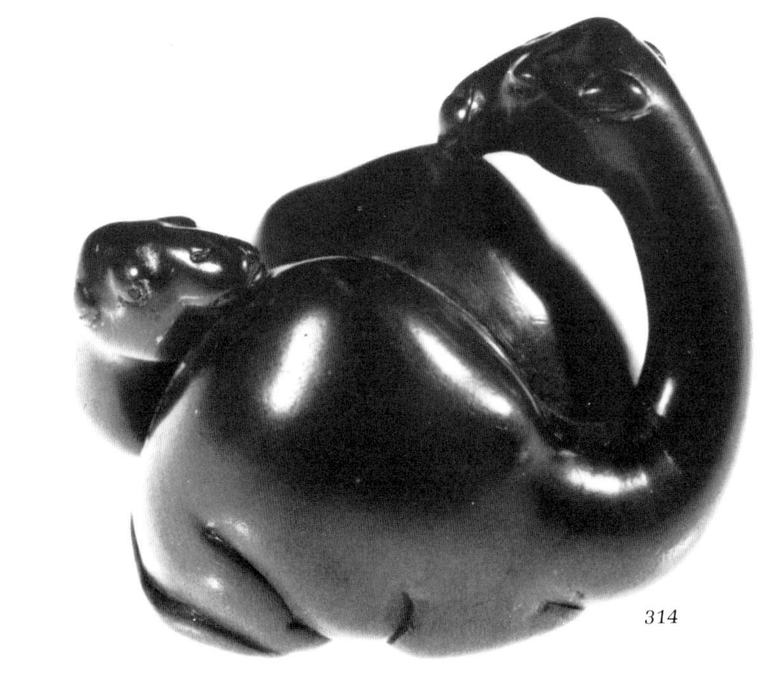

314

315

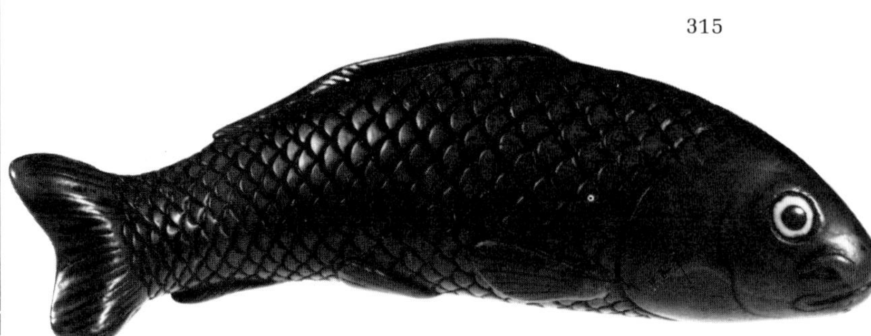

313
Cluster of monkeys. Wood.
Unsigned.
Late 18th century.
Length 6cm ($2\frac{1}{4}$in).
1945 10-17 666. Bequeathed by Oscar Raphael.

314
Two camels.
Wood, the eyes inlaid.
Unsigned.
Early 19th century.
Length 4.5cm ($1\frac{3}{4}$in).
1945 10-17 533. Bequeathed by Oscar Raphael.

For an almost identical example, *see* Frederick Meinertzhagen, *The Art of the Netsuke Carver*, no. 128.

315
Swimming carp.
Wood, the eyes inlaid in ivory with the pupils in horn.
Unsigned.
Late 18th century.
Length 7.6cm (3in).
F.1075. Franks Collection.

316
Two bamboo shoots, one hollowed out and containing a minute figure of Mōsō, visible through wormholes. Wood.
Unsigned.
19th century.
Height 5.25cm ($2\frac{1}{4}$in).
F.1006. Franks Collection.

Mōsō was one of the Chinese '24 Paragons of Filial Piety'. He gathered bamboo shoots in the depth of winter for his old mother.

317
Stylized hawk. Wood.
Unsigned.
Early 19th century.
Length 5.25cm ($2\frac{1}{4}$in).
1945 10-17 582. Bequeathed by Oscar Raphael.

318
Model of a Bizen pottery saké-bottle, stamped with a figure of the popular god Hotei. Wood.
Unsigned.
19th century.
Height 4.5cm ($1\frac{3}{4}$in).
F.369. Franks Collection.

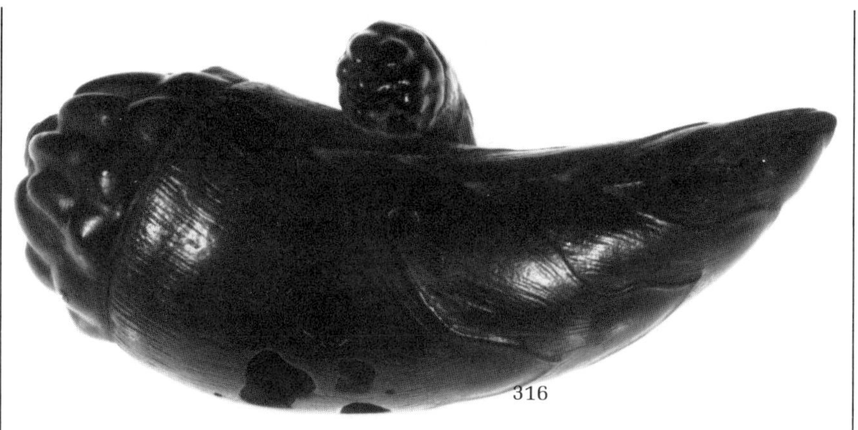
316

319
Pine cone, opening to reveal Jō and Uba, the type of an old couple. Wood.
Unsigned.
19th century.
Height 3.75cm ($1\frac{1}{2}$in).
F.1008. Franks Collection.

320
Rubbed ink stick, carved on one side with Daruma on a diaper ground, and on the other with characters in seal-script.
Ebony.
Unsigned.
Late 18th–early 19th century.
Length 5.75cm ($2\frac{1}{4}$in).
F.1056. Franks Collection.

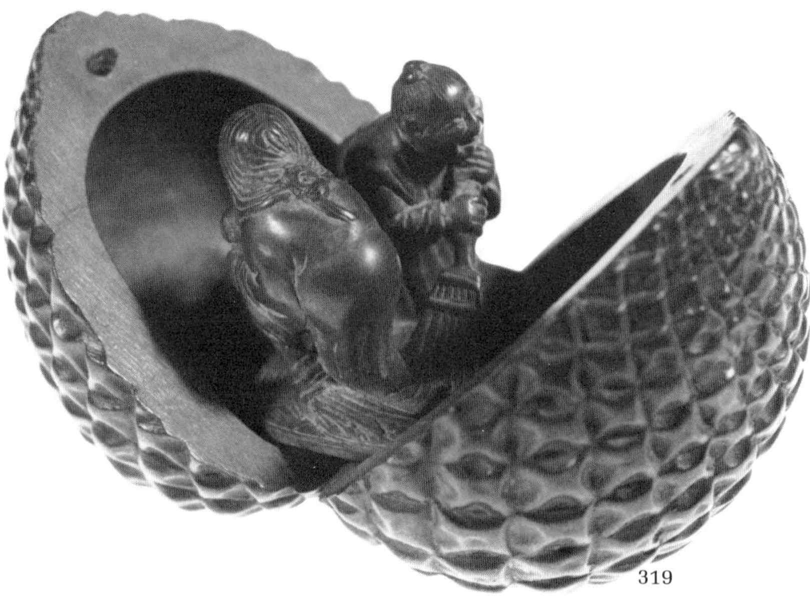
319

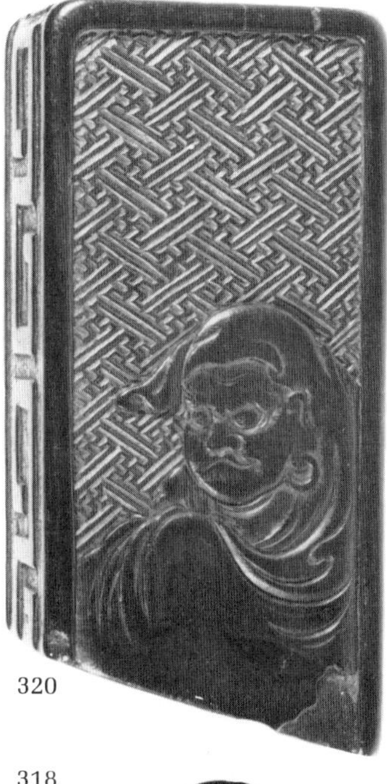
320

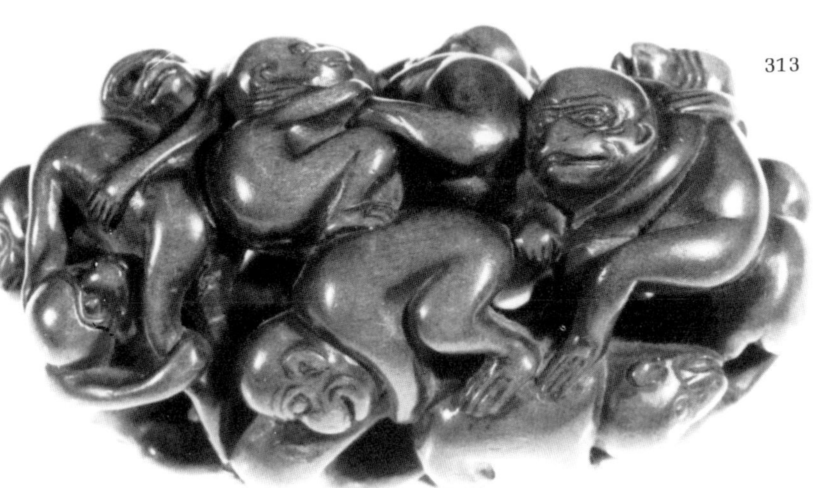
313

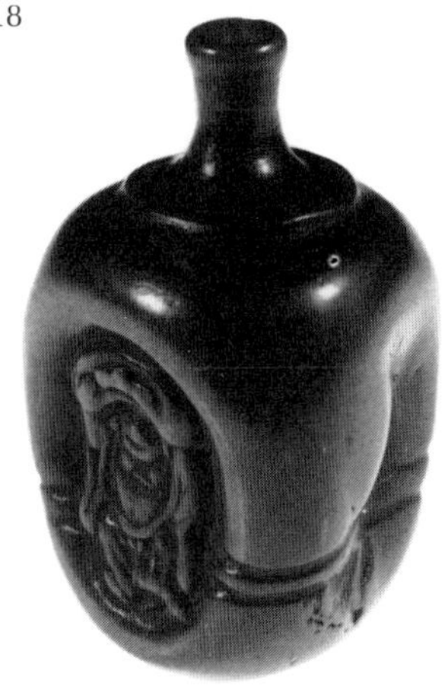
318

Unsigned: Ivory

321
Sennin with a gnarled staff and a gourd in his belt. The piece balances on one foot. Ivory.
Unsigned.
19th century.
Height 10cm (4in).
1930 12-17 63. Bequeathed by James Hilton.

322
Sennin holding a ?basket. Ivory.
Unsigned.
18th century.
Height 9.8cm (4in).
1945 10-17 559. Bequeathed by Oscar Raphael.

323
The *Sennin* Chōkarō standing with his gourd on his shoulders. Ivory.
Unsigned.
18th century.
Height 8.9cm (3½in).
1930 12-17 65. Bequeathed by James Hilton.

324
A *sennin*. Ivory.
Unsigned.
18th century.
Height 11.5cm (4½in).
1930 12-17 62. Bequeathed by James Hilton.

325
Gama Sennin with a string of cash in one hand, his toad perched on his shoulder. Ivory.
Unsigned.
18th century.
Height 10cm (4in).
1945 10-17 670. Bequeathed by Oscar Raphael.

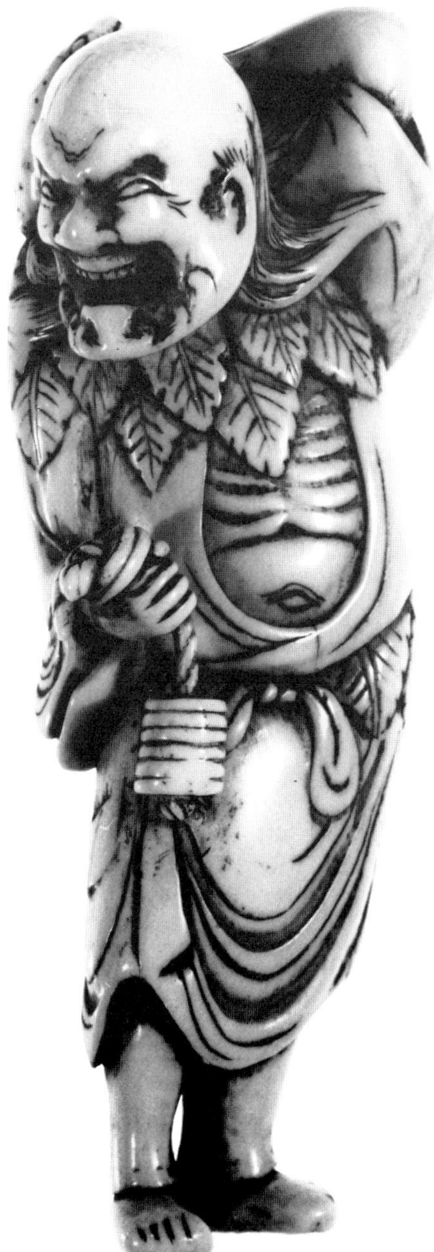

325

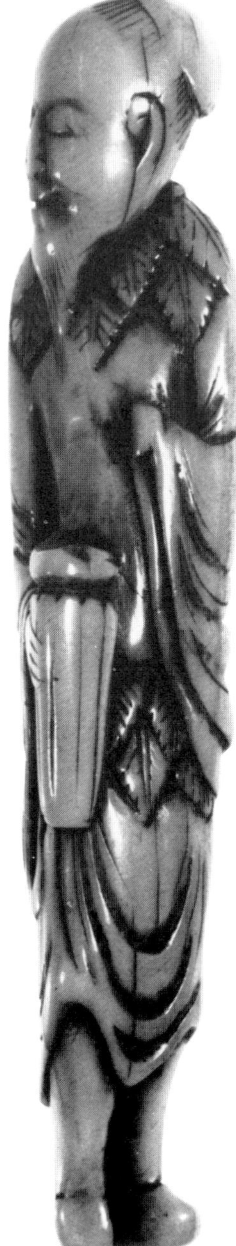

322

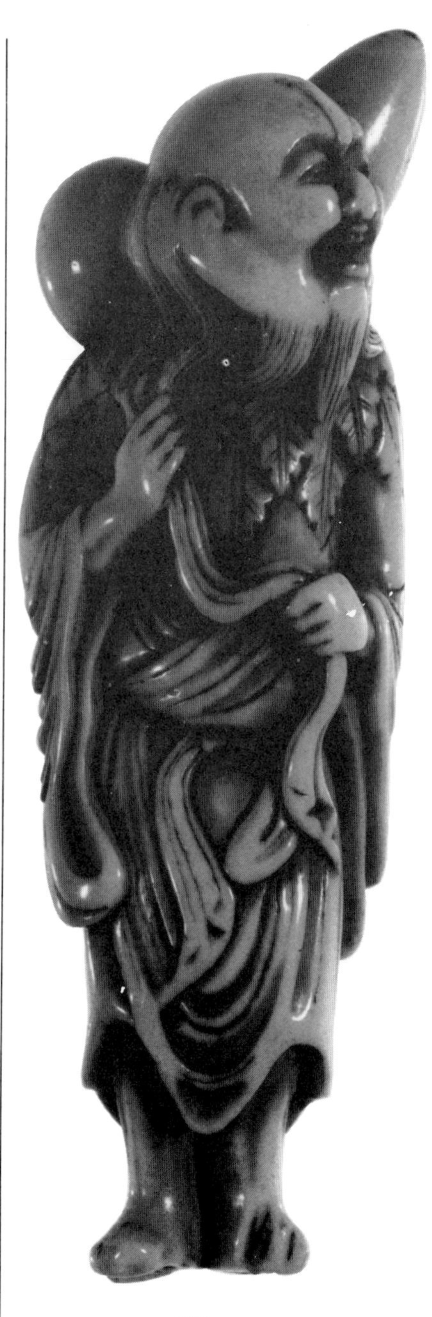

323

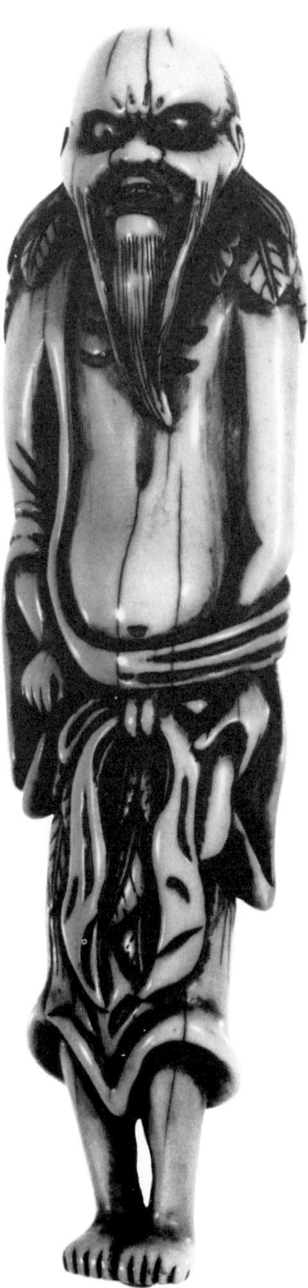

324

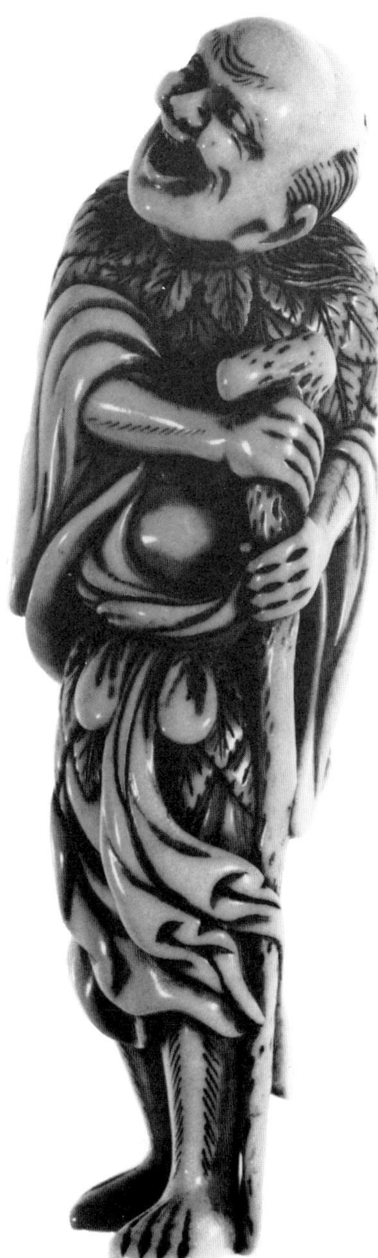

331

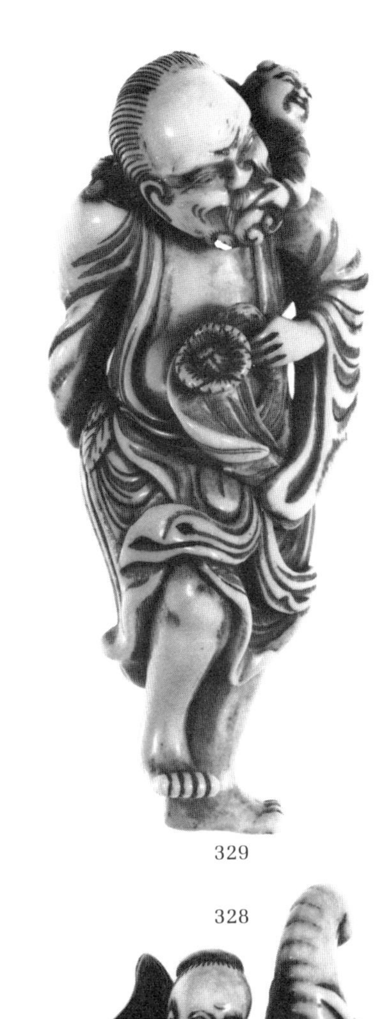

329

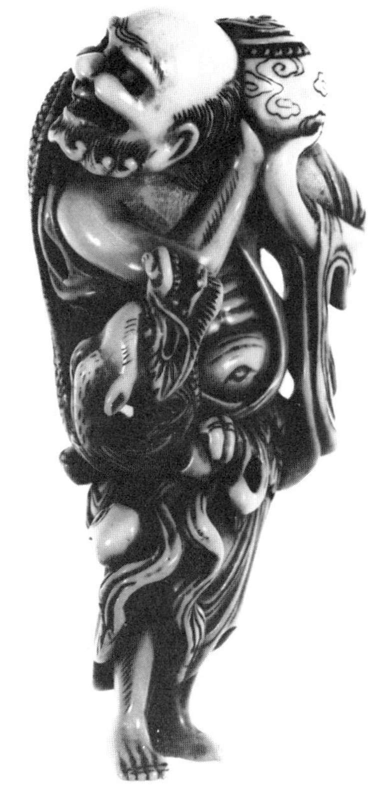

327

328

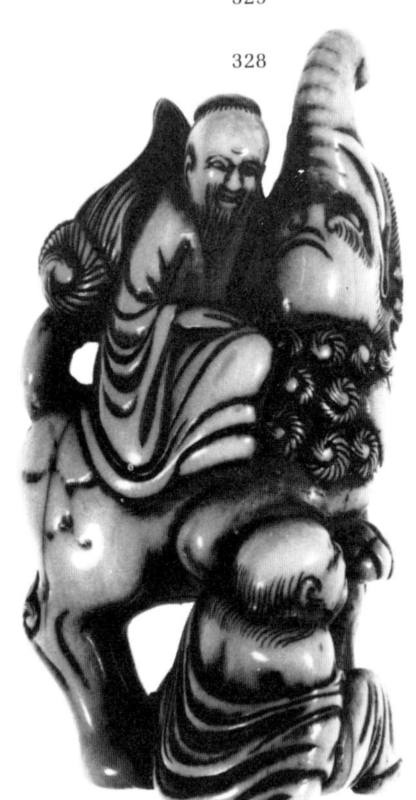

330

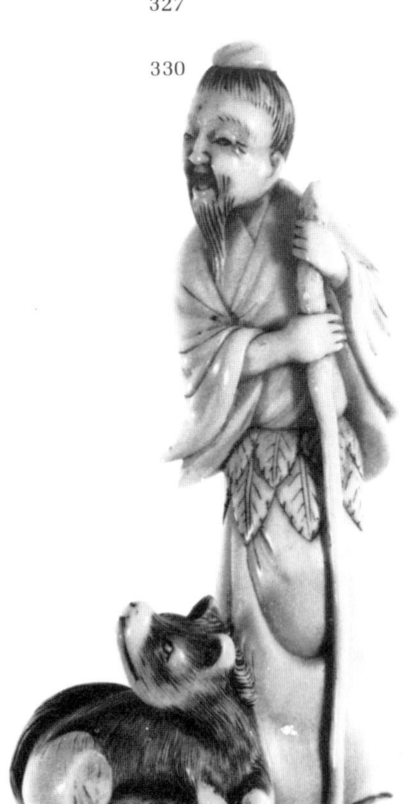

326
Chōkarō and his gourd and Gama Sennin with his toad. Ivory.
Unsigned.
Late 18th century.
Height 10.2cm (4in).
1930 12-17 64. Bequeathed by James Hilton.
Colour plate. page 13

327
The *rakan* Handaka Sonja, holding his bowl with the dragon emerging from it. Ivory.
Unsigned.
Late 18th century.
Height 8.9cm (3½in).
1930 12-17 49. Bequeathed by James Hilton.

328
Two Chinese Immortals, one riding on a *baku* (a legendary elephant-like creature). Ivory.
Unsigned.
Late 18th century.
Height 6.4cm (2½in).
1972 1-14 28. Bequeathed by Mrs Rosina Maria Howe.

329
Sennin, standing on one leg and holding a wilting flower, sucking the finger of the boy on his back. Ivory.
Unsigned.
Late 18th century.
Height 8.25cm (3¼in).
OA + 120. Franks Collection.

330
Sennin holding a staff, a fox with trifurcated tail beside him. Ivory.
Unsigned.
Early 19th century.
Height 7cm (2¾in).
OA + 121. Franks Collection.

The construction implies that the fox is bewitching or even turning into the *sennin*.
Colour plate. page 13

331
Tekkai Sennin. Ivory.
Unsigned.
18th century.
Height 10cm (4in).
1945 10-17 518. Bequeathed by Oscar Raphael.

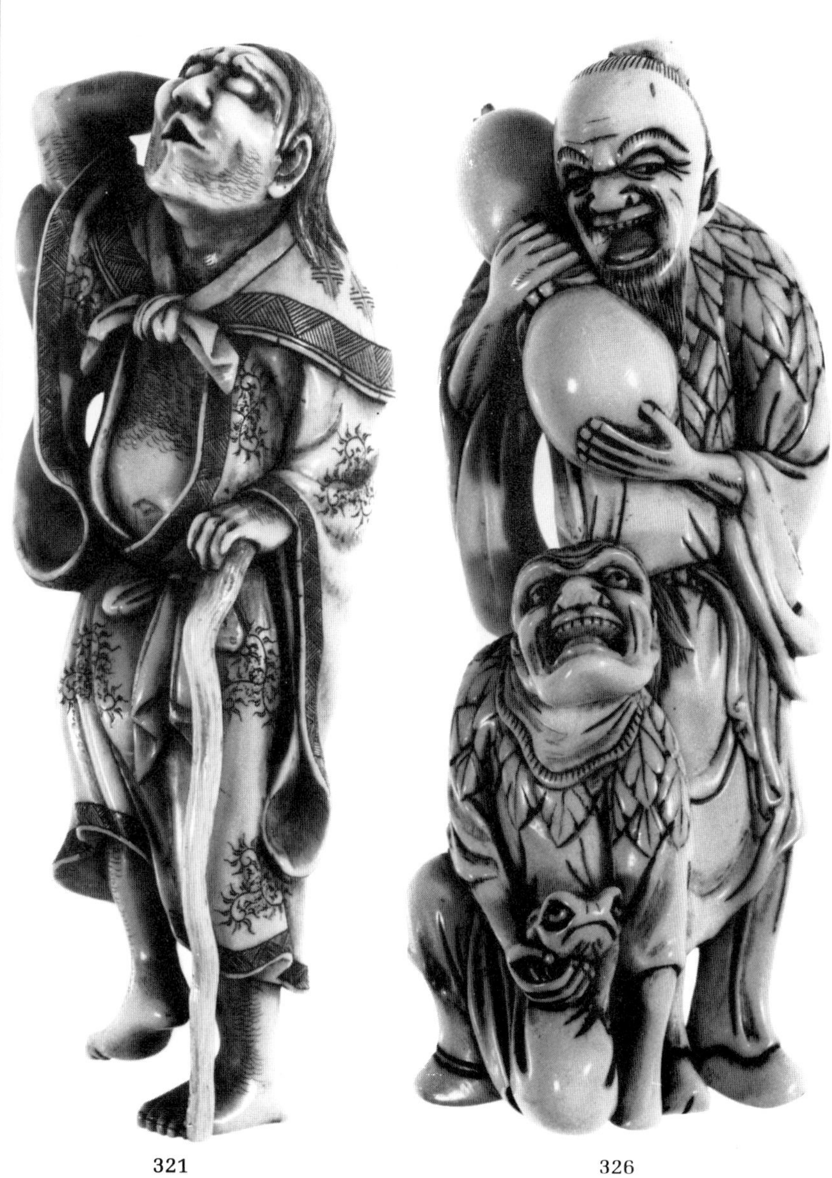

321 326

332
Sennin with gnarled staff, a gourd in his belt.
Ivory, deliberately stained, the mouth reddened.
Unsigned.
19th century.
Height 7.4cm ($2\frac{3}{4}$in).
F.740. Franks Collection.

333
Gama *Sennin* with a peach bough and his toad on his head.
Ivory, deliberately stained.
Unsigned.
19th century.
Height 10.2cm (4in).
F.57. Franks Collection.

334
Rakan seated on a rock with two gourds hanging from his shoulder. Signed Ryuzan in an inlaid rectangular cartouche on the base, added later.
18th century.
Height 5.3cm ($2\frac{1}{4}$in).
F.965. Franks Collection.

335
Daruma in flattened form, carved in half relief. Ivory.
Unsigned.
18th century.
Height 6cm ($2\frac{1}{4}$in).
1945 10-17 567. Bequeathed by Oscar Raphael.

Exhibited Red Cross, London, 1915, no. 23, illustrated pl. XLVII.

336
The popular gods Hotei and Daikoku as *sumō* wrestlers.
Ivory.
Unsigned.
18th century.
Height 7cm ($2\frac{3}{4}$in).
1945 10-17 596. Bequeathed by Oscar Raphael.

337
Chinese archer.
Ivory, deliberately stained.
Unsigned.
18th century.
Height 12.4cm ($4\frac{3}{4}$in).
1945 10-17 517. Bequeathed by Oscar Raphael.

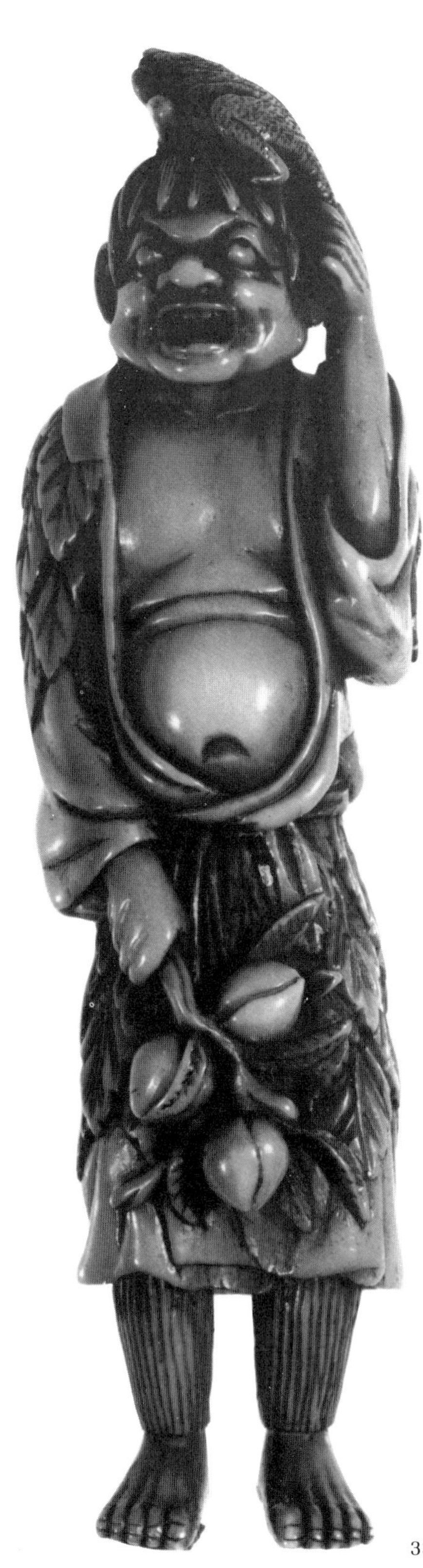

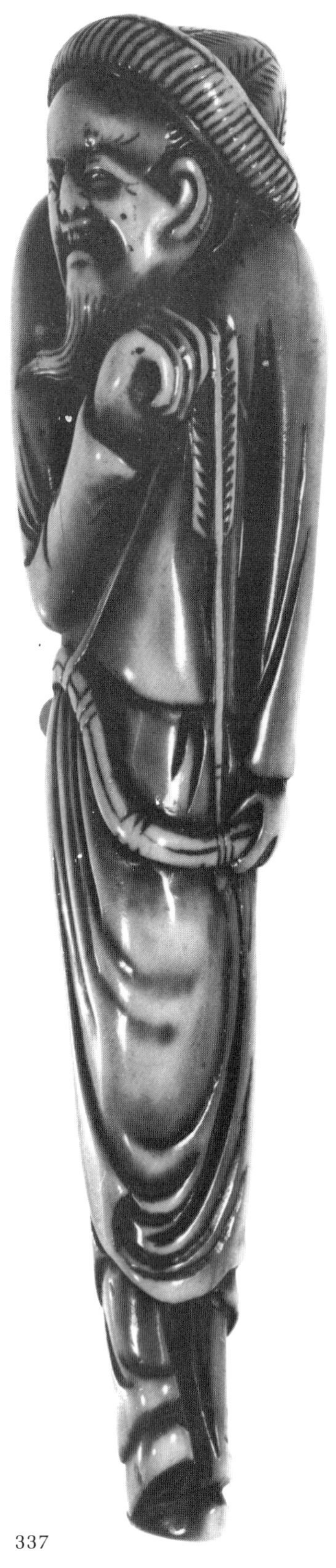

333 337

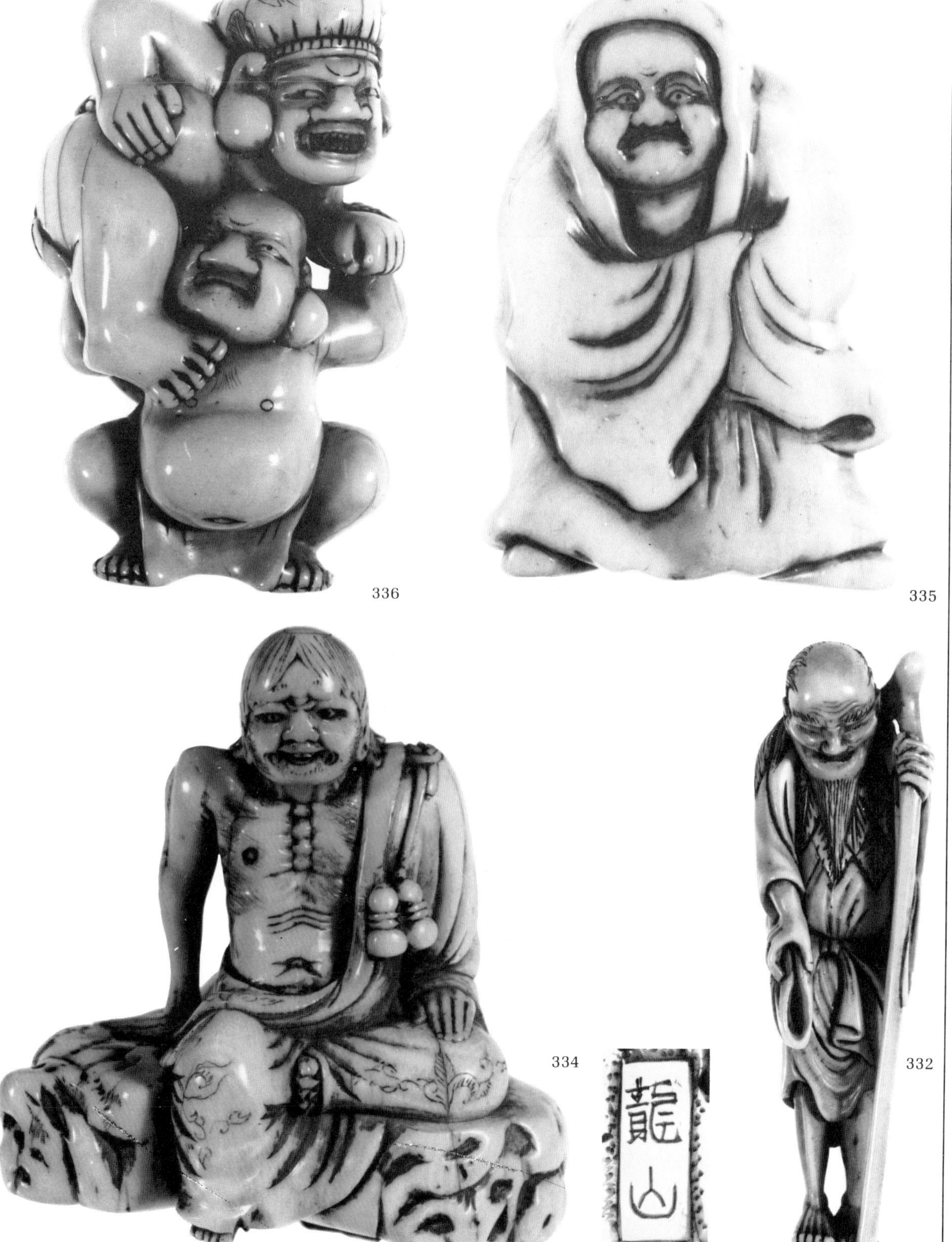

336

335

334

332

338
Kanzan and Jittoku examining a scroll with archaic Chinese characters. Ivory.
Unsigned.
Late 18th century.
Height 6.4cm ($2\frac{1}{2}$in).
1930 12-17 66. Bequeathed by James Hilton
Colour plate, page 13

339
The Chinese Emperor Meikō (Ming Huang) and his concubine Yōhiki (Yang Kuei-Fei) sharing a flute and a throne. Ivory.
Unsigned.
18th century.
Height 7.4cm (3in).
1945 10-17 595. Bequeathed by Oscar Raphael.

Ming Huang's partiality for his mistress was the most celebrated scandal of Far Eastern history.

340
Kanyū stroking his beard. Ivory.
Unsigned.
Late 18th century.
Height 9.5cm ($3\frac{1}{4}$in).
F.690. Franks Collection.

341
The Chinese hero Chao Yün on a horse, rescuing the son of his defeated master Liu Pei. Ivory.
Unsigned.
18th century.
Height 9.5cm ($3\frac{3}{4}$in).
1930 12-17 76. Bequeathed by James Hilton.
Colour plate, page 13

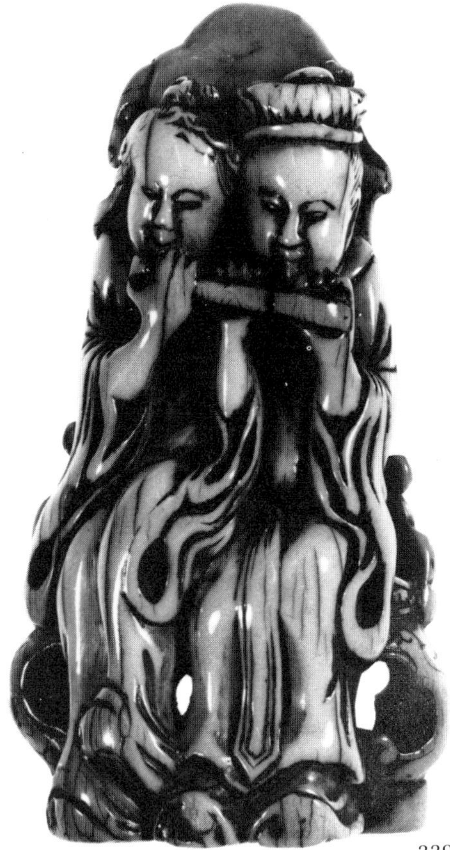
339

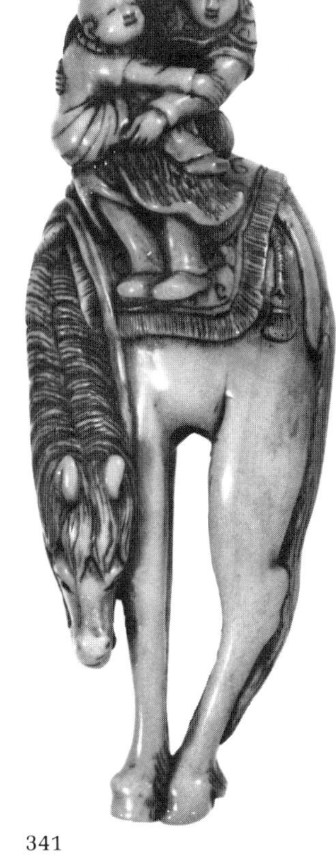
341

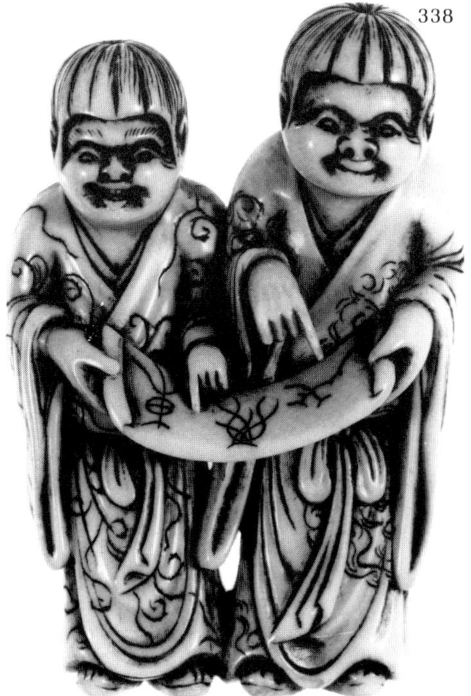
338

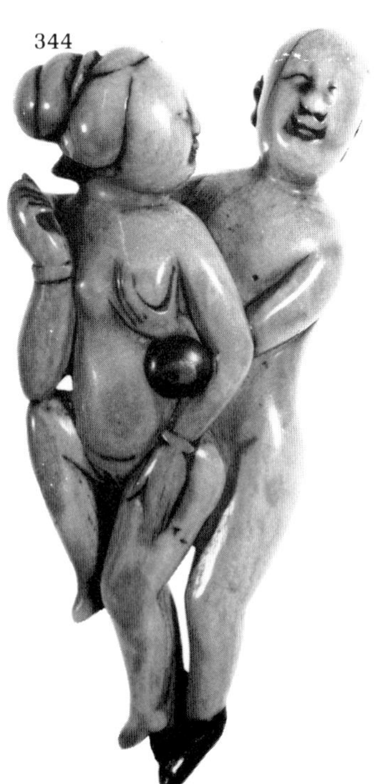
344

342
Shoki holding a tiny struggling demon in his hand while a bigger one climbs onto his shoulders. Ivory.
Unsigned.
18th century.
Height 13.35cm ($5\frac{1}{4}$in).
1945 10-17 600. Bequeathed by Oscar Raphael.
Colour plate, page 13

343
Two trackers pulling a tow-rope along a river bank.
Ivory, deliberately stained.
Unsigned.
18th century.
Length 6.4cm ($2\frac{1}{2}$in).
1945 10-17 641. Bequeathed by Oscar Raphael.

Exhibited Red Cross, London, 1915, no. 11, illustrated pl. XLVII.

344
Naked lovers, in the style of the 'medical' pieces, probably made in China.
Ivory, deliberately stained, a metal ring attached for the cord.
Unsigned.
18th century.
Length 8.9cm (4in).
1945 10-17 676. Bequeathed by Oscar Raphael.

For a similar example, *see* R. Bushell, *Netsuke, Familiar and Unfamiliar*, p. 112, no. 130.

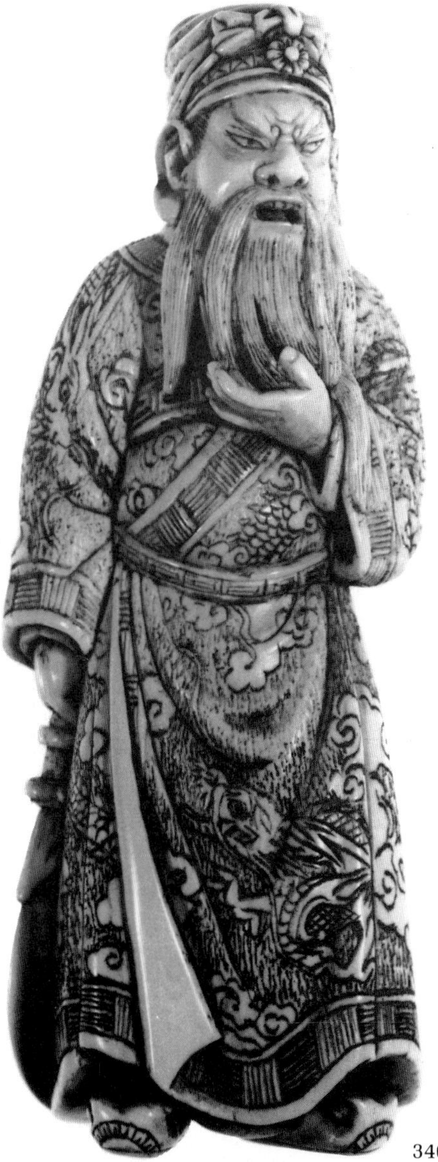

340

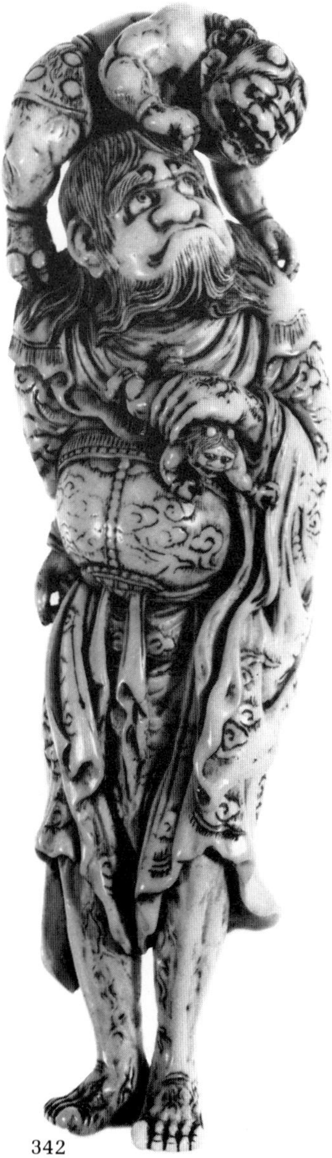

342

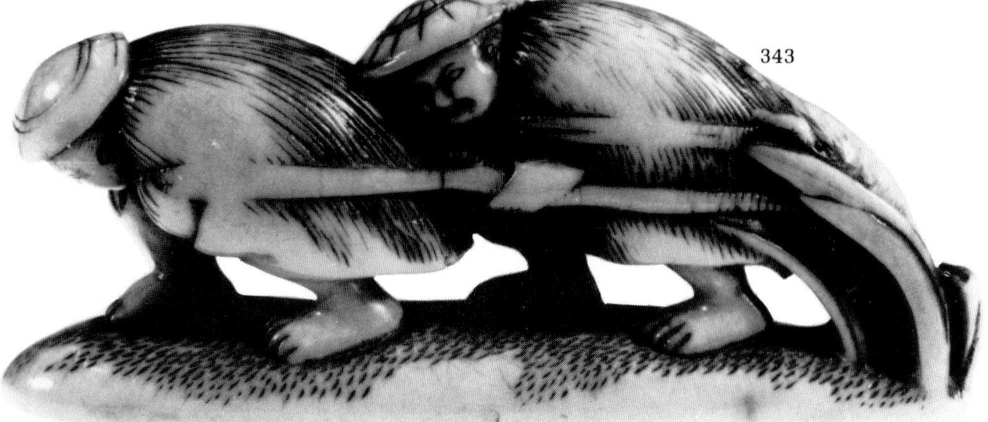
343

345
Sennin wearing a straw apron and holding a basket. Ivory.
Unsigned.
18th century.
Height 10.8cm ($4\frac{1}{4}$in).
1945 10-17 598. Bequeathed by Oscar Raphael.

346
Court lady of the Heian Period, her trailing robe tucked up behind. Ivory.
Unsigned.
18th century.
Height 11.5cm ($4\frac{1}{2}$in).
1945 10-17 597. Bequeathed by Oscar Raphael.

347
A street dancer with fan. Ivory.
Unsigned.
Early 19th century.
Height 8cm (3in).
1942 10-13 17. Bequeathed by Mrs Violet E. F. Becker.

348
A blind man attacked by a dog. He wears a tobacco pouch with a gourd netsuke. Ivory.
Unsigned.
19th century.
Height 3.75cm ($1\frac{1}{2}$in).
F.615. Franks Collection.

349
Itinerant saké-seller under a huge hat. Ivory.
Unsigned.
19th century.
Height 2.8cm (1in).
F.155. Franks Collection.

350
A young Chinese holding a coral handled umbrella. Ivory.
Unsigned.
18th century.
Height 11.5cm ($4\frac{1}{2}$in).
F.103. Franks Collection.

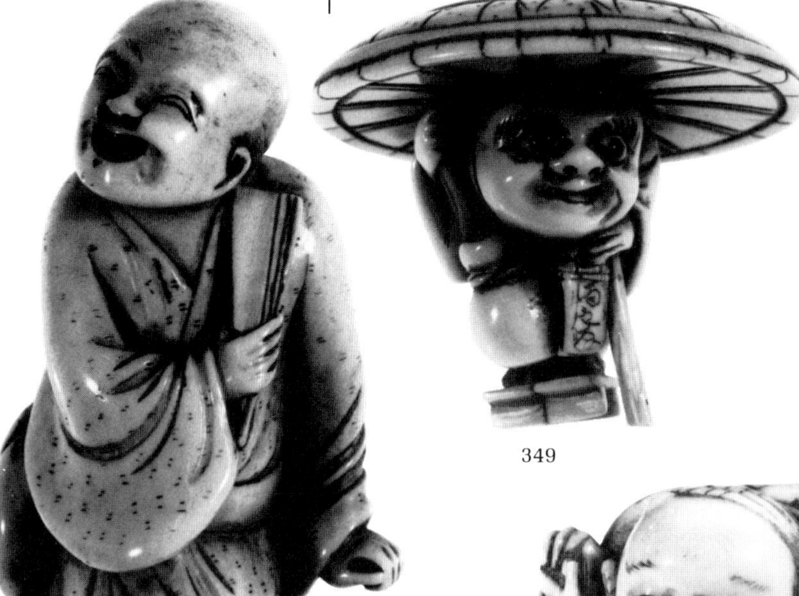

349

347

348

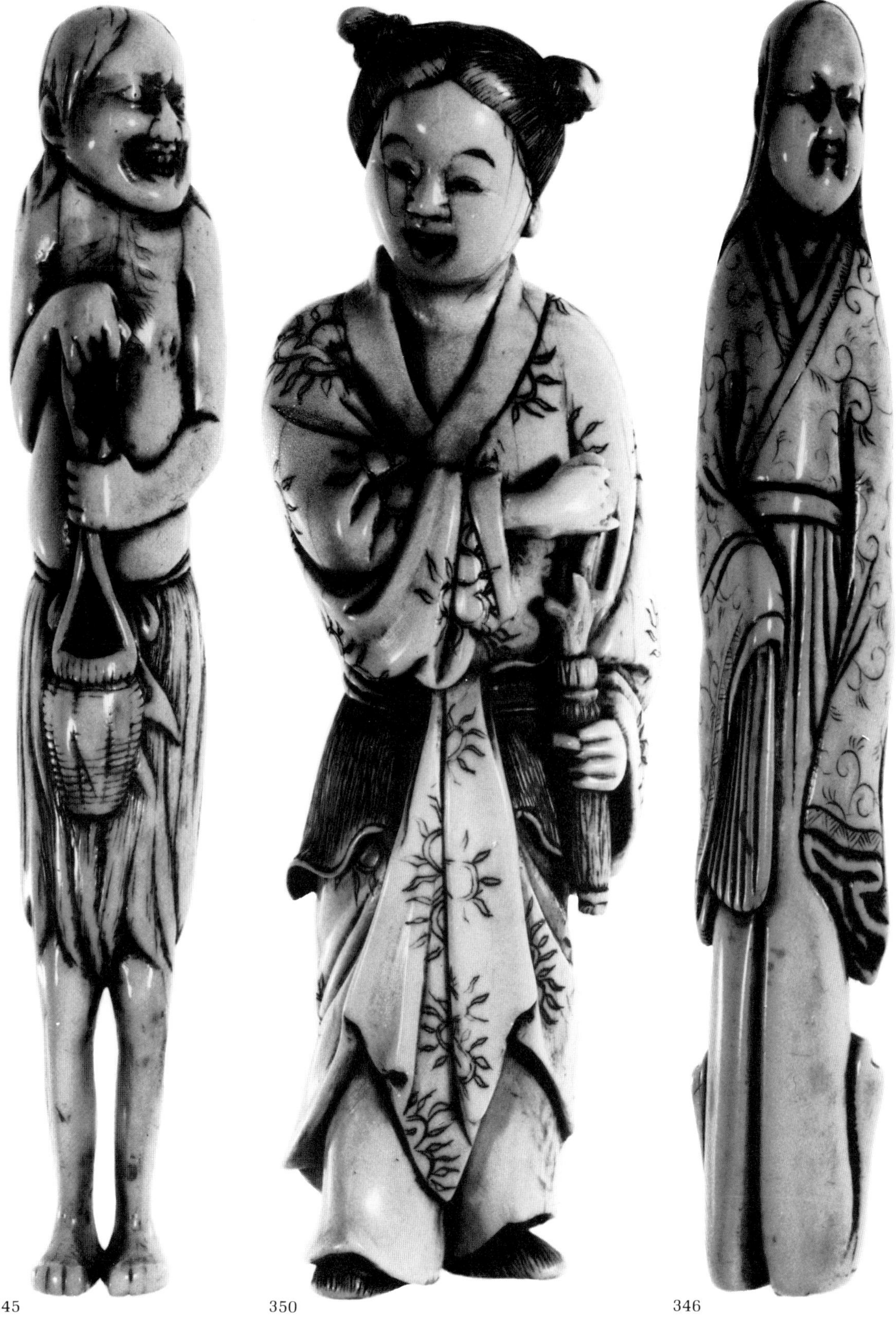

345 350 346

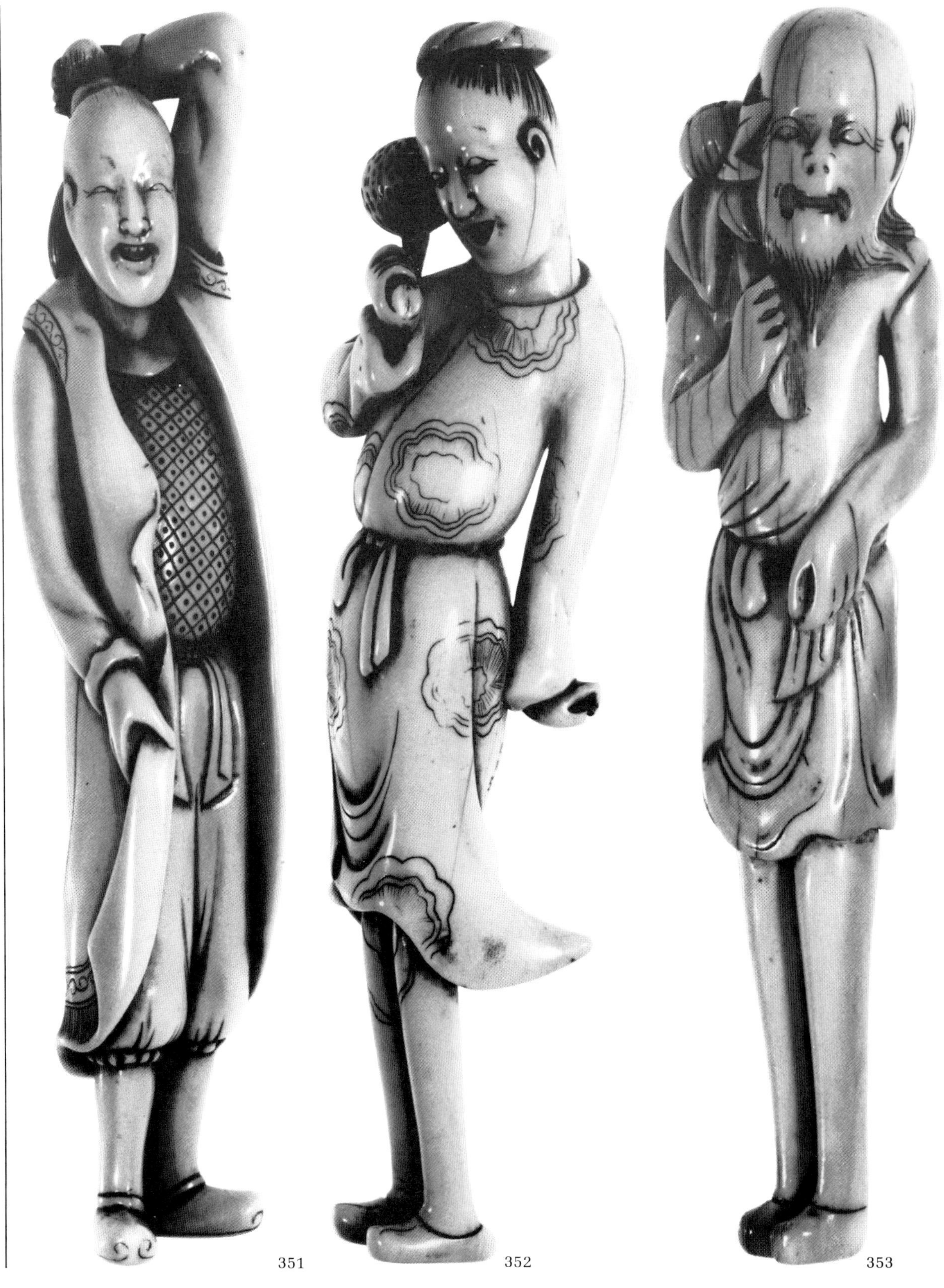

351

352

353

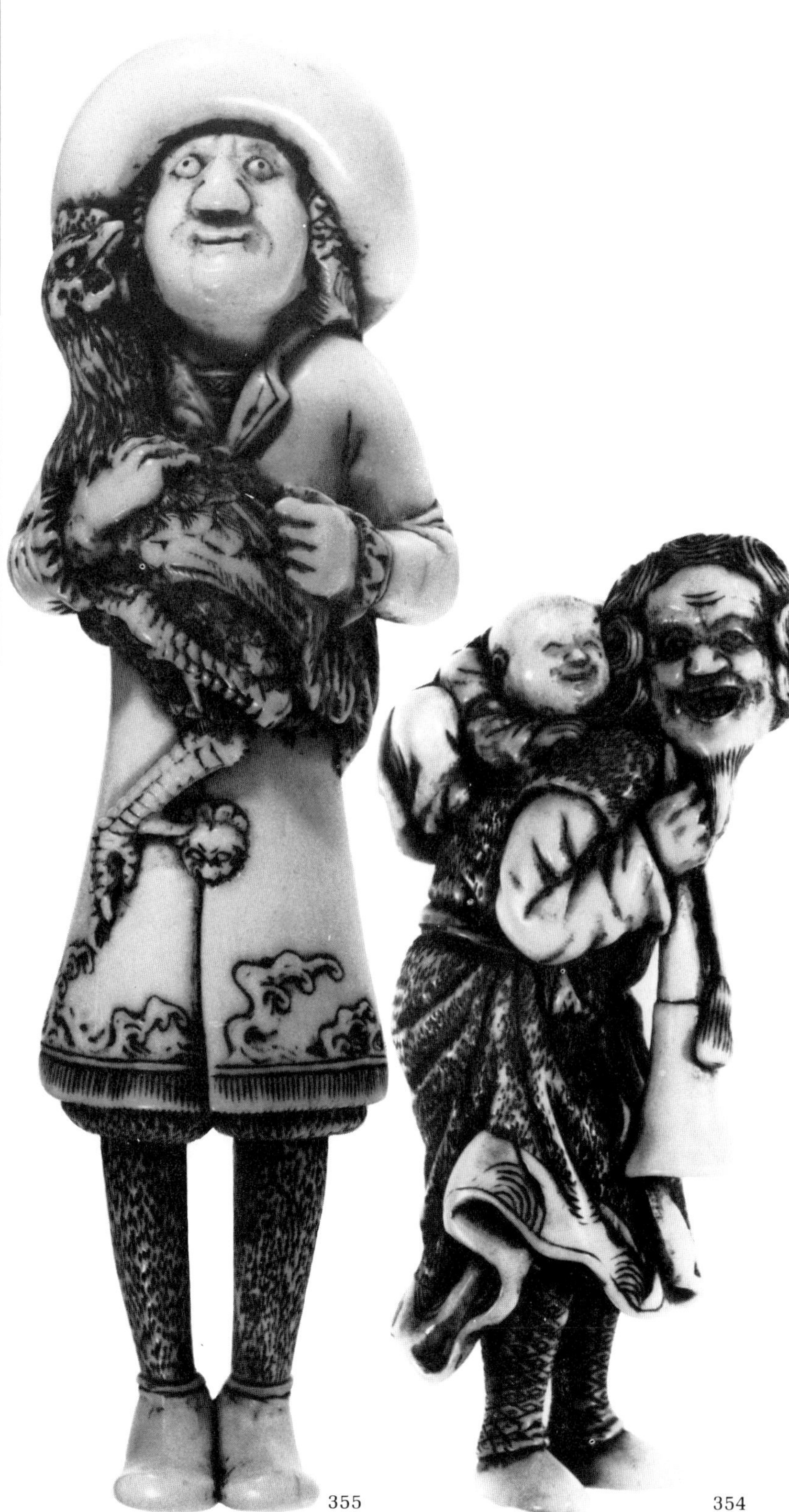
355 354

351
Chinese merchant. Ivory.
Unsigned.
18th century.
Height 11cm ($4\frac{1}{4}$in).
1945 10-17 537. Bequeathed by Oscar Raphael.

352
Young Chinese holding a flower. Ivory, metal button.
Unsigned.
18th century.
Height 13.3cm ($5\frac{3}{4}$in).
1945 10-17 558. Bequeathed by Oscar Raphael.

353
Sennin holding a lily over his shoulder. Ivory.
Unsigned.
18th century.
Height 12.1cm ($4\frac{3}{4}$in).
F.596. Franks Collection.

354
Chinaman with a trumpet, a boy on his back. Ivory.
Unsigned.
18th century.
Height 7cm ($2\frac{3}{4}$in).
F.563. Franks Collection.

355
Dutchman holding a cockerel. Ivory.
Unsigned.
18th century.
Height 11.8cm ($4\frac{3}{4}$in).
F.558. Franks Collection.

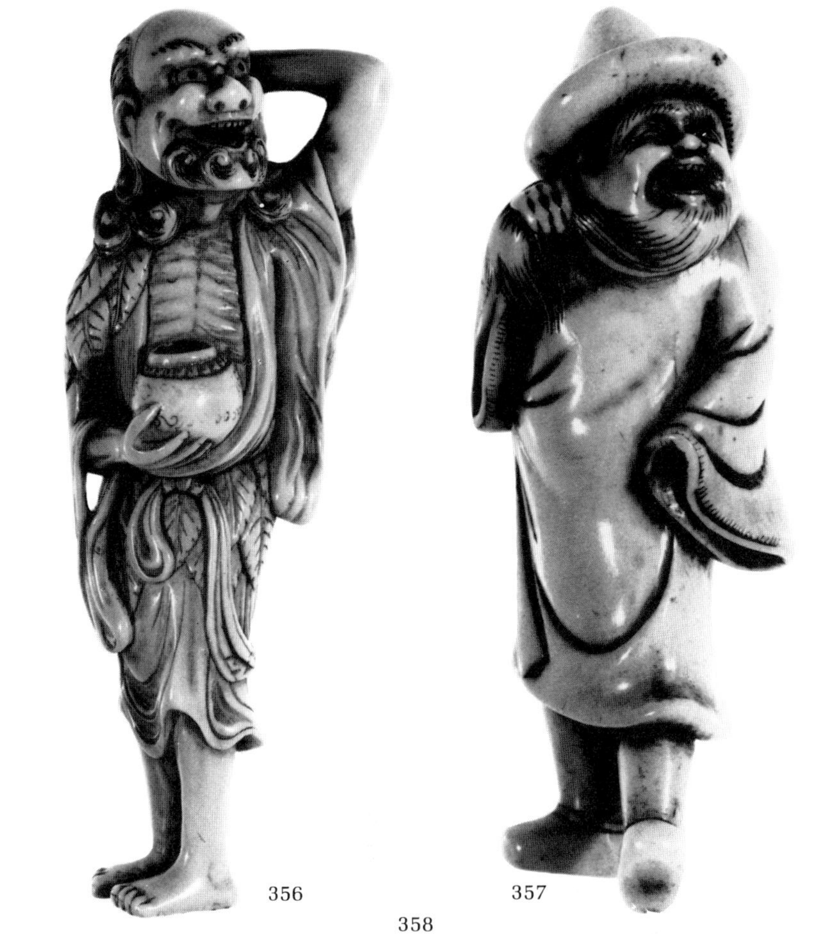

356 357

358

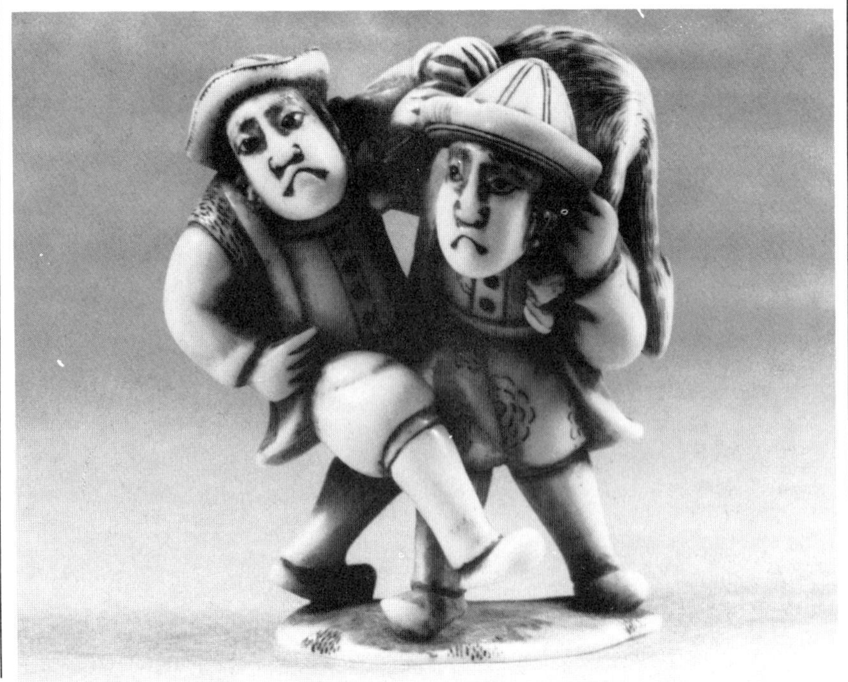

356
Sennin with begging bowl.
Ivory.
Unsigned.
18th century.
Height 11.5cm ($4\frac{1}{2}$in).
F.595. Franks Collection.

357
Chinaman holding his beard.
Ivory.
Unsigned.
18th century.
Height 7.6cm (3in).
1945 10-17 566. Bequeathed by Oscar Raphael.

358
Drunken Dutchmen, one with a dead deer over his shoulder.
Ivory, the eyes and buttons inlaid.
Unsigned.
Early 19th century.
Height 4.2cm ($1\frac{1}{4}$in).
F.562. Franks Collection.

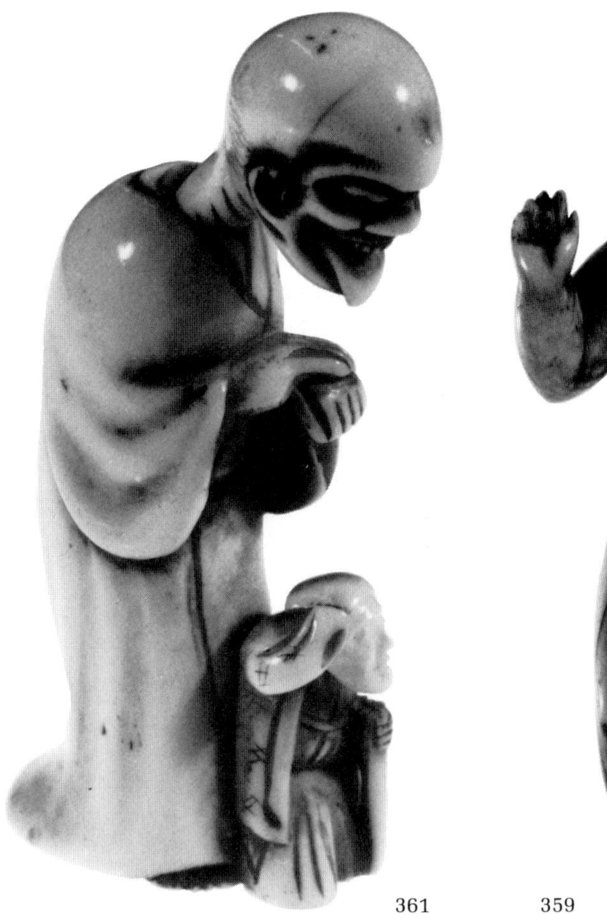

361 359

360

359
Christ Child with orb. Made for the Jesuits in Goa or Macao and converted into a netsuke. Such an overt Christian image could not have been openly used in

Japan during the proscription of Christianity (total 1639–1853), and this piece was probably made in the early seventeenth century. When it was converted to a netsuke is uncertain.
Ivory.
Unsigned.
17th century.
Height 6.7cm ($2\frac{1}{4}$in).
F.572. Franks Collection.

360
Netsuke carved in openwork with a female ghost in a willow tree. Ivory.
Unsigned.
19th century.
Length 4.5cm ($1\frac{3}{4}$in).
F.1158. Franks Collection.

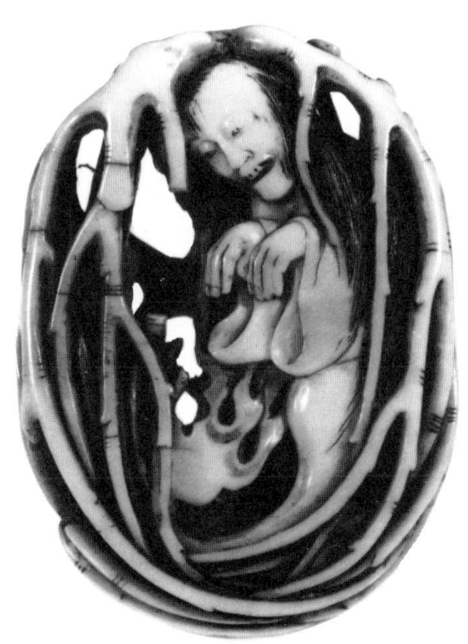

361
Huge *bakemono* with extendable neck looming over an unconcerned blind man. Ivory, the apparition's eyes inlaid.
Unsigned.
Early 19th century.
Height with neck extended 6.4cm ($2\frac{1}{2}$in).
F.758. Franks Collection.

For a similar example, in wood, see R. Bushell, *The Netsuke Handbook of Ueda Reikichi*, p. 141, no. 136.

362
Three foxes, one holding in its mouth a key, an attribute of the fox-god messenger, Inari. Ivory. Unsigned.
18th century.
Length 4.8cm (2in).
1945 10-17 521. Bequeathed by Oscar Raphael.
Exhibited Red Cross, London, 1915, no. 27, illustrated pl. XLVII.

363
Monkey with two peaches, leaning on a catfish ('earth-quake fish').
Ivory, the eyes of the fish inlaid.
Unsigned.
18th century.
Length 5.1cm (2in).
1953 12-17 5. Bequeathed by Mrs Helen Epstein.
For a similar example *see* N. K. Davey, *Netsuke*, no. 963.
A parody of the god Kadori Myōjin who keeps the great earthquake fish quiet with his gourd.

364
Rat on a dried fish.
Ivory, the eyes inlaid.
Unsigned.
Late 18th century.
Length 8.9cm (4in).
F.1076. Franks Collection.

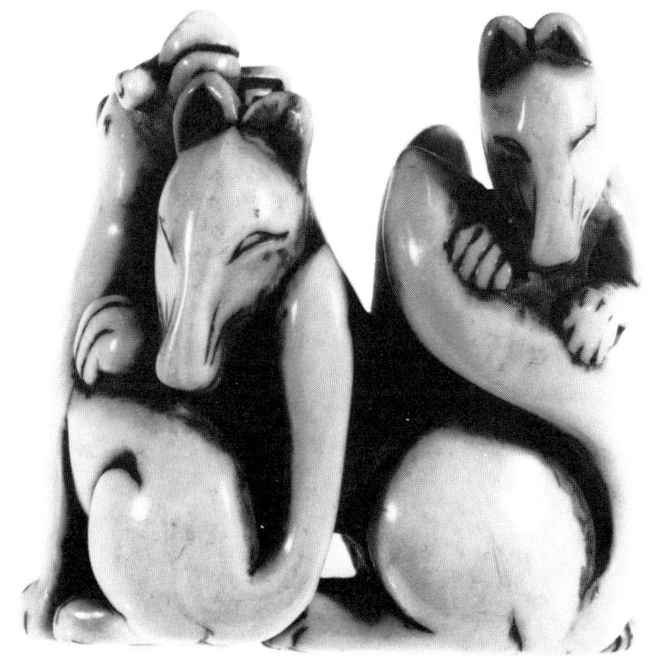

362

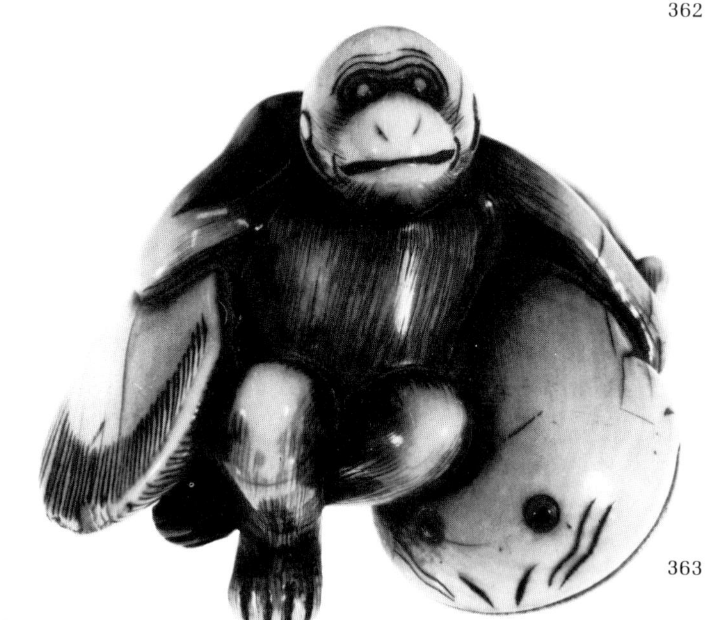

363

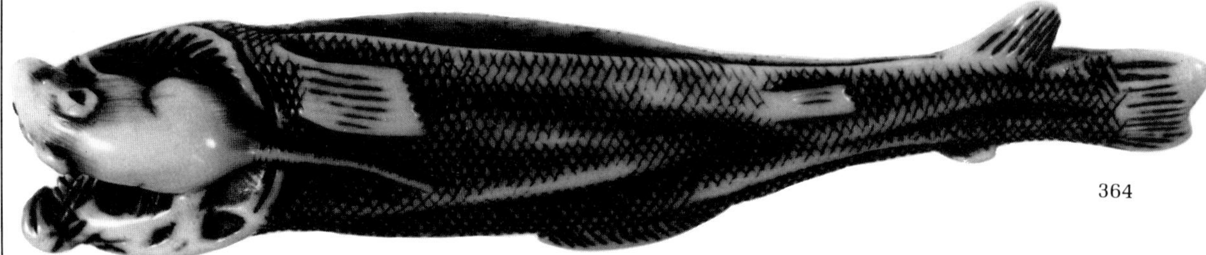

364

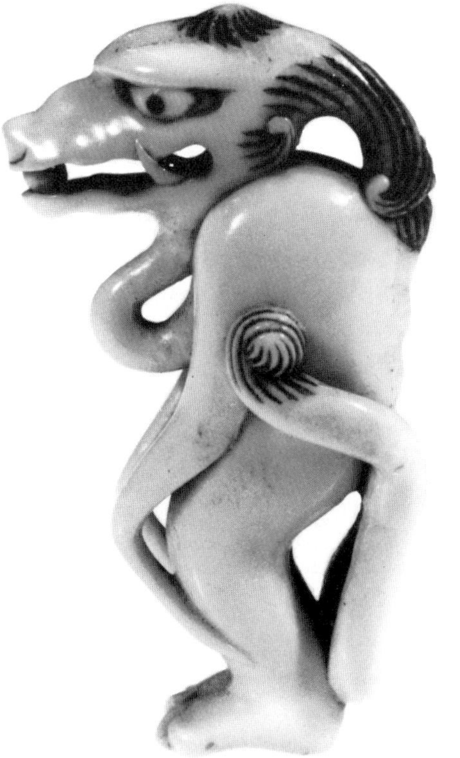

366

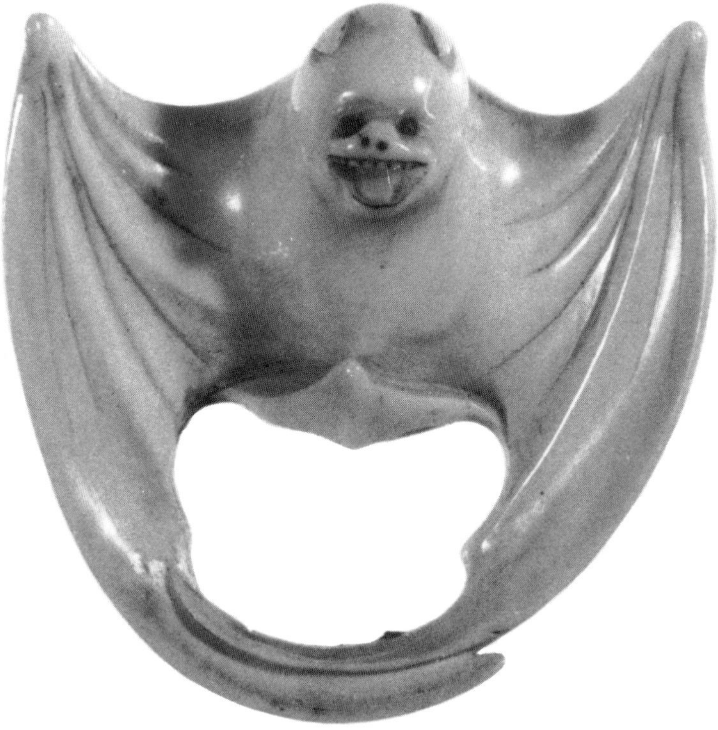

367

365
Lizard on a discarded hat, twined with creeper, on a base carved with a formal motif.
Ivory.
Unsigned.
19th century.
Diameter 4.2cm ($1\frac{3}{4}$in).
F.286. Franks Collection.

366
Bat.
Ivory, eyes inlaid.
Unsigned.
19th century.
Length 3.5cm ($1\frac{1}{4}$in).
F.688. Franks Collection.

367
Bakemono with lion-like body and long neck, with a ball in its jaws, from a design in the *Sōken Kishō*. Ivory.
Unsigned.
Probably 18th century.
Height 5.1cm (2in).
F.817. Franks Collection.

365

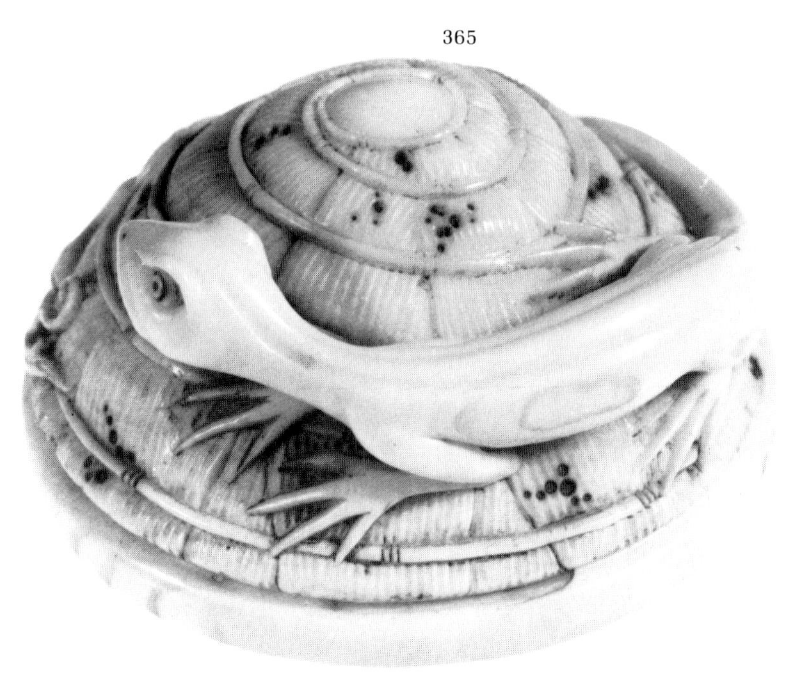

368
Sphere carved in semi-relief openwork in the style of Ryūsa with a *tengu* pursuing a phoenix.
Ivory, the eyes inlaid.
Unsigned.
19th century.
Diameter 4.5cm ($1\frac{3}{4}$in).
OA + 114

369
Tatebina doll. Ivory.
Unsigned.
Late 18th century.
Height 7.6cm (3in).
F.1053. Franks Collection.

370
Five worn-out coins. Ivory.
Unsigned.
19th century.
Length 4.5cm ($1\frac{3}{4}$in).
F.1124. Franks Collection.

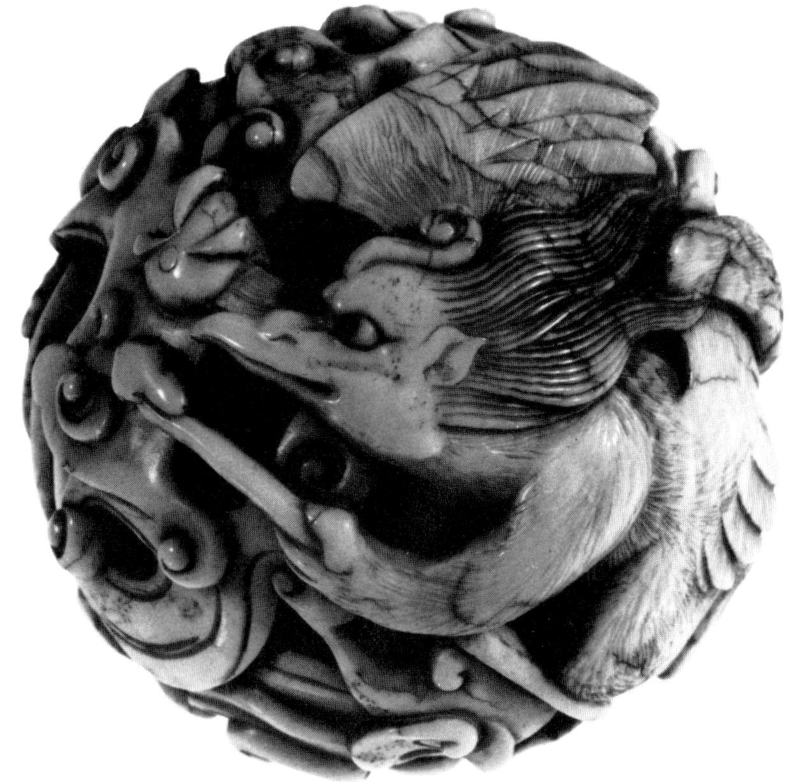
368

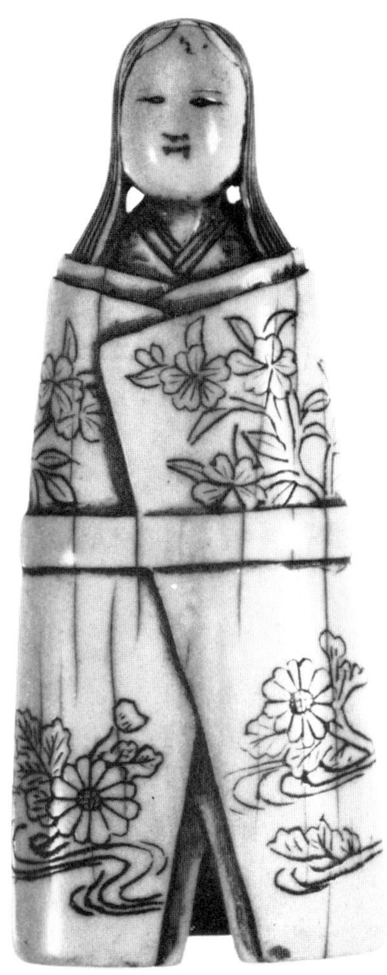
369

370
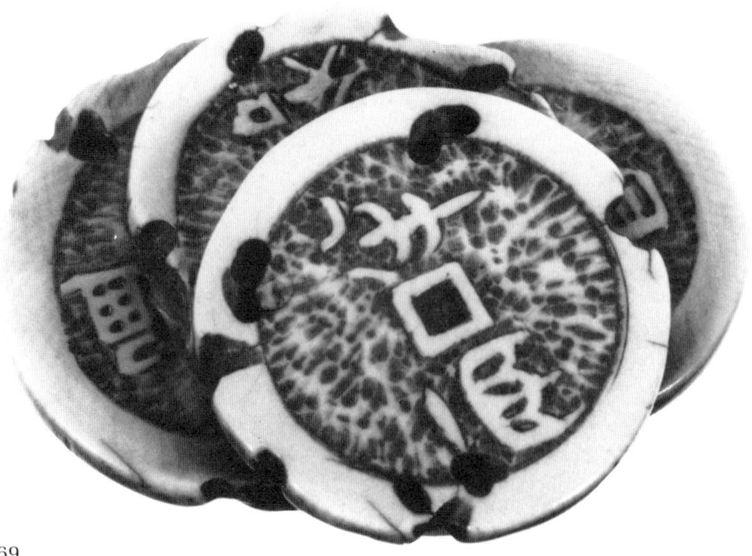

371
Shishi on an oval base.
Porcelain with straw and blue glazes.
Mikawachi ware.
19th century.
Length 4.2cm ($1\frac{3}{4}$in).
F.1461+. Franks Collection.

372
Frog on a closed umbrella.
Porcelain, glazed white, brown and grey.
Mikawachi ware.
19th century.
Length 6.4cm ($2\frac{1}{2}$in).
F.1498+. Franks Collection.

373
Gama Sennin, holding his toad in his left hand and a basket in his right.
Porcelain, matt-glazed to simulate ivory.
Stamped Masakazu on the back.
19th century.
Height 8.6cm ($3\frac{1}{4}$in).
F.1483+. Franks Collection.

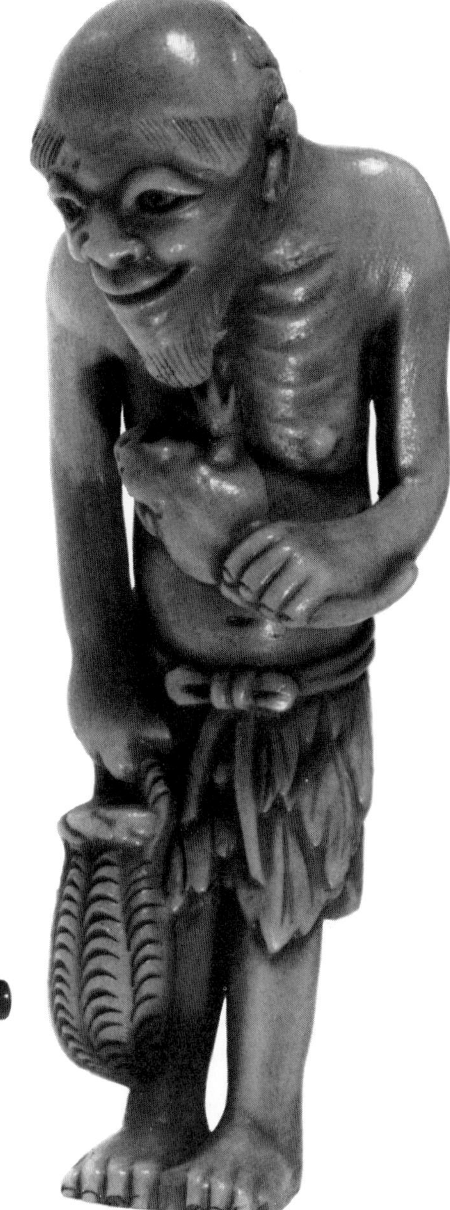

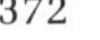

372

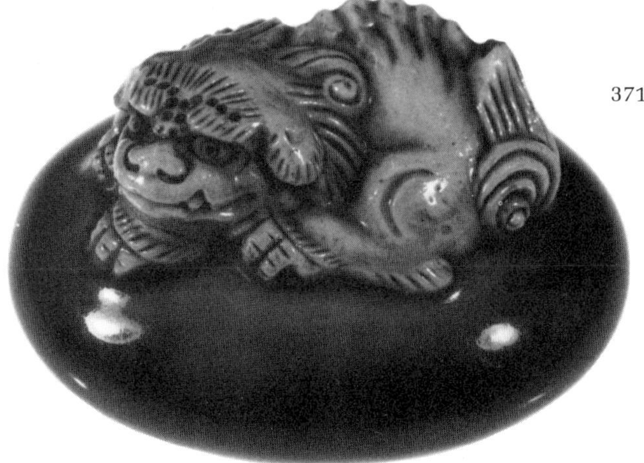

371

373

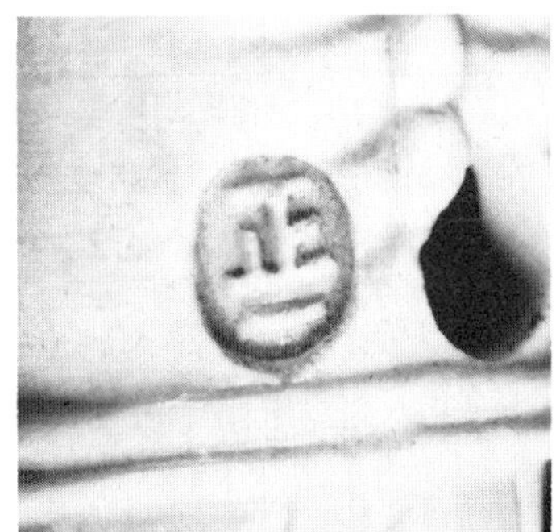

374
Snail on a crescent-shaped tile.
Porcelain, glazed in blue, white and grey.
Mikawachi ware.
19th century.
Length 6.4cm ($2\frac{1}{2}$in).
F.1464+. Franks Collection.

375
Manjū, decorated in underglaze blue with scrolling flowers and foliage.
Porcelain, with a garbled Chinese reign mark, Hsüan-tê and an unread seal.
Mikawachi ware.
19th century.
Diameter 4.1cm ($1\frac{3}{4}$in).
F.1433+. Franks Collection.

376
Puppy.
Porcelain glazed in white, with red, brown and black enamels.
Probably Mikawachi ware.
19th century.
Length 3.75cm ($1\frac{1}{2}$in).
F.1489+. Franks Collection.

377
Three tortoises.
Pottery with brown and grey glazes.
Signed Teiji in a gold-lacquer rectangular cartouche on the base.
Probably Mikawachi ware.
19th century.
Length 4.5cm ($1\frac{3}{4}$in).
F.1940B. Franks Collection.
Colour plate, page 24

378
Onna-Daruma (woman dressed as Daruma).
Unglazed pottery, with gilt and red-tinted details.
Bizen ware.
19th century.
Height 4.5cm ($1\frac{3}{4}$in).
F.1904. Franks Collection.

379
Okame.
Pottery, cream-glazed with coloured enamels.
Unread stamp on base.
Kyoto ware.
19th century.
Height 4.5cm ($1\frac{3}{4}$in).
F.1321A. Franks Collection.

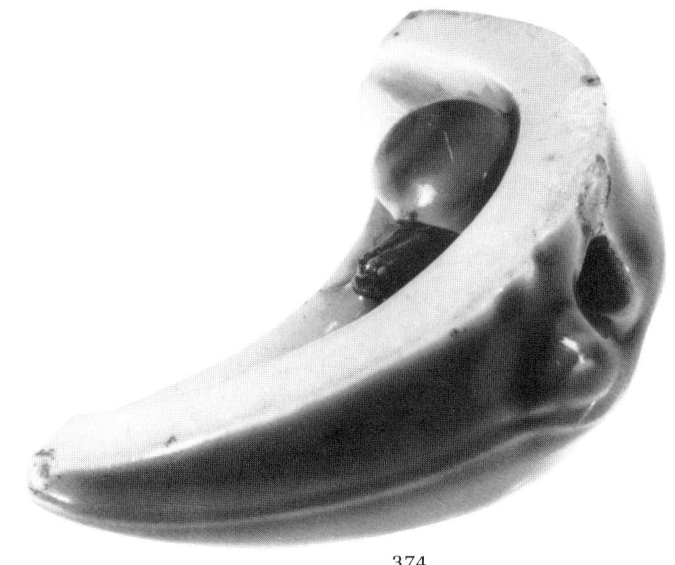

374

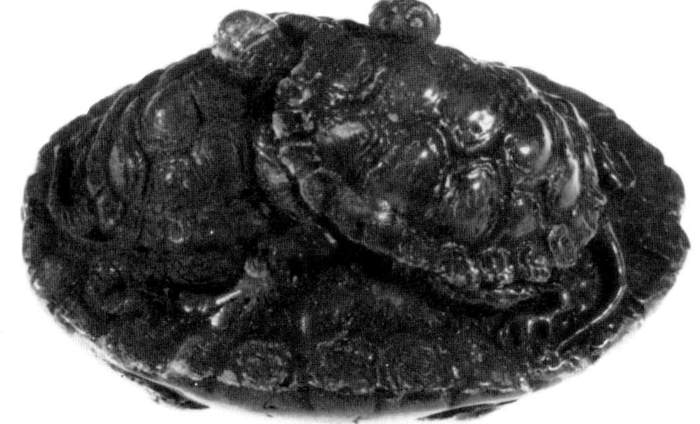

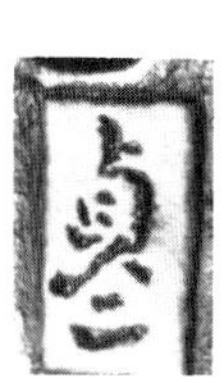

377

376

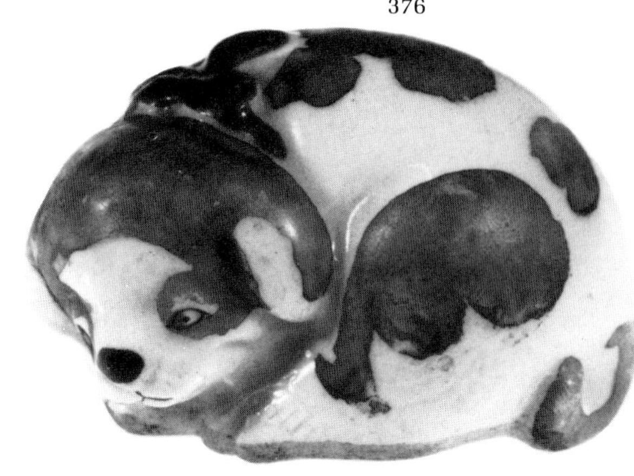

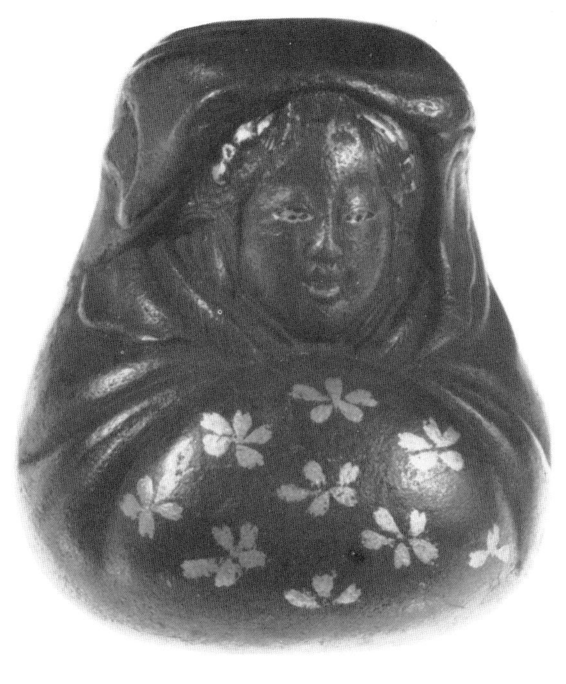

378

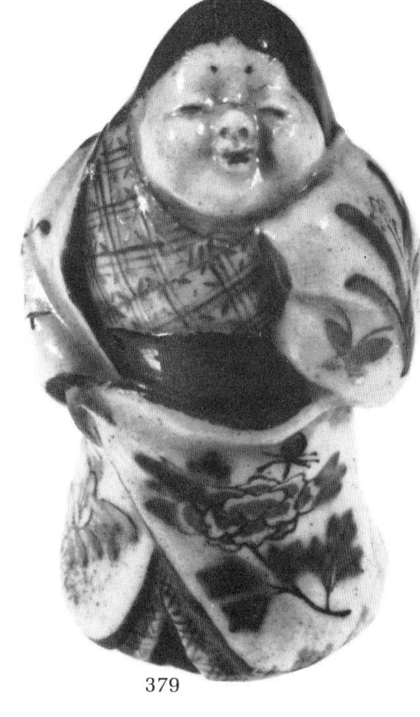

379

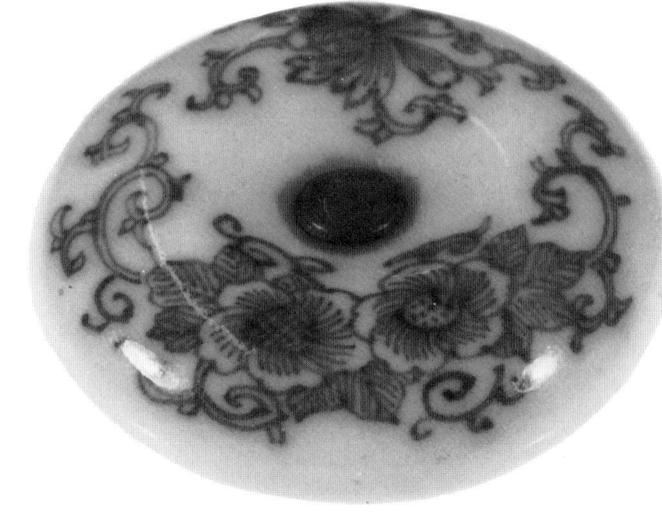

375

380
Dried fish, the rear part cut away to reveal the flesh, the back decorated with European letters. Lacquered wood, one cord-ring and the flesh in mother-of-pearl.
Unsigned, style of Ogawa Haritsu (Ritsuō).
18th century.
Length 11.4cm ($4\frac{1}{4}$in).
F.1078. Franks Collection.
For a similar example, *see* N. K. Davey, *Netsuke*, p. 425, no. 1268.

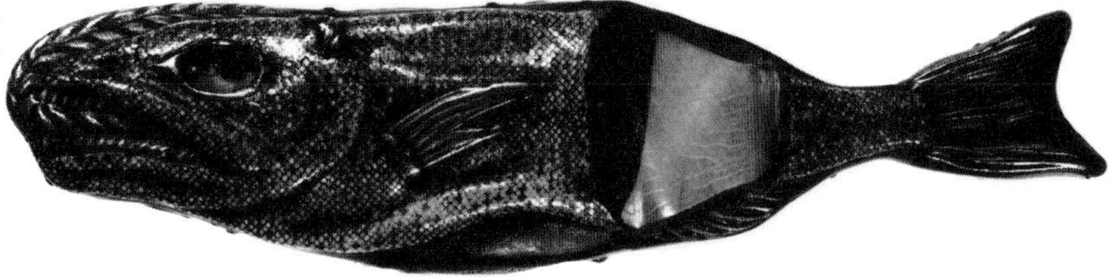

380

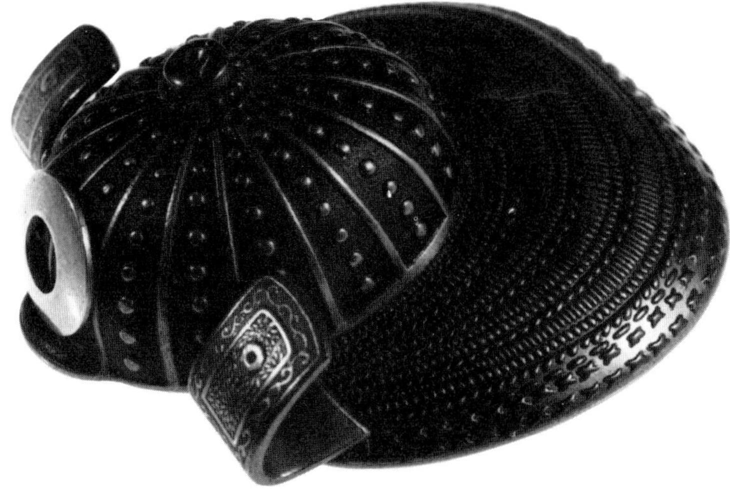

385

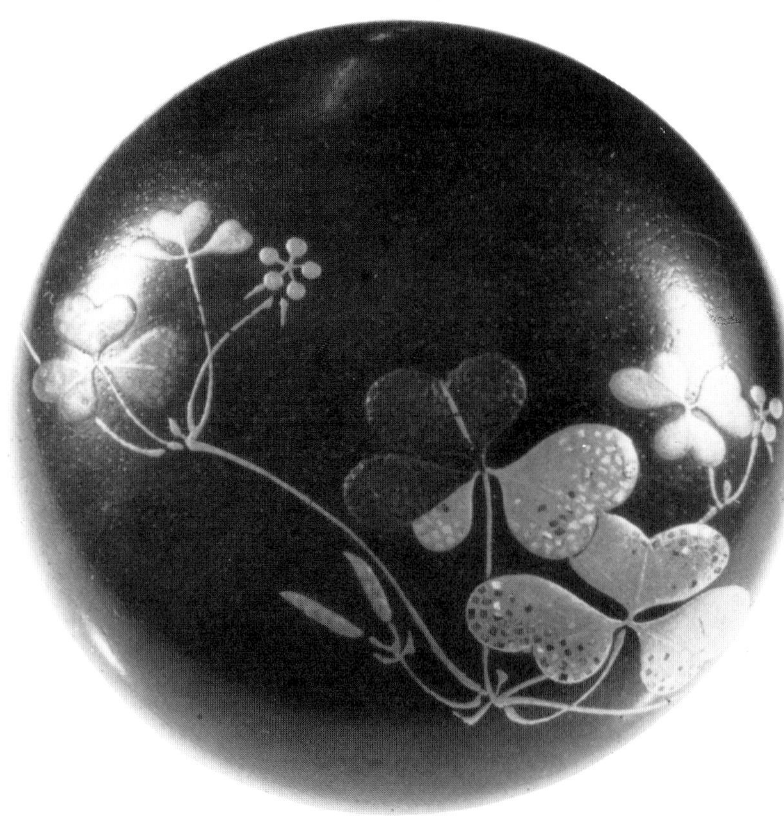

383

381
Manjū, decorated with a spider on a pod. Reddish-brown lacquer with grey-black decoration.
Signed with scratched characters Zeshin on the back.
19th century.
Width 3.25cm ($1\frac{1}{4}$in).
1928 7-17 9. Bequeathed by James Orange.

382
Manjū, decorated with a bird perched in a tree beside an old thatched cottage. Lacquer.
Signed with scratched characters Zeshin, on back.
Late 19th century.
Width 3.75cm ($1\frac{1}{2}$in).
1928 7-17 8. Bequeathed by James Orange.

383
Manjū, the top decorated with clover-grass. Wood, decorated with gold and black lacquer, with details in mother-of-pearl.
Signed with scratched characters Zeshin on the back.
19th century.
Diameter 3.5cm ($1\frac{1}{4}$in).
1928 7-17 7. Bequeathed by James Orange.

384
Manjū, decorated with bean pods and foliage.
Lacquer simulating iron, decoration in stained ivory, coloured lacquer, and mother-of-pearl.
Signed Issai in an oval cartouche on the back.
19th century.
Diameter 4.1cm ($1\frac{3}{4}$in).
F.542. Franks Collection.

385
Warrior's helmet, done in various lacquer techniques.
Metal boss and cord-ring.
Unsigned.
19th century.
Length 4.5cm ($1\frac{3}{4}$in).
1945 10-17 525. Bequeathed by Oscar Raphael.

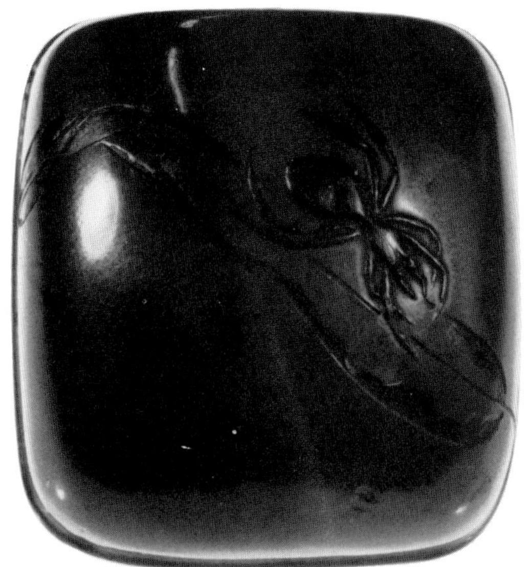

381

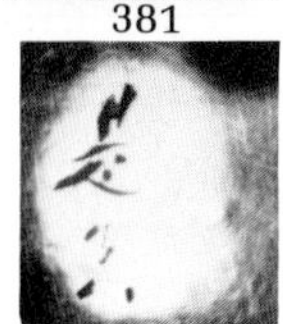

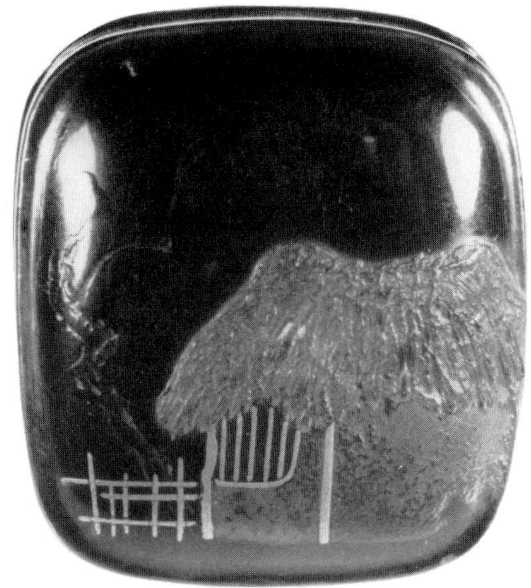

382

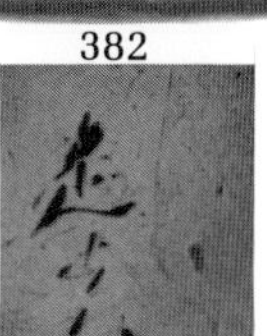

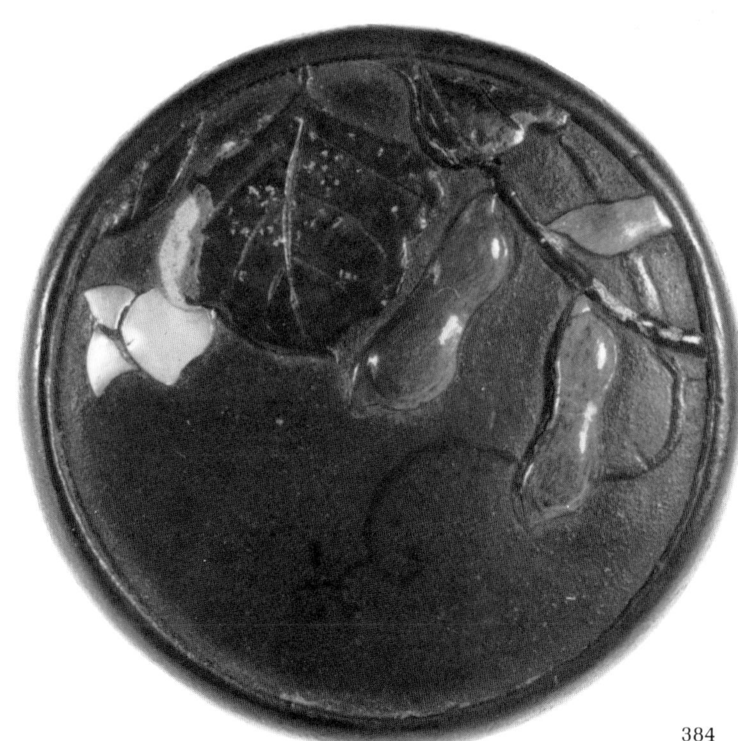

384

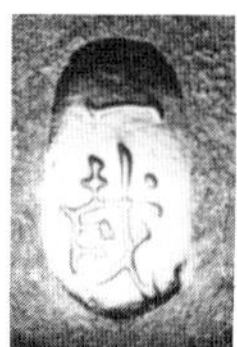

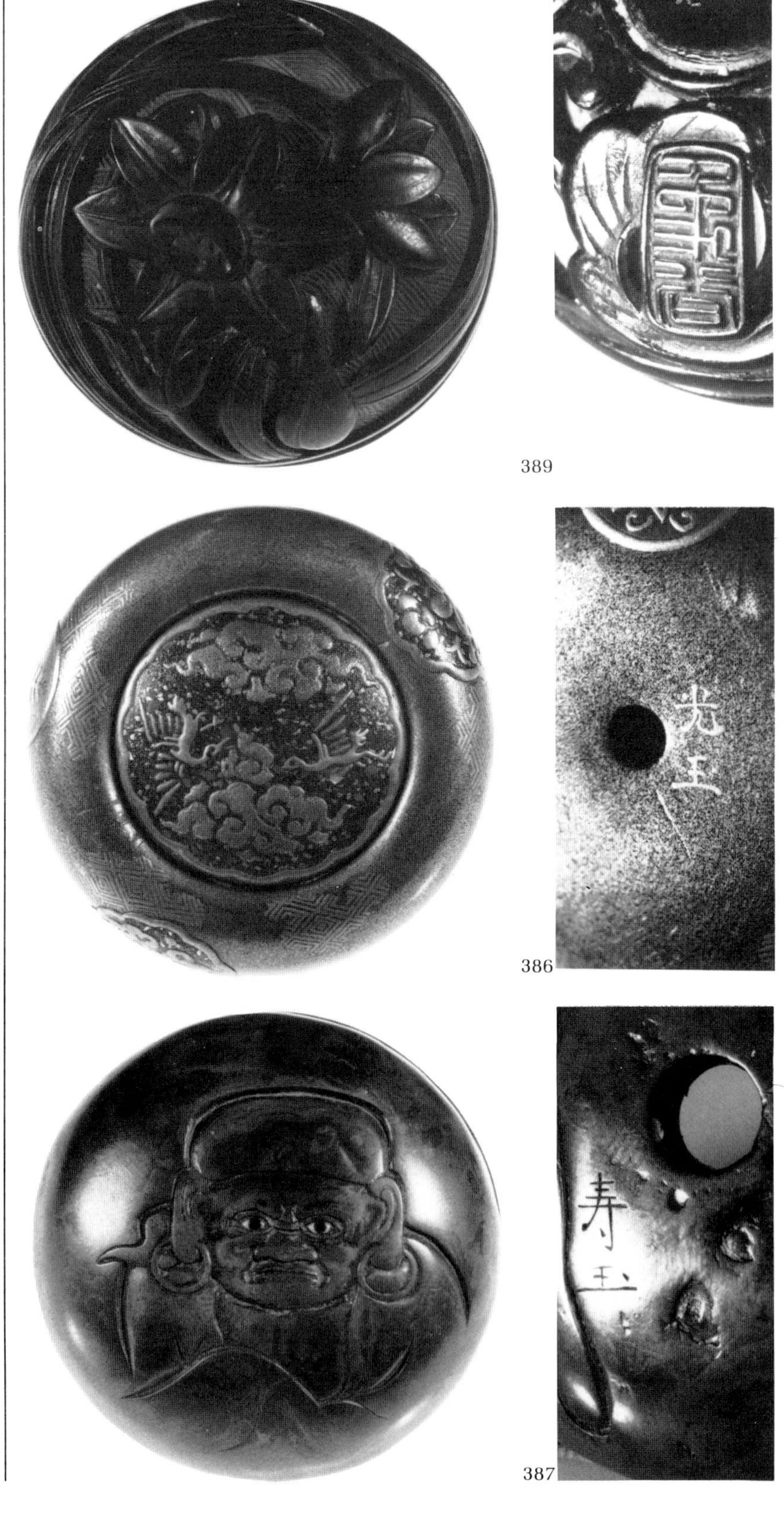

389

386

387

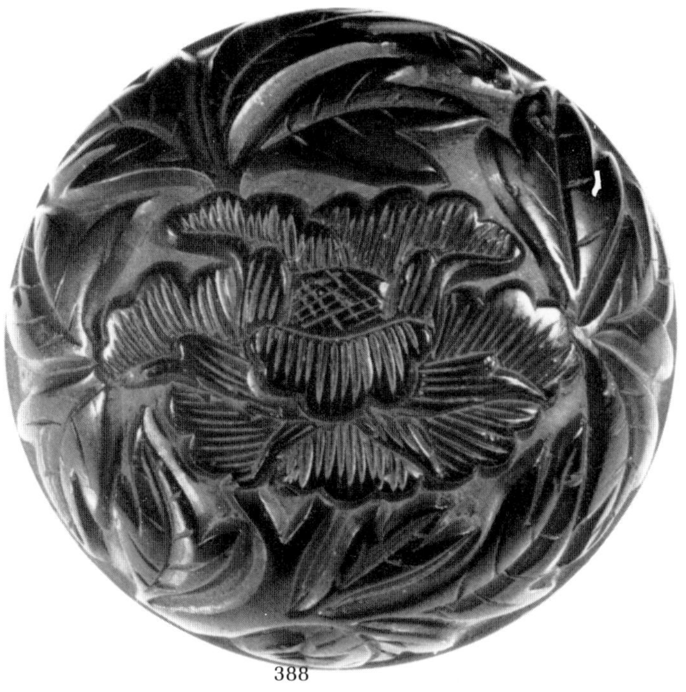
388

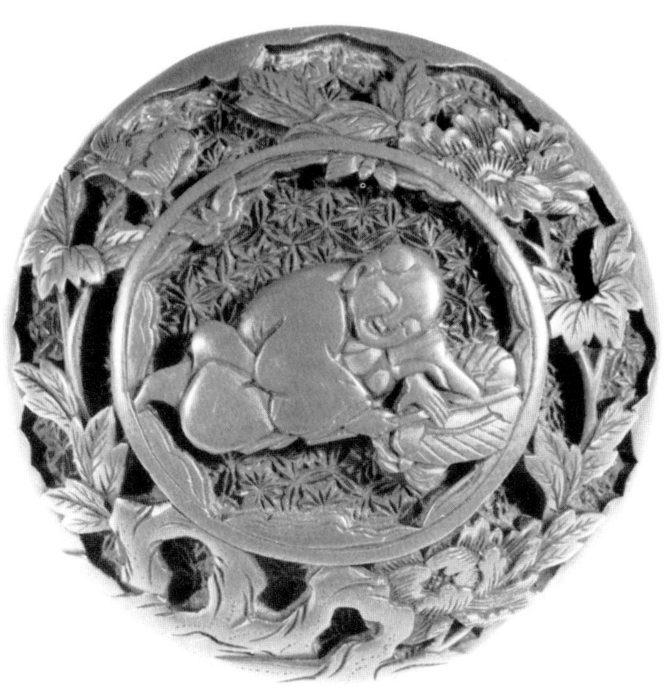
390

386
Kagamibuta shape, the plate decorated with birds flying among clouds, the bowl bearing various *mon* (heraldic devices). Lacquer with some mother-of-pearl.
Signed Kōgyoku.
19th century.
Diameter 3.75cm (1½in).
F.543. Franks Collection.

387
Manjū, incised on one side with Daruma and on the other with his fly-whisk.
Marbled red lacquer. Metal cord-attachment inside.
Signed with scratched characters Jūgyoku on the back.
19th century.
Diameter 4.5cm (1¾in).
F.1261. Franks Collection.

388
Manjū, decorated with chrysanthemums in carved black lacquer over a red ground.
Metal cord-ring inside.
Unsigned.
19th century.
Diameter 3.75cm (1½in).
OA + 303.

389
Manjū, decorated with narcissi on one side and scrolling on the other in carved black lacquer over a red ground.
Negoro finish inside.
Carved seal (unread) on back.
19th century.
Diameter 3.75cm (1½in).
F.1263. Franks Collection.

In the *negoro* technique red and black layers are superimposed and then rubbed to produce a mottled effect.

390
Manjū, decorated with a Chinese boy on one side and a bird and plum-blossom on the other.
Carved red lacquer (*tsuishū*).
Unsigned.
Early 19th century.
Diameter 4.2cm (1¾in).
F.1262. Franks Collection.

391
Shōjō dancer.
Carved red lacquer.
Signed Toyoyoshi in a rectangular cartouche on the base.
19th century.
Height 4.2cm ($1\frac{3}{4}$in).
1953 12-17 22. Bequeathed by Mrs Helen Epstein.

392
Mask of a demon with long hair. *Guri* lacquer.
Unsigned.
19th century.
Height 4.2cm ($1\frac{1}{4}$in).
1945 10-17 577. Bequeathed by Oscar Raphael.

393
Double gourd, carved with formal scrolls in *guri* lacquer. Metal mounts.
Unsigned.
19th century.
Length 5.1cm (2in).
1974 2-26 12. Given by Sir Harry Garner.

In the *guri* technique, different-coloured lacquers were laid on each other and then cut away in scrolling designs to reveal the layers.

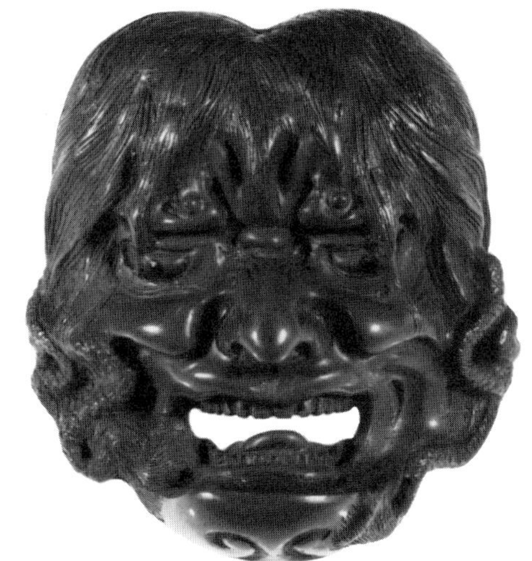

392

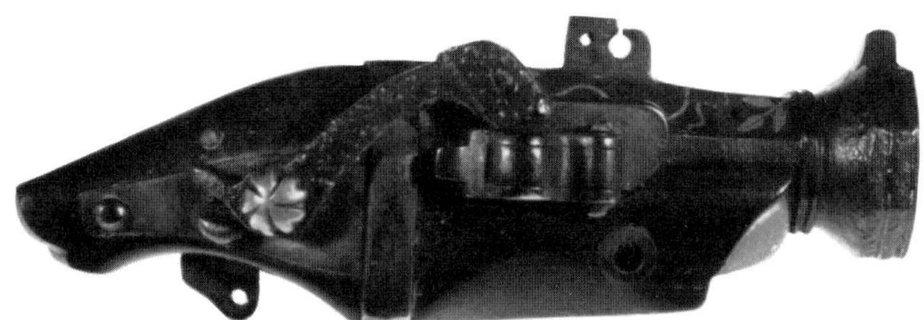

396

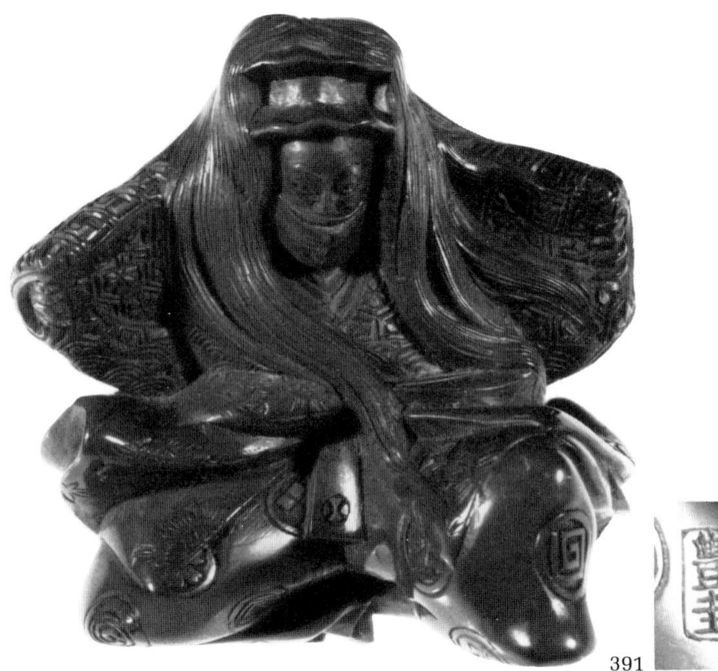

391

394
Manjū, formed of woven silver and *shakudō* alloy wires in a geometric design.
Unsigned.
19th century.
Diameter 3.5cm ($1\frac{1}{4}$in).
F.1309. Franks Collection.
For a similar example, see R. Bushell, *The Netsuke Handbook of Ueda Reikichi*, p. 26, no. 22.

395
Working tinder-box.
Brass, decorated with blossoms in copper and *shakudō* alloy.
Unsigned.
About 1800 AD.
Length 4.5cm ($1\frac{3}{4}$in).
F.1250. Franks Collection.

396
Model of a Western wall-gun.
Iron barrel with gold inlay, and wooden stock.
Unsigned.
Circa 1800 AD.
Length 4.5cm ($2\frac{3}{4}$in).
OA + 28.

397
Kagamibuta in the shape of a basket of molluscs.
Iron, partly gilt.
Unsigned.
19th century.
Diameter 3.75cm ($1\frac{1}{2}$in).
1945 10-17 629. Bequeathed by Oscar Raphael.

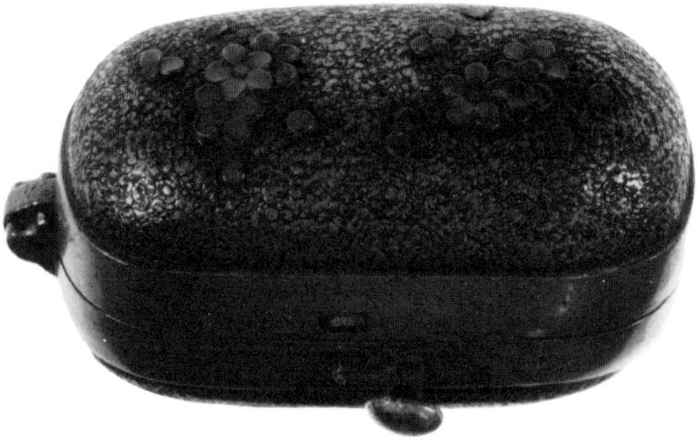

395

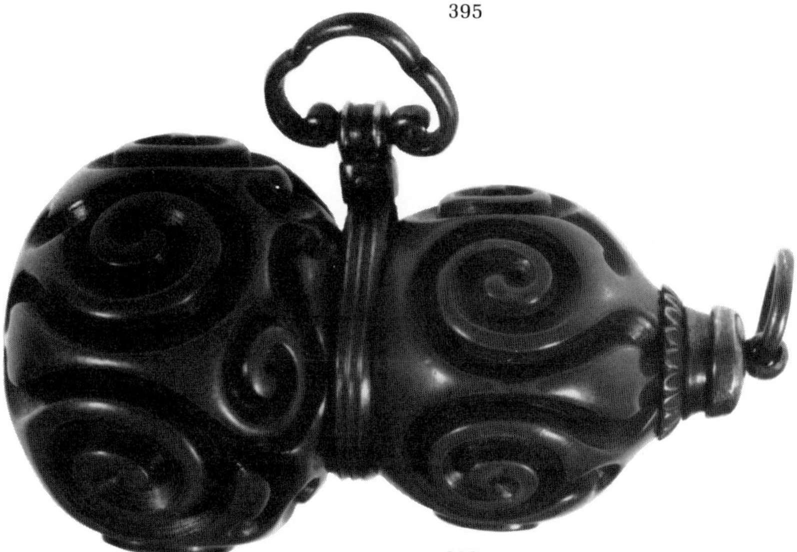

393

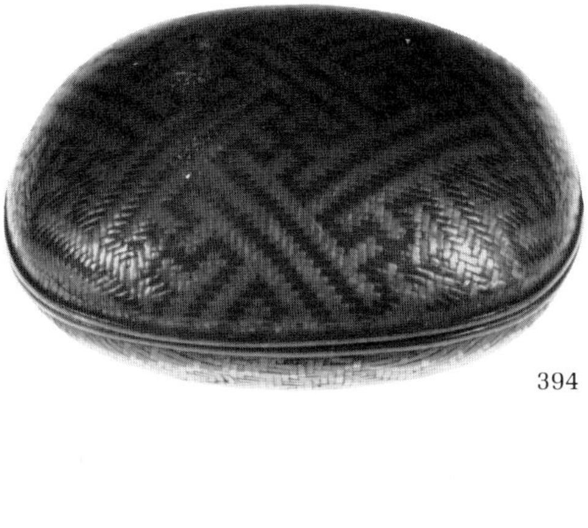

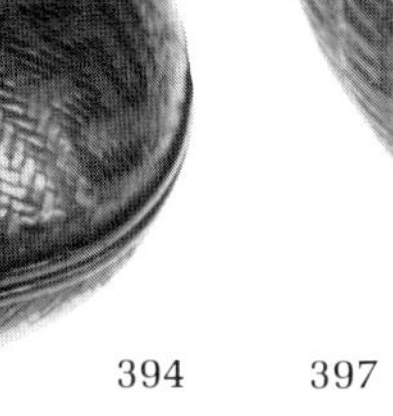

394

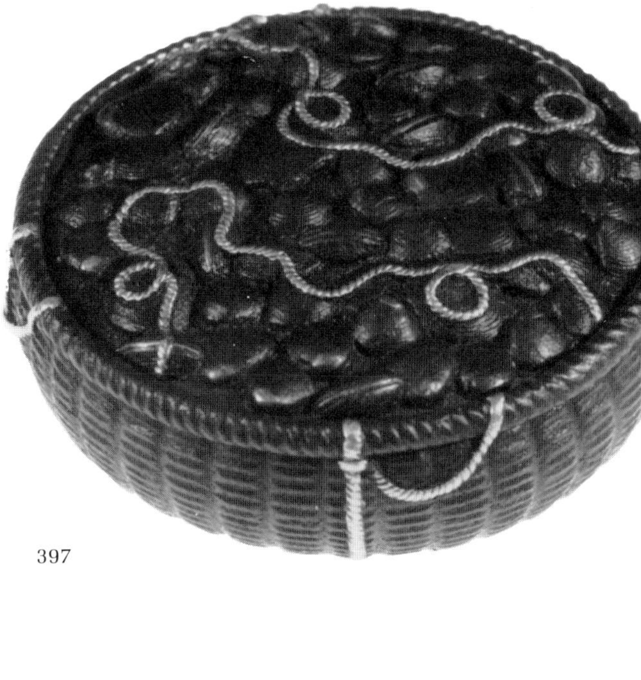

397

398
Ash-tray netsuke decorated with flowers and formal patterns.
Cloisonné enamel.
19th century.
Diameter 3.75cm ($1\frac{1}{2}$in).
F.387. Franks Collection.

399
Ox on a base.
Buffalo horn, the eyes inlaid.
Signed Hidemasa on the base.
19th century.
Height 3.5cm ($1\frac{1}{4}$in).
F.764. Franks Collection.

400
Cicada on a spray of foliage.
Buffalo horn.
Unsigned.
19th century.
Length 6cm ($2\frac{3}{4}$in).
F.1157. Franks Collection.

401
Rabbit.
Buffalo horn, the eyes inlaid in coral.
Unsigned.
19th century.
Height 2.5cm (1in).
OA + 308.

402
Peaches in semi-relief.
Amber, with gilt metal cord-attachments in chrysanthemum shape.
Unsigned.
19th century.
Width 6.7cm ($2\frac{3}{4}$in).
F.204. Franks Collection.

403
Peach.
Rock crystal.
Unsigned.
19th century.
Length 4.2cm ($1\frac{3}{4}$in).
F.1116. Franks Collection.

404
The natural jaw of a wolf, the *himotoshi* formed by an iron pin, passing through the bone.
Length 7cm ($3\frac{3}{4}$in).
OA + 29.

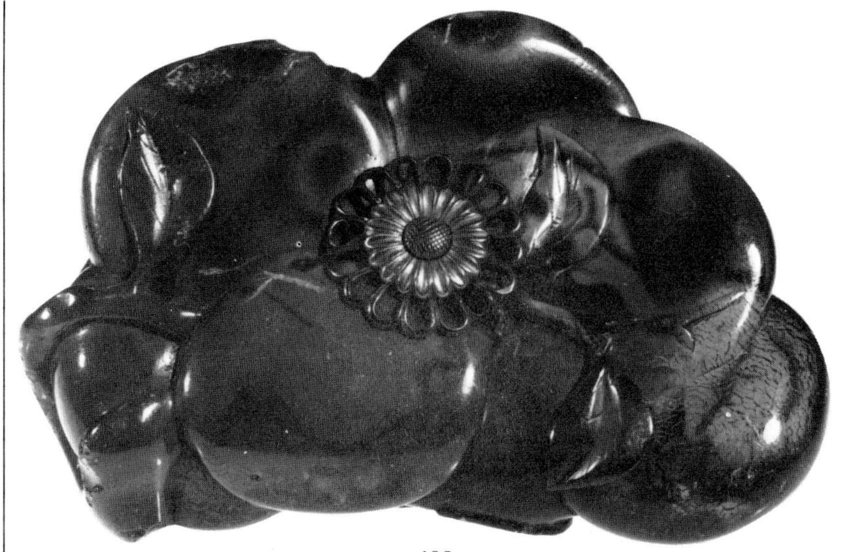
402

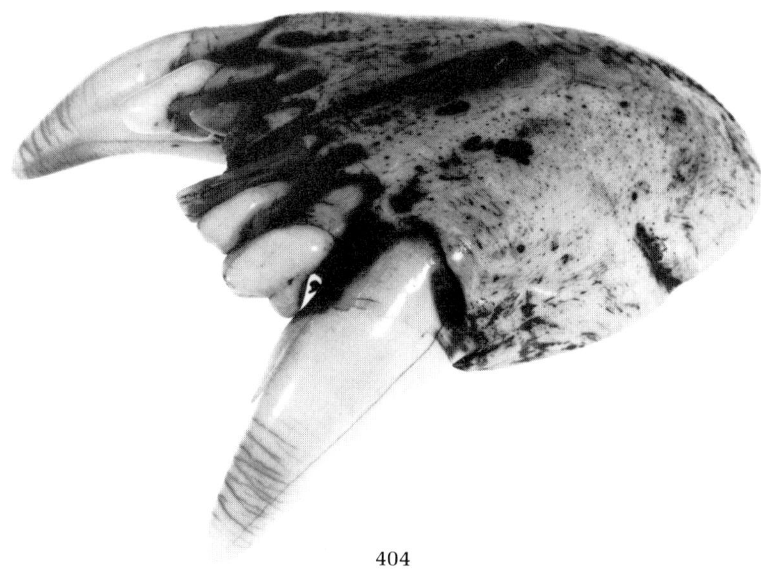
404

398
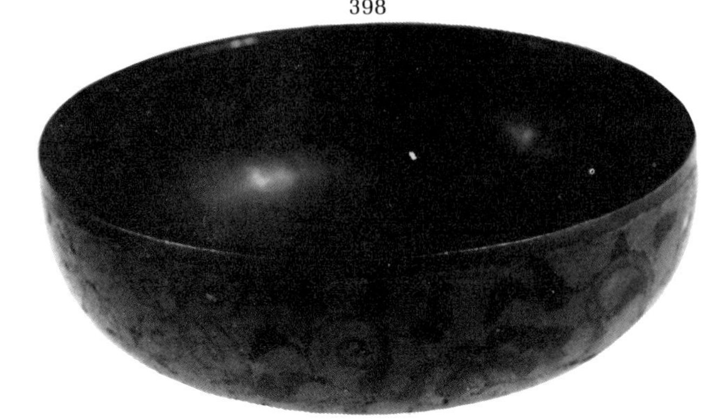

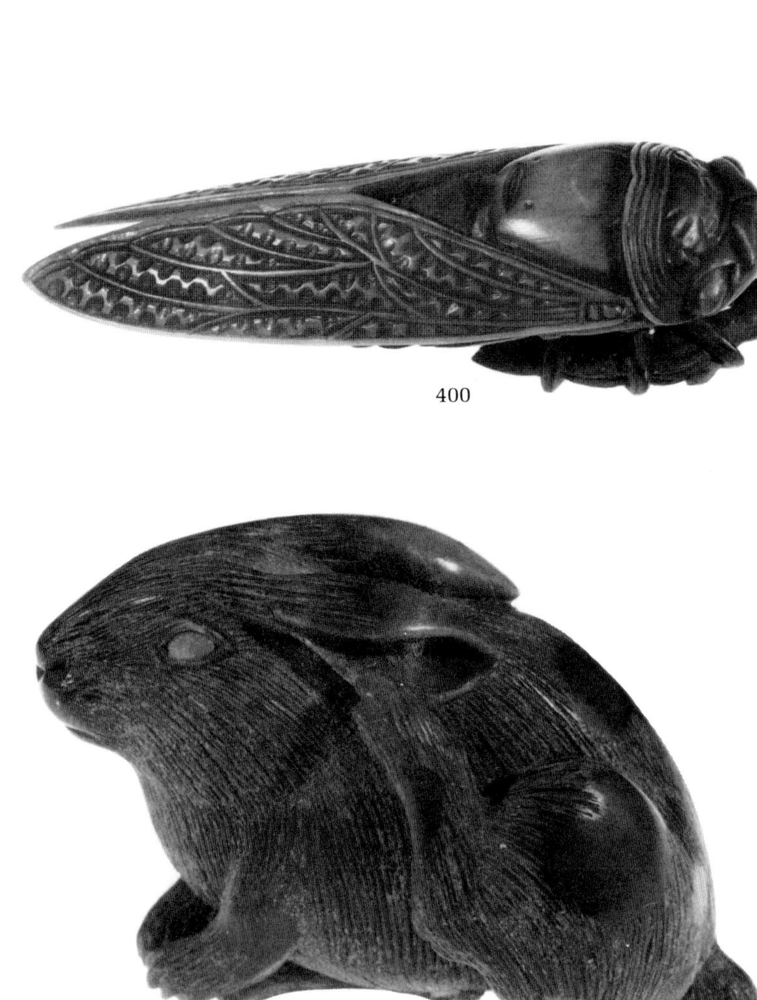

400

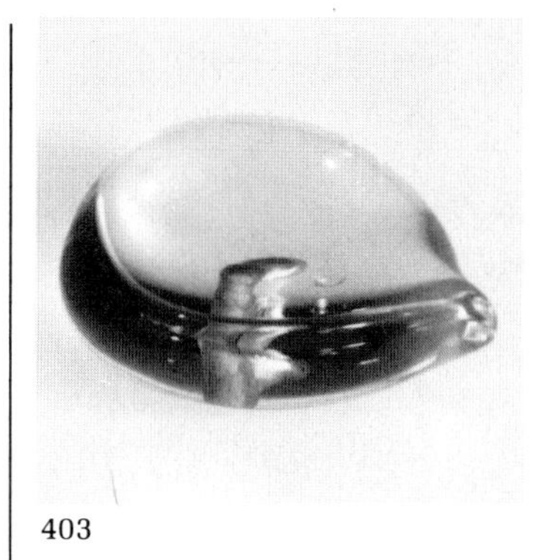

403

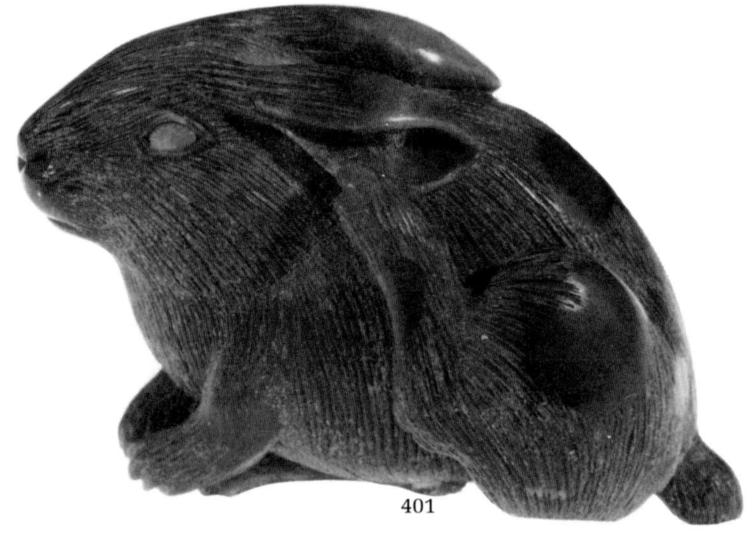

401

399

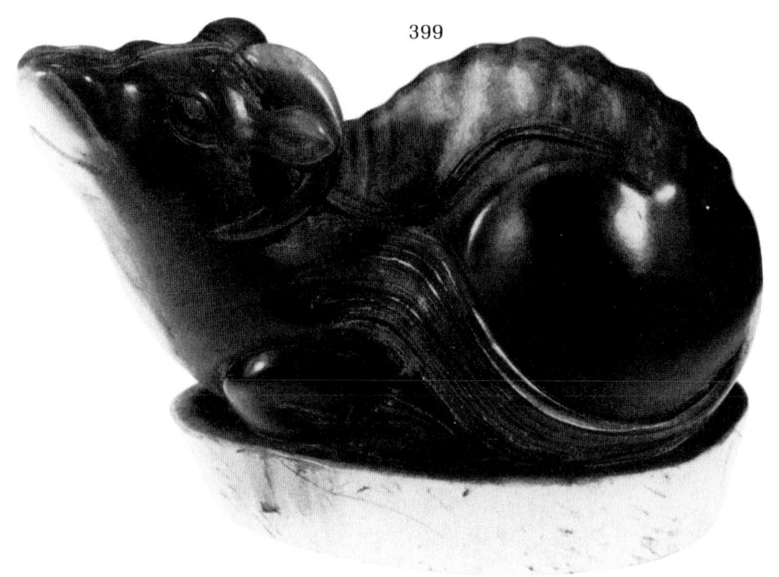

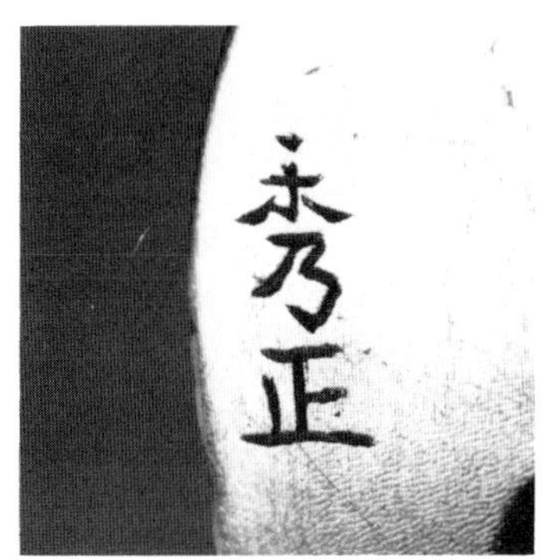

Publications Quoted

Behrens Collection. W. L. Joly, *Catalogue of the W. L. Behrens Collection*. London, 1922.

Red Cross Catalogue. W. L. Joly and K. Tomita, *Japanese Art and Handicraft* (An illustrated record of the Loan Exhibition held in aid of the British Red Cross). London, 1915.

R. Bushell, *The Netsuke Handbook of Ueda Reikichi*. Tokyo, 1961.

R. Bushell, *Collectors' Netsuke*. Tokyo, 1971.

N. K. Davey, *Netsuke* (A comprehensive study based on the M. T. Hindson Collection). London, 1974.

Meinertzhagen Index. A card index of some 12,000 netsuke seen and recorded by Frederick Meinertzhagen. Now kept in the British Museum, Department of Oriental Antiquities.

Inaba, Tsūryū. *Sōken Kishō*. Osaka, 1781. (Includes the earliest account of netsuke-makers.)

Amma. Blind masseur, frequently seen in netsuke working on a client or trying to lift a large stone (which may be intended to represent a gigantic testicle). Wall-eyed masks also represent *amma*.

Badger (Tanuki). Considered in Japan a malevolent and tricky creature, fond of distending its stomach or scrotum to huge size and beating on it as a drum. An iron kettle turned into a badger in the story of the *bambuku chagama*, and it is also found disguised as a priest.

Bakemono. 'Apparitions', a name for any ghost outside the regular demons and mythical creatures.

Bekakō (or **Bekankō**). Gesture of derision made by pulling down the lower eyelid with one finger, usually made by children and Dutchmen in netsuke.

Benkei. Legendary giant who was defeated by the young hero Yoshitsune and became his faithful follower. They are often shown together by a post of the Gojō Bridge in Kyoto where they fought. Benkei is sometimes seen carrying the great bell of the Miidera Temple which he stole for the rival monks of Hieizan.

Benten. One of the seven gods of good fortune, shown playing a lute.

Chōkarō. One of the eight Chinese immortals, he carried a gourd in which his magical horse slept at night. A favourite subject for netsuke.

Clam's Breath. Sometimes called 'Clam's dream', a vision of the dragon king's underwater palace exhaled from an open clam-shell. Other scenes are also shown in clam-shells as a vehicle for the netsuke carver's ingenuity.

Daikoku. One of the seven gods of good fortune, symbolized by a rat, a mallet, and a *daikon* (large white radish).

Daruma. Founder of Zen Buddhism, said to have sat and meditated for many years and lost the use of his legs, hence the legless Daruma dolls and snow-men favoured by Japanese children. He has bushy eyebrows, a beard, and often carries a flywhisk. He is a frequent subject for netsuke, especially humorous ones.

Dutchmen. Dutch traders, restricted to the tiny island of Deshima off Nagasaki during the Isolation, are common netsuke subjects.

Ebisu. One of the seven gods of good fortune, usually shown with a fish or fishing-tackle.

Endō Morito. Shown doing penance behind a freezing water-fall for having mistakenly killed his mistress.

Fox. Considered a magical creature in Japan, frequently found dressed as a priest or woman. The fox symbolizes the Shintō rice-god Inari.

Gama Sennin. The sennin with a toad, usually on his shoulder or head.

Handaka Sonja. One of the Rakan. He is shown in netsuke with a great dragon emerging from his begging bowl.

Hannya. Woman who turned into a demon with horns, usually carved as a mask-netsuke.

Himotoshi. The cord-holes of a netsuke.

Hotei. Most commonly portrayed of the seven gods of good fortune, grossly fat, bald, very cheerful, and often attended by children who sometimes appear from his sack.

Ikkaku Sennin. The sennin with a horn. Of Indian origin, he was renowned for his holiness and chastity, but was trapped into losing it by a princess of the court. He is usually shown carrying her on his back after she had grown tired.

Jittoku see **Kanzan**.

Jō and Uba. Typical old couple, Jō being the man and Uba the woman. They are often shown by the old pine tree at Takasago, which they are said to haunt as the spirits of ancient lovers who died there at a great age. Jō often carries a rake, and Uba a broom.

Kagamibuta. A type of netsuke with a decorated metal disk inserted in a *manjū* case.

Kakihan. 'Written seal', a very cursive style of written characters used as a subsidiary signature by some netsuke-makers. It is rarely readable in isolation.

Kannon. Bodhisattva of Mercy, the most popular of the orthodox Buddhist deities in Japan, where she is always feminine in the Edo period.

Kanyū (more correctly **Kan'u** in Japanese). One of the three military heroes of the Chinese Han Dynasty, shown as a warrior of majestic appearance stroking his beard and holding a long, curved halberd.

Kanzan and Jittoku. Chinese youths symbolizing the permeation of Zen doctrine into all aspects of life. Kanzan holds a scroll, representing learning, while Jittoku upholds labour by wielding a broom.

Kappa. Mythical water creature, with a monkey-like head and frog-like body, said to attack human beings in the water. It is often shown with a hollow in the top of its head where its vital fluids are kept. It is frequently portrayed with its leg caught in a clam shell.

Koto. A long stringed instrument played horizontally on the ground.

Manjū. A round, flat, rice-cake still eaten in Japan. It gave its name to a type of netsuke of similar shape.

Manzai. A popular street-dance performed by one, two or three people, sometimes with lion-dog costume.

Momotarō. The peach boy, found in a peach-stone by a childless old couple. He travelled with a monkey, pheasant and dog to fight a giant. This story is probably the best known among Japanese children.

Okame. Goddess who tempted the sun-goddess from her cave by her antics in the ancient Japanese legend. She is a favourite netsuke subject with her puffed-up cheeks and slit-eyes, and is often shown in ridiculous or bawdy situations. Okame masks are also common.

Oni. A demon, small and horned, often pursued by Shoki or pelted with beans at the new year.

Ono no Komachi. Ninth century AD poetess, one of the 'Six Great Poets' of Japanese literature. Her life fell from beauty and fame to aged poverty. She is most often portrayed as an old woman, seated unrecognized by the road-side, and sometimes as a young woman washing a written paper in water to show a dishonest rival had only just added to it.

Rakan. The sixteen apostles of the Buddha. They all have long ears, large eyebrows, bald heads, and heavily lined faces, and were as popular as the sennin as netsuke subjects. *See also* Handaka Sonja.

Sambasō. Dance of Shintō origin, done by two performers with masks, fans, and tall hats.

Sennin. 'Hermit man'. Name for Chinese holy men of the mountains and a very popular subject for netsuke, after the eighteenth century publication of illustrated books about them. They comprise both Taoist and Buddhist figures, and are usually portrayed with beard and long hair, carrying a staff, and dressed in a skirt of leaves. Sennin with particular attributes are listed separately.

Seven Gods of Good Fortune. Popular deities of mainly Buddhist origin, very common netsuke subjects, where they are sometimes shown together in the 'treasure ship'. They are Benten, Bishamon, Daikoku, Ebisu, Fukurokujū, Hotei and Jūrōjin.

Shakudō. Alloy of copper with a small amount of gold, pickled to a lustrous blue-black. Used as an inlay on **Kagamibuta** netsuke.

Shiba Onkō. Chinese boy who rescued his friend from drowning in a huge jar of water by smashing it. The subject became 'hob in the well' on eighteenth century European porcelain.

Shishi. Lion-dog, often shown with a ball. These creatures were both guardians of temples and symbols of the Chinese scholar. As the latter they are a very common subject for netsuke, especially when surmounting a seal.

Shōjō. Mythical, almost human creatures with red hair, always in a cheerfully drunken state.

Shoki. 'The Demon Queller', shown as a Chinese T'ang Dynasty warrior with a strongly winged cap and a long sword. He is frequently made a fool of by the small demons he pursues, and is a very common netsuke subject.

Tekkai Sennin. One of the eight immortals, he took the form of a beggar leaning on an iron staff. He is usually shown gazing upwards, perhaps to receive wisdom from Lao Tze in heaven.

Tengu. Mythical creature with eagle's beak, wings and claws but a more-or-less human body. Another sort had a very long nose, and this was the type the hero Yoshitsune associated with in the forests in his fugitive days. They were more humorous than malevolent.

Tōbōsaku. Legendary Chinese who achieved immortality by eating the peaches of the Goddess Seiōbō. He is shown as an old man with a peach.

Uba *see* **Jō.**

Zodiac. Represented by twelve creatures in cyclic order. Each year was dedicated in turn to one of them, and netsuke in the form of the creature of one's birth-year were popular. They are, in order, rat, ox, tiger, hare or rabbit, dragon, snake, horse, sheep or goat, monkey, cock or bird, dog, pig.

ŌSAKA. Main port of Japan in the Edo period, centre of the rice and money markets. Ōsaka seems to have been the earliest place of carved netsuke manufacture, especially of the tall eighteenth century figures of Chinese subjects.

Dōraku. Early nineteenth century, probably also signed Dōrakusai. Worked in ivory and wood.

Dōshō (1828–84). Preferred ivory, which he sometimes inlaid. His shapes are very compact.

Gechū. Mentioned in the Sōken Kishō (1781).

Hidemasa. Early nineteenth century, worked mainly in ivory, the robes being decorated with scrolling. He had at least one pupil using the same name and characters.

Kaigyokusai Masatsugu (1813–92). Worked in fine quality ivory, perhaps the most technically skilled of all netsuke carvers. His later work was intricate, like the 'clam's breath' palace type, and every detail of his work is perfect. Preferred not to bore holes but to incorporate the *himotoshi* into the design. He was very widely copied in his own lifetime, especially by his many pupils.

Kōhōsai (died about 1907). Worked in ivory only, but sometimes lacquered.

Kokusai Sanshō (1871–1936). Preferred pale woods.

Masahiro (Mid-nineteenth century). Pupil of Mitsuhiro, often carved a boy pushing a Daruma snowman.

Masatsugu. Early nineteenth century, thought to have been a pupil of Hidemasa. Should not be confused with Kaigyokusai Masatsugu.

Mitsuhiro (1810–75). Preferred single subjects; worked mainly in ivory, delicately stained and engraved.

Nagamachi Shūzan. Late eighteenth century. So named to distinguish him from Yoshimura Shūzan (*see* Introduction), whose practice of painting over the wood he copied. His work is similar to the *Nara-ningyō*, (simply carved folk netsuke) but more refined.

Shigemasa. Early nineteenth century, preferred ivory.

Tsuji. Mentioned in the *Sōken Kishō* (1781), specialized in wood figures. His one-character signature is very unobtrusive.

KYOTO. Capital of Japan from 793 until 1867, but not the seat of actual government from 1601 onwards. It remained the centre of the court and of higher culture, especially painting, and of traditional crafts. There is a soft, restrained, self-contained quality about the netsuke as of the other arts of Kyoto. They tend to favour animal subjects.

Hakuryū. Mid-nineteenth century, specialized in ivory animals, especially very spirited tigers with brilliantly inlaid eyes. His work has force rather than finesse.

Kagetoshi. Worked during the second quarter of the nineteenth century. It is not absolutely certain that he worked in Kyoto. He was well-known for his very intricate but compact carvings in wood or ivory of crowded groups of buildings, animals or figures. The British Museum has a sketchbook of his designs.

Kōseki (1871–1948). Buddhist sculptor who studied traditional styles and copied them with great skill. Not basically a netsuke carver, but produced a few of superb quality for Western collectors, the first recorded example of such a practice. The British Museum has a few larger sculptural works by him.

Masanao. Mentioned in the *Sōken Kishō* (1781). Worked in wood and ivory, and specialized in birds and animals. He was very widely copied. He should not be confused with Masanao of Yamada.

Mitsuharu. Mentioned in the *Sōken Kishō* (1781). He preferred vegetable subjects but also did good animals in the style of Tomotada.

Mitsuhide. Early nineteenth century, preferred wood. He was well-known for his monkeys and and other animals.

Okatomo. Mentioned in the *Sōken Kishō* (1781). A pupil of Tomotada, he worked mainly in ivory and specialized in animals. His best known design, very much copied, is of two quail and millet stalks. This was a design based on the paintings of the official court artists of the Tosa School.

Okatori. Brother of Okatomo, worked late eighteenth century. He specialized in animals, but his reputation was less than his brother's and his work consequently less copied.

Rantei. Dates uncertain, probably first half of the nineteenth century. Preferred animals in fine ivory, often stained for effect, and with skilfully inlaid eyes.

Tomotada. Mentioned in the *Sōken Kishō* (1781). Worked mainly in ivory, and specialized in animals, particular his famous cattle subjects which were very widely copied.

Yasutada. Late eighteenth century, worked in the style of Tomotada.

EDO (Tokyo). Seat of government from 1601 until 1867. In 1867 the Emperors moved there and it became the official capital, renamed Tokyo. Edo was the biggest city in the world by the eighteenth century, a great metropolis of consumers. Lacking artistic traditions, its crafts tended to be original, sophisticated and sometimes slick. It became much the largest producer of netsuke in the early nineteenth century, and many studios worked there. Mask-netsuke and *kagamibuta* were Edo specialities, and there is more racy humour than in other centres. Carvers were often drawn in from other centres.

Chōgetsu (1826–92). School of Tomochika, worked in wood, ivory and horn.

Gyokuyōsai. Mid-nineteenth century, well-known for vegetable subjects and for figures of Daruma.

Hakuunsai. Mid-nineteenth century, favoured masks and *manjū* in ivory.

Hōjitsu (died in 1872). Noted for his very elegant and compact figure-netsuke.

Itsumin. Mid-nineteenth century, favoured wood carvings of animals. He also did large carvings.

Joryū. Late eighteenth century, did figures in wood and ivory.

Jūgyoku. Mid-nineteenth century, noted for his extreme realism in both ivory and wood in various subjects.

Kōjitsu (1833–93). Pupil of Hōjitsu, he specialized in ivory, especially *manjū*.

Kōmin. Late nineteenth century, noted for tortoises carved in tortoiseshell and for netsuke in wood.

Kōsai (Moritoshi). Late nineteenth century, specialized in masks and ivory *manjū* in sunk relief.

Masatoshi (Kikugawa). Mid- to late nineteenth century. Carved *manjū* in ivory, often with designs taken from books.

Minkoku. Late eighteenth century, worked in ivory and wood, as did his pupil of the same name. It is hard to distinguish the work of these two carvers.

Miwa. Mentioned in the *Sōken Kishō* (1781), well known for his tall figures in wood. There were at least two other makers using this name after him, and it is not easy to distinguish them.

Ryōmin. Mid-nineteenth century, worked mainly in ivory and specialized in *manjū*. Founded a large school.

Ryūkei. Mid-nineteenth century, worked in wood and ivory, the latter often stained. Was officially awarded the Buddhist title of *Hokkyō*.

Shūgetsu. Mentioned in the *Sōken Kishō* (1781), but succeeded by three generations using the same name. He was a Kanō School painter of some reputation, like Yoshimura Shūzan. All the Shūgetsu carvers used wood.

Shūmin. Late eighteenth century, pupil of Sh (getsu. He and his pupil of the same name worked in wood. They tended to rim the *himotoshi* in ivory.

Tōkoku. Mid- to late nineteenth century. Self-taught carver in many materials, often inlaid. Had a number of successors of the same name.

Tomochika (1800–73). Specialized in ivory carvings of striking design, often taken from books like Hokusai's *Manga*. Had two successors of the same name.

Uman, Deme. Mentioned in *Sōken Kishō* (1781). Best-known member of the Deme family which specialized in masks.

Zemin. Nineteenth century, a rare artist about whom nothing is known.

Zeshin (1807–91). Painter of the Shijō School and eminent lacquerer. He did a few *hako* and *manjū* netsuke in a very refined style.

ASAKUSA DISTRICT OF EDO. The carvers of this district, known as the Bohemian quarter of Edo, used the cheap material antler (stagshorn). They were remarkably adept at turning the flaws of the material to artistic use. The netsuke tend to be humorous.

Kokusai. Third quarter of the nineteenth century, founder of the style using antler.

Masayuki (Hōshunsai). Nineteenth century. Best known for his *mokugyō* (temple bell) subjects in antler.

Rensai. Mid- to late nineteenth century. There were three makers of this name, but the first seems to have signed simply 'Ren'. Specialized in animal subjects.

WAKAYAMA. Castle-town in Kii Province, south of Ōsaka, headquarters of a branch of the ruling Tokugawa family, and a centre of Chinese learning and culture.

Issai (Ogasawara). Mentioned in the *Sōken Kishō* (1781). Said to have worked mainly in ivory.

IWASHIRO. Province of central northern Japan, corresponding to modern Fukushima Prefecture.

Issan (Hidari). Early nineteenth century, worked in wood, specialized in animals and mythical beasts.

Sari. Late eighteenth century. Worked in wood, preferred shells, reptiles, and amphibians.

NAGOYA. Castle-town, capital of Mino province, and a great stronghold of one of the principal branches of the ruling Tokugawa family. The Nagoya carvers preferred wood and concentrated on very naturalistic subjects. They disliked boring cord-holes and tried to use natural features of the design to accommodate the cord.

Ittan. Mid-nineteenth century. Noted for his small but intricately carved figures and animals in stained wood.

Masanobu (Fujiwara). Born 1838. Worked in ivory, specializing in ivory landscapes carved within or on a natural object or *manjū*.

Tadatoshi. Early nineteenth century. A follower of Tametaka.

Tadayoshi. Mid-nineteenth century. The most celebrated of the Nagoya carvers, he made mostly living creatures or vegetables in wood. He was awarded the Buddhist title of Hōgan.

Tametaka. Mentioned in the *Sōken Kishō* (1781). His compact figures and animals are distinguished by raised-work carving (*Ukibori*) on the surface.

HIDA. Inland province to the north of Nagoya. The carvers nearly always worked in wood and preferred natural subjects. Hida was the place of origin of the simply-carved style called ittōbori ('one-cut carving').

Sukenaga. Worked about 1820–30 in Takayama.

TSU. Principal town of Ise Province on the eastern seaboard of the Kii peninsula. The carvers of this region (as with the neighbouring Yamada, Gifu and Nagoya areas) worked mainly in the fine softwoods which abounded in the local forests.

Kokei. Follower of Minkō, but his animals are more naturalistic.

Minkō. Mentioned in the *Sōken Kishō* (1781). Very famous for his tigers, of which large numbers were made by his studio and signed by him. Used brass to inlay eyes.

YAMADA. Town of Ise Province on the eastern seaboard of the Kii peninsula, home of the Masanao studio.

Masakatsu (1840–89). Son of the first Masanao.

Masanao. There was a whole line of makers using this name, and all working mainly in boxwood on animal subjects. The first Masanao lived 1815–90. The successive generations seem to become more polished but less spirited.

KAGA. Province on the Japan Sea coast, north-east from Kyoto. It was the stronghold of the Maeda family, the most powerful of the fiefs who had opposed the Tokugawa government, and its capital town of Kanazawa had a very independent cultural tradition.

Tameoto. Late eighteenth century. Worked in the town of Komatsu near Kanazawa.

ECHIZEN. Remote province on the north-west coast of the Japan Sea.

Sessai (1821–79). Came from Mikuni. Most of his work is rather grotesquely powerful and is in wood.

IWAMI. Province of Western Japan on the Japan Sea coast. The carvers of this maritime and wooded area had a very distinct style. They preferred natural subjects, especially insects and amphibians, often carved on a small part of a tusk or long tooth. They also tended to add very long inscriptions.

Gambun. Early nineteenth century. Favoured vegetable subjects done in *umimatsu* (sea-pine) and other rare materials, with tiny metal insects.

Gohō. Late eighteenth century. Well known for frogs and shells.

HAKATA. Important town in Kyūshū, now incorporated in the city of Fukuoka. Had a sculptural tradition in the well-known Hakata dolls.

Otoman. Mid-nineteenth century. Specialized in ivory animals, especially tigers with stripes indicated by staining.

TAMBA. Inland province to the north-west of Kyoto, a traditional source of fine craftsmen.

Toyomasa (1773–1856). A man of wide culture, he carved a variety of subjects in wood, the eyes inlaid in tortoiseshell. He had a son using the same name.

Concordance of Registration Numbers

Registration Number	*Catalogue Number*	*Registration Number*	*Catalogue Number*	*Registration Number*	*Catalogue Number*	*Registration Number*	*Catalogue Number*
OA + 24	244	F.346	40	F.726	240	F.994	86
OA + 28	396	F.351	151	F.732	296	F.1006	316
OA + 29	404	F.356	263	F.733	289	F.1008	319
OA + 114	368	F.357	261	F.740	332	F.1009	96
OA + 120	329	F.359	274	F.744	292	F.1017	291
OA + 121	330	F.369	318	F.747	239	F.1019	235
OA + 124	80	F.371	149	F.754	209	F.1037	137
OA + 226	158	F.385	152	F.756	307	F.1040	290
OA + 303	388	F.387	398	F.758	361	F.1046	28
OA + 308	401	F.395	123	F.760	224	F.1051	248
OA + 312	9	F.400	251	F.761	223	F.1053	369
OA + 540	256	F.409	243	F.762	172	F.1054	258
S.35	130	F.411	22	F.763	49	F.1055	116
S.48	7	F.437	18	F.764	399	F.1056	320
W.419	252	F.438	101	F.765	68	F.1057	160
W.425	122	F.443	156	F.770	66	F.1063	137
F.54	214	F.465	107	F.772	46	F.1065	128
F.57	333	F.481	142	F.774	63	F.1066	245
F.63	298	F.484	91	F.778	74	F.1067	232
F.77A	67	F.492	207	F.782	43	F.1070	81
F.102	282	F.493	120	F.783	133	F.1075	315
F.103	350	F.535	228	F.786	176	F.1076	364
F.108	145	F.542	384	F.789	54	F.1078	380
F.128	167	F.543	386	F.790	61	F.1079	170
F.135	57	F.558	355	F.791	15	F.1084	212
F.145	197	F.562	358	F.794	19	F.1090	48
F.149	118	F.563	354	F.795	30	F.1091	210
F.155	349	F.567	104	F.800	190	F.1094	179
F.159	105	F.569	302	F.801	216	F.1102	52
F.160	106	F.571	110	F.802	164	F.1105	312
F.166	92	F.572	359	F.805	178	F.1106	246
F.174	187	F.574	121	F.806	75	F.1108	71
F.175	237	F.577	47	F.809	157	F.1109	189
F.202	20	F.580	113	F.810	161	F.1110	148
F.204	402	F.595	356	F.816	44	F.1111	193
F.221	65	F.596	353	F.817	367	F.1112	6
F.227	202	F.601	226	F.819	109	F.1113	191
F.231	79	F.602	233	F.820	208	F.1115	25
F.236	58	F.605	188	F.823	183	F.1116	403
F.245	171	F.615	348	F.842	37	F.1117	119
F.246	203	F.629	255	F.852	184	F.1119	72
F.253	78	F.631	143	F.853	112	F.1123	169
F.256	69	F.638	98	F.863	108	F.1124	370
F.257	225	F.663	219	F.874	33	F.1127	2
F.258	215	F.666	194	F.883	200	F.1133	268
F.259	155	F.670	62	F.884	11	F.1135	265
F.262	238	F.672	204	F.887	199	F.1154	154
F.268	13	F.674	174	F.895	165	F.1156	220
F.269	185	F.676	206	F.897	24	F.1157	400
F.277	117	F.679	21	F.900	211	F.1158	360
F.282	114	F.681	90	F.905	166	F.1162	180
F.286	365	F.683	77	F.927	173	F.1174	83
F.291	103	F.686	73	F.928	4	F.1183	270
F.296	247	F.688	366	F.928A	134	F.1185	266
F.301	159	F.689	295	F.949	254	F.1196	275
F.311	181	F.690	340	F.965	334	F.1216	124
F.319	36	F.691	231	F.967	3	F.1218	125
F.324	168	F.692	99	F.969	136	F.1227	132
F.328	29	F.693	56	F.990	5	F.1230	242

Registration Number	Catalogue Number
F.1232	196
F.1250	395
F.1253	100
F.1256	221
F.1261	387
F.1262	390
F.1263	389
F.1294	279
F.1306	280
F.1309	394
F.1321A	379
F.1433 +	375
F.1434	102
F.1447	273
F.1448	272
F.1449	271
F.1461 +	371
F.1464 +	374
F.1483 +	373
F.1489 +	376
F.1498 +	372
F.1674	186
F.1904	378
F.1940B	377
1912 10-12 2	306
1912 10-12 4	1
1912 10-12 5	309
1912 10-12 6	41
1912 10-12 7	95
1912 10-12 8	97
1912 10-12 13	213
1912 10-12 16	230
1928 7-17 7	383
1928 7-17 8	382
1928 7-17 9	381
1930 12-17 49	327
1930 12-17 60	31
1930 12-17 62	324
1930 12-17 63	331
1930 12-17 64	326
1930 12-17 65	323
1930 12-17 66	338
1930 12-17 74	51
1930 12-17 76	341
1930 12-17 81	131
1930 12-17 91	60
1930 12-17 93	50
1930 12-17 96	153
1930 12-17 98	177
1930 12-17 108	192
1942 10-13 17	347
1942 10-13 19	205
1945 10-17 515	283
1945 10-17 516	12
1945 10-17 517	337
1945 10-17 518	321
1945 10-17 519	59
1945 10-17 520	55
1945 10-17 521	362
1945 10-17 523	127
1945 10-17 524	257
1945 10-17 525	385
1945 10-17 530	88
1945 10-17 531	285
1945 10-17 532	129
1945 10-17 533	314
1945 10-17 535	297
1945 10-17 537	351
1945 10-17 542	260
1945 10-17 543	310
1945 10-17 551	16
1945 10-17 554	281
1945 10-17 555	276
1945 10-17 558	352
1945 10-17 559	322
1945 10-17 565	45
1945 10-17 566	357
1945 10-17 567	335
1945 10-17 571	94
1945 10-17 573	284
1945 10-17 576	311
1945 10-17 577	392
1945 10-17 578	262
1945 10-17 580	146
1945 10-17 581	147
1945 10-17 582	317
1945 10-17 583	267
1945 10-17 585	236
1945 10-17 586	303
1945 10-17 589	35
1945 10-17 591	70
1945 10-17 592	23
1945 10-17 595	339
1945 10-17 596	336
1945 10-17 597	346
1945 10-17 598	345
1945 10-17 600	342
1945 10-17 601	39
1945 10-17 602	126
1945 10-17 603	53
1945 10-17 605	8
1945 10-17 606	26
1945 10-17 612	163
1945 10-17 614	89
1045 10-17 616	115
1945 10-17 617	140
1945 10-17 619	286
1945 10-17 620	305
1945 10-17 621	259
1945 10-17 622	287
1945 10-17 623	304
1945 10-17 626	269
1945 19-17 627	264
1945 10-17 628	42
1945 10-17 629	397
1945 10-17 630	277
1945 10-17 633	139
1945 10-17 634	85
1945 10-17 635	84
1945 10-17 638	135
1945 10-17 641	343
1945 10-17 643	222
1945 10-17 645	162
1945 10-17 646	253
1945 10-17 647	293
1945 10-17 648	249
1945 10-17 649	288
1945 10-17 650	294
1945 10-17 651	308
1945 10-17 652	241
1945 10-17 653	111
1945 10-17 654	229
1945 10-17 656	278
1945 10-17 657	144
1945 10-17 659	150
1945 10-17 661	27
1945 10-17 662	218
1945 10-17 663	17
1945 10-17 664	250
1945 10-17 666	313
1945 10-17 667	234
1945 10-17 669	217
1945 10-17 670	325
1945 10-17 671	301
1945 10-17 673	300
1945 10-17 676	344
1948 10-19 5	175
1953 12-17 1	38
1953 12-17 5	363
1953 12-17 6	10
1953 12-17 8	34
1953 12-17 10	64
1953 12-17 11	138
1953 12-17 12	201
1953 12-17 13	195
1953 12-17 14	182
1953 12-17 15	198
1953 12-17 16	227
1953 12-17 17	87
1953 12-17 22	391
1956 10-19 7	299
1972 1-14 6	76
1972 1-14 9	82
1972 1-14 19	14
1972 1-14 28	328
1972 1-14 47	32
1974 2-26 12	393

Index *References are to numbers of the objects in the catalogue*